The Quran With Tafsir Ibn Kathir Part 1 of 30 Al Fatiha 001 To Al Baqarah 141

The Quran With Tafsir Ibn Kathir
Part 1 of 30
Al Fatiha 001 To
Al Baqarah 141

With
Arabic Script, Transliteration of Arabic, Meaning in
English and Ibn Kathir's Abridged Tafsir (Explanation)

Muhammad Saed Abdul-Rahman

BSc, DipHE

MSA Publication Limited

© Muhammad Saed Abdul-Rahman, 2011
ISBN 978-1-86179-828-2

All Rights reserved

British Library Cataloguing in Publication Data. A Catalogue record for this book is available from the British Library

Designed, Typeset and produced by:
MSA Publication Limited, 4 Bello Close, Herne Hill,
London SE24 9BW
United Kingdom

Cover design: Houriyah Abdul-Rahman

TABLE OF CONTENTS

TABLE OF CONTENTS .... **V**

PRELUDE .... **XV**

    OPENING SERMAN XV
    OUR MISSION XVI
    BIOGRAPHY OF HAFIZ IBN KATHIR (701 H - 774 H) XVI
        Ibn Kathir's Teachers xvi
        Ibn Kathir's Students.. xvii
        Ibn Kathir's Books xviii
        Ibn Kathir's Death xix

PREFACE .... **XXI**

    ABOUT THIS BOOK XXI
    PERFORMING PROSTRATION WHILE READING THE QUR'AN XXI

PART 1 FULL ARABIC TEXT **1**

INTRODUCTION TO CHAPTER (SURAH) 1: AL-FATIHAH (THE OPENING) **13**

    IBN KATHIR'S INTRODUCTION 13
        The Meaning of Al-Fatihah and its Various Names.................................... 13
        How many Ayat does Al-Fatihah contain 14
        The Number of Words and Letters in Al-Fatihah 14
        The Reason it is called Umm Al-Kitab 14
        Virtues of Al-Fatihah 15
        Al-Fatihah and the Prayer 18
        Explaining this Hadith 20
        Reciting Al-Fatihah is required in Every Rak`ah of the Prayer 21
        The Tafsir of Isti`adhah (seeking Refuge).. 21
        Seeking Refuge before reciting the Qur'an.. 23
        Seeking Refuge with Allah when One is Angry 25
        Is the Isti`adhah (seeking Refuge) required 26
        Virtues of the Isti`adhah 26
        What does Isti`adhah mean... 27
        Why the Devil is called Shaytan 28
        The Meaning of Ar-Rajim 29

CHAPTER (SURAH) 1: AL-FATIHAH (THE OPENING), VERSES 001–007 .... **30**

    Surah: 1 Ayah: 1 .... *30*
        Tafsir Ibn Kathir 30
        Bismillah is the First Ayah of Al-Fatihah... 30
        Basmalah aloud in the Prayer 31
        The Virtue of Al-Fatihah.. 33
        Basmalah is recommended before performing any Deed 33

    The Meaning of "Allah 34
    The Meaning of Ar-Rahman Ar-Rahim - the Most Gracious, the Most Merciful.. 35
Surah: 1 Ayah: 2... 38
    Tafsir Ibn Kathir 38
        The Meaning of Al-Hamd 38
        The Difference between Praise and Thanks.. 38
        The Statements of the Salaf about Al-Hamd.. 38
        The Virtues of Al-Hamd 39
        Al before Hamd encompasses all Types of Thanks and Appreciation for Allah ... 40
        The Meaning of Ar-Rabb, the Lord.. 40
        The Meaning of Al-`Alamin 40
        Why is the Creation called `Alam 41
Surah: 1 Ayah: 3... 41
    Tafsir Ibn Kathir 41
Surah: 1 Ayah: 4... 42
    Tafsir Ibn Kathir 42
        Indicating Sovereignty on the Day of Judgment 42
        The Meaning of Yawm Ad-Din 42
        Allah is Al-Malik (King or Owner) 43
        The Meaning of Ad-Din 43
Surah: 1 Ayah: 5, Ayah: 6 & Ayah: 7... 44
    Tafsir Ibn Kathir 45
        The Linguistic and Religious Meaning of `Ibadah... 45
        The Merit of stating the Object of the Action before the Doer of the Act, and the Merit of these Negations 45
        Al-Fatihah indicates the Necessity of praising Allah. It is required in every Prayer. 45
        Tawhid Al-Uluhiyyah 47
        Tawhid Ar-Rububiyyah.. 48
        Allah called His Prophet (Peace be upon him) an `Abd 48
        Encouraging the Performance of the Acts of Worship during Times of Distress . 48
        Why Praise was mentioned First... 49
        The Meaning of As-Sirat Al-Mustaqim, the Straight Path. 50
        The Faithful ask for and abide by Guidance 51
        The Summary of Al-Fatihah 53
        The Bounties are because of Allah, not the Deviations 54
        Saying Amin 55

INTRODUCTION TO CHAPTER (SURAH) 2: AL-BAQARAH (THE COW) 57

    IBN KATHIR'S INTRODUCTION 57
        The Virtues of Surat Al-Baqarah.. 57
        Virtues of Surat Al-Baqarah and Surat Al `Imran... 59
        Surat Al-Baqarah was revealed in Al-Madinah 62

CHAPTER (SURAH) 2: AL-BQARAH (THE COW), VERSES 001-141.......................... 63

Table of Contents

Surah: 2 Ayah: 1 63
Tafsir Ibn Kathir 63
- The Discussion of the Individual Letters 63
- The Letters at the Beginning of Surahs 64
- These Letters testify to the Miraculous Qur'an 64

Surah: 2 Ayah: 2 66
Tafsir Ibn Kathir 66
- There is no Doubt in the Qur'an 66
- Guidance is granted to Those Who have Taqwa 67
- The Meaning of Al-Muttaqin 67
- There are Two Types of Hidayah (Guidance) 68
- Meaning of Taqwa 68

Surah: 2 Ayah: 3 69
Tafsir Ibn Kathir 69
- The Meaning of Iman (Belief, Faith) 69
- The Meaning of Al-Ghayb 70
- Meaning of Iqamat As-Salah 71
- The Meaning of "Spending" in this Ayah 72
- The Meaning of Salah 73

Surah: 2 Ayah: 4 73
Tafsir Ibn Kathir 73
- Attributes of the Believers 73

Surah: 2 Ayah: 5 75
Tafsir Ibn Kathir 75
- Guidance and Success are awarded to the Believers 75

Surah: 2 Ayah: 6 76
Tafsir Ibn Kathir 76

Surah: 2 Ayah: 7 77
Tafsir Ibn Kathir 77
- Meaning of Khatama 77
- The Meaning of Ghishawah 79

Surah: 2 Ayahs: 8 & 9 79
Tafsir Ibn Kathir 80
- The Hypocrites 80
- Meaning of Nifaq 80
- The Beginning of Hypocrisy 80
- The Tafsir of Aya 2:8 (& Aya 2:9) 81

Surah: 2 Ayah: 10 82
Tafsir Ibn Kathir 83
- The Meaning of 'Disease' in this Ayah 83

Surah: 2 Ayah: 11 & Ayah: 12 85
Tafsir Ibn Kathir 85
- Meaning of Mischief 85
- Types of Mischief that the Hypocrites commit 85

Surah: 2 Ayah: 13 86
   Tafsir Ibn Kathir 87
      Types of Mischief that the Hypocrites commit (Continued) 87
Surah: 2 Ayah: 14 & Ayah: 15 87
   Tafsir Ibn Kathir 88
      The Hypocrites' Cunning and Deceit 88
      Human and Jinn Devils 88
      The Meaning of 'Mocking 88
      The Hypocrites suffering for their Plots 89
      Meaning of 'Leaves them increasing in their deviation to wander blindly 89
Surah: 2 Ayah: 16 90
   Tafsir Ibn Kathir 90
Surah: 2 Ayah: 17 & Ayah: 18 91
   Tafsir Ibn Kathir 91
      The Example of the Hypocrites 91
Surah: 2 Ayah: 19 & Ayah: 20 92
   Tafsir Ibn Kathir 93
      Another Parable of the Hypocrites 93
      Types of Believers and Types of Disbelievers 95
      Types of Hearts 96
Surah: 2 Ayah: 21 & Ayah: 22 98
   Tafsir Ibn Kathir 99
      Tawhid Al-Uluhiyyah 99
      A Hadith with the same Meaning 100
      Signs of Allah's Existence 102
Surah: 2 Ayah: 23 & Ayah: 24 103
   Tafsir Ibn Kathir 104
      The Message of Messenger of Allah is True 104
      The Challenge 104
      Examples of the Miracle of the Qur'an 106
      The Qur'an is the Greatest Miracle given to the Prophet 108
      Meaning of 'Stones' 108
      Jahannam (Hellfire) exists now 109
Surah: 2 Ayah: 25 110
   Tafsir Ibn Kathir 111
      Rewards of Righteous Believers 111
      The similarity between the Fruits of Paradise 112
      The Wives of the People of Paradise are Pure 112
Surah: 2 Ayah: 26 & Ayah: 27 113
   Tafsir Ibn Kathir 113
      A Parable about the Life of This World 114
      The Meaning of 'Loss' 117
Surah: 2 Ayah: 28 118
   Tafsir Ibn Kathir 118

Table of Contents

Surah: 2 Ayah: 29 .... *119*
   Tafsir Ibn Kathir 119
      Evidence of Allah's Ability 119
      The Beginning of the Creation 119
      The Earth was created before Heaven 120
      Spreading the Earth out after the Heavens were created 120

Surah: 2 Ayah: 30 .... *121*
   Tafsir Ibn Kathir 121
      Adam and His Children inhabited the Earth, Generation after Generation 121
      The Obligation of appointing a Khalifah and some related Issues 123

Surah: 2 Ayah: 31, Ayah: 32 & Ayah: 33 .... *124*
   Tafsir Ibn Kathir 125
      The Virtue of Adam over the Angels 125
      Adam's Virtue of Knowledge is demonstrated 128

Surah: 2 Ayah: 34 .... *129*
   Tafsir Ibn Kathir 130
      Honoring Adam when the Angels prostrated before Him 130
      The Prostration was before Adam but the Obedience was to Allah 130

Surah: 2 Ayah: 35 & Ayah: 36 .... *131*
   Tafsir Ibn Kathir 132
      Adam was honored again 132
      Hawwa' was created before Adam entered Paradise 132
      Allah tests Adam 133
      Adam was very Tall 134
      Adam remained in Paradise for an Hour 134
      A Doubt and a Rebuttal 135

Surah: 2 Ayah: 37 .... *135*
   Tafsir Ibn Kathir 135
      Adam repents and supplicates to Allah 135

Surah: 2 Ayah: 38 & Ayah: 39 .... *136*
   Tafsir Ibn Kathir 137

Surah: 2 Ayah: 40 & Ayah: 41 .... *137*
   Tafsir Ibn Kathir 138
      Encouraging the Children of Israel to embrace Islam 138
      Israel is Prophet Ya'qub (Jacob) 138
      Allah's Blessings for the Children of Israel 139
      Reminding the Children of Israel of Allah's Covenant with Them 139

Surah: 2 Ayah: 42 & Ayah: 43 .... *141*
   Tafsir Ibn Kathir 141
      The Prohibition of hiding the Truth and distorting It with Falsehood 141

Surah: 2 Ayah: 44 .... *142*
   Tafsir Ibn Kathir 143
      The Condemnation of commanding Others to observe Righteousness while ignoring Righteousness 143

Surah: 2 Ayah: 45 & Ayah: 46 .... *145*
    Tafsir Ibn Kathir 145
        The Support that comes with Patience and Prayer.. 145
Surah: 2 Ayah: 47 .... *147*
    Tafsir Ibn Kathir 147
        Reminding the Children of Israel that They were preferred above the Other Nations.. 147
        The Ummah of Muhammad is Better than the Children of Israel...................... 148
Surah: 2 Ayah: 48 .... *148*
    Tafsir Ibn Kathir 148
        Neither Intercession, Ransom, or Assistance will be accepted on behalf of the Disbelievers.. 149
Surah: 2 Ayah: 49 & Ayah: 50 .... *151*
    Tafsir Ibn Kathir 151
        The Children of Israel were saved from Pharaoh and His Army Who drowned. 151
        Fasting the Day of 'Ashura 153
Surah: 2 Ayah: 51, Ayah: 52 & Ayah: 53 .... *153*
    Tafsir Ibn Kathir 154
        The Children of Israel worshipped the Calf... 154
Surah: 2 Ayah: 54 .... *154*
    Tafsir Ibn Kathir 155
        The Children of Israel kill each other in Repentance 155
Surah: 2 Ayah: 55 & Ayah: 56 .... *156*
    Tafsir Ibn Kathir 156
        The Best among the Children of Israel ask to see Allah; their subsequent Death and Resurrection... 156
Surah: 2 Ayah: 57 .... *158*
    Tafsir Ibn Kathir 158
        The Shade, the Manna and the Quail 158
        The Virtue of Muhammad's Companions over the Companions of all Other Prophets... 160
Surah: 2 Ayah: 58 & Ayah: 59 .... *160*
    Tafsir Ibn Kathir 161
        The Jews were Rebellious instead of Appreciative when They gained Victory.. 161
Surah: 2 Ayah: 60 .... *164*
    Tafsir Ibn Kathir 164
        Twelve Springs gush forth.. 164
Surah: 2 Ayah: 61 .... *165*
    Tafsir Ibn Kathir 166
        The Children of Israel preferred Foods inferior to Manna and Quails 166
        Covering the Jews in Humiliation and Misery.. 167
        Meaning of Kibr 168
Surah: 2 Ayah: 62 .... *168*
    Tafsir Ibn Kathir 169

Table of Contents

- Faith and doing Righteous Deeds equals Salvation in all Times 169
- The Meaning of Mu'min, or Believer 169
- Why the Jews were called 'Yahud 169
- why the christians were called nasara 169
- The Sabi'un or Sabians 170

Surah: 2 Ayah: 63 & Ayah: 64 .... *170*
- Tafsir Ibn Kathir 171
- Taking the Covenant from the Jews 171

Surah: 2 Ayah: 65 & Ayah: 66 .... *172*
- Tafsir Ibn Kathir 172
- The Jews breach the Sanctity of the Sabbath 172
- The Monkeys and Swine that exist now are not the Descendants of Those that were transformed 173

Surah: 2 Ayah: 67 .... *174*
- Tafsir Ibn Kathir 174
- The Story of the murdered Israeli Man and the Cow 174

Surah: 2 Ayah: 68, Ayah: 69, Ayah: 70 & Ayah: 71 .... *175*
- Tafsir Ibn Kathir 176
- The Stubbornness of the Jews regarding the Cow; Allah made the Matter difficult for Them 176

Surah: 2 Ayah: 72 & Ayah: 73 .... *177*
- Tafsir Ibn Kathir 178
- Bringing the murdered Man back to Life 178

Surah: 2 Ayah: 74 .... *179*
- Tafsir Ibn Kathir 179
- The Harshness of the Jews 179
- Solid Inanimate Objects possess a certain Degree of Awareness 180

Surah: 2 Ayah: 75, Ayah: 76 & Ayah: 77 .... *182*
- Tafsir Ibn Kathir 183
- There was little Hope that the Jews Who lived during the Time of the Prophet could have believed 183
- The Jews knew the Truth of the Prophet, but disbelieved in Him 184

Surah: 2 Ayah: 78 & Ayah: 79 .... *185*
- Tafsir Ibn Kathir 185
- The Meaning of 'Ummi 185
- The Explanation of Amani 186
- Woe unto Those Criminals among the Jews 186

Surah: 2 Ayah: 80 .... *187*
- Tafsir Ibn Kathir 187
- The Jews hope They will only remain in the Fire for a Few Days 187

Surah: 2 Ayah: 81 & Ayah: 82 .... *189*
- Tafsir Ibn Kathir 190
- When Small Sins gather, They bring about Destruction 190

Surah: 2 Ayah: 83 .... *191*

Tafsir Ibn Kathir 191
    The Covenant that Allah took from the Children of Israel 191
Surah: 2 Ayah: 84, Ayah: 85 & Ayah: 86 .... *194*
    Tafsir Ibn Kathir 195
    The Terms of the Covenant and their Breach of It 195
Surah: 2 Ayah: 87 .... *197*
    Tafsir Ibn Kathir 197
        The Arrogance of the Jews who denied and killed Their Prophets 197
        Jibril is Ruh Al-Qudus 198
        The Jews tried to kill the Prophet 199
Surah: 2 Ayah: 88 .... *199*
    Tafsir Ibn Kathir 199
Surah: 2 Ayah: 89 .... *200*
    Tafsir Ibn Kathir 201
        The Jews were awaiting the Prophet's coming, but They disbelieved in Him when He was sent 201
Surah: 2 Ayah: 90 .... *202*
    Tafsir Ibn Kathir 202
Surah: 2 Ayah: 91 & Ayah: 92 .... *203*
    Tafsir Ibn Kathir 204
        Although The Jews denied the Truth, They claimed to be Believers! 204
Surah: 2 Ayah: 93 .... *205*
    Tafsir Ibn Kathir 206
        The Jews rebel after Allah took Their Covenant and raised the Mountain above Their Heads 206
Surah: 2 Ayah: 94, Ayah: 95 & Ayah: 96 .... *206*
    Tafsir Ibn Kathir 207
        Calling the Jews to invoke Allah to destroy the Unjust Party 207
        Disbelievers wish They could live longer 209
Surah: 2 Ayah: 97 & Ayah: 98 .... *209*
    Tafsir Ibn Kathir 210
        The Jews are the Enemies of Jibril 210
        Choosing Some Angels to believe in over Others is Disbelief like choosing Some Prophets over Others 211
Surah: 2 Ayah: 99, Ayah: 100, Ayah: 101, Ayah: 102 & Ayah: 103 .... *214*
    Tafsir Ibn Kathir 215
        Proofs of Muhammad's Prophethood 215
        The Jews break Their Covenants 216
        The Jews abandoned the Book of Allah and practiced Magic 216
        Magic existed before Sulayman (Solomon) 216
        The Story of Harut and Marut, and the Explanation that They were Angels 217
        Learning Magic is Kufr 219
        Causing a Separation between the Spouses is One of the Effects of Magic 220
        Allah's Appointed Term supercedes Everything 220

Table of Contents

Surah: 2 Ayah: 104 & Ayah: 105 221
   Tafsir Ibn Kathir 222
      Manners in Speech 222
      The extreme Enmity that the Disbelievers and the People of the Book have against Muslims 224

Surah: 2 Ayah: 106 & Ayah: 107 224
   Tafsir Ibn Kathir 225
      The Meaning of Naskh 225
      Naskh occurs even though the Jews deny it 226

Surah: 2 Ayah: 108 227
   Tafsir Ibn Kathir 228
      The Prohibition of Unnecessary Questions 228

Surah: 2 Ayah: 109 & Ayah: 110 230
   Tafsir Ibn Kathir 230
      The Prohibition of following the Ways of the People of the Book 230
      The Encouragement to perform Good Deeds 232

Surah: 2 Ayah: 111, Ayah: 112 & Ayah: 113 232
   Tafsir Ibn Kathir 233
      The Hopes of the People of the Book 233
      The Jews and Christians dispute among Themselves out of Disbelief and Stubbornness 236

Surah: 2 Ayah: 114 237
   Tafsir Ibn Kathir 237
      Of the Most Unjust are Those Who prevent People from the Masjids and strive for their Ruin 237
      The Good News that Islam shall prevail 239

Surah: 2 Ayah: 115 240
   Tafsir Ibn Kathir 240
      Facing the Qiblah (Direction of the Prayer) 240
      The Qiblah for the People of Al-Madinah is what is between the East and the West 242

Surah: 2 Ayah: 116 & Ayah: 117 242
   Tafsir Ibn Kathir 243
      Refuting the Claim that Allah has begotten a Son 243
      Everything is within Allah's Grasp 244
      The Meaning of Badi' 245

Surah: 2 Ayah: 118 246
   Tafsir Ibn Kathir 247

Surah: 2 Ayah: 119 248
   Tafsir Ibn Kathir 248
      The Description of the Prophet in the Tawrah 249

Surah: 2 Ayah: 120 & Ayah: 121 249
   Tafsir Ibn Kathir 250
      The Meaning of Correct Tilawah 251

Surah: 2 Ayah: 122 & Ayah: 123 253
   Tafsir Ibn Kathir 253
Surah: 2 Ayah: 124 254
   Tafsir Ibn Kathir 254
     Ibrahim Al-Khalil was an Imam for the People 254
     What were the Words that Ibrahim was tested with 255
     The Unjust do not qualify for Allah's Promise 257
Surah: 2 Ayah: 125 (continued), Ayah: 126, Ayah: 127 & Ayah: 128 257
   bn Kathir's Tafsir 259
     The Virtue of Allah's House 259
     Allah described the House as a safe resort and refuge, for those who visit it are safe, even if they had committed acts of evil. This honor comes from the honor of the person who built it first, Khalil Ar-Rahman, just as Allah said, ... 259
     The Command to purify the House 262
     Makkah is a Sacred Area 263
     Ibrahim invokes Allah to make Makkah an Area of Safety and Sustenance 265
     Building the Ka'bah and asking Allah to accept This Deed 268
     The Story of rebuilding the House by Quraysh before the Messenger of Allah was sent as Prophet 271
     The Dispute regarding Who should place the Black Stone in Its Place 272
     Ibn Az-Zubayr rebuilds Al-Ka'bah the way the Prophet wished 273
     An Ethiopian will destroy the Ka'bah just before the Last Hour 275
     The Meaning of Manasik 277
Surah: 2 Ayah: 129 278
   Tafsir Ibn Kathir 278
     Ibrahim's Supplication that Allah sends the Prophet 278
     The Meaning of Al-Kitab wal-Hikmah 279
Surah: 2 Ayah: 130, Ayah: 131 & Ayah: 132 280
   Tafsir Ibn Kathir 280
     Only the Fools deviate from Ibrahim's Religion 280
     Adhering to Tawhid until Death 282
Surah: 2 Ayah: 133 & Ayah: 134 283
   Tafsir Ibn Kathir 284
     Ya`qub's Will and Testament to His Children upon His Death 284
Surah: 2 Ayah: 135 285
   Tafsir Ibn Kathir 286
Surah: 2 Ayah: 136 286
   Tafsir Ibn Kathir 287
     The Muslim believes in all that Allah `revealed and all the Prophets 287
Surah: 2 Ayah: 137 & 2 Ayah: 138 288
   Tafsir Ibn Kathir 288
Surah: 2 Ayah: 139 Ayah: 140 & Ayah: 141 289
   Tafsir Ibn Kathir 290

PRELUDE

Opening Serman

Indeed, all praise is due to Allah. We praise Him and seek His help and forgiveness. We seek refuge with Allah from our soul's evil and our wrong doings. He whom Allah guides, no one can misguide; and he whom He misguides, no one can guide

I bear witness that there is no (true) god except Allah – alone without a partner, and I bear witness that Muhammad (peace and blessings of Allah be upon him) is His 'abd (servant) and messenger.

يَٰٓأَيُّهَا ٱلَّذِينَ ءَامَنُوا۟ ٱتَّقُوا۟ ٱللَّهَ حَقَّ تُقَاتِهِۦ وَلَا تَمُوتُنَّ إِلَّا وَأَنتُم مُّسْلِمُونَ

O you who believe! Fear Allâh (by doing all that He has ordered and by abstaining from all that He has forbidden) as He should be feared. (Obey Him, be thankful to Him, and remember Him always), and die not except in a state of Islâm (as Muslims (with complete submission to Allâh)).

يَٰٓأَيُّهَا ٱلنَّاسُ ٱتَّقُوا۟ رَبَّكُمُ ٱلَّذِى خَلَقَكُم مِّن نَّفْسٍ وَٰحِدَةٍ وَخَلَقَ مِنْهَا زَوْجَهَا وَبَثَّ مِنْهُمَا رِجَالًا كَثِيرًا وَنِسَآءً ۚ وَٱتَّقُوا۟ ٱللَّهَ ٱلَّذِى تَسَآءَلُونَ بِهِۦ وَٱلْأَرْحَامَ ۚ إِنَّ ٱللَّهَ كَانَ عَلَيْكُمْ رَقِيبًا

O mankind! Be dutiful to your Lord, Who created you from a single person (Adam), and from him (Adam) He created his wife (Hawwâ (Eve)) and from them both He created many men and women; and fear Allâh through Whom you demand (your mutual rights), and (do not cut the relations of) the wombs (kinship). Surely, Allâh is Ever an All-Watcher over you.

يُصْلِحْ لَكُمْ أَعْمَٰلَكُمْ وَيَغْفِرْ لَكُمْ ذُنُوبَكُمْ ۗ وَمَن يُطِعِ ٱللَّهَ وَرَسُولَهُۥ فَقَدْ فَازَ فَوْزًا عَظِيمًا

He will direct you to do righteous good deeds and will forgive you your sins. And whosoever obeys Allâh and His Messenger (peace be upon him), he has indeed achieved a great achievement (i.e. he will be saved from the Hell-fire and will be admitted to Paradise).

Indeed, the best speech is Allah's Book and the best guidance is Muhammad's () guidance. The worst affairs (of religion) are those innovated (by people), for every such innovation is an act of misguidance leading to the Fire

Our Mission

Our mission is to gather in one place, for the English-speaking public, all relevant information needed to make the Qur'an more understandable and easier to study. This book tries to do this by providing the following:

1. The Arabic Text for those who are able to read Arabic
2. Transliteration of the Arabic text for those who are unable to read the Arabic script. This will give them a sample of the sound of the Qur'an, which they could not otherwise comprehend from reading the English meaning.
3. The meaning of the qur'an (translated by Dr. Muhammad Taqi-ud-Din Al-Hilali, Ph.D. and Dr. Muhammad Muhsin Khan)
4. Explanation (abridged Tafsir) by Ibn Kathir (translated by Safi-ur-Rahman al-Mubarakpuri)

We hope that by doing this an ordinary English-speaker will be able to pick up a copy of this book and study and comprehend The Glorious Qur'an in a way that is acceptable to the understanding of the Rightly-guided Muslim Ummah (Community).

Biography of Hafiz Ibn Kathir
(701 H - 774 H)

By the Honored Shaykh `Abdul-Qadir Al-Arna'ut, may Allah protect him.

He is the respected Imam, Abu Al-Fida', `Imad Ad-Din Isma il bin 'Umar bin Kathir Al-Qurashi Al-Busrawi - Busraian in origin; Dimashqi in training, learning and residence.

Ibn Kathir was born in the city of Busra in 701 H. His father was the Friday speaker of the village, but he died while Ibn Kathir was only four years old. Ibn Kathir's brother, Shaykh Abdul-Wahhab, reared him and taught him until he moved to Damascus in 706 H., when he was five years old.

Ibn Kathir's Teachers

Ibn Kathir studied Fiqh - Islamic jurisprudence - with Burhan Ad-Din, Ibrahim bin `Abdur-Rahman Al-Fizari, known as Ibn Al-Firkah (who died in 729 H). Ibn Kathir heard Hadiths from `Isa bin Al-Mutim, Ahmad bin Abi Talib, (Ibn Ash-Shahnah) (who died in 730 H), Ibn Al-Hajjar, (who died in 730 H), and the Hadith narrator of Ash-Sham (modern day Syria and surrounding areas); Baha

Ad-Din Al-Qasim bin Muzaffar bin `Asakir (who died in 723 H), and Ibn Ash-Shirdzi, Ishaq bin Yahya Al-Ammuddi, also known as `Afif Ad-Din, the Zahiriyyah Shaykh who died in 725 H, and Muhammad bin Zarrad. He remained with Jamal Ad-Din, Yusuf bin Az-Zaki AlMizzi who died in 724 H, he benefited from his knowledge and also married his daughter. He also read with Shaykh Al-Islam, Taqi Ad-Din Ahmad bin `Abdul-Halim bin `Abdus-Salam bin Taymiyyah who died in 728 H. He also read with the Imam Hafiz and historian Shams Ad-Din, Muhammad bin Ahmad bin Uthman bin Qaymaz Adh-Dhahabi, who died in 748 H. Also, Abu Musa Al-Qarafai, Abu Al-Fath Ad-Dabbusi and 'Ali bin `Umar As-Suwani and others who gave him permission to transmit the knowledge he learned with them in Egypt.

In his book, Al-Mu jam Al-Mukhtas, Al-Hafiz Adh-Dhaliabi wrote that Ibn Kathir was, "The Imam, scholar of jurisprudence, skillful scholar of Hadith, renowned Fagih and scholar of Tafsir who wrote several beneficial books."

Further, in Ad-Durar Al-Kdminah, Al-Hafiz Ibn Hajar AlAsqalani said, "Ibn Kathir worked on the subject of the Hadith in the areas of texts and chains of narrators. He had a good memory, his books became popular during his lifetime, and people benefited from them after his death."

Also, the renowned historian Abu Al-Mahasin, Jamal Ad-Din Yusuf bin Sayf Ad-Din (Ibn Taghri Bardi), said in his book, AlManhal As-Safi, "He is the Shaykh, the Imam, the great scholar `Imad Ad-Din Abu Al-Fida'. He learned extensively and was very active in collecting knowledge and writing. He was excellent in the areas of Fiqh, Tafsfr and Hadith. He collected knowledge, authored (books), taught, narrated Hadith and wrote. He had immense knowledge in the fields of Hadith, Tafsir, Fiqh, the Arabic language, and so forth. He gave Fatawa (religious verdicts) and taught until he died, may Allah grant him mercy. He was known for his precision and vast knowledge, and as a scholar of history, Hadith and Tafsir."

Ibn Kathir's Students

Ibn Hajji was one of Ibn Kathir's students, and he described Ibn Kathir: "He had the best memory of the Hadith texts. He also had the most knowledge concerning the narrators and authenticity, his contemporaries and teachers admitted to these qualities. Every time I met him I gained some benefit from him."

Also, Ibn Al-`Imad Al-Hanbali said in his book, Shadhardt Adh-Dhahab, "He is the renowned Hafiz `Imad Ad-Din, whose memory was excellent, whose forgetfulness was miniscule, whose understanding was adequate, and who had good knowledge in the Arabic language." Also, Ibn Habib said about Ibn Kathir, "He heard knowledge and collected it and wrote various books. He brought comfort to the ears with his Fatwas and narrated Hadith and brought benefit to other people. The papers that contained his Fatwas were transmitted to the various (Islamic) provinces. Further, he was known for his precision and encompassing knowledge."

Ibn Kathir's Books

1 - One of the greatest books that Ibn Kathir wrote was his Tafsir of the Noble Qur'an, which is one of the best Tafsir that rely on narrations [of Ahadith, the Tafsir of the Companions, etc.]. The Tafsir by Ibn Kathir was printed many times and several scholars have summarized it.

2- The History Collection known as Al-Biddyah, which was printed in 14 volumes under the name Al-Bidayah wanNihdyah, and contained the stories of the Prophets and previous nations, the Prophet's Seerah (life story) and Islamic history until his time. He also added a book Al-Fitan, about the Signs of the Last Hour.

3- At-Takmil ft Ma`rifat Ath-Thiqat wa Ad-Du'afa wal Majdhil which Ibn Kathir collected from the books of his two Shaykhs Al-Mizzi and Adh-Dhahabi; Al-Kdmal and Mizan Al-Ftiddl. He added several benefits regarding the subject of Al-Jarh and AtT'adil.

4- Al-Hadi was-Sunan ft Ahadith Al-Masdnfd was-Sunan which is also known by, Jami` Al-Masdnfd. In this book, Ibn Kathir collected the narrations of Imams Ahmad bin Hanbal, Al-Bazzar, Abu Ya`la Al-Mawsili, Ibn Abi Shaybah and from the six collections of Hadith: the Two Sahihs [Al-Bukhari and Muslim] and the Four Sunan [Abu Dawud, At-Tirmidhi, AnNasa and Ibn Majah]. Ibn Kathir divided this book according to areas of Fiqh.

5-Tabaqat Ash-Shaf iyah which also contains the virtues of Imam Ash-Shafi.

6- Ibn Kathir wrote references for the Ahadith of Adillat AtTanbfh, from the Shafi school of Fiqh.

7- Ibn Kathir began an explanation of Sahih Al-Bukhari, but he did not finish it.

8- He started writing a large volume on the Ahkam (Laws), but finished only up to the Hajj rituals.

9- He summarized Al-Bayhaqi's 'Al-Madkhal. Many of these books were not printed.

10- He summarized `Ulum Al-Hadith, by Abu `Amr bin AsSalah and called it Mukhtasar `Ulum Al-Hadith. Shaykh Ahmad Shakir, the Egyptian Muhaddith, printed this book along with his commentary on it and called it Al-Ba'th Al-Hathfth fi Sharh Mukhtasar `Ulum Al-Hadith.

11- As-Sfrah An-Nabawiyyah, which is contained in his book Al-Biddyah, and both of these books are in print.

12- A research on Jihad called Al-Ijtihad ft Talabi Al-Jihad, which was printed several times.

Ibn Kathir's Death

Al-Hafiz Ibn Hajar Al-Asgalani said, "Ibn Kathir lost his sight just before his life ended. He died in Damascus in 774 H." May Allah grant mercy upon Ibn Kathir and make him among the residents of His Paradise.

PREFACE

In the name of Allah, Most Gracious, Most Merciful.

About this book

The previous publication of this book included some background information to the chapters of the Qur'an by an Islamic scholar known as Abul Ala Maududi. This information was used to shed more light on the chapters by giving a summery of why each chapter was given its name, It's period of revelation and the circumstances surrounding its revelatiom. However, some Muslims objected to the inclusion of the contributions of Maududi.

In this new publication of Tafsir Ibn Kathir, we have removed all traces of the contribution of Abul Ala Maududi. Personally, I do not know the reasons for the objections to Maududi, but this work concerns only the tafsir of Ibn Kathir, so we have not included anything from Maududi in it. We have also corrected all the typing and formatting errors found in the previous publication. We have not alter the structure of the book. The reader is still able to read the full Arabic Text of the thirty Parts of the Qur'an and follow its meanings in the English language. The transliteration of the Arabic text should also give the reader a taste of the sound of the original Arabic.

May Almighty Allah accept this effort from us, and make it a source of blessings for us in this world and in the next. I bear witness that there is none worthy of worship but Allah and I bear witness that Muhammad (may the peace and blessings of Allah be upon him) is the slave and messenger of Allah.

Performing Prostration While Reading the Qur'an

Question:

Could you please give a list of the Qur'anic verses when a prostration is recommended? What happens if we read these verses and not perform a prostration?

A. Jalil

Answer:

There are 15 verses in the Qur'an that mention prostration before God Almighty as a good action by God-fearing believers. Therefore, it is strongly recommended to perform such a prostration when we read or listen to any of these verses, whether during prayer or in any situation.

Some scholars are of the view that even if one has not performed ablution, one should prostrate oneself. These verses are given here, starting with the Arabic title of the surah which is followed by two numbers, the first indicating the surah, and the second indicating the verse,: Al-Araf 7: 206; Al-Raad 13: 15; Al-Nahl 16: 50; Al-Isra 17: 109; Maryam 19: 58; Al-Hajj 22: 18 & 22: 77; Al-Furqan 25: 60; Al-Naml 27: 26; Al-Sajdah 32: 15; Saad 38: 25; Fussilat 41: 38; Al-Najm 53: 62; Al-Inshiqaq 84: 21 and Al-Alaq 96: 19.

If you do not perform a prostration when you read or listen to any of these verses, you have done badly because you miss out on the reward of performing a prostration for God. You incur no sin and violate no divine order.

Reference:
http://archive.arabnews.com/?page=5&section=0&article=97811&d=1&m=7&y=2007

Tafsir Ibn Kathir Juz' 1 (Part 1): Chapter (Surah) 1: Al-Fatihah (The Opening) 001 To Chapter (Surah) 2: Al-Baqarah (The Cow) 141

PART 1 FULL ARABIC TEXT

Chapter (Surah) 1: Al-Fatihah 001-007

﴿ بِسْمِ اللَّهِ الرَّحْمَـنِ الرَّحِيمِ ۝ الْحَمْدُ لِلَّهِ رَبِّ الْعَـلَمِينَ ۝ الرَّحْمَـنِ الرَّحِيمِ ۝ مَـلِكِ يَوْمِ الدِّينِ ۝ إِيَّاكَ نَعْبُدُ وَإِيَّاكَ نَسْتَعِينُ ۝ اهْدِنَا الصِّرَاطَ الْمُسْتَقِيمَ ۝ صِرَاطَ الَّذِينَ أَنْعَمْتَ عَلَيْهِمْ غَيْرِ الْمَغْضُوبِ عَلَيْهِمْ وَلاَ الضَّآلِّينَ ۝ ﴾

(Al-Fatiha 001-007)

Chapter (Surah) 2: Al-Baqarah 001-141

بِسْمِ اللَّهِ الرَّحْمَنِ الرَّحِيمِ

﴿ الم ۝ ذَلِكَ الْكِتَـبُ لاَ رَيْبَ فِيهِ هُدًى لِلْمُتَّقِينَ ۝ الَّذِينَ يُؤْمِنُونَ بِالْغَيْبِ وَيُقِيمُونَ الصَّلَوةَ وَمِمَّا رَزَقْنَـهُمْ يُنفِقُونَ ۝ وَالَّذِينَ يُؤْمِنُونَ بِمَآ أُنزِلَ إِلَيْكَ وَمَآ أُنزِلَ مِن قَبْلِكَ وَبِالأَخِرَةِ هُمْ يُوقِنُونَ ۝ أُوْلَـئِكَ عَلَى هُدًى مِّن رَّبِّهِمْ وَأُوْلَـئِكَ هُمُ الْمُفْلِحُونَ ۝ إِنَّ الَّذِينَ كَفَرُواْ سَوَآءٌ عَلَيْهِمْ ءَأَنذَرْتَهُمْ أَمْ لَمْ تُنذِرْهُمْ لاَ يُؤْمِنُونَ ۝ خَتَمَ اللَّهُ عَلَى قُلُوبِهمْ وَعَلَى سَمْعِهِمْ وَعَلَى أَبْصَـرِهِمْ غِشَـوَةٌ وَلَهُمْ عَذَابٌ عظِيمٌ ۝ وَمِنَ النَّاسِ مَن يَقُولُ ءَامَنَّا بِاللَّهِ وَبِالْيَوْمِ الأَخِرِ وَمَا هُم بِمُؤْمِنِينَ ۝ يُخَـدِعُونَ اللَّهَ وَالَّذِينَ ءَامَنُواْ وَمَا يَخْدَعُونَ إِلاَّ أَنفُسَهُمْ وَمَا يَشْعُرُونَ ۝ فِى قُلُوبِهِم مَّرَضٌ فَزَادَهُمُ اللَّهُ مَرَضاً

وَلَهُمْ عَذَابٌ أَلِيمٌ بِمَا كَانُوا يَكْذِبُونَ ۝ وَإِذَا قِيلَ لَهُمْ لَا تُفْسِدُوا فِي الْأَرْضِ قَالُوا إِنَّمَا نَحْنُ مُصْلِحُونَ ۝ أَلَا إِنَّهُمْ هُمُ الْمُفْسِدُونَ وَلَٰكِن لَّا يَشْعُرُونَ ۝ وَإِذَا قِيلَ لَهُمْ آمِنُوا كَمَا آمَنَ النَّاسُ قَالُوا أَنُؤْمِنُ كَمَا آمَنَ السُّفَهَاءُ ۗ أَلَا إِنَّهُمْ هُمُ السُّفَهَاءُ وَلَٰكِن لَّا يَعْلَمُونَ ۝ وَإِذَا لَقُوا الَّذِينَ آمَنُوا قَالُوا آمَنَّا وَإِذَا خَلَوْا إِلَىٰ شَيَاطِينِهِمْ قَالُوا إِنَّا مَعَكُمْ إِنَّمَا نَحْنُ مُسْتَهْزِئُونَ ۝ اللَّهُ يَسْتَهْزِئُ بِهِمْ وَيَمُدُّهُمْ فِي طُغْيَانِهِمْ يَعْمَهُونَ ۝ أُولَٰئِكَ الَّذِينَ اشْتَرَوُا الضَّلَالَةَ بِالْهُدَىٰ فَمَا رَبِحَت تِّجَارَتُهُمْ وَمَا كَانُوا مُهْتَدِينَ ۝ مَثَلُهُمْ كَمَثَلِ الَّذِي اسْتَوْقَدَ نَارًا فَلَمَّا أَضَاءَتْ مَا حَوْلَهُ ذَهَبَ اللَّهُ بِنُورِهِمْ وَتَرَكَهُمْ فِي ظُلُمَاتٍ لَّا يُبْصِرُونَ ۝ صُمٌّ بُكْمٌ عُمْيٌ فَهُمْ لَا يَرْجِعُونَ ۝ أَوْ كَصَيِّبٍ مِّنَ السَّمَاءِ فِيهِ ظُلُمَاتٌ وَرَعْدٌ وَبَرْقٌ يَجْعَلُونَ أَصَابِعَهُمْ فِي آذَانِهِم مِّنَ الصَّوَاعِقِ حَذَرَ الْمَوْتِ ۚ وَاللَّهُ مُحِيطٌ بِالْكَافِرِينَ ۝ يَكَادُ الْبَرْقُ يَخْطَفُ أَبْصَارَهُمْ ۖ كُلَّمَا أَضَاءَ لَهُم مَّشَوْا فِيهِ وَإِذَا أَظْلَمَ عَلَيْهِمْ قَامُوا ۚ وَلَوْ شَاءَ اللَّهُ لَذَهَبَ بِسَمْعِهِمْ وَأَبْصَارِهِمْ ۚ إِنَّ اللَّهَ عَلَىٰ كُلِّ شَيْءٍ قَدِيرٌ ۝ يَا أَيُّهَا النَّاسُ اعْبُدُوا رَبَّكُمُ الَّذِي خَلَقَكُمْ وَالَّذِينَ مِن قَبْلِكُمْ لَعَلَّكُمْ تَتَّقُونَ ۝ الَّذِي جَعَلَ لَكُمُ الْأَرْضَ فِرَاشًا وَالسَّمَاءَ بِنَاءً وَأَنزَلَ مِنَ السَّمَاءِ مَاءً فَأَخْرَجَ بِهِ مِنَ الثَّمَرَاتِ رِزْقًا لَّكُمْ ۖ فَلَا تَجْعَلُوا لِلَّهِ أَندَادًا وَأَنتُمْ تَعْلَمُونَ ۝ وَإِن كُنتُمْ فِي رَيْبٍ مِّمَّا نَزَّلْنَا عَلَىٰ عَبْدِنَا فَأْتُوا بِسُورَةٍ مِّن مِّثْلِهِ وَادْعُوا شُهَدَاءَكُم مِّن دُونِ اللَّهِ إِن كُنتُمْ صَادِقِينَ ۝ فَإِن لَّمْ تَفْعَلُوا وَلَن تَفْعَلُوا فَاتَّقُوا النَّارَ الَّتِي وَقُودُهَا النَّاسُ وَالْحِجَارَةُ ۖ أُعِدَّتْ لِلْكَافِرِينَ ۝ وَبَشِّرِ الَّذِينَ آمَنُوا وَعَمِلُوا

ٱلصَّٰلِحَٰتِ أَنَّ لَهُمْ جَنَّٰتٍ تَجْرِى مِن تَحْتِهَا ٱلْأَنْهَٰرُ ۖ كُلَّمَا رُزِقُوا۟ مِنْهَا مِن ثَمَرَةٍ رِّزْقًا ۙ قَالُوا۟ هَٰذَا ٱلَّذِى رُزِقْنَا مِن قَبْلُ ۖ وَأُتُوا۟ بِهِۦ مُتَشَٰبِهًا ۖ وَلَهُمْ فِيهَآ أَزْوَٰجٌ مُّطَهَّرَةٌ ۖ وَهُمْ فِيهَا خَٰلِدُونَ ۝ إِنَّ ٱللَّهَ لَا يَسْتَحْىِۦٓ أَن يَضْرِبَ مَثَلًا مَّا بَعُوضَةً فَمَا فَوْقَهَا ۚ فَأَمَّا ٱلَّذِينَ ءَامَنُوا۟ فَيَعْلَمُونَ أَنَّهُ ٱلْحَقُّ مِن رَّبِّهِمْ ۖ وَأَمَّا ٱلَّذِينَ كَفَرُوا۟ فَيَقُولُونَ مَاذَآ أَرَادَ ٱللَّهُ بِهَٰذَا مَثَلًا ۘ يُضِلُّ بِهِۦ كَثِيرًا وَيَهْدِى بِهِۦ كَثِيرًا ۚ وَمَا يُضِلُّ بِهِۦٓ إِلَّا ٱلْفَٰسِقِينَ ۝ ٱلَّذِينَ يَنقُضُونَ عَهْدَ ٱللَّهِ مِنۢ بَعْدِ مِيثَٰقِهِۦ وَيَقْطَعُونَ مَآ أَمَرَ ٱللَّهُ بِهِۦٓ أَن يُوصَلَ وَيُفْسِدُونَ فِى ٱلْأَرْضِ ۚ أُو۟لَٰٓئِكَ هُمُ ٱلْخَٰسِرُونَ ۝ كَيْفَ تَكْفُرُونَ بِٱللَّهِ وَكُنتُمْ أَمْوَٰتًا فَأَحْيَٰكُمْ ۖ ثُمَّ يُمِيتُكُمْ ثُمَّ يُحْيِيكُمْ ثُمَّ إِلَيْهِ تُرْجَعُونَ ۝ هُوَ ٱلَّذِى خَلَقَ لَكُم مَّا فِى ٱلْأَرْضِ جَمِيعًا ثُمَّ ٱسْتَوَىٰٓ إِلَى ٱلسَّمَآءِ فَسَوَّىٰهُنَّ سَبْعَ سَمَٰوَٰتٍ ۚ وَهُوَ بِكُلِّ شَىْءٍ عَلِيمٌ ۝ وَإِذْ قَالَ رَبُّكَ لِلْمَلَٰٓئِكَةِ إِنِّى جَاعِلٌ فِى ٱلْأَرْضِ خَلِيفَةً ۖ قَالُوٓا۟ أَتَجْعَلُ فِيهَا مَن يُفْسِدُ فِيهَا وَيَسْفِكُ ٱلدِّمَآءَ وَنَحْنُ نُسَبِّحُ بِحَمْدِكَ وَنُقَدِّسُ لَكَ ۖ قَالَ إِنِّىٓ أَعْلَمُ مَا لَا تَعْلَمُونَ ۝ وَعَلَّمَ ءَادَمَ ٱلْأَسْمَآءَ كُلَّهَا ثُمَّ عَرَضَهُمْ عَلَى ٱلْمَلَٰٓئِكَةِ فَقَالَ أَنۢبِـُٔونِى بِأَسْمَآءِ هَٰٓؤُلَآءِ إِن كُنتُمْ صَٰدِقِينَ ۝ قَالُوا۟ سُبْحَٰنَكَ لَا عِلْمَ لَنَآ إِلَّا مَا عَلَّمْتَنَآ ۖ إِنَّكَ أَنتَ ٱلْعَلِيمُ ٱلْحَكِيمُ ۝ قَالَ يَٰٓـَٔادَمُ أَنۢبِئْهُم بِأَسْمَآئِهِمْ ۖ فَلَمَّآ أَنۢبَأَهُم بِأَسْمَآئِهِمْ قَالَ أَلَمْ أَقُل لَّكُمْ إِنِّىٓ أَعْلَمُ غَيْبَ ٱلسَّمَٰوَٰتِ وَٱلْأَرْضِ وَأَعْلَمُ مَا تُبْدُونَ وَمَا كُنتُمْ تَكْتُمُونَ ۝ وَإِذْ قُلْنَا لِلْمَلَٰٓئِكَةِ ٱسْجُدُوا۟ لِءَادَمَ فَسَجَدُوٓا۟ إِلَّآ إِبْلِيسَ أَبَىٰ وَٱسْتَكْبَرَ وَكَانَ مِنَ ٱلْكَٰفِرِينَ ۝ وَقُلْنَا يَٰٓـَٔادَمُ ٱسْكُنْ أَنتَ وَزَوْجُكَ ٱلْجَنَّةَ وَكُلَا

مِنْهَا رَغَدًا حَيْثُ شِئْتُمَا وَلَا تَقْرَبَا هَـٰذِهِ ٱلشَّجَرَةَ فَتَكُونَا مِنَ ٱلظَّـٰلِمِينَ ۝ فَأَزَلَّهُمَا ٱلشَّيْطَـٰنُ عَنْهَا فَأَخْرَجَهُمَا مِمَّا كَانَا فِيهِ ۖ وَقُلْنَا ٱهْبِطُوا۟ بَعْضُكُمْ لِبَعْضٍ عَدُوٌّ ۖ وَلَكُمْ فِى ٱلْأَرْضِ مُسْتَقَرٌّ وَمَتَـٰعٌ إِلَىٰ حِينٍ ۝ فَتَلَقَّىٰٓ ءَادَمُ مِن رَّبِّهِۦ كَلِمَـٰتٍ فَتَابَ عَلَيْهِ ۚ إِنَّهُۥ هُوَ ٱلتَّوَّابُ ٱلرَّحِيمُ ۝ قُلْنَا ٱهْبِطُوا۟ مِنْهَا جَمِيعًا ۖ فَإِمَّا يَأْتِيَنَّكُم مِّنِّى هُدًى فَمَن تَبِعَ هُدَاىَ فَلَا خَوْفٌ عَلَيْهِمْ وَلَا هُمْ يَحْزَنُونَ ۝ وَٱلَّذِينَ كَفَرُوا۟ وَكَذَّبُوا۟ بِـَٔايَـٰتِنَآ أُو۟لَـٰٓئِكَ أَصْحَـٰبُ ٱلنَّارِ ۖ هُمْ فِيهَا خَـٰلِدُونَ ۝ يَـٰبَنِىٓ إِسْرَٰٓءِيلَ ٱذْكُرُوا۟ نِعْمَتِىَ ٱلَّتِىٓ أَنْعَمْتُ عَلَيْكُمْ وَأَوْفُوا۟ بِعَهْدِىٓ أُوفِ بِعَهْدِكُمْ وَإِيَّـٰىَ فَٱرْهَبُونِ ۝ وَءَامِنُوا۟ بِمَآ أَنزَلْتُ مُصَدِّقًا لِّمَا مَعَكُمْ وَلَا تَكُونُوٓا۟ أَوَّلَ كَافِرٍۭ بِهِۦ ۖ وَلَا تَشْتَرُوا۟ بِـَٔايَـٰتِى ثَمَنًا قَلِيلًا وَإِيَّـٰىَ فَٱتَّقُونِ ۝ وَلَا تَلْبِسُوا۟ ٱلْحَقَّ بِٱلْبَـٰطِلِ وَتَكْتُمُوا۟ ٱلْحَقَّ وَأَنتُمْ تَعْلَمُونَ ۝ وَأَقِيمُوا۟ ٱلصَّلَوٰةَ وَءَاتُوا۟ ٱلزَّكَوٰةَ وَٱرْكَعُوا۟ مَعَ ٱلرَّٰكِعِينَ ۝ ۞ أَتَأْمُرُونَ ٱلنَّاسَ بِٱلْبِرِّ وَتَنسَوْنَ أَنفُسَكُمْ وَأَنتُمْ تَتْلُونَ ٱلْكِتَـٰبَ ۚ أَفَلَا تَعْقِلُونَ ۝ وَٱسْتَعِينُوا۟ بِٱلصَّبْرِ وَٱلصَّلَوٰةِ ۚ وَإِنَّهَا لَكَبِيرَةٌ إِلَّا عَلَى ٱلْخَـٰشِعِينَ ۝ ٱلَّذِينَ يَظُنُّونَ أَنَّهُم مُّلَـٰقُوا۟ رَبِّهِمْ وَأَنَّهُمْ إِلَيْهِ رَٰجِعُونَ ۝ يَـٰبَنِىٓ إِسْرَٰٓءِيلَ ٱذْكُرُوا۟ نِعْمَتِىَ ٱلَّتِىٓ أَنْعَمْتُ عَلَيْكُمْ وَأَنِّى فَضَّلْتُكُمْ عَلَى ٱلْعَـٰلَمِينَ ۝ وَٱتَّقُوا۟ يَوْمًا لَّا تَجْزِى نَفْسٌ عَن نَّفْسٍ شَيْـًٔا وَلَا يُقْبَلُ مِنْهَا شَفَـٰعَةٌ وَلَا يُؤْخَذُ مِنْهَا عَدْلٌ وَلَا هُمْ يُنصَرُونَ ۝ وَإِذْ نَجَّيْنَـٰكُم مِّنْ ءَالِ فِرْعَوْنَ يَسُومُونَكُمْ سُوٓءَ ٱلْعَذَابِ يُذَبِّحُونَ أَبْنَآءَكُمْ وَيَسْتَحْيُونَ نِسَآءَكُمْ ۚ وَفِى ذَٰلِكُم بَلَآءٌ مِّن رَّبِّكُمْ عَظِيمٌ ۝ وَإِذْ فَرَقْنَا بِكُمُ ٱلْبَحْرَ فَأَنجَيْنَـٰكُمْ وَأَغْرَقْنَآ ءَالَ فِرْعَوْنَ وَأَنتُمْ تَنظُرُونَ ۝ وَإِذْ وَٰعَدْنَا مُوسَىٰٓ أَرْبَعِينَ

لَيْلَةً ثُمَّ ٱتَّخَذْتُمُ ٱلْعِجْلَ مِنۢ بَعْدِهِۦ وَأَنتُمْ ظَٰلِمُونَ ۝ ثُمَّ عَفَوْنَا عَنكُم مِّنۢ بَعْدِ ذَٰلِكَ لَعَلَّكُمْ تَشْكُرُونَ ۝ وَإِذْ ءَاتَيْنَا مُوسَى ٱلْكِتَٰبَ وَٱلْفُرْقَانَ لَعَلَّكُمْ تَهْتَدُونَ ۝ وَإِذْ قَالَ مُوسَىٰ لِقَوْمِهِۦ يَٰقَوْمِ إِنَّكُمْ ظَلَمْتُمْ أَنفُسَكُم بِٱتِّخَاذِكُمُ ٱلْعِجْلَ فَتُوبُوٓا۟ إِلَىٰ بَارِئِكُمْ فَٱقْتُلُوٓا۟ أَنفُسَكُمْ ذَٰلِكُمْ خَيْرٌ لَّكُمْ عِندَ بَارِئِكُمْ فَتَابَ عَلَيْكُمْ إِنَّهُۥ هُوَ ٱلتَّوَّابُ ٱلرَّحِيمُ ۝ وَإِذْ قُلْتُمْ يَٰمُوسَىٰ لَن نُّؤْمِنَ لَكَ حَتَّىٰ نَرَى ٱللَّهَ جَهْرَةً فَأَخَذَتْكُمُ ٱلصَّٰعِقَةُ وَأَنتُمْ تَنظُرُونَ ۝ ثُمَّ بَعَثْنَٰكُم مِّنۢ بَعْدِ مَوْتِكُمْ لَعَلَّكُمْ تَشْكُرُونَ ۝ وَظَلَّلْنَا عَلَيْكُمُ ٱلْغَمَامَ وَأَنزَلْنَا عَلَيْكُمُ ٱلْمَنَّ وَٱلسَّلْوَىٰ كُلُوا۟ مِن طَيِّبَٰتِ مَا رَزَقْنَٰكُمْ وَمَا ظَلَمُونَا وَلَٰكِن كَانُوٓا۟ أَنفُسَهُمْ يَظْلِمُونَ ۝ وَإِذْ قُلْنَا ٱدْخُلُوا۟ هَٰذِهِ ٱلْقَرْيَةَ فَكُلُوا۟ مِنْهَا حَيْثُ شِئْتُمْ رَغَدًا وَٱدْخُلُوا۟ ٱلْبَابَ سُجَّدًا وَقُولُوا۟ حِطَّةٌ نَّغْفِرْ لَكُمْ خَطَٰيَٰكُمْ وَسَنَزِيدُ ٱلْمُحْسِنِينَ ۝ فَبَدَّلَ ٱلَّذِينَ ظَلَمُوا۟ قَوْلًا غَيْرَ ٱلَّذِى قِيلَ لَهُمْ فَأَنزَلْنَا عَلَى ٱلَّذِينَ ظَلَمُوا۟ رِجْزًا مِّنَ ٱلسَّمَآءِ بِمَا كَانُوا۟ يَفْسُقُونَ ۝ ۞ وَإِذِ ٱسْتَسْقَىٰ مُوسَىٰ لِقَوْمِهِۦ فَقُلْنَا ٱضْرِب بِّعَصَاكَ ٱلْحَجَرَ فَٱنفَجَرَتْ مِنْهُ ٱثْنَتَا عَشْرَةَ عَيْنًا قَدْ عَلِمَ كُلُّ أُنَاسٍ مَّشْرَبَهُمْ كُلُوا۟ وَٱشْرَبُوا۟ مِن رِّزْقِ ٱللَّهِ وَلَا تَعْثَوْا۟ فِى ٱلْأَرْضِ مُفْسِدِينَ ۝ وَإِذْ قُلْتُمْ يَٰمُوسَىٰ لَن نَّصْبِرَ عَلَىٰ طَعَامٍ وَٰحِدٍ فَٱدْعُ لَنَا رَبَّكَ يُخْرِجْ لَنَا مِمَّا تُنۢبِتُ ٱلْأَرْضُ مِنۢ بَقْلِهَا وَقِثَّآئِهَا وَفُومِهَا وَعَدَسِهَا وَبَصَلِهَا قَالَ أَتَسْتَبْدِلُونَ ٱلَّذِى هُوَ أَدْنَىٰ بِٱلَّذِى هُوَ خَيْرٌ ٱهْبِطُوا۟ مِصْرًا فَإِنَّ لَكُم مَّا سَأَلْتُمْ وَضُرِبَتْ عَلَيْهِمُ ٱلذِّلَّةُ وَٱلْمَسْكَنَةُ وَبَآءُو بِغَضَبٍ مِّنَ ٱللَّهِ ذَٰلِكَ بِأَنَّهُمْ كَانُوا۟ يَكْفُرُونَ

بِـَٔايَٰتِ ٱللَّهِ وَيَقْتُلُونَ ٱلنَّبِيِّـۧنَ بِغَيْرِ ٱلْحَقِّ ۗ ذَٰلِكَ بِمَا عَصَوا۟ وَّكَانُوا۟ يَعْتَدُونَ ۝ إِنَّ ٱلَّذِينَ ءَامَنُوا۟ وَٱلَّذِينَ هَادُوا۟ وَٱلنَّصَٰرَىٰ وَٱلصَّٰبِـِٔينَ مَنْ ءَامَنَ بِٱللَّهِ وَٱلْيَوْمِ ٱلْـَٔاخِرِ وَعَمِلَ صَٰلِحًا فَلَهُمْ أَجْرُهُمْ عِندَ رَبِّهِمْ وَلَا خَوْفٌ عَلَيْهِمْ وَلَا هُمْ يَحْزَنُونَ ۝ وَإِذْ أَخَذْنَا مِيثَٰقَكُمْ وَرَفَعْنَا فَوْقَكُمُ ٱلطُّورَ خُذُوا۟ مَآ ءَاتَيْنَٰكُم بِقُوَّةٍ وَٱذْكُرُوا۟ مَا فِيهِ لَعَلَّكُمْ تَتَّقُونَ ۝ ثُمَّ تَوَلَّيْتُم مِّنۢ بَعْدِ ذَٰلِكَ ۖ فَلَوْلَا فَضْلُ ٱللَّهِ عَلَيْكُمْ وَرَحْمَتُهُۥ لَكُنتُم مِّنَ ٱلْخَٰسِرِينَ ۝ وَلَقَدْ عَلِمْتُمُ ٱلَّذِينَ ٱعْتَدَوْا۟ مِنكُمْ فِى ٱلسَّبْتِ فَقُلْنَا لَهُمْ كُونُوا۟ قِرَدَةً خَٰسِـِٔينَ ۝ فَجَعَلْنَٰهَا نَكَٰلًا لِّمَا بَيْنَ يَدَيْهَا وَمَا خَلْفَهَا وَمَوْعِظَةً لِّلْمُتَّقِينَ ۝ وَإِذْ قَالَ مُوسَىٰ لِقَوْمِهِۦٓ إِنَّ ٱللَّهَ يَأْمُرُكُمْ أَن تَذْبَحُوا۟ بَقَرَةً ۖ قَالُوٓا۟ أَتَتَّخِذُنَا هُزُوًا ۖ قَالَ أَعُوذُ بِٱللَّهِ أَنْ أَكُونَ مِنَ ٱلْجَٰهِلِينَ ۝ قَالُوا۟ ٱدْعُ لَنَا رَبَّكَ يُبَيِّن لَّنَا مَا هِىَ ۚ قَالَ إِنَّهُۥ يَقُولُ إِنَّهَا بَقَرَةٌ لَّا فَارِضٌ وَلَا بِكْرٌ عَوَانٌۢ بَيْنَ ذَٰلِكَ ۖ فَٱفْعَلُوا۟ مَا تُؤْمَرُونَ ۝ قَالُوا۟ ٱدْعُ لَنَا رَبَّكَ يُبَيِّن لَّنَا مَا لَوْنُهَا ۚ قَالَ إِنَّهُۥ يَقُولُ إِنَّهَا بَقَرَةٌ صَفْرَآءُ فَاقِعٌ لَّوْنُهَا تَسُرُّ ٱلنَّٰظِرِينَ ۝ قَالُوا۟ ٱدْعُ لَنَا رَبَّكَ يُبَيِّن لَّنَا مَا هِىَ إِنَّ ٱلْبَقَرَ تَشَٰبَهَ عَلَيْنَا وَإِنَّآ إِن شَآءَ ٱللَّهُ لَمُهْتَدُونَ ۝ قَالَ إِنَّهُۥ يَقُولُ إِنَّهَا بَقَرَةٌ لَّا ذَلُولٌ تُثِيرُ ٱلْأَرْضَ وَلَا تَسْقِى ٱلْحَرْثَ مُسَلَّمَةٌ لَّا شِيَةَ فِيهَا ۚ قَالُوا۟ ٱلْـَٰٔنَ جِئْتَ بِٱلْحَقِّ ۚ فَذَبَحُوهَا وَمَا كَادُوا۟ يَفْعَلُونَ ۝ وَإِذْ قَتَلْتُمْ نَفْسًا فَٱدَّٰرَٰءْتُمْ فِيهَا ۖ وَٱللَّهُ مُخْرِجٌ مَّا كُنتُمْ تَكْتُمُونَ ۝ فَقُلْنَا ٱضْرِبُوهُ بِبَعْضِهَا ۚ كَذَٰلِكَ يُحْىِ ٱللَّهُ ٱلْمَوْتَىٰ وَيُرِيكُمْ ءَايَٰتِهِۦ لَعَلَّكُمْ تَعْقِلُونَ ۝ ثُمَّ قَسَتْ قُلُوبُكُم مِّنۢ بَعْدِ ذَٰلِكَ فَهِىَ كَٱلْحِجَارَةِ أَوْ أَشَدُّ قَسْوَةً ۚ وَإِنَّ مِنَ ٱلْحِجَارَةِ لَمَا

يَتَفَجَّرُ مِنْهُ ٱلْأَنْهَٰرُ ۚ وَإِنَّ مِنْهَا لَمَا يَشَّقَّقُ فَيَخْرُجُ مِنْهُ ٱلْمَآءُ ۚ وَإِنَّ مِنْهَا لَمَا يَهْبِطُ مِنْ خَشْيَةِ ٱللَّهِ ۗ وَمَا ٱللَّهُ بِغَٰفِلٍ عَمَّا تَعْمَلُونَ ۝ أَفَتَطْمَعُونَ أَن يُؤْمِنُوا۟ لَكُمْ وَقَدْ كَانَ فَرِيقٌ مِّنْهُمْ يَسْمَعُونَ كَلَٰمَ ٱللَّهِ ثُمَّ يُحَرِّفُونَهُۥ مِنۢ بَعْدِ مَا عَقَلُوهُ وَهُمْ يَعْلَمُونَ ۝ وَإِذَا لَقُوا۟ ٱلَّذِينَ ءَامَنُوا۟ قَالُوٓا۟ ءَامَنَّا وَإِذَا خَلَا بَعْضُهُمْ إِلَىٰ بَعْضٍ قَالُوٓا۟ أَتُحَدِّثُونَهُم بِمَا فَتَحَ ٱللَّهُ عَلَيْكُمْ لِيُحَآجُّوكُم بِهِۦ عِندَ رَبِّكُمْ ۚ أَفَلَا تَعْقِلُونَ ۝ أَوَلَا يَعْلَمُونَ أَنَّ ٱللَّهَ يَعْلَمُ مَا يُسِرُّونَ وَمَا يُعْلِنُونَ ۝ وَمِنْهُمْ أُمِّيُّونَ لَا يَعْلَمُونَ ٱلْكِتَٰبَ إِلَّآ أَمَانِىَّ وَإِنْ هُمْ إِلَّا يَظُنُّونَ ۝ فَوَيْلٌ لِّلَّذِينَ يَكْتُبُونَ ٱلْكِتَٰبَ بِأَيْدِيهِمْ ثُمَّ يَقُولُونَ هَٰذَا مِنْ عِندِ ٱللَّهِ لِيَشْتَرُوا۟ بِهِۦ ثَمَنًا قَلِيلًا ۖ فَوَيْلٌ لَّهُم مِّمَّا كَتَبَتْ أَيْدِيهِمْ وَوَيْلٌ لَّهُم مِّمَّا يَكْسِبُونَ ۝ وَقَالُوا۟ لَن تَمَسَّنَا ٱلنَّارُ إِلَّآ أَيَّامًا مَّعْدُودَةً ۚ قُلْ أَتَّخَذْتُمْ عِندَ ٱللَّهِ عَهْدًا فَلَن يُخْلِفَ ٱللَّهُ عَهْدَهُۥٓ ۖ أَمْ تَقُولُونَ عَلَى ٱللَّهِ مَا لَا تَعْلَمُونَ ۝ بَلَىٰ مَن كَسَبَ سَيِّئَةً وَأَحَٰطَتْ بِهِۦ خَطِيٓـَٔتُهُۥ فَأُو۟لَٰٓئِكَ أَصْحَٰبُ ٱلنَّارِ ۖ هُمْ فِيهَا خَٰلِدُونَ ۝ وَٱلَّذِينَ ءَامَنُوا۟ وَعَمِلُوا۟ ٱلصَّٰلِحَٰتِ أُو۟لَٰٓئِكَ أَصْحَٰبُ ٱلْجَنَّةِ ۖ هُمْ فِيهَا خَٰلِدُونَ ۝ وَإِذْ أَخَذْنَا مِيثَٰقَ بَنِىٓ إِسْرَٰٓءِيلَ لَا تَعْبُدُونَ إِلَّا ٱللَّهَ وَبِٱلْوَٰلِدَيْنِ إِحْسَانًا وَذِى ٱلْقُرْبَىٰ وَٱلْيَتَٰمَىٰ وَٱلْمَسَٰكِينِ وَقُولُوا۟ لِلنَّاسِ حُسْنًا وَأَقِيمُوا۟ ٱلصَّلَوٰةَ وَءَاتُوا۟ ٱلزَّكَوٰةَ ثُمَّ تَوَلَّيْتُمْ إِلَّا قَلِيلًا مِّنكُمْ وَأَنتُم مُّعْرِضُونَ ۝ وَإِذْ أَخَذْنَا مِيثَٰقَكُمْ لَا تَسْفِكُونَ دِمَآءَكُمْ وَلَا تُخْرِجُونَ أَنفُسَكُم مِّن دِيَٰرِكُمْ ثُمَّ أَقْرَرْتُمْ وَأَنتُمْ تَشْهَدُونَ ۝ ثُمَّ أَنتُمْ هَٰٓؤُلَآءِ تَقْتُلُونَ أَنفُسَكُمْ وَتُخْرِجُونَ فَرِيقًا مِّنكُم مِّن دِيَٰرِهِمْ تَظَٰهَرُونَ عَلَيْهِم بِٱلْإِثْمِ

وَٱلْعُدْوَٰنِ وَإِن يَأْتُوكُمْ أُسَٰرَىٰ تُفَٰدُوهُمْ وَهُوَ مُحَرَّمٌ عَلَيْكُمْ إِخْرَاجُهُمْ ۚ أَفَتُؤْمِنُونَ بِبَعْضِ ٱلْكِتَٰبِ وَتَكْفُرُونَ بِبَعْضٍ ۚ فَمَا جَزَآءُ مَن يَفْعَلُ ذَٰلِكَ مِنكُمْ إِلَّا خِزْيٌ فِى ٱلْحَيَوٰةِ ٱلدُّنْيَا ۖ وَيَوْمَ ٱلْقِيَٰمَةِ يُرَدُّونَ إِلَىٰٓ أَشَدِّ ٱلْعَذَابِ ۗ وَمَا ٱللَّهُ بِغَٰفِلٍ عَمَّا تَعْمَلُونَ ۝ أُو۟لَٰٓئِكَ ٱلَّذِينَ ٱشْتَرَوُا۟ ٱلْحَيَوٰةَ ٱلدُّنْيَا بِٱلْءَاخِرَةِ ۖ فَلَا يُخَفَّفُ عَنْهُمُ ٱلْعَذَابُ وَلَا هُمْ يُنصَرُونَ ۝ وَلَقَدْ ءَاتَيْنَا مُوسَى ٱلْكِتَٰبَ وَقَفَّيْنَا مِنۢ بَعْدِهِۦ بِٱلرُّسُلِ ۖ وَءَاتَيْنَا عِيسَى ٱبْنَ مَرْيَمَ ٱلْبَيِّنَٰتِ وَأَيَّدْنَٰهُ بِرُوحِ ٱلْقُدُسِ ۗ أَفَكُلَّمَا جَآءَكُمْ رَسُولٌۢ بِمَا لَا تَهْوَىٰٓ أَنفُسُكُمُ ٱسْتَكْبَرْتُمْ فَفَرِيقًا كَذَّبْتُمْ وَفَرِيقًا تَقْتُلُونَ ۝ وَقَالُوا۟ قُلُوبُنَا غُلْفٌۢ ۚ بَل لَّعَنَهُمُ ٱللَّهُ بِكُفْرِهِمْ فَقَلِيلًا مَّا يُؤْمِنُونَ ۝ وَلَمَّا جَآءَهُمْ كِتَٰبٌ مِّنْ عِندِ ٱللَّهِ مُصَدِّقٌ لِّمَا مَعَهُمْ وَكَانُوا۟ مِن قَبْلُ يَسْتَفْتِحُونَ عَلَى ٱلَّذِينَ كَفَرُوا۟ فَلَمَّا جَآءَهُم مَّا عَرَفُوا۟ كَفَرُوا۟ بِهِۦ ۚ فَلَعْنَةُ ٱللَّهِ عَلَى ٱلْكَٰفِرِينَ ۝ بِئْسَمَا ٱشْتَرَوْا۟ بِهِۦٓ أَنفُسَهُمْ أَن يَكْفُرُوا۟ بِمَآ أَنزَلَ ٱللَّهُ بَغْيًا أَن يُنَزِّلَ ٱللَّهُ مِن فَضْلِهِۦ عَلَىٰ مَن يَشَآءُ مِنْ عِبَادِهِۦ ۖ فَبَآءُو بِغَضَبٍ عَلَىٰ غَضَبٍ ۚ وَلِلْكَٰفِرِينَ عَذَابٌ مُّهِينٌ ۝ وَإِذَا قِيلَ لَهُمْ ءَامِنُوا۟ بِمَآ أَنزَلَ ٱللَّهُ قَالُوا۟ نُؤْمِنُ بِمَآ أُنزِلَ عَلَيْنَا وَيَكْفُرُونَ بِمَا وَرَآءَهُۥ وَهُوَ ٱلْحَقُّ مُصَدِّقًا لِّمَا مَعَهُمْ ۗ قُلْ فَلِمَ تَقْتُلُونَ أَنۢبِيَآءَ ٱللَّهِ مِن قَبْلُ إِن كُنتُم مُّؤْمِنِينَ ۝ ۞ وَلَقَدْ جَآءَكُم مُّوسَىٰ بِٱلْبَيِّنَٰتِ ثُمَّ ٱتَّخَذْتُمُ ٱلْعِجْلَ مِنۢ بَعْدِهِۦ وَأَنتُمْ ظَٰلِمُونَ ۝ وَإِذْ أَخَذْنَا مِيثَٰقَكُمْ وَرَفَعْنَا فَوْقَكُمُ ٱلطُّورَ خُذُوا۟ مَآ ءَاتَيْنَٰكُم بِقُوَّةٍ وَٱسْمَعُوا۟ ۖ قَالُوا۟ سَمِعْنَا وَعَصَيْنَا وَأُشْرِبُوا۟ فِى قُلُوبِهِمُ ٱلْعِجْلَ بِكُفْرِهِمْ ۚ قُلْ بِئْسَمَا يَأْمُرُكُم بِهِۦٓ إِيمَٰنُكُمْ إِن كُنتُم

مُؤْمِنِينَ ۝ قُلْ إِن كَانَتْ لَكُمُ ٱلدَّارُ ٱلْأَخِرَةُ عِندَ ٱللَّهِ خَالِصَةً مِّن دُونِ ٱلنَّاسِ فَتَمَنَّوُا۟ ٱلْمَوْتَ إِن كُنتُمْ صَٰدِقِينَ ۝ وَلَن يَتَمَنَّوْهُ أَبَدًۢا بِمَا قَدَّمَتْ أَيْدِيهِمْ ۚ وَٱللَّهُ عَلِيمٌۢ بِٱلظَّٰلِمِينَ ۝ وَلَتَجِدَنَّهُمْ أَحْرَصَ ٱلنَّاسِ عَلَىٰ حَيَوٰةٍ وَمِنَ ٱلَّذِينَ أَشْرَكُوا۟ ۚ يَوَدُّ أَحَدُهُمْ لَوْ يُعَمَّرُ أَلْفَ سَنَةٍ وَمَا هُوَ بِمُزَحْزِحِهِۦ مِنَ ٱلْعَذَابِ أَن يُعَمَّرَ ۗ وَٱللَّهُ بَصِيرٌۢ بِمَا يَعْمَلُونَ ۝ قُلْ مَن كَانَ عَدُوًّۭا لِّجِبْرِيلَ فَإِنَّهُۥ نَزَّلَهُۥ عَلَىٰ قَلْبِكَ بِإِذْنِ ٱللَّهِ مُصَدِّقًۭا لِّمَا بَيْنَ يَدَيْهِ وَهُدًۭى وَبُشْرَىٰ لِلْمُؤْمِنِينَ ۝ مَن كَانَ عَدُوًّۭا لِّلَّهِ وَمَلَٰٓئِكَتِهِۦ وَرُسُلِهِۦ وَجِبْرِيلَ وَمِيكَىٰلَ فَإِنَّ ٱللَّهَ عَدُوٌّۭ لِّلْكَٰفِرِينَ ۝ وَلَقَدْ أَنزَلْنَآ إِلَيْكَ ءَايَٰتٍۭ بَيِّنَٰتٍ ۖ وَمَا يَكْفُرُ بِهَآ إِلَّا ٱلْفَٰسِقُونَ ۝ أَوَكُلَّمَا عَٰهَدُوا۟ عَهْدًۭا نَّبَذَهُۥ فَرِيقٌۭ مِّنْهُم ۚ بَلْ أَكْثَرُهُمْ لَا يُؤْمِنُونَ ۝ وَلَمَّا جَآءَهُمْ رَسُولٌۭ مِّنْ عِندِ ٱللَّهِ مُصَدِّقٌۭ لِّمَا مَعَهُمْ نَبَذَ فَرِيقٌۭ مِّنَ ٱلَّذِينَ أُوتُوا۟ ٱلْكِتَٰبَ كِتَٰبَ ٱللَّهِ وَرَآءَ ظُهُورِهِمْ كَأَنَّهُمْ لَا يَعْلَمُونَ ۝ وَٱتَّبَعُوا۟ مَا تَتْلُوا۟ ٱلشَّيَٰطِينُ عَلَىٰ مُلْكِ سُلَيْمَٰنَ ۖ وَمَا كَفَرَ سُلَيْمَٰنُ وَلَٰكِنَّ ٱلشَّيَٰطِينَ كَفَرُوا۟ يُعَلِّمُونَ ٱلنَّاسَ ٱلسِّحْرَ وَمَآ أُنزِلَ عَلَى ٱلْمَلَكَيْنِ بِبَابِلَ هَٰرُوتَ وَمَٰرُوتَ ۚ وَمَا يُعَلِّمَانِ مِنْ أَحَدٍ حَتَّىٰ يَقُولَآ إِنَّمَا نَحْنُ فِتْنَةٌۭ فَلَا تَكْفُرْ ۖ فَيَتَعَلَّمُونَ مِنْهُمَا مَا يُفَرِّقُونَ بِهِۦ بَيْنَ ٱلْمَرْءِ وَزَوْجِهِۦ ۚ وَمَا هُم بِضَآرِّينَ بِهِۦ مِنْ أَحَدٍ إِلَّا بِإِذْنِ ٱللَّهِ ۚ وَيَتَعَلَّمُونَ مَا يَضُرُّهُمْ وَلَا يَنفَعُهُمْ ۚ وَلَقَدْ عَلِمُوا۟ لَمَنِ ٱشْتَرَىٰهُ مَا لَهُۥ فِى ٱلْأَخِرَةِ مِنْ خَلَٰقٍۢ ۚ وَلَبِئْسَ مَا شَرَوْا۟ بِهِۦٓ أَنفُسَهُمْ ۚ لَوْ كَانُوا۟ يَعْلَمُونَ ۝ وَلَوْ أَنَّهُمْ ءَامَنُوا۟ وَٱتَّقَوْا۟ لَمَثُوبَةٌۭ مِّنْ عِندِ ٱللَّهِ خَيْرٌۭ ۖ لَّوْ كَانُوا۟ يَعْلَمُونَ ۝ يَٰٓأَيُّهَا ٱلَّذِينَ

ءَامَنُوا۟ لَا تَقُولُوا۟ رَٰعِنَا وَقُولُوا۟ ٱنظُرْنَا وَٱسْمَعُوا۟ ۗ وَلِلْكَٰفِرِينَ عَذَابٌ أَلِيمٌ ۝ مَّا يَوَدُّ ٱلَّذِينَ كَفَرُوا۟ مِنْ أَهْلِ ٱلْكِتَٰبِ وَلَا ٱلْمُشْرِكِينَ أَن يُنَزَّلَ عَلَيْكُم مِّنْ خَيْرٍ مِّن رَّبِّكُمْ ۗ وَٱللَّهُ يَخْتَصُّ بِرَحْمَتِهِۦ مَن يَشَآءُ ۚ وَٱللَّهُ ذُو ٱلْفَضْلِ ٱلْعَظِيمِ ۝ مَا نَنسَخْ مِنْ ءَايَةٍ أَوْ نُنسِهَا نَأْتِ بِخَيْرٍ مِّنْهَآ أَوْ مِثْلِهَآ ۗ أَلَمْ تَعْلَمْ أَنَّ ٱللَّهَ عَلَىٰ كُلِّ شَىْءٍ قَدِيرٌ ۝ أَلَمْ تَعْلَمْ أَنَّ ٱللَّهَ لَهُۥ مُلْكُ ٱلسَّمَٰوَٰتِ وَٱلْأَرْضِ ۗ وَمَا لَكُم مِّن دُونِ ٱللَّهِ مِن وَلِىٍّ وَلَا نَصِيرٍ ۝ أَمْ تُرِيدُونَ أَن تَسْـَٔلُوا۟ رَسُولَكُمْ كَمَا سُئِلَ مُوسَىٰ مِن قَبْلُ ۗ وَمَن يَتَبَدَّلِ ٱلْكُفْرَ بِٱلْإِيمَٰنِ فَقَدْ ضَلَّ سَوَآءَ ٱلسَّبِيلِ ۝ وَدَّ كَثِيرٌ مِّنْ أَهْلِ ٱلْكِتَٰبِ لَوْ يَرُدُّونَكُم مِّنۢ بَعْدِ إِيمَٰنِكُمْ كُفَّارًا حَسَدًا مِّنْ عِندِ أَنفُسِهِم مِّنۢ بَعْدِ مَا تَبَيَّنَ لَهُمُ ٱلْحَقُّ ۖ فَٱعْفُوا۟ وَٱصْفَحُوا۟ حَتَّىٰ يَأْتِىَ ٱللَّهُ بِأَمْرِهِۦٓ ۗ إِنَّ ٱللَّهَ عَلَىٰ كُلِّ شَىْءٍ قَدِيرٌ ۝ وَأَقِيمُوا۟ ٱلصَّلَوٰةَ وَءَاتُوا۟ ٱلزَّكَوٰةَ ۚ وَمَا تُقَدِّمُوا۟ لِأَنفُسِكُم مِّنْ خَيْرٍ تَجِدُوهُ عِندَ ٱللَّهِ ۗ إِنَّ ٱللَّهَ بِمَا تَعْمَلُونَ بَصِيرٌ ۝ وَقَالُوا۟ لَن يَدْخُلَ ٱلْجَنَّةَ إِلَّا مَن كَانَ هُودًا أَوْ نَصَٰرَىٰ ۗ تِلْكَ أَمَانِيُّهُمْ ۗ قُلْ هَاتُوا۟ بُرْهَٰنَكُمْ إِن كُنتُمْ صَٰدِقِينَ ۝ بَلَىٰ مَنْ أَسْلَمَ وَجْهَهُۥ لِلَّهِ وَهُوَ مُحْسِنٌ فَلَهُۥٓ أَجْرُهُۥ عِندَ رَبِّهِۦ وَلَا خَوْفٌ عَلَيْهِمْ وَلَا هُمْ يَحْزَنُونَ ۝ وَقَالَتِ ٱلْيَهُودُ لَيْسَتِ ٱلنَّصَٰرَىٰ عَلَىٰ شَىْءٍ وَقَالَتِ ٱلنَّصَٰرَىٰ لَيْسَتِ ٱلْيَهُودُ عَلَىٰ شَىْءٍ وَهُمْ يَتْلُونَ ٱلْكِتَٰبَ ۗ كَذَٰلِكَ قَالَ ٱلَّذِينَ لَا يَعْلَمُونَ مِثْلَ قَوْلِهِمْ ۚ فَٱللَّهُ يَحْكُمُ بَيْنَهُمْ يَوْمَ ٱلْقِيَٰمَةِ فِيمَا كَانُوا۟ فِيهِ يَخْتَلِفُونَ ۝ وَمَنْ أَظْلَمُ مِمَّن مَّنَعَ مَسَٰجِدَ ٱللَّهِ أَن يُذْكَرَ فِيهَا ٱسْمُهُۥ وَسَعَىٰ فِى خَرَابِهَآ ۚ أُو۟لَٰٓئِكَ مَا كَانَ لَهُمْ أَن

يَدْخُلُوهَا إِلَّا خَآئِفِينَ ۚ لَهُمْ فِى ٱلدُّنْيَا خِزْىٌ وَلَهُمْ فِى ٱلْءَاخِرَةِ عَذَابٌ عَظِيمٌ ﴿١١٤﴾ وَلِلَّهِ ٱلْمَشْرِقُ وَٱلْمَغْرِبُ ۚ فَأَيْنَمَا تُوَلُّوا۟ فَثَمَّ وَجْهُ ٱللَّهِ ۚ إِنَّ ٱللَّهَ وَٰسِعٌ عَلِيمٌ ﴿١١٥﴾ وَقَالُوا۟ ٱتَّخَذَ ٱللَّهُ وَلَدًا ۗ سُبْحَٰنَهُۥ ۖ بَل لَّهُۥ مَا فِى ٱلسَّمَٰوَٰتِ وَٱلْأَرْضِ ۖ كُلٌّ لَّهُۥ قَٰنِتُونَ ﴿١١٦﴾ بَدِيعُ ٱلسَّمَٰوَٰتِ وَٱلْأَرْضِ ۖ وَإِذَا قَضَىٰٓ أَمْرًا فَإِنَّمَا يَقُولُ لَهُۥ كُن فَيَكُونُ ﴿١١٧﴾ وَقَالَ ٱلَّذِينَ لَا يَعْلَمُونَ لَوْلَا يُكَلِّمُنَا ٱللَّهُ أَوْ تَأْتِينَآ ءَايَةٌ ۗ كَذَٰلِكَ قَالَ ٱلَّذِينَ مِن قَبْلِهِم مِّثْلَ قَوْلِهِمْ ۘ تَشَٰبَهَتْ قُلُوبُهُمْ ۗ قَدْ بَيَّنَّا ٱلْءَايَٰتِ لِقَوْمٍ يُوقِنُونَ ﴿١١٨﴾ إِنَّآ أَرْسَلْنَٰكَ بِٱلْحَقِّ بَشِيرًا وَنَذِيرًا ۖ وَلَا تُسْـَٔلُ عَنْ أَصْحَٰبِ ٱلْجَحِيمِ ﴿١١٩﴾ وَلَن تَرْضَىٰ عَنكَ ٱلْيَهُودُ وَلَا ٱلنَّصَٰرَىٰ حَتَّىٰ تَتَّبِعَ مِلَّتَهُمْ ۗ قُلْ إِنَّ هُدَى ٱللَّهِ هُوَ ٱلْهُدَىٰ ۗ وَلَئِنِ ٱتَّبَعْتَ أَهْوَآءَهُم بَعْدَ ٱلَّذِى جَآءَكَ مِنَ ٱلْعِلْمِ ۙ مَا لَكَ مِنَ ٱللَّهِ مِن وَلِىٍّ وَلَا نَصِيرٍ ﴿١٢٠﴾ ٱلَّذِينَ ءَاتَيْنَٰهُمُ ٱلْكِتَٰبَ يَتْلُونَهُۥ حَقَّ تِلَاوَتِهِۦٓ أُو۟لَٰٓئِكَ يُؤْمِنُونَ بِهِۦ ۗ وَمَن يَكْفُرْ بِهِۦ فَأُو۟لَٰٓئِكَ هُمُ ٱلْخَٰسِرُونَ ﴿١٢١﴾ يَٰبَنِىٓ إِسْرَٰٓءِيلَ ٱذْكُرُوا۟ نِعْمَتِىَ ٱلَّتِىٓ أَنْعَمْتُ عَلَيْكُمْ وَأَنِّى فَضَّلْتُكُمْ عَلَى ٱلْعَٰلَمِينَ ﴿١٢٢﴾ وَٱتَّقُوا۟ يَوْمًا لَّا تَجْزِى نَفْسٌ عَن نَّفْسٍ شَيْـًٔا وَلَا يُقْبَلُ مِنْهَا عَدْلٌ وَلَا تَنفَعُهَا شَفَٰعَةٌ وَلَا هُمْ يُنصَرُونَ ﴿١٢٣﴾ ۞ وَإِذِ ٱبْتَلَىٰٓ إِبْرَٰهِـۧمَ رَبُّهُۥ بِكَلِمَٰتٍ فَأَتَمَّهُنَّ ۖ قَالَ إِنِّى جَاعِلُكَ لِلنَّاسِ إِمَامًا ۖ قَالَ وَمِن ذُرِّيَّتِى ۖ قَالَ لَا يَنَالُ عَهْدِى ٱلظَّٰلِمِينَ ﴿١٢٤﴾ وَإِذْ جَعَلْنَا ٱلْبَيْتَ مَثَابَةً لِّلنَّاسِ وَأَمْنًا وَٱتَّخِذُوا۟ مِن مَّقَامِ إِبْرَٰهِـۧمَ مُصَلًّى ۖ وَعَهِدْنَآ إِلَىٰٓ إِبْرَٰهِـۧمَ وَإِسْمَٰعِيلَ أَن طَهِّرَا بَيْتِىَ لِلطَّآئِفِينَ وَٱلْعَٰكِفِينَ وَٱلرُّكَّعِ ٱلسُّجُودِ ﴿١٢٥﴾ وَإِذْ قَالَ إِبْرَٰهِـۧمُ رَبِّ ٱجْعَلْ هَٰذَا بَلَدًا ءَامِنًا وَٱرْزُقْ أَهْلَهُۥ مِنَ ٱلثَّمَرَٰتِ مَنْ ءَامَنَ مِنْهُم بِٱللَّهِ وَٱلْيَوْمِ

ٱلْأَخِرِ قَالَ وَمَن كَفَرَ فَأُمَتِّعُهُ قَلِيلًا ثُمَّ أَضْطَرُّهُ إِلَىٰ عَذَابِ ٱلنَّارِ وَبِئْسَ ٱلْمَصِيرُ ۝ وَإِذْ يَرْفَعُ إِبْرَٰهِمُ ٱلْقَوَاعِدَ مِنَ ٱلْبَيْتِ وَإِسْمَٰعِيلُ رَبَّنَا تَقَبَّلْ مِنَّآ إِنَّكَ أَنتَ ٱلسَّمِيعُ ٱلْعَلِيمُ ۝ رَبَّنَا وَٱجْعَلْنَا مُسْلِمَيْنِ لَكَ وَمِن ذُرِّيَّتِنَآ أُمَّةً مُّسْلِمَةً لَّكَ وَأَرِنَا مَنَاسِكَنَا وَتُبْ عَلَيْنَآ إِنَّكَ أَنتَ ٱلتَّوَّابُ ٱلرَّحِيمُ ۝ رَبَّنَا وَٱبْعَثْ فِيهِمْ رَسُولًا مِّنْهُمْ يَتْلُواْ عَلَيْهِمْ ءَايَٰتِكَ وَيُعَلِّمُهُمُ ٱلْكِتَٰبَ وَٱلْحِكْمَةَ وَيُزَكِّيهِمْ إِنَّكَ أَنتَ ٱلْعَزِيزُ ٱلْحَكِيمُ ۝ وَمَن يَرْغَبُ عَن مِّلَّةِ إِبْرَٰهِمَ إِلَّا مَن سَفِهَ نَفْسَهُ وَلَقَدِ ٱصْطَفَيْنَٰهُ فِى ٱلدُّنْيَا وَإِنَّهُۥ فِى ٱلْءَاخِرَةِ لَمِنَ ٱلصَّٰلِحِينَ ۝ إِذْ قَالَ لَهُۥ رَبُّهُۥٓ أَسْلِمْ قَالَ أَسْلَمْتُ لِرَبِّ ٱلْعَٰلَمِينَ ۝ وَوَصَّىٰ بِهَآ إِبْرَٰهِمُ بَنِيهِ وَيَعْقُوبُ يَٰبَنِىَّ إِنَّ ٱللَّهَ ٱصْطَفَىٰ لَكُمُ ٱلدِّينَ فَلَا تَمُوتُنَّ إِلَّا وَأَنتُم مُّسْلِمُونَ ۝ أَمْ كُنتُمْ شُهَدَآءَ إِذْ حَضَرَ يَعْقُوبَ ٱلْمَوْتُ إِذْ قَالَ لِبَنِيهِ مَا تَعْبُدُونَ مِنۢ بَعْدِى قَالُوا۟ نَعْبُدُ إِلَٰهَكَ وَإِلَٰهَ ءَابَآئِكَ إِبْرَٰهِمَ وَإِسْمَٰعِيلَ وَإِسْحَٰقَ إِلَٰهًا وَٰحِدًا وَنَحْنُ لَهُۥ مُسْلِمُونَ ۝ تِلْكَ أُمَّةٌ قَدْ خَلَتْ لَهَا مَا كَسَبَتْ وَلَكُم مَّا كَسَبْتُمْ وَلَا تُسْـَٔلُونَ عَمَّا كَانُوا۟ يَعْمَلُونَ ۝ وَقَالُوا۟ كُونُوا۟ هُودًا أَوْ نَصَٰرَىٰ تَهْتَدُوا۟ قُلْ بَلْ مِلَّةَ إِبْرَٰهِمَ حَنِيفًا وَمَا كَانَ مِنَ ٱلْمُشْرِكِينَ ۝ قُولُوٓا۟ ءَامَنَّا بِٱللَّهِ وَمَآ أُنزِلَ إِلَيْنَا وَمَآ أُنزِلَ إِلَىٰٓ إِبْرَٰهِمَ وَإِسْمَٰعِيلَ وَإِسْحَٰقَ وَيَعْقُوبَ وَٱلْأَسْبَاطِ وَمَآ أُوتِىَ مُوسَىٰ وَعِيسَىٰ وَمَآ أُوتِىَ ٱلنَّبِيُّونَ مِن رَّبِّهِمْ لَا نُفَرِّقُ بَيْنَ أَحَدٍ مِّنْهُمْ وَنَحْنُ لَهُۥ مُسْلِمُونَ ۝ فَإِنْ ءَامَنُوا۟ بِمِثْلِ مَآ ءَامَنتُم بِهِۦ فَقَدِ ٱهْتَدَوا۟ وَّإِن تَوَلَّوْا۟ فَإِنَّمَا هُمْ فِى شِقَاقٍ فَسَيَكْفِيكَهُمُ ٱللَّهُ وَهُوَ ٱلسَّمِيعُ ٱلْعَلِيمُ ۝ صِبْغَةَ ٱللَّهِ وَمَنْ أَحْسَنُ مِنَ ٱللَّهِ صِبْغَةً وَنَحْنُ لَهُۥ

عَبِدُونَ ۝ قُلْ أَتُحَآجُّونَنَا فِى ٱللَّهِ وَهُوَ رَبُّنَا وَرَبُّكُمْ وَلَنَآ أَعْمَـٰلُنَا وَلَكُمْ أَعْمَـٰلُكُمْ وَنَحْنُ لَهُۥ مُخْلِصُونَ ۝ أَمْ تَقُولُونَ إِنَّ إِبْرَٰهِـۧمَ وَإِسْمَـٰعِيلَ وَإِسْحَـٰقَ وَيَعْقُوبَ وَٱلْأَسْبَاطَ كَانُوا۟ هُودًا أَوْ نَصَـٰرَىٰ قُلْ ءَأَنتُمْ أَعْلَمُ أَمِ ٱللَّهُ وَمَنْ أَظْلَمُ مِمَّن كَتَمَ شَهَـٰدَةً عِندَهُۥ مِنَ ٱللَّهِ وَمَا ٱللَّهُ بِغَـٰفِلٍ عَمَّا تَعْمَلُونَ ۝ تِلْكَ أُمَّةٌ قَدْ خَلَتْ لَهَا مَا كَسَبَتْ وَلَكُم مَّا كَسَبْتُمْ وَلَا تُسْـَٔلُونَ عَمَّا كَانُوا۟ يَعْمَلُونَ ۝

INTRODUCTION TO CHAPTER (SURAH) 1: AL-FATIHAH (THE OPENING)

Ibn Kathir's Introduction

The Meaning of Al-Fatihah and its Various Names

This Surah is called Al-Fatihah, that is, the Opener of the Book, the Surah with which prayers are begun. It is also called, Umm Al-Kitab (the Mother of the Book), according to the majority of the scholars. In an authentic Hadith recorded by At-Tirmidhi, who graded it Sahih, Abu Hurayrah said that the Messenger of Allah said,

«الْحَمْدُ لِلَّهِ رَبِّ الْعَالَمِينَ أُمُّ الْقُرْآنِ وَأُمُّ الْكِتَابِ وَالسَّبْعُ الْمَثَانِي وَالْقُرْآنُ الْعَظِيمُ»

(Al-Hamdu lillahi Rabbil-`Alamin is the Mother of the Qur'an, the Mother of the Book, and the seven repeated Ayat of the Glorious Qur'an.)

It is also called Al-Hamd and As-Salah, because the Prophet said that his Lord said,

«قَسَمْتُ الصَّلَاةَ بَيْنِي وَبَيْنَ عَبْدِي نِصْفَيْنِ، فَإِذَا قَالَ الْعَبْدُ: الْحَمْدُ لِلَّهِ رَبِّ الْعَالَمِينَ، قَالَ اللَّهُ: حَمِدَنِي عَبْدِي»

(`The prayer (i.e., Al-Fatihah) is divided into two halves between Me and My servants.' When the servant says, `All praise is due to Allah, the Lord of existence,' Allah says, 'My servant has praised Me.')

Al-Fatihah was called the Salah, because reciting it is a condition for the correctness of Salah - the prayer. Al-Fatihah was also called Ash-Shifa' (the Cure).

It is also called Ar-Ruqyah (remedy), since in the Sahih, there is the narration of Abu Sa`id telling the the story of the Companion who used Al-Fatihah as a remedy for the tribal chief who was poisoned. Later, the Messenger of Allah said to a Companion,

$$\text{«وَمَا يُدْرِيكَ أَنَّهَا رُقْيَةٌ»}$$

(How did you know that it is a Ruqyah)

Al-Fatihah was revealed in Makkah as Ibn `Abbas, Qatadah and Abu Al-`Aliyah stated. Allah said,

$$[\text{وَلَقَدْ ءاتَيْنَـكَ سَبْعًا مِّنَ الْمَثَانِي}]$$

(And indeed, We have bestowed upon you the seven Mathani) (seven repeatedly recited verses), (i.e. Surat Al-Fatihah) (15:87). Allah knows best.

How many Ayat does Al-Fatihah contain

There is no disagreement over the view that Al-Fatihah contains seven Ayat. According to the majority of the reciters of Al-Kufah, a group of the Companions, the Tabi`in, and a number of scholars from the successive generations, the Bismillah is a separate Ayah in its beginning. We will mention this subject again soon, if Allah wills, and in Him we trust.

The Number of Words and Letters in Al-Fatihah

The scholars say that Al-Fatihah consists of twenty-five words, and that it contains one hundred and thirteen letters.

The Reason it is called Umm Al-Kitab

In the beginning of the Book of Tafsir, in his Sahih, Al-Bukhari said; "It is called Umm Al-Kitab, because the Qur'an starts with it and because the prayer is started by reciting it." It was also said that it is called Umm Al-Kitab, because it contains the meanings of the entire Qur'an. Ibn Jarir said, "The Arabs call every comprehensive matter that contains several specific areas an Umm. For instance, they call the skin that surrounds the brain, Umm Ar-Ra's. They also call the flag that gathers the ranks of the army an Umm." He also said, "Makkah was called Umm Al-Qura, (the Mother of the Villages) because it is the grandest and the leader of all villages. It was also said that the earth was made starting from Makkah."

Chapter 1: Al-Fatihah, Verses 001 to 007

Further, Imam Ahmad recorded that Abu Hurayrah narrated about Umm Al-Qur'an that the Prophet said,

«هِيَ أُمُّ الْقُرْآنِ وَهِيَ السَّبْعُ الْمَثَانِي وَهِيَ الْقُرْآنُ الْعَظِيمُ»

(It is Umm Al-Qur'an, the seven repeated (verses) and the Glorious Qur'an.)

Also, Abu Ja`far, Muhammad bin Jarir At-Tabari recorded Abu Hurayrah saying that the Messenger of Allah said about Al-Fatihah,

«هِيَ أُمُّ الْقُرْآنِ وَهِيَ فَاتِحَةُ الْكِتَابِ وَهِيَ السَّبْعُ الْمَثَانِي»

(It is Umm Al-Qur'an, Al-Fatihah of the Book (the Opener of the Qur'an) and the seven repeated (verses).)

Virtues of Al-Fatihah

Imam Ahmad bin Hanbal recorded in the Musnad that Abu Sa`id bin Al-Mu`alla said, "I was praying when the Prophet called me, so I did not answer him until I finished the prayer. I then went to him and he said, (What prevented you from coming) I said, 'O Messenger of Allah ! I was praying.' He said, (`Didn't Allah say),

[يَأَيُّهَا الَّذِينَ ءَامَنُوا اسْتَجِيبُوا لِلَّهِ وَلِلرَّسُولِ إِذَا دَعَاكُمْ لِمَا يُحْيِيكُمْ]

(O you who believe! Answer Allah (by obeying Him) and (His) Messenger when he () calls you to that which gives you life) He then said,

«لَأُعَلِّمَنَّكَ أَعْظَمَ سُورَةٍ فِي الْقُرْآنِ قَبْلَ أَنْ تَخْرُجَ مِنَ الْمَسْجِدِ»

(I will teach you the greatest Surah in the Qur'an before you leave the Masjid.) He held my hand and when he was about to leave the Masjid, I said, `O Messenger of Allah! You said: I will teach you the greatest Surah in the Qur'an.' He said, (Yes.)

[الْحَمْدُ لِلَّهِ رَبِّ الْعَالَمِينَ]

(Al-Hamdu lillahi Rabbil-`Alamin)"

«نَعَمْ هِيَ السَّبْعُ الْمَثَانِي وَالْقُرْآنُ الْعَظِيمُ الَّذِي أُوتِيتُهُ»

(It is the seven repeated (verses) and the Glorious Qur'an that I was given.)"

Al-Bukhari, Abu Dawud, An-Nasa'i and Ibn Majah also recorded this Hadith.

Also, Imam Ahmad recorded that Abu Hurayrah said, "The Messenger of Allah went out while Ubayy bin Ka`b was praying and said, (O Ubayy!) Ubayy did not answer him. The Prophet said, (O Ubayy!) Ubayy prayed faster then went to the Messenger of Allah saying, `Peace be unto you, O Messenger of Allah!' He said, (Peace be unto you. O Ubayy, what prevented you from answering me when I called you) He said, `O Messenger of Allah! I was praying.' He said, (Did you not read among what Allah has sent down to me,)

$$[اسْتَجِيبُواْ لِلَّهِ وَلِلرَّسُولِ إِذَا دَعَاكُمْ لِمَا يُحْيِيكُمْ]$$

(Answer Allah (by obeying Him) and (His) Messenger when he () calls you to that which gives you life) He said, `Yes, O Messenger of Allah! I will not do it again.' the Prophet said,

$$«أَتُحِبُّ أَنْ أُعَلِّمَكَ سُورَةً لَمْ تَنْزِلْ لَا فِي التَّوْرَاةِ وَلَا فِي الْإِنْجِيلِ وَلَا فِي الزَّبُورِ وَلَا فِي الْفُرْقَانِ مِثْلَهَا؟»$$

(Would you like me to teach you a Surah the likes of which nothing has been revealed in the Tawrah, the Injil, the Zabur (Psalms) or the Furqan (the Qur'an)) He said, `Yes, O Messenger of Allah!' The Messenger of Allah said, (I hope that I will not leave through this door until you have learned it.) He (Ka`b) said, `The Messenger of Allah held my hand while speaking to me. Meanwhile I was slowing down fearing that he might reach the door before he finished his conversation. When we came close to the door, I said: O Messenger of Allah ! What is the Surah that you have promised to teach me' He said, (What do you read in the prayer.) Ubayy said, `So I recited Umm Al-Qur'an to him.' He said,

$$«وَالَّذِي نَفْسِي بِيَدِهِ مَا أَنْزَلَ اللَّهُ فِي التَّوْرَاةِ وَلَا فِي الْإِنْجِيلِ وَلَا فِي الزَّبُورِ وَلَا فِي الْفُرْقَانِ مِثْلَهَا إِنَّهَا السَّبْعُ الْمَثَانِي»$$

(By Him in Whose Hand is my soul! Allah has never revealed in the Tawrah, the Injil, the Zabur or the Furqan a Surah like it. It is the seven repeated verses that I was given.)"

Also, At-Tirmidhi recorded this Hadith and in his narration, the Prophet said,

«إِنَّهَا مِنَ السَّبْعِ الْمَثَانِي وَالْقُرْآنِ الْعَظِيمِ الَّذِي أُعْطِيتُهُ»

(It is the seven repeated verses and the Glorious Qur'an that I was given.) At-Tirmidhi then commented that this Hadith is Hasan Sahih.

There is a similar Hadith on this subject narrated from Anas bin Malik Further, `Abdullah, the son of Imam Ahmad, recorded this Hadith from Abu Hurayrah from Ubayy bin Ka`b, and he mentioned a longer but similar wording for the above Hadith. In addition, At-Tirmidhi and An-Nasa'i recorded this Hadith from Abu Hurayrah from Ubayy bin Ka`b who said that the Messenger of Allah said,

«مَا أَنْزَلَ اللهُ فِي التَّوْرَاةِ وَلَا فِي الْإِنْجِيلِ مِثْلَ أُمِّ الْقُرْآنِ وَهِيَ السَّبْعُ الْمَثَانِي وَهِيَ مَقْسُومَةٌ بَيْنِي وَبَيْنَ عَبْدِي نِصْفَيْنِ»

(Allah has never revealed in the Tawrah or the Injil anything similar to Umm Al-Qur'an.

It is the seven repeated verses and it is divided into two halves between Allah and His servant.)

This is the wording reported by An-Nasa'i. At-Tirmidhi said that this Hadith is Hasan Gharib.

Also, Imam Ahmad recorded that Ibn Jabir said, "I went to the Messenger of Allah after he had poured water (for purification) and said, `Peace be unto you, O Messenger of Allah!' He did not answer me. So I said again, `Peace be unto you, O Messenger of Allah!' Again, he did not answer me, so I said again, `Peace be unto you, O Messenger of Allah!' Still he did not answer me. The Messenger of Allah went while I was following him, until he arrived at his residence. I went to the Masjid and sat there sad and depressed. The Messenger of Allah came out after he performed his purification and said, (Peace and Allah's mercy be unto you, peace and Allah's mercy be unto you, peace and Allah's mercy be unto you.) He then said, (O `Abdullah bin Jabir! Should I inform you of the best Surah in the Qur'an) I said, `Yes, O Messenger of Allah!' He said, (Read, `All praise be to Allah, the Lord of the existence,' until you finish it.)" This Hadith has a good chain of narrators.

Some scholars relied on this Hadith as evidence that some Ayat and Surahs have more virtues than others.

Furthermore, in the chapter about the virtues of the Qur'an, Al-Bukhari recorded that Abu Sa`id Al-Khudri said, "Once, we were on a journey when a female servant came and said, `The leader of this area has been poisoned and our people are away. Is there a healer among you' Then a man whose healing expertise did not interest us stood for her, he read a Ruqyah for him, and he was healed. The chief gave him thirty sheep as a gift and some milk. When he came back to us we said to him, `You know of a (new) Ruqyah, or did you do this before' He said, `I only used Umm Al-Kitab as Ruqyah.' We said, `Do not do anything further until we ask the Messenger of Allah.' When we went back to Al-Madinah we mentioned what had happened to the Prophet . The Prophet said,

«وَمَا كَانَ يُدْرِيهِ أَنَّهَا رُقْيَةٌ اقْسِمُوا وَاضْرِبُوا لِي بِسَهْمٍ»

(Who told him that it is a Ruqyah Divide (the sheep) and reserve a share for me.)"

Also, Muslim recorded in his Sahih, and An-Nasa'i in his Sunan that Ibn `Abbas said, "While Jibril (Gabriel) was with the Messenger of Allah , he heard a noise from above. Jibril lifted his sight to the sky and said, `This is a door in heaven being open, and it has never been opened before now.' An angel descended from that door and came to the Prophet and said, `Receive the glad tidings of two lights that you have been given, which no other Prophet before you was given: the Opening of the Book and the last (three) Ayat of Surat Al-Baqarah. You will not read a letter of them, but will gain its benefit.'" This is the wording collected by An-Nasa'i (Al-Kubra 5:12) and Muslim recorded similar wording (1:554).

Al-Fatihah and the Prayer

Muslim recorded that Abu Hurayrah said that the Prophet said,

«مَنْ صَلَّى صَلَاةً لَمْ يَقْرَأْ فِيهَا أُمَّ الْقُرْآنِ فَهِيَ خِدَاجٌ ثَلَاثًا غَيْرُ تَمَامٍ»

(Whoever performs any prayer in which he did not read Umm Al-Qur'an, then his prayer is incomplete.) He said it thrice.

Abu Hurayrah was asked, "[When] we stand behind the Imam" He said, "Read it to yourself, for I heard the Messenger of Allah say,

«قَالَ اللَّهُ عَزَّ وَجَلَّ: قَسَمْتُ الصَّلَاةَ بَيْنِي وَبَيْنَ عَبْدِي نِصْفَيْنِ وَلِعَبْدِي مَا سَأَلَ فَإِذَا قَالَ:

[الْحَمْدُ لِلَّهِ رَبِّ الْعَالَمِينَ]، قَالَ اللهُ: حَمِدَنِي عَبْدِي وَإِذَا قَالَ:

Chapter 1: Al-Fatihah, Verses 001 to 007   19

[الرَّحْمَنِ الرَّحِيمِ]، قَالَ اللهُ: أَثْنَى عَلَيَّ عَبْدِي، فَإِذَا قَالَ:

[مَالِكِ يَوْمِ الدِّينِ]، قَالَ اللهُ: مَجَّدَنِي عَبْدِي وَقَالَ مَرَّةً: فَوَّضَ إِلَيَّ عَبْدِي فَإِذَا قَالَ:

[إِيَّاكَ نَعْبُدُ وَإِيَّاكَ نَسْتَعِينُ]، قَالَ: هَذَا بَيْنِي وَبَيْنَ عَبْدِي وَلِعَبْدِي مَا سَأَلَ، فَإِذَا قَالَ:

[اهْدِنَا الصِّرَاطَ الْمُسْتَقِيمَ - صِرَاطَ الَّذِينَ أَنْعَمْتَ عَلَيْهِمْ غَيْرِ الْمَغْضُوبِ عَلَيْهِمْ وَلاَ الضَّالِّينَ]، قَالَ اللهُ: هَذَا لِعَبْدِي وَلِعَبْدِي مَا سَأَلَ»

(Allah, the Exalted, said, `I have divided the prayer (Al-Fatihah) into two halves between Myself and My servant, and My servant shall have what he asks for.' If he says,

[الْحَمْدُ لِلَّهِ رَبِّ الْعَالَمِينَ]

(All praise and thanks be to Allah, the Lord of existence.)

Allah says, `My servant has praised Me.' When the servant says,

[الرَّحْمَنِ الرَّحِيمِ]

(The Most Gracious, the Most Merciful.)

Allah says, `My servant has glorified Me.' When he says,

[مَالِكِ يَوْمِ الدِّينِ]

(The Owner of the Day of Recompense.) Allah says, `My servant has glorified Me,' or `My servant has related all matters to Me.' When he says,

$$[\text{إِيَّاكَ نَعْبُدُ وَإِيَّاكَ نَسْتَعِينُ}]$$

(You (alone) we worship, and You (alone) we ask for help.) Allah says, `This is between Me and My servant, and My servant shall acquire what he sought.' When he says,

$$[\text{اهْدِنَا الصِّرَاطَ الْمُسْتَقِيمَ – صِرَاطَ الَّذِينَ أَنْعَمْتَ عَلَيْهِمْ غَيْرِ الْمَغْضُوبِ عَلَيْهِمْ وَلاَ الضَّآلِّينَ}]$$

(Guide us to the straight path. The way of those on whom You have granted Your grace, not (the way) of those who earned Your anger, nor of those who went astray), Allah says, `This is for My servant, and My servant shall acquire what he asked for.')."

These are the words of An-Nasa'i, while both Muslim and An-Nasa'i collected the following wording, "A half of it is for Me and a half for My servant, and My servant shall acquire what he asked for."

Explaining this Hadith

The last Hadith used the word [Salah] `prayer' in reference to reciting the Qur'an, (Al-Fatihah in this case) just as Allah said in another Ayah,

$$[\text{وَلاَ تَجْهَرْ بِصَلاَتِكَ وَلاَ تُخَافِتْ بِهَا وَابْتَغِ بَيْنَ ذَلِكَ سَبِيلاً}]$$

(And offer your Salah (prayer) neither aloud nor in a low voice, but follow a way between.) meaning, with your recitation of the Qur'an, as the Sahih related from Ibn `Abbas. Also, in the last Hadith, Allah said, "I have divided the prayer between Myself and My servant into two halves, a half for Me and a half for My servant. My servant shall have what he asked for." Allah next explained the division that involves reciting Al-Fatihah, demonstrating the importance of reciting the Qur'an during the prayer, which is one of the prayer's greatest pillars. Hence, the word `prayer' was used here although only a part of it was actually being referred to, that is, reciting the Qur'an. Similarly, the word `recite' was used where prayer is meant, as demonstrated by Allah's statement,

$$[\text{وَقُرْءَانَ الْفَجْرِ إِنَّ قُرْءَانَ الْفَجْرِ كَانَ مَشْهُودًا}]$$

(And recite the Qur'an in the early dawn. Verily, the recitation of the Qur'an in the early dawn is ever witnessed.) in reference to the Fajr prayer. The Two Sahihs recorded that the angels of the night and the day attend this prayer.

Reciting Al-Fatihah is required in Every Rak`ah of the Prayer

All of these facts testify to the requirement that reciting the Qur'an (Al-Fatihah) in the prayer is required, and there is a consensus between the scholars on this ruling. The Hadith that we mentioned also testifies to this fact, for the Prophet said,

«مَنْ صَلَّى صَلَاةً لَمْ يَقْرَأْ فِيهَا بِأُمِّ الْقُرْآنِ فَهِيَ خِدَاجٌ»

(Whoever performs any prayer in which he did not recite Umm Al-Qur'an, his prayer is incomplete.)

Also, the Two Sahihs recorded that `Ubadah bin As-Samit said that the Messenger of Allah said,

«لَا صَلَاةَ لِمَنْ لَمْ يَقْرَأْ بِفَاتِحَةِ الْكِتَابِ»

(There is no prayer for whoever does not recite the Opening of the Book.)

Also, the Sahihs of Ibn Khuzaymah and Ibn Hibban recorded that Abu Hurayrah said that the Messenger of Allah said,

«لَا تُجْزِئُ صَلَاةٌ لَا يُقْرَأُ فِيهَا بِأُمِّ الْقُرْآنِ»

(The prayer during which Umm Al-Qur'an is not recited is invalid.)

There are many other Hadiths on this subject. Therefore, reciting the Opening of the Book, during the prayer by the Imam and those praying behind him, is required in every prayer, and in every Rak`ah.

The Tafsir of Isti`adhah (seeking Refuge)

Allah said,

[خُذِ الْعَفْوَ وَأْمُرْ بِالْعُرْفِ وَأَعْرِضْ عَنِ الْجَاهِلِينَ - وَإِمَّا يَنزَغَنَّكَ مِنَ الشَّيْطَانِ نَزْغٌ فَاسْتَعِذْ بِاللَّهِ إِنَّهُ سَمِيعٌ عَلِيمٌ]

(Show forgiveness, enjoin what is good, and stay away from the foolish (i.e. don't punish them). And if an evil whisper comes to you from Shaytan (Satan), then seek refuge with Allah. Verily, He is Hearing, Knowing) (7:199-200),

[ادْفَعْ بِالَّتِى هِىَ أَحْسَنُ السَّيِّئَةَ نَحْنُ أَعْلَمُ بِمَا يَصِفُونَ - وَقُلْ رَّبِّ أَعُوذُ بِكَ مِنْ هَمَزَاتِ الشَّيَطِينِ - وَأَعُوذُ بِكَ رَبِّ أَن يَحْضُرُونِ]

(Repel evil with that which is better. We are Best-Acquainted with things they utter. And say: "My Lord! I seek refuge with You from the whisperings (suggestions) of the Shayatin (devils). And I seek refuge with You, My Lord! lest they should come near me.") (23:96-98) and,

[وَلاَ تَسْتَوِى الْحَسَنَةُ وَلاَ السَّيِّئَةُ ادْفَعْ بِالَّتِى هِىَ أَحْسَنُ فَإِذَا الَّذِى بَيْنَكَ وَبَيْنَهُ عَدَاوَةٌ كَأَنَّهُ وَلِىٌّ حَمِيمٌ - وَمَا يُلَقَّاهَا إِلاَّ الَّذِينَ صَبَرُواْ وَمَا يُلَقَّاهَآ إِلاَّ ذُو حَظٍّ عَظِيمٍ - وَإِمَّا يَنزَغَنَّكَ مِنَ الشَّيْطَنِ نَزْغٌ فَاسْتَعِذْ بِاللَّهِ إِنَّهُ هُوَ السَّمِيعُ الْعَلِيمُ]

(Repel (an evil) with one which is better, then verily he with whom there was enmity between you, (will become) as though he was a close friend. But none is granted it except those who are patient - and none is granted it except the owner of the great portion (of happiness in the Hereafter, i.e. Paradise and of a high moral character) in this world. And if an evil whisper from Shaytan tries to turn you away (O Muhammad) (from doing good), then seek refuge in Allah. Verily, He is the Hearing, the Knowing.) (41:34-36) These are the only three Ayat that carry this meaning. Allah commanded that we be lenient human enemy, so that his soft nature might make him an ally and a supporter. He also commanded that we seek refuge from the satanic enemy, because the devil does not relent in his enmity if we treat him with kindness and leniency. The devil only seeks the destruction of the Son of Adam due to the vicious enmity and hatred he has always had towards man's father, Adam. Allah said,

[يَبَنِى آدَمَ لاَ يَفْتِنَنَّكُمُ الشَّيْطَنُ كَمَآ أَخْرَجَ أَبَوَيْكُم مِّنَ الْجَنَّةِ]

(O Children of Adam! Let not Shaytan deceive you, as he got your parents [Adam and Hawwa' (Eve)] out of Paradise) (7:27),

[إِنَّ الشَّيْطَنَ لَكُمْ عَدُوٌّ فَاتَّخِذُوهُ عَدُوّاً إِنَّمَا يَدْعُو حِزْبَهُ لِيَكُونُواْ مِنْ أَصْحَبِ السَّعِيرِ]

(Surely, Shaytan is an enemy to you, so take (treat) him as an enemy. He only invites his Hizb (followers) that they may become the dwellers of the blazing Fire) (35:6) and,

[أَفَتَتَّخِذُونَهُ وَذُرِّيَّتَهُ أَوْلِيَآءَ مِن دُونِى وَهُمْ لَكُمْ عَدُوٌّ بِئْسَ لِلظَّـلِمِينَ بَدَلاً]

(Will you then take him (Iblis) and his offspring as protectors and helpers rather than Me while they are enemies to you What an evil is the exchange for the Zalimun (polytheists, and wrongdoers, etc)) (18:50).

The devil assured Adam that he wanted to advise him, but he was lying. Hence, how would he treat us after he had vowed,

[فَبِعِزَّتِكَ لأُغْوِيَنَّهُمْ أَجْمَعِينَ إِلاَّ عِبَادَكَ مِنْهُمُ الْمُخْلَصِينَ]

("By Your might, then I will surely, mislead them all. Except Your chosen servants among them (i.e. faithful, obedient, true believers of Islamic Monotheism).") (38:82-83)

Also, Allah said,

[فَإِذَا قَرَأْتَ الْقُرْءَانَ فَاسْتَعِذْ بِاللَّهِ مِنَ الشَّيْطَنِ الرَّجِيمِ]

[إِنَّهُ لَيْسَ لَهُ سُلْطَانٌ عَلَى الَّذِينَ ءَامَنُواْ وَعَلَى رَبِّهِمْ يَتَوَكَّلُونَ - إِنَّمَا سُلْطَنُهُ عَلَى الَّذِينَ يَتَوَلَّوْنَهُ وَالَّذِينَ هُم بِهِ مُشْرِكُونَ]

(So when you [want to] recite the Qur'an, seek refuge with Allah from Shaytan, the outcast (the cursed one). Verily, he has no power over those who believe and put their trust only in their Lord (Allah). His power is only over those who obey and follow him (Satan), and those who join partners with Him.) (16:98-100).

Seeking Refuge before reciting the Qur'an

Allah said,

[فَإِذَا قَرَأْتَ الْقُرْءَانَ فَاسْتَعِذْ بِاللَّهِ مِنَ الشَّيْطَنِ الرَّجِيمِ]

(So when you [want to] recite the Qur'an, seek refuge with Allah from Shaytan, the outcast (the cursed one).) meaning, before you recite the Qur'an. Similarly, Allah said,

$$[\text{إِذَا قُمْتُمْ إِلَى الصَّلوةِ فَاغْسِلُواْ وُجُوهَكُمْ وَأَيْدِيَكُمْ}]$$

(When you intend to offer As-Salah (the prayer), wash your faces and your hands (forearms)) (5:6) meaning, before you stand in prayer, as evident by the Hadiths that we mentioned. Imam Ahmad recorded that Abu Sa`id Al-Khudri said, "When the Messenger of Allah would stand up in prayer at night, he would start his prayer with the Takbir (saying "Allahu Akbar"; Allah is Greater) and would then supplicate,

«سُبْحَانَكَ اللَّهُمَّ وَبِحَمْدِكَ، وَتَبَارَكَ اسْمُكَ، وَتَعَالَى جَدُّكَ، وَلَا إِلَهَ غَيْرُكَ»

(All praise is due to You, O Allah, and also the thanks. Blessed be Your Name, Exalted be Your sovereignty, and there is no deity worthy of worship except You.)

He would then say thrice,

«لَا إِلَهَ إِلَّا اللهُ»

ثَلَاثًا

(There is no deity worthy of worship except Allah,).

He would then say,

«أَعُوذُ بِاللهِ السَّمِيعِ الْعَلِيمِ مِنَ الشَّيْطَانِ الرَّجِيمِ مِنْ هَمْزِهِ وَنَفْخِهِ وَنَفْثِهِ»

(I seek refuge with Allah, the Hearing, the Knowing, from the cursed Satan, from his coercion, lures to arrogance and poems.)."

The four collectors of the Sunan recorded this Hadith, which At-Tirmidhi considered the most famous Hadith on this subject.

Abu Dawud and Ibn Majah recorded that Jubayr bin Mut`im said that his father said, "When the Messenger of Allah started the prayer, he said,

«اللهُ أَكْبَرُ كَبِيرًا ثَلَاثًا الْحَمْدُ لِلهِ كَثِيرًا ثَلَاثًا سُبْحَانَ اللهِ بُكْرَةً وَأَصِيلًا ثَلَاثًا اللَّهُمَّ إِنِّي أَعُوذُ بِكَ مِنَ الشَّيْطَانِ الرَّجِيمِ مِنْ هَمْزِهِ وَنَفْخِهِ وَنَفْثِهِ»

(Allah is the Greater, truly the Greatest (thrice); all praise is due to Allah always (thrice); and all praise is due to Allah day and night (thrice). O Allah! I seek refuge with You from the cursed Satan, from his Hamz, Nafkh and Nafth.).'' `Amr said, "The Hamz means asphyxiation, the Nafkh means arrogance, and the Nafth means poetry." Also, Ibn Majah recorded that `Ali bin Al-Mundhir said that Ibn Fudayl narrated that `Ata' bin As-Sa'ib said that Abu `Abdur-Rahman As-Sulami said that Ibn Mas`ud said that the Prophet said,

«اللَّهُمَّ إِنِّي أَعُوذُ بِكَ مِنَ الشَّيْطَانِ الرَّجِيمِ وَهَمْزِهِ وَنَفْخِهِ وَنَفْثِهِ»

(O Allah! I seek refuge with You from the cursed devil, from his Hamz, Nafkh and Nafth.)

He said, "The Hamz means death, the Nafkh means arrogance, and the Nafth means poetry."

Seeking Refuge with Allah when One is Angry

In his Musnad, Al-Hafiz Abu Ya`la Ahmad bin `Ali bin Al-Muthanna Al-Mawsili reported that Ubayy bin Ka`b said, "Two men disputed with each other in the presence of the Messenger of Allah and the nose of one of them became swollen because of extreme anger. The Messenger of Allah said,

«إِنِّي لَأَعْلَمُ شَيْئًا لَوْ قَالَهُ لَذَهَبَ عَنْهُ مَا يَجِدُ: أَعُوذُ بِاللهِ مِنَ الشَّيْطَانِ الرَّجِيمِ»

(I know of some words that if he said them, what he feels will go away, 'I seek refuge with Allah from the cursed Satan.')"

An-Nasa'i also recorded this Hadith in his book, Al-Yawm wal-Laylah.

Al-Bukhari recorded that Sulayman bin Surad said, "Two men disputed in the presence of the Prophet while we were sitting with him. One of them was cursing the other fellow and his face turned red due to anger. The Prophet said,

«إِنِّي لَأَعْلَمُ كَلِمَةً لَوْ قَالَهَا لَذَهَبَ عَنْهُ مَا يَجِدُ، لَوْ قَالَ: أَعُوذُ بِاللهِ مِنَ الشَّيْطَانِ الرَّجِيمِ»

(I know of a statement which if he said it, will make what he feels disappear, `I seek refuge with Allah from the cursed Satan.') They said to the man, `Do you not hear what the Messenger of Allah is saying' He said, `I am not insane.'" Also, Muslim, Abu Dawud and An-Nasa'i recorded this Hadith.

There are many other Hadiths about seeking refuge with Allah. One can find this subject in the books on supplication and the virtues of righteous, good deeds.

Is the Isti`adhah (seeking Refuge) required

The majority of the scholars state that reciting the Isti`adhah (in the prayer and when reciting the Qur'an) is recommended and not required, and therefore, not reciting it does not constitute a sin. However, Ar-Razi recorded that `Ata' bin Abi Rabah said that the Isti`adhah is required in the prayer and when one reads the Qur'an. In support of `Ata's statement, Ar-Razi relied upon the apparent meaning of the Ayah,

[فَاسْتَعِذْ]

(Then seek refuge.) He said that the Ayah contains a command that requires implementation. Also, the Prophet always said the Isti`adhah. In addition, the Isti`adhah wards off the evil of Satan, which is neccessary, the rule is that the means needed to implement a requirement of the religion is itself also required. And when one says, "I seek refuge with Allah from the cursed devil." Then this will suffice.

Virtues of the Isti`adhah

The Isti`adhah cleanses the mouth from the foul speech that it has indulged in. It also purifies the mouth and prepares it to recite the speech of Allah. Further, the Isti`adhah entails seeking Allah's help and acknowledging His ability to do everything. The Isti`adhah also affirms the servant's meekness, weakness and inability to face the enemy of his inner evil, whom Allah alone, Who created this enemy, is able to repel and defeat. This enemy does not accept kindness, unlike the human enemy. There are three Ayat in the Qur'an that affirm this fact. Also, Allah said,

[إِنَّ عِبَادِى لَيْسَ لَكَ عَلَيْهِمْ سُلْطَنٌ وَكَفَى بِرَبِّكَ وَكِيلاً]

(Verily, My servants (i.e. the true believers of Islamic Monotheism) - you have no authority over them. And sufficient is your Lord as a Guardian.) (17:65).

We should state here that the believers, whom the human enemies kill, become martyrs, while those who fall victim to the inner enemy - Satan - become bandits. Further, the believers who are defeated by the apparent enemy - disbelievers - gain a reward, while those defeated by the inner enemy earn a sin and become misguided. Since Satan sees man where man cannot see him, it is befitting that the believers seek refuge from Satan with Whom Satan cannot see. The Isti`adhah is a form of drawing closer to Allah and seeking refuge with Him from the evil of every evil creature.

What does Isti`adhah mean

Isti`adhah means, "I seek refuge with Allah from the cursed Satan so that he is prevented from affecting my religious or worldly affairs, or hindering me from adhering to what I was commanded, or luring me into what I was prohibited from." Indeed, only Allah is able to prevent the evil of Satan from touching the son of Adam. This is why Allah allowed us to be lenient and kind with the human devil, so that his soft nature might cause him to refrain from the evil he is indulging in. However, Allah required us to seek refuge with Him from the evil of Satan, because he neither accepts bribes nor does kindness affect him, for he is pure evil. Thus, only He Who created Satan is able to stop his evil. This meaning is reiterated in only three Ayat in the Qur'an. Allah said in Surat Al-A`raf,

[خُذِ الْعَفْوَ وَأْمُرْ بِالْعُرْفِ وَأَعْرِضْ عَنِ الْجَاهِلِينَ]

(Show forgiveness, enjoin what is good, and turn away from the foolish (i.e. don't punish them).) (7:199)

This is about dealing with human beings. He then said in the same Surah,

[وَإِمَّا يَنزَغَنَّكَ مِنَ الشَّيْطَنِ نَزْغٌ فَاسْتَعِذْ بِاللَّهِ إِنَّهُ سَمِيعٌ عَلِيمٌ]

(And if an evil whisper comes to you from Shaytan, then seek refuge with Allah. Verily, He is Hearing, Knowing (7: 200).)

Allah also said in Surat Al-Mu'minun,

[ادْفَعْ بِالَّتِي هِيَ أَحْسَنُ السَّيِّئَةَ نَحْنُ أَعْلَمُ بِمَا يَصِفُونَ - وَقُلْ رَبِّ أَعُوذُ بِكَ مِنْ هَمَزَاتِ الشَّيَاطِينِ - وَأَعُوذُ بِكَ رَبِّ أَن يَحْضُرُونِ]

(Repel evil with that which is better. We are Best-Acquainted with the things they utter. And say: "My Lord! I seek refuge with You from the whisperings (suggestions) of the Shayatin (devils). And I seek refuge with You, My Lord! lest they should come near me." (23:96-98).)

Further, Allah said in Surat As-Sajdah,

[وَلاَ تَسْتَوِى الْحَسَنَةُ وَلاَ السَّيِّئَةُ ادْفَعْ بِالَّتِى هِىَ أَحْسَنُ فَإِذَا الَّذِى بَيْنَكَ وَبَيْنَهُ عَدَاوَةٌ كَأَنَّهُ وَلِىٌّ حَمِيمٌ - وَمَا يُلَقَّاهَا إِلاَّ الَّذِينَ صَبَرُواْ وَمَا يُلَقَّاهَآ إِلاَّ ذُو حَظٍّ عَظِيمٍ - وَإِمَّا يَنزَغَنَّكَ مِنَ الشَّيْطَنِ نَزْغٌ فَاسْتَعِذْ بِاللَّهِ إِنَّهُ هُوَ السَّمِيعُ الْعَلِيمُ]

(The good deed and the evil deed cannot be equal. Repel (the evil) with one which is better, then verily he, between whom and you there was enmity, (will become) as though he was a close friend. But none is granted it (the above quality) except those who are patient - and none is granted it except the owner of the great portion (of happiness in the Hereafter, i.e. Paradise and of a high moral character) in this world. And if an evil whisper from Shaytan tries to turn you away (from doing good), then seek refuge in Allah. Verily, He is the Hearing, the Knowing) (41:34-36).

Why the Devil is called Shaytan

In the Arabic language, Shaytan is derived from Shatana, which means the far thing. Hence, the Shaytan has a different nature than mankind, and his sinful ways are far away from every type of righteousness. It was also said that Shaytan is derived from Shata, (literally `burned'), because it was created from fire. Some scholars said that both meanings are correct, although they state that the first meaning is more plausible. Further, Siybawayh (the renowned Arab linguistic) said, "The Arabs say, `So-and-so has Tashaytan,' when he commits the act of the devils. If Shaytan was derived from Shata, they would have said, Tashayyata (rather than Tashaytan)." Hence, Shaytan is derived from the word that means, far away. This is why they call those who are rebellious (or mischievous) from among the Jinns and mankind a `Shaytan'. Allah said,

[وَكَذَلِكَ جَعَلْنَا لِكُلِّ نِبِىٍّ عَدُوّاً شَيَطِينَ الإِنْسِ وَالْجِنِّ يُوحِى بَعْضُهُمْ إِلَى بَعْضٍ زُخْرُفَ الْقَوْلِ غُرُوراً]

(And so We have appointed for every Prophet enemies - Shayatin (devils) among mankind and Jinn, inspiring one another with adorned speech as a delusion (or by way of deception)) (6:112).

In addition, the Musnad by Imam Ahmad records that Abu Dharr said that the Messenger of Allah said,

«يَا أَبَا ذَرَ تَعَوَّذْ بِاللَّهِ مِنْ شَيَاطِينِ الْإِنْسِ وَالْجِنِّ»

(O Abu Dharr! Seek refuge with Allah from the devils of mankind and the Jinns.) Abu Dharr said, "I asked him, `Are there human devils' He said, (Yes.)" Furthermore, it is recorded in Sahih Muslim that Abu Dharr said that the Messenger of Allah said,

«يَقْطَعُ الصَّلَاةَ الْمَرْأَةُ وَالْحِمَارُ وَالْكَلْبُ الْأَسْوَدُ»

(The woman, the donkey and the black dog interrupt the prayer (if they pass in front of those who do not pray behind a Sutrah, i.e. a barrier).) Abu Dharr said, "I said, `What is the difference between the black dog and the red or yellow dog' He said,

«الْكَلْبُ الْأَسْوَدُ شَيْطَانٌ»

(The black dog is a devil.).''

Also, Ibn Jarir At-Tabari recorded that `Umar bin Al-Khattab once rode a Berthawn (huge camel) which started to proceed arrogantly. `Umar kept striking the animal, but the animal kept walking in an arrogant manner. `Umar dismounted the animal and said, "By Allah! You have carried me on a Shaytan. I did not come down from it until after I had felt something strange in my heart." This Hadith has an authentic chain of narrators.

The Meaning of Ar-Rajim

Ar-Rajim means, being expelled from all types of righteousness. Allah said,

[وَلَقَدْ زَيَّنَّا السَّمَاءَ الدُّنْيَا بِمَصَابِيحَ وَجَعَلْنَاهَا رُجُوماً لِّلشَّيَاطِينِ]

(And indeed We have adorned the nearest heaven with lamps, and We have made such lamps Rujuman (as missiles) to drive away the Shayatin (devils)) (67:5).

Allah also said,

[إِنَّا زَيَّنَّا السَّمَاءَ الدُّنْيَا بِزِينَةٍ الْكَوَاكِبِ - وَحِفْظاً مِّن كُلِّ شَيْطَنٍ مَّارِدٍ - لاَّ يَسَّمَّعُونَ إِلَى الْمَلَإِ الْأَعْلَى وَيُقْذَفُونَ مِن كُلِّ جَانِبٍ - دُحُوراً وَلَهُمْ

عَذَابٌ وَاصِبٌ - إِلاَّ مَنْ خَطِفَ الْخَطْفَةَ فَأَتْبَعَهُ شِهَابٌ ثَاقِبٌ]

(Verily, We have adorned the near heaven with the stars (for beauty). And to guard against every rebellious devil. They cannot listen to the higher group (angels) for they are pelted from every side. Outcast, and theirs is a constant (or painful) torment. Except such as snatch away something by stealing, and they are pursued by a flaming fire of piercing brightness) (37:6-10).

Further, Allah said,

[وَلَقَدْ جَعَلْنَا فِى السَّمَاءِ بُرُوجًا وَزَيَّنَّاهَا لِلنَّاظِرِينَ - وَحَفِظْنَاهَا مِن كُلِّ شَيْطَنٍ رَّجِيمٍ - إِلاَّ مَنِ اسْتَرَقَ السَّمْعَ فَأَتْبَعَهُ شِهَابٌ مُّبِينٌ]

(And indeed, We have put the big stars in the heaven and We beautified it for the beholders. And We have guarded it (near heaven) from every Shaytan Rajim (outcast Shaytan). Except him (devil) who steals the hearing then he is pursued by a clear flaming fire.) (15:16-18).

There are several similar Ayat. It was also said that Rajim means, the person who throws or bombards things, because the devil throws doubts and evil thoughts in people's hearts. The first meaning is more popular and accurate.

CHAPTER (SURAH) 1: AL-FATIHAH (THE OPENING), VERSES 001–007

Surah: 1 Ayah: 1

﴿ بِسْمِ ٱللَّهِ ٱلرَّحْمَـٰنِ ٱلرَّحِيمِ ۝ ﴾

1. In the Name of Allâh, the Most Gracious, the Most Merciful.

Transliteration

1. Bismi All<u>a</u>hi alrra<u>h</u>m<u>a</u>ni alrra<u>h</u>eemi

Tafsir Ibn Kathir

Bismillah is the First Ayah of Al-Fatihah

The Companions started the Book of Allah with Bismillah:

(1. In the Name of Allah, the Most Gracious, the Most Merciful.)

The scholars also agree that Bismillah is a part of an Ayah in Surat An-Naml (chapter 27). They disagree over whether it is a separate Ayah before every

Surah, or if it is an Ayah, or a part of an Ayah, included in every Surah where the Bismillah appears in its beginning. Ad-Daraqutni also recorded a Hadith from Abu Hurayrah from the Prophet that supports this Hadith by Ibn Khuzaymah. Also, similar statements were attributed to `Ali, Ibn `Abbas and others.

The opinion that Bismillah is an Ayah of every Surah, except Al-Bara'ah (chapter 9), was attributed to (the Companions) Ibn `Abbas, Ibn `Umar, Ibn Az-Zubayr, Abu Hurayrah and `Ali. This opinion was also attributed to the Tabi`in: `Ata', Tawus, Sa`id bin Jubayr, Makhul and Az-Zuhri. This is also the view of `Abdullah bin Al-Mubarak, Ash-Shafi`i, Ahmad bin Hanbal, (in one report from him) Ishaq bin Rahwayh and Abu `Ubayd Al-Qasim bin Salam. On the other hand, Malik, Abu Hanifah and their followers said that Bismillah is not an Ayah in Al-Fatihah or any other Surah. Dawud said that it is a separate Ayah in the beginning of every Surah, not part of the Surah itself, and this opinion was also attributed to Ahmad bin Hanbal.

Basmalah aloud in the Prayer

As for Basmalah aloud during the prayer, those who did not agree that it is a part of Al-Fatihah, state that the Basmalah should not be aloud. The scholars who stated that Bismillah is a part of every Surah (except chapter 9) had different opinions; some of them, such as Ash-Shafi`i, said that one should recite Bismillah with Al-Fatihah aloud. This is also the opinion of many among the Companions, the Tabi`in and the Imams of Muslims from the Salaf and the later generations. For instance, this is the opinion of Abu Hurayrah, Ibn `Umar, Ibn `Abbas, Mu`awiyah, `Umar and `Ali - according to Ibn `Abdul-Barr and Al-Bayhaqi. Also, the Four Khalifahs - as Al-Khatib reported - were said to have held this view although the report from them is contradicted. The Tabi`in scholars who gave this Tafsir include Sa`id bin Jubayr, `Ikrimah, Abu Qilabah, Az-Zuhri, `Ali bin Al-Hasan, his son Muhammad, Sa`id bin Al-Musayyib, `Ata', Tawus, Mujahid, Salim, Muhammad bin Ka`b Al-Qurazi, Abu Bakr bin Muhammad bin `Amr bin Hazm, Abu Wa'il, Ibn Sirin, Muhammad bin Al-Munkadir, `Ali bin `Abdullah bin `Abbas, his son Muhammad, Nafi` the freed slave of Ibn `Umar, Zayd bin Aslam, `Umar bin `Abdul-Aziz, Al-Azraq bin Qays, Habib bin Abi Thabit, Abu Ash-Sha`tha', Makhul and `Abdullah bin Ma`qil bin Muqarrin. Also, Al-Bayhaqi added `Abdullah bin Safwan, and Muhammad bin Al-Hanafiyyah to this list. In addition, Ibn `Abdul-Barr added `Amr bin Dinar.

The proof that these scholars relied on is that, since Bismillah is a part of Al-Fatihah, it should be recited aloud like the rest of Al-Fatihah. Also, An-Nasa'i recorded in his Sunan, Ibn Hibban and Ibn Khuzaymah in their Sahihs and Al-Hakim in the Mustadrak, that Abu Hurayrah once performed the prayer and recited Bismillah aloud. After he finished the prayer, he said, "Among you, I perform the prayer that is the closest to the prayer of the Messenger of Allah ." Ad-Daraqutni, Al-Khatib and Al-Bayhaqi graded this Hadith Sahih Furthermore, in Sahih Al-Bukhari it is recorded that Anas bin Malik was asked about the recitation of the Prophet . He said, "His recitation was unhurried." He then demonstrated that and recited, while lengthening the recitation of Bismillah Ar-Rahman Ar-Rahim, Also, in the Musnad of Imam Ahmad, the Sunan of Abu Dawud, the Sahih of Ibn Hibban and the Mustadrak of Al-Hakim - it is recorded that Umm Salamah said, "The Messenger of Allah used to distinguish each Ayah during his recitation,

(In the Name of Allah, the Most Gracious, the Most Merciful. All praise and thanks be to Allah, the Lord of all that exists, the Most Gracious, the Most Merciful. The Owner of the Day of Recompense.)"

Ad-Daraqutni graded the chain of narration for this Hadith Sahih Furthermore, Imam Abu `Abdullah Ash-Shafi`i and Al-Hakim in his Mustadrak, recorded that Mu`awiyah led the prayer in Al-Madinah and did not recite the Bismillah. The Muhajirin who were present at that prayer criticized that. When Mu`awiyah led the following prayer, he recited the Bismillah aloud.

The Hadiths mentioned above provide sufficient proof for the opinion that the Bismillah is recited aloud. As for the opposing evidences and the scientific analysis of the narrations mentioned their weaknesses or otherwise it is not our desire to discuss this subject at this time.

Other scholars stated that the Bismillah should not be recited aloud in the prayer, and this is the established practice of the Four Khalifahs, as well as `Abdullah bin Mughaffal and several scholars among the Tabi`in and later generations. It is also the Madhhab (view) of Abu Hanifah, Ath-Thawri and Ahmad bin Hanbal.

Imam Malik stated that the Bismillah is not recited aloud or silently. This group based their view upon what Imam Muslim recorded that `A'ishah said that the Messenger of Allah used to start the prayer by reciting the Takbir (Allahu Akbar; Allah is Greater) and then recite,

(All praise and thanks be to Allah, the Lord of all that exists.) (Ibn Abi Hatim 1:12).

Also, the Two Sahihs recorded that Anas bin Malik said, "I prayed behind the Prophet , Abu Bakr, `Umar and `Uthman and they used to start their prayer with,

(All praise and thanks be to Allah, the Lord of all that exists.)

Muslim added, "And they did not mention,

(In the Name of Allah, the Most Gracious, the Most Merciful) whether in the beginning or the end of the recitation." Similar is recorded in the Sunan books from `Abdullah bin Mughaffal, may Allah be pleased with him.

These are the opinions held by the respected Imams, and their statements are similar in that they agree that the prayer of those who recite Al-Fatihah aloud or in secret is correct. All the favor is from Allah.

The Virtue of Al-Fatihah

Imam Ahmad recorded in his Musnad, that a person who was riding behind the Prophet said, "The Prophet's animal tripped, so I said, `Cursed Shaytan.' The Prophet said,

«لَا تَقُلْ: تَعِسَ الشَّيْطَانُ، فَإِنَّكَ إِذَا قُلْتَ: تَعِسَ الشَّيْطَانُ، تَعَاظَمَ وَقَالَ: بِقُوَّتِي صَرَعْتُهُ، وَإِذَا قُلْتَ: بِاسْمِ اللهِ تَصَاغَرَ حَتَى يَصِيرَ مِثْلَ الذُّبَابِ»

(Do not say, 'Cursed Shaytan,' for if you say these words, Satan becomes arrogant and says, 'With my strength I made him fall.' When you say, 'Bismillah,' Satan will become as small as a fly.)

Further, An-Nasa'i recorded in his book Al-Yawm wal-Laylah, and also Ibn Marduwyah in his Tafsir that Usamah bin `Umayr said, "I was riding behind the Prophet..." and he mentioned the rest of the above Hadith. The Prophet said in this narration,

«لَا تَقُلْ هَكَذَا فَإِنَّهُ يَتَعَاظَمُ حَتَّى يَكُونَ كَالْبَيْتِ، وَلَكِنْ قُلْ: بِسْمِ اللهِ، فَإِنَّهُ يَصْغَرُ حَتَّى يَكُونَ كَالذُّبَابَةِ»

(Do not say these words, because then Satan becomes larger; as large as a house. Rather, say, 'Bismillah,' because Satan then becomes as small as a fly.)

This is the blessing of reciting Bismillah.

Basmalah is recommended before performing any Deed

Basmalah (reciting Bismillah) is recommended before starting any action or deed. For instance, Basmalah is recommended before starting a Khutbah (speech).

The Basmalah is also recommended before one enters the place where he wants to relieve himself, there is a Hadith concerning this practice. Further, Basmalah is recommended at the beginning of ablution, for Imam Ahmad and the Sunan compilers recorded that Abu Hurayrah, Sa`id bin Zayd and Abu Sa`id narrated from the Prophet ,

«لَا وُضُوءَ لِمَنْ لَمْ يَذْكُرِ اسْمَ اللهِ عَلَيْهِ»

(There is no valid ablution for he who did not mention Allah's Name in it.)

This Hadith is Hasan (good). Also, the Basmalah is recommended before eating, for Muslim recorded in his Sahih that the Messenger of Allah said to `Umar bin Abi Salamah while he was a child under his care,

«قُلْ بِسْمِ اللهِ وَكُلْ بِيَمِينِكَ وَكُلْ مِمَّا يَلِيكَ»

(Say Bismillah, eat with your right hand and eat from whatever is next to you.)

Some of the scholars stated that Basmalah before eating is obligatory. Basmalah before having sexual intercourse is also recommended. The Two Sahihs recorded that Ibn `Abbas said that the Messenger of Allah said,

«لَوْ أَنَّ أَحَدَكُمْ إِذَا أَرَادَ أَنْ يَأْتِيَ أَهْلَهُ قَالَ: بِسْمِ اللهِ اللَّهُمَّ جَنِّبْنَا الشَّيْطَانَ وَجَنِّبِ الشَّيْطَانَ مَا رَزَقْتَنَا، فَإِنَّهُ إِنْ يُقَدَّرْ بَيْنَهُمَا وَلَدٌ لَمْ يَضُرَّهُ الشَّيْطَانُ أَبَدًا»

(If anyone of you before having sexual relations with his wife says, 'In the Name of Allah. O Allah! Protect us from Satan and also protect what you grant us (meaning the coming offspring) from Satan,' and if it is destined that they should have a child then, Satan will never be able to harm that child.)

The Meaning of "Allah

Allah is the Name of the Lord, the Exalted. It is said that Allah is the Greatest Name of Allah, because it is referred to when describing Allah by the various attributes. For instance, Allah said,

(He is Allah, beside Whom La ilaha illa Huwa (none has the right to be worshipped but He) the Knower of the unseen and the seen. He is the Most Gracious, the Most Merciful. He is Allah, beside Whom La ilaha illa Huwa, the King, the Holy, the One free from all defects, the Giver of security, the Watcher over His creatures, the Almighty, the Compeller, the Supreme. Glory be to Allah! (High is He) above all that they associate as partners with Him. He is Allah, the Creator, the Inventor of all things, the Bestower of forms. To Him belong the Best Names. All that is in the heavens and the earth glorify Him. And He is the Almighty, the Wise) (59:22-24).

Chapter 1: Al-Fatihah, Verses 001 to 007

Hence, Allah mentioned several of His Names as Attributes for His Name Allah. Similarly, Allah said,

(And (all) the Most Beautiful Names belong to Allah, so call on Him by them) (7:180), and,

(Say (O Muhammad :) "Invoke Allah or invoke the Most Gracious (Allah), by whatever name you invoke Him (it is the same), for to Him belong the Best Names.") (17:110)

Also, the Two Sahihs recorded that Abu Hurayrah said that the Messenger of Allah said,

«إِنَّ لِلَّهِ تِسْعَةً وَتِسْعِينَ اسْمًا، مِائَةً إِلَّا وَاحِدًا، مَنْ أَحْصَاهَا دَخَلَ الْجَنَّةَ»

(Allah has ninety-nine Names, one hundred minus one, whoever counts (and preserves) them, will enter Paradise.)

These Names were mentioned in a Hadith recorded by At-Tirmidhi and Ibn Majah, and there are several differences between these two narrations.

The Meaning of Ar-Rahman Ar-Rahim - the Most Gracious, the Most Merciful

Ar-Rahman and Ar-Rahim are two names derived from Ar-Rahmah (the mercy), but Rahman has more meanings that pertain to mercy than Ar-Rahim. There is a statement by Ibn Jarir that indicates that there is a consensus on this meaning. Further, Al-Qurtubi said, "The proof that these names are derived (from Ar-Rahmah), is what At-Tirmidhi recorded - and graded Sahih from `Abdur-Rahman bin `Awf that he heard the Messenger of Allah say,

«قَالَ اللهُ تَعَالَى: أَنَا الرَّحْمَنُ خَلَقْتُ الرَّحِمَ وَشَقَقْتُ لَهَا اسْمًا مِنِ اسْمِي، فَمَنْ وَصَلَهَا وَصَلْتُهُ وَمَنْ قَطَعَها قَطَعْتُهُ»

(Allah the Exalted said, 'I Am Ar-Rahman. I created the Raham (womb, i.e. family relations) and derived a name for it from My Name. Hence, whoever keeps it, I will keep ties to him, and whoever severs it, I will sever ties with him.') He then said, "This is a text that indicates the derivation." He then said, "The Arabs denied the name Ar-Rahman, because of their ignorance about Allah and His attributes."

Al-Qurtubi said, "It was said that both Ar-Rahman and Ar-Rahim have the same meaning, such as the words Nadman and Nadim, as Abu `Ubayd has stated. Abu `Ali Al-Farisi said, `Ar-Rahman, which is exclusively for Allah, is a name that encompasses every type of mercy that Allah has. Ar-Rahim is what effects the believers, for Allah said,

(And He is ever Rahim (merciful) to the believers.)' (33:43) Also, Ibn `Abbas said - about Ar-Rahman and Ar-Rahim, `They are two soft names, one of them is softer than the other (meaning it carries more implications of mercy).'''

Ibn Jarir said; As-Surri bin Yahya At-Tamimi narrated to me that `Uthman bin Zufar related that Al-`Azrami said about Ar-Rahman and Ar-Rahim, "He is Ar-Rahman with all creation and Ar-Rahim with the believers." Hence. Allah's statements,

(Then He rose over (Istawa) the Throne (in a manner that suits His majesty), Ar-Rahman) (25:59),) and,

(Ar-Rahman (Allah) rose over (Istawa) the (Mighty) Throne (in a manner that suits His majesty).) (20:5)

Allah thus mentioned the Istawa - rising over the Throne - along with His Name Ar-Rahman, to indicate that His mercy encompasses all of His creation. Allah also said,

(And He is ever Rahim (merciful) to the believers), thus encompassing the believers with His Name Ar-Rahim. They said, "This testifies to the fact that Ar-Rahman carries a broader scope of meanings pertaining to the mercy of Allah with His creation in both lives. Meanwhile, Ar-Rahim is exclusively for the believers." Yet, we should mention that there is a supplication that reads,

«رَحْمَنَ الدُّنْيَا وَالْآخِرَةِ وَرَحِيمَهُمَا»

(The Rahman and the Rahim of this life and the Hereafter)

Allah's Name Ar-Rahman is exclusively His. For instance, Allah said,

(Say (O Muhammad): "Invoke Allah or invoke Ar-Rahman (Allah), by whatever name you invoke Him (it is the same), for to Him belong the Best Names) (17:110),) and,

(And ask (O Muhammad) those of Our Messengers whom We sent before you: "Did We ever appoint alihah (gods) to be worshipped besides Ar-Rahman (Most Gracious, Allah)") (43:45).

Further, when Musaylimah the Liar called himself the Rahman of Yamamah, Allah made him known by the name `Liar' and exposed him. Hence, whenever Musaylimah is mentioned, he is described as `the Liar'. He became an example for lying among the residents of the cities and villages and the residents of the deserts, the bedouins.

Therefore, Allah first mentioned His Name - Allah - that is exclusively His and described this Name by Ar-Rahman, which no one else is allowed to use, just as Allah said,

(Say (O Muhammad): "Invoke Allah or invoke Ar-Rahman (Allah), by whatever name you invoke Him (it is the same), for to Him belong the Best Names.") (17:110)

Only Musaylimah and those who followed his misguided ways described Musaylimah by Ar-Rahman.

As for Allah's Name Ar-Rahim, Allah has described others by it. For instance, Allah said,

(Verily, there has come unto you a Messenger (Muhammad) from amongst yourselves (i.e. whom you know well). It grieves him that you should receive any injury or difficulty. He (Muhammad) is anxious over you (to be rightly guided) for the believers (he is) kind (full of pity), and Rahim (merciful)) (9:128).

Allah has also described some of His creation using some of His other Names. For instance, Allah said,

(Verily, We have created man from Nutfah (drops) of mixed semen (sexual discharge of man and woman), in order to try him, so We made him hearer (Sami`) and seer (Basir) (76:2).

In conclusion, there are several of Allah's Names that are used as names for others besides Allah. Further, some of Allah's Names are exclusive for Allah alone, such as Allah, Ar-Rahman, Al-Khaliq (the Creator), Ar-Raziq (the Sustainer), and so forth.

Hence, Allah started the Tasmiyah (meaning, `In the Name of Allah, Most Gracious Most Merciful') with His Name, Allah, and described Himself as Ar-Rahman, (Most Gracious) which is softer and more general than Ar-Rahim. The most honorable Names are mentioned first, just as Allah did here.

A Hadith narrated by Umm Salamah stated that the recitation of the Messenger of Allah was slow and clear, letter by letter,

(In the Name of Allah, the Most Gracious, the Most Merciful. All the praises and thanks be to Allah, the Lord of all that exists. The Most Gracious, the Most Merciful. The Owner of the Day of Recompense) (1:1-4).

And this is how a group of scholars recite it. Others connected the recitation of the Tasmiyah to Al-Hamd.

Surah: 1 Ayah: 2

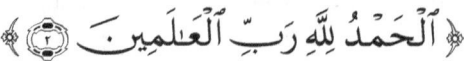

2. All the praises and thanks be to Allâh, the Lord of the 'Alamîn (mankind, jinn and all that exists).

Transliteration

2. Alhamdu lillahi rabbi alAAalameena

Tafsir Ibn Kathir

The Meaning of Al-Hamd

Abu Ja`far bin Jarir said, "The meaning of

(Al-Hamdu Lillah) (all praise and thanks be to Allah) is: all thanks are due purely to Allah, alone, not any of the objects that are being worshipped instead of Him, nor any of His creation. These thanks are due to Allah's innumerable favors and bounties, that only He knows the amount of. Allah's bounties include creating the tools that help the creation worship Him, the physical bodies with which they are able to implement His commands, the sustenance that He provides them in this life, and the comfortable life He has granted them, without anything or anyone compelling Him to do so. Allah also warned His creation and alerted them about the means and methods with which they can earn eternal dwelling in the residence of everlasting happiness. All thanks and praise are due to Allah for these favors from beginning to end."

Further, Ibn Jarir commented on the Ayah,

(Al-Hamdu Lillah), that it means, "A praise that Allah praised Himself with, indicating to His servants that they too should praise Him, as if Allah had said, `Say: All thanks and praise is due to Allah.' It was said that the statement,

(All praise and thanks be to Allah), entails praising Allah by mentioning His most beautiful Names and most honorable Attributes. When one proclaims, `All thanks are due to Allah,' he will be thanking Him for His favors and bounties."

The Difference between Praise and Thanks

Hamd is more general, in that it is a statement of praise for one's characteristics, or for what he has done. Thanks are given for what was done, not merely for characteristics.

The Statements of the Salaf about Al-Hamd

Hafs mentioned that `Umar said to `Ali, "We know La ilaha illallah, Subhan Allah and Allahu Akbar. What about Al-Hamdu Lillah" `Ali said, "A statement that Allah liked for Himself, was pleased with for Himself and He likes that it be repeated." Also, Ibn `Abbas said, "Al-Hamdu Lillah is the statement of appreciation. When the servant says Al-Hamdu Lillah, Allah says, `My servant has praised Me." Ibn Abi Hatim recorded this Hadith.

The Virtues of Al-Hamd

Imam Ahmad bin Hanbal recorded that Al-Aswad bin Sari` said, "I said, `O Messenger of Allah! Should I recite to you words of praise for My Lord, the Exalted, that I have collected' He said,

«أَمَا إِنَّ رَبَّكَ يُحِبُّ الْحَمْدَ»

(Verily, your Lord likes Al-Hamd.)"

An-Nasa'i also recorded this Hadith. Furthermore, Abu `Isa At-Tirmidhi, An-Nasa'i and Ibn Majah recorded that Musa bin Ibrahim bin Kathir related that Talhah bin Khirash said that Jabir bin `Abdullah said that the Messenger of Allah said,

«أَفْضَلُ الذِّكْرِ لَا إِلَهَ إِلَّا اللهُ، وَأَفْضَلُ الدُّعَاءِ الْحَمْدُ لِلهِ»

(The best Dhikr (remembering Allah) is La ilaha illallah and the best supplication is Al-Hamdu Lillah.)

At-Tirmidhi said that this Hadith is Hasan Gharib. Also, Ibn Majah recorded that Anas bin Malik said that the Messenger of Allah said,

«مَا أَنْعَمَ اللهُ عَلَى عَبْدٍ نِعْمَةً فَقَالَ: الْحَمْدُ لِلهِ، إِلَّا كَانَ الَّذِي أَعْطَى أَفْضَلَ مِمَّا أَخَذَ»

(No servant is blessed by Allah and says,`Al-Hamdu Lillah', except that what he was given is better than that which he has himself acquired.) Further, in his Sunan, Ibn Majah recorded that Ibn `Umar said that the Messenger of Allah said,

«إِنَّ عَبْدًا مِنْ عِبَادِ اللهِ قَالَ: يَا رَبِّ لَكَ الْحَمْدُ كَمَا يَنْبَغِي لِجَلَالِ وَجْهِكَ وَعَظِيمِ سُلْطَانِكَ. فَعَضَلَتْ بِالْمَلَكَيْنِ فَلَمْ يَدْرِيَا كَيْفَ يَكْتُبَانِهَا فَصَعِدَا إِلَى اللهِ فَقَالَا: يَا رَبَّنَا إِنَّ عَبْدًا قَدْ قَالَ مَقَالَةً لَا نَدْرِي كَيْفَ نَكْتُبُهَا، قَالَ اللهُ، وَهُوَ أَعْلَمُ بِمَا قَالَ عَبْدُهُ: مَاذَا قَالَ عَبْدِي؟ قَالَا: يَا

رَبٍّ إِنَّهُ قَالَ: لَكَ الْحَمْدُ يَا رَبِّ كَمَا يَنْبَغِي لِجَلَالِ وَجْهِكَ وَعَظِيمِ سُلْطَانِكَ. فَقَالَ اللهُ لَهُمَا: اكْتُبَاهَا كَمَا قَالَ عَبْدِي، حَتَّى يَلْقَانِي فَأَجْزِيَهِ بِهَا.»

(A servant of Allah once said, `O Allah! Yours is the Hamd that is suitable for the grace of Your Face and the greatness of Your Supreme Authority.' The two angels were confused as to how to write these words. They ascended to Allah and said, `O our Lord! A servant has just uttered a statement and we are unsure how to record it for him.' Allah said while having more knowledge in what His servant has said, 'What did My servant say' They said, `He said, `O Allah! Yours is the Hamd that is suitable for the grace of Your Face and the greatness of Your Supreme Authority.' Allah said to them, `Write it as My servant has said it, until he meets Me and then I shall reward him for it.)

Al before Hamd encompasses all Types of Thanks and Appreciation for Allah

The letters Alif and Lam before the word Hamd serve to encompass all types of thanks and appreciation for Allah, the Exalted. A Hadith stated,

«اللَّهُمَّ لَكَ الْحَمْدُ كُلُّهُ، وَلَكَ الْمُلْكُ كُلُّهُ، وَبِيَدِكَ الْخَيْرُ كُلُّهُ، وَإِلَيْكَ يُرْجَعُ الْأَمْرُ كُلُّهُ»

(O Allah! All of Al-Hamd is due to You, You own all the ownership, all types of good are in Your Hand and all affairs belong to You.)

The Meaning of Ar-Rabb, the Lord

Ar-Rabb is the owner who has full authority over his property. Ar-Rabb, linguistically means, the master or the one who has the authority to lead. All of these meanings are correct for Allah. When it is alone, the word Rabb is used only for Allah. As for other than Allah, it can be used to say Rabb Ad-Dar, the master of such and such object. Further, it was reported that Ar-Rabb is Allah's Greatest Name.

The Meaning of Al-`Alamin

Al-`Alamin is plural for `Alam, which encompasses everything in existence except Allah. The word `Alam is itself a plural word, having no singular form. The `Alamin are different creations that exist in the heavens and the earth, on land and at sea. Every generation of creation is called an `Alam. Al-Farra` and Abu `Ubayd said, "`Alam includes all that has a mind, the Jinns, mankind, the angels and the devils, but not the animals." Also, Zayd bin Aslam and Abu Muhaysin said, `Alam includes all that Allah has created with a soul." Further, Qatadah said about,

(The Lord of the `Alamin), "Every type of creation is an `Alam." Az-Zajjaj also said, "Alam encompasses everything that Allah created, in this life and in the Hereafter." Al-Qurtubi commented, "This is the correct meaning, that the `Alam encompasses everything that Allah created in both worlds. Similarly, Allah said,

(Fir`awn (Pharaoh) said: "And what is the Lord of the `Alamin" Musa (Moses) said: "The Lord of the heavens and the earth, and all that is between them, if you seek to be convinced with certainty") (26:23-24).

Why is the Creation called `Alam

`Alam is derived from `Alamah, that is because it is a sign testifying to the existence of its Creator and to His Oneness."

Surah: 1 Ayah: 3

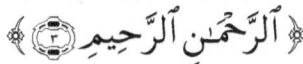

3. The Most Gracious, the Most Merciful.

Transliteration

3. Alrrahmani alrraheemi

Tafsir Ibn Kathir

(Ar-Rahman (the Most Gracious), Ar-Rahim (the Most Merciful)) We explained these Names in the Basmalah. Al-Qurtubi said, "Allah has described Himself by `Ar-Rahman, Ar-Rahim' after saying `the Lord of the Alamin', so His statement here includes a warning, and then an encouragement. Similarly, Allah said,

(Declare (O Muhammad) unto My servants, that truly, I am the Oft-Forgiving, the Most Merciful. And that My torment is indeed the most painful torment.) (15:49-50) Allah said,

(Surely, your Lord is swift in retribution, and certainly He is Oft-Forgiving, Most Merciful.) (6:165)

Hence, Rabb contains a warning while Ar-Rahman Ar-Rahim encourages. Further, Muslim recorded in his Sahih that the Messenger of Allah said,

«لَوْ يَعْلَمُ الْمُؤْمِنُ مَا عِنْدَ اللهِ مِنَ الْعُقُوبَةِ مَا طَمِعَ فِي جَنَّتِهِ أَحَدٌ، وَلَوْ

«يَعْلَمُ الْكَافِرُ مَا عِنْدَ اللهِ مِنَ الرَّحْمَةِ مَا قَنَطَ مِنْ رَحْمَتِهِ أَحَدٌ»

(If the believer knew what punishment Allah has, none would have hope in acquiring His Paradise, and if the disbeliever knew what mercy Allah has, none will lose hope of earning His mercy.)

Surah: 1 Ayah: 4

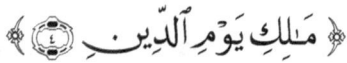

4. The Only Owner (and the Only Ruling Judge) of the Day of Recompense (i.e. the Day of Resurrection)

Transliteration

4. Maliki yawmi alddeeni

Tafsir Ibn Kathir

Indicating Sovereignty on the Day of Judgment

Allah mentioned His sovereignty of the Day of Resurrection, but this does not negate His sovereignty over all other things. For Allah mentioned that He is the Lord of existence, including this earthly life and the Hereafter. Allah only mentioned the Day of Recompense here because on that Day, no one except Him will be able to claim ownership of anything whatsoever. On that Day, no one will be allowed to speak without His permission. Similarly, Allah said,

(The Day that Ar-Ruh (Jibril (Gabriel) or another angel) and the angels will stand forth in rows, they will not speak except him whom the Most Gracious (Allah) allows, and he will speak what is right.) (78:38),

(And all voices will be humbled for the Most Gracious (Allah), and nothing shall you hear but the low voice of their footsteps.)(20:108), and,

(On the Day when it comes, no person shall speak except by His (Allah's) leave. Some among them will be wretched and (others) blessed) (11:105).

Ad-Dahhak said that Ibn `Abbas commented, "Allah says, `On that Day, no one owns anything that they used to own in the world.'"

The Meaning of Yawm Ad-Din

Ibn `Abbas said, "Yawm Ad-Din is the Day of Recompense for the creatures, meaning the Day of Judgment. On that Day, Allah will reckon the creation for their deeds, evil for evil, good for good, except for those whom He pardons." In addition, several other Companions, Tabi`in and scholars of the Salaf, said similarly, for this meaning is apparent and clear from the Ayah.

Allah is Al-Malik (King or Owner)

Allah is the True Owner (Malik) (of everything and everyone). Allah said,

(He is Allah, beside Whom La ilaha illa Huwa, the King, the Holy, the One free from all defects) (59:23).

Also, the Two Sahihs recorded Abu Hurayrah saying that the Prophet said,

«أَخْنَعُ اسْمٍ عِنْدَ اللهِ رَجُلٌ تَسَمَّى بِمَلِكِ الْأَمْلَاكِ وَلَا مَالِكَ إِلَّا اللهُ»

(The most despicable name to Allah is a person who calls himself the king of kings, while there are no owners except Allah.)

Also the Two Sahihs recorded that the Messenger of Allah said,

«يَقْبِضُ اللهُ الْأَرْضَ وَيَطْوِي السَّمَاءَ بِيَمِينِهِ ثُمَّ يَقُولُ: أَنَا الْمَلِكُ، أَيْنَ مُلُوكُ الْأَرْضِ؟ أَيْنَ الْجَبَّارُونَ؟ أَيْنَ الْمُتَكَبِّرُونَ؟»

((On the Day of Judgement) Allah will grasp the earth and fold up the heavens with His Right Hand and proclaim, 'I Am the King! Where are the kings of the earth Where are the tyrants Where are the arrogant')

Also, in the the Glorious Qur'an;

(Whose is the kingdom this Day Allah's, the One, the Irresistible.)(40:16).

As for calling someone other than Allah a king in this life, then it is done as a figure of speech. For instance, Allah said,

(Indeed Allah appointed Talut (Saul) as a king over you.) (2:247),

(As there was a king behind them)(18:79), and,

When He made Prophets among you, and made you kings)5:20(.

Also, the Two Sahihs recorded,

«مِثْلُ الْمُلُوكِ عَلَى الْأَسِرَّةِ»

(Just like kings reclining on their thrones)

The Meaning of Ad-Din

Ad-Din means the reckoning, the reward or punishment. Similarly, Allah said,

(On that Day Allah will pay them the (Dinahum) recompense (of their deeds) in full) (24:25), and,

(Shall we indeed (be raised up) to receive reward or punishment (according to our deeds)) (37:53). A Hadith stated,

«الْكَيِّسُ مَنْ دَانَ نَفْسَهُ وَعَمِلَ لِمَا بَعْدَ الْمَوتِ»

(The wise person is he who reckons himself and works for (his life) after death.) meaning, he holds himself accountable. Also, `Umar said, "Hold yourself accountable before you are held accountable, weigh yourselves before you are weighed, and be prepared for the biggest gathering before He Whose knowledge encompasses your deeds,

(That Day shall you be brought to Judgement, not a secret of yours will be hidden) (69:18)."

Surah: 1 Ayah: 5, Ayah: 6 & Ayah: 7

﴿ إِيَّاكَ نَعْبُدُ وَإِيَّاكَ نَسْتَعِينُ ﴾

5. You (Alone) we worship, and You (Alone) we ask for help (for each and everything).

﴿ اهْدِنَا الصِّرَاطَ الْمُسْتَقِيمَ ﴾

6. Guide us to the Straight Way.

﴿ صِرَاطَ الَّذِينَ أَنْعَمْتَ عَلَيْهِمْ غَيْرِ الْمَغْضُوبِ عَلَيْهِمْ وَلَا الضَّالِّينَ ﴾

7. The Way of those on whom You have bestowed Your Grace, not (the way) of those who earned Your Anger (such as the Jews), nor of those who went astray (such as the Christians).

Transliteration

5. Iyyaka naAAbudu wa-iyyaka nastaAAeenu 6. Ihdina alssirata almustaqeema 7. Sirata allatheena anAAamta AAalayhim ghayri almaghdoobi AAalayhim wala alddalleena

Tafsir Ibn Kathir

The Linguistic and Religious Meaning of `Ibadah

Linguistically, `Ibadah means subdued. For instance, a road is described as Mu`abbadah, meaning, `paved'. In religious terminology, `Ibadah implies the utmost love, humility and fear.

The Merit of stating the Object of the Action before the Doer of the Act, and the Merit of these Negations

"You...", means, we worship You alone and none else, and rely on You alone and none else. This is the perfect form of obedience and the entire religion is implied by these two ideas. Some of the Salaf said, Al-Fatihah is the secret of the Qur'an, while these words are the secret of Al-Fatihah,

(5. You we worship, and You we ask for help.)

The first part is a declaration of innocence from Shirk (polytheism), while the second negates having any power or strength, displaying the recognition that all affairs are controlled by Allah alone. This meaning is reiterated in various instances in the Qur'an. For instance, Allah said,

(So worship Him (O Muhammad) and put your trust in Him. And your Lord is not unaware of what you (people) do.) (11:123),

(Say: "He is the Most Gracious (Allah), in Him we believe, and in Him we put our trust.") (67:29),

((He alone is) the Lord of the east and the west; La ilaha illa Huwa (none has the right to be worshipped but He).

So take Him alone as Wakil (Disposer of your affairs)), (73:9), and,

(You we worship, and You we ask for help).

We should mention that in this Ayah, the type of speech here changes from the third person to direct speech by using the Kaf in the statement Iyyaka (You). This is because after the servant praised and thanked Allah, he stands before Him, addressing Him directly;

(You we worship, and You we ask for help).

Al-Fatihah indicates the Necessity of praising Allah. It is required in every Prayer.

The beginning of Surat Al-Fatihah contains Allah's praise for Himself by His most beautiful Attributes and indicates to His servants that, they too, should praise Him in the same manner. Hence, the prayer is not valid unless one recites Al-Fatihah, if he is able. The Two Sahihs recorded that `Ubadah bin As-Samit said that the Messenger of Allah said,

«لَا صَلَاةَ لِمَنْ لَمْ يَقْرَأْ بِفَاتِحَةِ الْكِتَابِ»

(There is no valid prayer for whoever does not recite Al-Fatihah of the Book.)

Also, it is recorded in Sahih Muslim that Abu Hurayrah said that the Messenger of Allah said,

«يَقُولُ اللَّهُ تَعَالَى: قَسَمْتُ الصَّلَاةَ بَيْنِي وَبَيْنَ عَبْدِي نِصْفَيْنِ، فَنِصْفُهَا لِي وَنِصْفُهَا لِعَبْدِي وَلِعَبْدِي مَا سَأَلَ، إِذَا قَالَ الْعَبْدُ:

«الْحَمْدُ للَّهِ رَبِّ الْعَالَمِينَ»

قَالَ اللَّهُ: أَثْنَى عَلَيَّ عَبْدِي فَإِذَا قَالَ:

[مَلِكِ يَوْمِ الدِّينِ]، قَالَ اللَّهُ: مَجَّدَنِي عَبْدِي، وَإِذَا قَالَ:

[إِيَّاكَ نَعْبُدُ وَإِيَّاكَ نَسْتَعِينُ]، قَالَ: هَذَا بَيْنِي وَبَيْنَ عَبْدِي، وَلِعَبْدِي مَا سَأَلَ، فَإِذَا قَالَ:

[اهْدِنَا الصِّرَاطَ الْمُسْتَقِيمَ]

Chapter 1: Al-Fatihah, Verses 001 to 007

[صِرَاطَ الَّذِينَ أَنْعَمْتَ عَلَيْهِمْ غَيْرِ الْمَغْضُوبِ عَلَيْهِمْ وَلاَ الضَّالِّينَ]،

قَالَ: هذَا لِعَبْدِي، وَلِعَبْدِي مَا سَأَلَ»

(Allah said, `I divided the prayer into two halves between Myself and My servant, one half is for Me and one half for My servant. My servant shall have what he asks for.' When the servant says,

[الْحَمْدُ لِلَّهِ رَبِّ الْعَالَمِينَ]

(All praise and thanks be to Allah, the Lord of all that exists.), Allah says, `My servant has praised Me.' When the servant says,

[الرَّحْمَنِ الرَّحِيمِ]

(The Most Gracious, the Most Merciful), Allah says, `My servant has praised Me.' When the servant says,

[مَلِكِ يَوْمِ الدِّينِ]

(The Owner of the Day of Recompense), Allah says, `My servant has glorified Me.' If the servant says,

[إِيَّاكَ نَعْبُدُ وَإِيَّاكَ نَسْتَعِينُ]

(You we worship, and You we ask for help), Allah says, `This is between Me and My servant, and My servant shall have what he asked.' If the servant says,

[اهْدِنَا الصِّرَاطَ الْمُسْتَقِيمَ - صِرَاطَ الَّذِينَ أَنْعَمْتَ عَلَيْهِمْ غَيْرِ الْمَغْضُوبِ عَلَيْهِمْ وَلاَ الضَّالِّينَ]

(Guide us to the straight path. The path of those on whom You have bestowed Your grace, not (that) of those who have earned Your anger, nor of those who went astray), Allah says, `This is for My servant, and My servant shall have what he asked.')

Tawhid Al-Uluhiyyah

Ad-Dahhak narrated that Ibn `Abbas said,

(You we worship) means, "It is You whom we single out, Whom we fear and Whom we hope in, You alone, our Lord, and none else.

Tawhid Ar-Rububiyyah

(And You we ask for help), to obey you and in all of our affairs." Further, Qatadah said that the Ayah,

(You we worship, and You we ask for help) "Contains Allah's command to us to perform sincere worship for Him and to seek His aid concerning all of our affairs." Allah mentioned,

(You we worship) before,

(And You we ask for help), because the objective here is the worship, while Allah's help is the tool to implement this objective. Certainly, one first takes care of the most important aspects and then what is less important, and Allah knows best.

Allah called His Prophet (Peace be upon him) an `Abd

Allah called His Messenger an `Abd (servant) when He mentioned sending down His Book, the Prophet's involvement in inviting to Him, and when mentioning the Isra' (overnight journey from Makkah to Jerusalem and then to heaven), and these are the Prophet's most honorable missions. Allah said,

(All praise and thanks be to Allah, Who has sent down to His servant (Muhammad) the Book (the Qur'an)) (18:1),

(And when the servant of Allah (Muhammad) stood up invoking Him (his Lord - Allah in prayer)), (72:19) and,

(Glorified (and Exalted) be He (Allah) (above all that they associate with Him) Who took His servant (Muhammad) for a journey by night) (17:1).

Encouraging the Performance of the Acts of Worship during Times of Distress

Allah also recommended that His Prophet resort to acts of worship during times when he felt distressed because of the disbelievers who defied and denied him. Allah said,

(Indeed, We know that your breast is straitened at what they say. So glorify the praises of your Lord and be of those who prostrate themselves (to Him). And worship your Lord until there comes unto you the certainty (i.e. death)) (15:97-99).

Why Praise was mentioned First

Since the praise of Allah, Who is being sought for help, was mentioned, it was appropriate that one follows the praise by asking for his need. We stated that Allah said,

«فَنِصْفُهَا لِي وَنِصْفُهَا لِعَبْدِي، وَلِعَبْدِي مَا سَأَلَ»

(One half for Myself and one half for My servant, and My servant shall have what he asked.)

This is the best method for seeking help, by first praising the one whom help is sought from and then asking for His aid, and help for one's self, and for his Muslim brethren by saying.

(Guide us to the straight path.)

This method is more appropriate and efficient in bringing about a positive answer to the pleas, and this is why Allah recommended this better method.

Asking for help may take the form of conveying the condition of the person who is seeking help. For instance, the Prophet Moses said,

(My Lord! Truly, I am in need of whatever good that You bestow on me!) (28:24).

Also, one may first mention the attributes of whoever is being asked, such as what Dhun-Nun said,

(La ilaha illa Anta (none has the right to be worshipped but You (O Allah)), Glorified (and Exalted) be You (above all that they associate with You)! Truly, I have been of the wrongdoers) (21:87).

Further, one may praise Him without mentioning what he needs. The Meaning of Guidance mentioned in the Surah

The guidance mentioned in the Surah implies being directed and guided to success. Allah said,

(Guide us to the straight path) meaning guide, direct, lead and grant us the correct guidance. Also,

(And shown him the two ways (good and evil)) (90:10), means, `We explained to him the paths of good and evil.' Also, Allah said,

(He (Allah) chose him (as an intimate friend) and guided him to a straight path) (16:121), and,

(And lead them on to the way of flaming Fire (Hell)) (37:23). Similarly, Allah said,

(And verily, you (O Muhammad) are indeed guiding (mankind) to the straight path) (42:52), and,

(All praise and thanks be to Allah, Who has guided us to this) (7:43), meaning, guided us and directed us and qualified us for this end - Paradise.

The Meaning of As-Sirat Al-Mustaqim, the Straight Path.

As for the meaning of As-Sirat Al-Mustaqim, Imam Abu Ja`far At-Tabari said, "The Ummah agreed that Sirat Al-Mustaqim, is the clear path without branches, according to the language of the Arabs. For instance, Jarir bin `Atiyah Al-Khatafi said in a poem, `The Leader of the faithful is on a path that will remain straight even though the other paths are crooked." At-Tabari also stated that, "There are many evidences to this fact." At-Tabari then proceeded, "The Arabs use the term, Sirat in reference to every deed and statement whether righteous or wicked. Hence the Arabs would describe the honest person as being straight and the wicked person as being crooked. The straight path mentioned in the Qur'an refers to Islam.

Imam Ahmad recorded in his Musnad that An-Nawwas bin Sam`an said that the Prophet said,

«ضَرَبَ اللهُ مَثَلًا صِرَاطًا مُسْتَقِيمًا، وَعَلَى جَنْبَتَي الصِّرَاطِ سُورَانِ فِيهِمَا أَبْوَابٌ مُفَتَّحَةٌ، وَعَلَى الْأَبْوَابِ سُتُورٌ مُرْخَاةٌ، وَعَلَى بَابِ الصِّرَاطِ دَاعٍ يَقُولُ: يَاأَيُّهَا النَّاسُ ادْخُلُوا الصِّرَاطَ جَمِيعًا وَلَا تَعَوَّجُوا، وَدَاعٍ يَدْعُو مِنْ فَوْقِ الصِّرَاطِ، فَإِذَا أَرَادَ الْإِنْسَانُ أَنْ يَفْتَحَ شَيْئًا مِنْ تِلْكَ الْأَبْوَابِ قَالَ: وَيْحَكَ لَا تَفْتَحْهُ فَإِنَّكَ إِنْ فَتَحْتَهُ تَلِجْهُ فَالصِّرَاطُ: الْإِسْلَامُ وَالسُّورَانِ: حُدُودُ اللهِ وَالْأَبْوَابُ الْمُفَتَّحَةُ مَحَارِمُ اللهِ وَذَلِكَ الدَّاعِي عَلَى رَأْسِ الصِّرَاطِ كِتَابُ اللهِ، وَالدَّاعِي مِنْ فَوْقِ الصِّرَاطِ وَاعِظُ اللهِ فِي قَلْبِ كُلِّ مُسْلِمٍ»

(Allah has set an example: a Sirat (straight path) that is surrounded by two walls on both sides, with several open doors within the walls covered with curtains. There is a caller on the gate of the Sirat who heralds, 'O people! Stay on the path and do not deviate from it.' Meanwhile, a caller from above the path is also warning any person who wants to open any of these doors, 'Woe unto you! Do not open it, for if you open it you will pass through.' The straight path is Islam, the two walls are Allah's set limits, while the doors resemble what Allah has prohibited. The caller on the gate of the Sirat is the Book of Allah, while the caller above the Sirat is Allah's admonishment in the heart of every Muslim.)

The Faithful ask for and abide by Guidance

If someone asks, "Why does the believer ask Allah for guidance during every prayer and at other times, while he is already properly guided Has he not already acquired guidance"

The answer to these questions is that if it were not a fact that the believer needs to keep asking for guidance day and night, Allah would not have directed him to invoke Him to acquire the guidance. The servant needs Allah the Exalted every hour of his life to help him remain firm on the path of guidance and to make him even more firm and persistent on it. The servant does not have the power to benefit or harm himself, except by Allah's permission. Therefore, Allah directed the servant to invoke Him constantly, so that He provides him with His aid and with firmness and success. Indeed, the happy person is he whom Allah guides to ask of Him. This is especially the case if a person urgently needs Allah's help day or night. Allah said,

(O you who believe! Believe in Allah, and His Messenger (Muhammad), and the Book (the Qur'an) which He has sent down to His Messenger, and the Scripture which He sent down to those before (him)) (4:16).

Therefore, in this Ayah Allah commanded the believers to believe, and this command is not redundant since what is sought here is firmness and continuity of performing the deeds that help one remain on the path of faith. Also, Allah commanded His believing servants to proclaim,

(Our Lord! Let not our hearts deviate (from the truth) after You have guided us, and grant us mercy from You. Truly, You are the Bestower.) (3:8). Hence,

(Guide us to the straight way) means, "Make us firm on the path of guidance and do not allow us to deviate from it."

(7. The way of those upon whom You have bestowed Your grace, not (that) of those who earned Your anger, nor of those who went astray).

We mentioned the Hadith in which the servant proclaims,

(Guide us to the straight way) and Allah says, "This is for My servant, and My servant shall acquire what he asks for." Allah's statement.

(The way of those upon whom You have bestowed Your grace) defines the path. `Those upon whom Allah has bestowed His grace' are those mentioned in Surat An-Nisa' (chapter 4), when Allah said,

(And whoever obeys Allah and the Messenger (Muhammad), then they will be in the company of those on whom Allah has bestowed His grace, the Prophets, the Siddiqin (the truly faithful), the martyrs, and the righteous. And how excellent these companions are! Such is the bounty from Allah, and Allah is sufficient to know) (4:69-70).

Allah's statement,

(Not (the way) of those who earned Your anger, nor of those who went astray) meaning guide us to the straight path, the path of those upon whom you have bestowed Your grace, that is, the people of guidance, sincerity and obedience to Allah and His Messengers. They are the people who adhere to Allah's commandments and refrain from committing what He has prohibited. But, help us to avoid the path of those whom Allah is angry with, whose intentions are corrupt, who know the truth, yet deviate from it. Also, help us avoid the path of those who were led astray, who lost the true knowledge and, as a result, are wandering in misguidance, unable to find the correct path. Allah asserted that the two paths He described here are both misguided when He repeated the negation `not'. These two paths are the paths of the Christians and Jews, a fact that the believer should beware of so that he avoids them. The path of the believers is knowledge of the truth and abiding by it. In comparison, the Jews abandoned practicing the religion, while the Christians lost the true knowledge. This is why `anger' descended upon the Jews, while being described as `led astray' is more appropriate of the Christians. Those who know, but avoid implementing the truth, deserve the anger, unlike those who are ignorant. The Christians want to seek the true knowledge, but are unable to find it because they did not seek it from its proper resources.

This is why they were led astray. We should also mention that both the Christians and the Jews have earned the anger and are led astray, but the anger is one of the attributes more particular of the Jews. Allah said about the Jews,

(Those (Jews) who incurred the curse of Allah and His wrath) (5:60).

The attribute that the Christians deserve most is that of being led astray, just as Allah said about them,

(Who went astray before and who misled many, and strayed (themselves) from the right path) (5:77).

There are several Hadiths and reports from the Salaf on this subject. Imam Ahmad recorded that `Adi bin Hatim said, "The horsemen of the Messenger of Allah seized my paternal aunt and some other people. When they brought them to the Messenger of Allah , they were made to stand in line before him.

My aunt said, `O Messenger of Allah! The supporter is far away, the offspring have stopped coming and I am an old woman, unable to serve. Grant me your favor, may Allah grant you His favor.' He said, `Who is your supporter' She said, `Adi bin Hatim.' He said, `The one who ran away from Allah and His Messenger' She said, `So, the Prophet freed me.' When the Prophet came back, there was a man next to him, I think that he was `Ali, who said to her, `Ask him for a means of transportation.' She asked the Prophet , and he ordered that she be given an animal.

" `Adi then said, "Later on, she came to me and said, `He (Muhammad) has done a favor that your father (who was a generous man) would never have done. So and-so person came to him and he granted him his favor, and so-and-so came to him and he granted him his favor.' So I went to the Prophet and found that some women and children were gathering with him, so close that I knew that he was not a king like Kisra (King of Persia) or Caesar. He said, `O `Adi! What made you run away, so that La ilaha illallah is not proclaimed Is there a deity worthy of worship except Allah What made you run away, so that Allahu Akbar (Allah is the Greater) is not proclaimed Is there anything Greater than Allah' I proclaimed my Islam and I saw his face radiate with pleasure and he said:

«إِنَّ الْمَغْضُوبَ عَلَيْهِمُ الْيَهُودُ وَ إِنَّ الضَّالِينَ النَّصَارَى»

(Those who have earned the anger are the Jews and those who are led astray are the Christians.)"

This Hadith was also collected by At-Tirmidhi who said that it is Hasan Gharib.

Also, when Zayd bin `Amr bin Nufayl went with some of his friends - before Islam - to Ash-Sham seeking the true religion, the Jews said to him, "You will not become a Jew unless you carry a share of the anger of Allah that we have earned." He said, "I am seeking to escape Allah's anger." Also, the Christians said to him, "If you become one of us you will carry a share in Allah's discontent." He said, "I cannot bear it." So he remained in his pure nature and avoided worshipping the idols and the polytheistic practices. He became neither a Jew, nor Christian. As for his companions, they became Christians because they found it more pure than Judaism. Waraqah bin Nawfal was among these people until Allah guided him by the hand of His Prophet, when he was sent as Prophet, and Waraqah believed in the revelation that was sent to the Prophet (may Allah be pleased with him).

The Summary of Al-Fatihah

The honorable Surah Al-Fatihah contains seven Ayat including the praise and thanks of Allah, glorifying Him and praising Him by mentioning His most Beautiful Names and most high Attributes. It also mentions the Hereafter, which is the Day of Resurrection, and directs Allah's servants to ask of Him, invoking Him and declaring that all power and strength comes from Him. It also calls to the sincerity of the worship of Allah alone, singling Him out in His divinity, believing in His perfection, being free from the need of any partners, having no rivals nor equals. Al-Fatihah directs the believers to invoke Allah to guide them to the straight path, which is the true religion, and to help them remain on that path in this life, and to pass over the actual Sirat (bridge over hell that everyone must pass over) on the Day of Judgment. On that Day, the believers will be directed to the gardens of comfort in the company of the Prophets, the truthful ones, the martyrs and the righteous. Al-Fatihah also encourages performing good deeds, so that the believers will be in the company of the good-doers on the Day of Resurrection. The Surah also warns against following the paths of misguidance, so that one does not end up being gathered with those who indulge in sin, on the Day of Resurrection, including those who have earned the anger and those who were led astray.

The Bounties are because of Allah, not the Deviations

Allah said,

(The way of those upon whom you have bestowed Your grace), when He mentioned His favor. On mentioning anger, Allah said,

(Not (that) of those who earned Your anger), without mentioning the subject, although it is He Who has sent down the anger on them, just as Allah stated in another Ayah,

(Have you (O Muhammad) not seen those (hypocrites) who take as friends a people upon whom is the wrath of Allah (i.e. Jews)) (58:14).

Also, Allah relates the misguidance of those who indulged in it, although they were justly misguided according to Allah's appointed destiny. For instance, Allah said,

(He whom Allah guides, he is the rightly-guided; but he whom He sends astray, for him you will find no Wali (guiding friend) to lead him (to the right path)) (18:17)

and,

(Whomsoever Allah sends astray, none can guide him; and He lets them wander blindly in their transgression) (7:186).

These and several other Ayat testify to the fact that Allah alone is the One Who guides and misguides, contrary to the belief of the Qadariyyah sect, who claimed that the servants choose and create their own destiny. They rely on some unclear Ayat avoiding what is clear and contradicts their desires. Theirs, is the method of the people who follow their lust, desire and wickedness. An authentic Hadith narrated,

»إِذَا رَأَيْتُمُ الَّذِينَ يَتَّبِعُونَ مَا تَشَابَهَ مِنْهُ فَأُولَئِكَ الَّذِينَ سَمَّى اللهُ فَاحْذَرُوهُمْ«

(When you see those who follow what is not so clear in it (the Qur'an), then they are those whom Allah has mentioned (refer to 3:7). Hence, avoid them.)

The Prophet was referring to Allah's statement,

(So as for those in whose hearts there is a deviation (from the truth) they follow that which is not entirely clear thereof, seeking Al-Fitnah (polytheism and trials), and seeking for its hidden meanings)(3:7).

Verily, no innovator in the religion could ever rely on any authentic evidence in the Qur'an that testifies to his innovation. The Qur'an came to distinguish between truth and falsehood, and guidance and misguidance. The Qur'an does not contain any discrepancies or contradictions, because it is a revelation from the Most Wise, Worthy of all praise.

Saying Amin

It is recommended to say Amin after finishing the recitation of Al-Fatihah. Amin means, "O Allah! Accept our invocation." The evidence that saying Amin is recommended is contained in what Imams Ahmad, Abu Dawud and At-Tirmidhi recorded, that Wa'il bin Hujr said, "I heard the Messenger of Allah recite,

[غَيْرِ الْمَغْضُوبِ عَلَيْهِمْ وَلاَ الضَّآلِّينَ]

(Not (that) of those who earned Your anger, nor of those who went astray), and he said `Amin' extending it with his voice."

Abu Dawud's narration added, "Raising his voice with it." At-Tirmidhi then commented that this Hadith is Hasan and was also narrated from `Ali and Ibn Mas`ud. Also, Abu Hurayrah narrated that whenever the Messenger of Allah would recite,

[غَيْرِ الْمَغْضُوبِ عَلَيْهِمْ وَلاَ الضَّآلِّينَ]

(Not (the way) of those who earned Your anger, nor of those who went astray), He would say Amin until those who were behind him in the first line could hear him.

Abu Dawud and Ibn Majah recorded this Hadith with the addition, "Then the Masjid would shake because of (those behind the Prophet) reciting Amin." Also, Ad-Daraqutni recorded this Hadith and commented that it is Hasan.

Further, Bilal narrated that he said, "O Messenger of Allah! Do not finish saying Amin before I can join you." This was recorded by Abu Dawud.

In addition, Abu Nasr Al-Qushayri narrated that Al-Hasan and Ja`far As-Sadiq stressed the `m' in Amin.

Saying Amin is recommended for those who are not praying (when reciting Al-Fatihah) and is strongly recommended for those who are praying, whether alone or behind the Imam. The Two Sahihs recorded that the Messenger of Allah said,

«إِذَا أَمَّنَ الْإِمَامُ فَأَمِّنُوا، فَإِنَّهُ مَنْ وَافَقَ تَأْمِينُهُ تَأْمِينَ الْمَلَائِكَةِ غُفِرَ لَهُ مَا تَقَدَّمَ مِنْ ذَنْبِهِ»

(When the Imam says, ' Amin', then say, 'Amin', because whoever says, Amin' with the angels, his previous sins will be forgiven.)

Muslim recorded that the Messenger of Allah said,

«إِذَا قَالَ أَحَدُكُمْ فِي الصَّلَاةِ: آمِينَ، وَالْمَلَائِكَةُ فِي السَّمَاءِ: آمِينَ، فَوَافَقَتْ إِحْدَاهُمَا الْأُخْرَى غُفِرَ لَهُ مَا تَقَدَّمَ مِنْ ذَنْبِهِ»

(When any of you says in the prayer, 'Amin ` and the angels in heaven say, `Amin', in unison, his previous sins will be forgiven.)

It was said that the Hadith talks about both the angels and the Muslims saying Amin at the same time. The Hadith also refers to when the Amins said by the angels and the Muslims are equally sincere (thus bringing about forgiveness).

Further, it is recorded in Sahih Muslim that Abu Musa related that the Prophet said,

«إِذَا قَالَ يَعْنِي الْإِمَامَ : وَلَا الضَّالِّينَ، فَقُولُوا: آمِينَ، يُحِبْكُمُ اللهُ»

(When the Imam says, `Walad-dallin', say, `Amin' and Allah will answer your invocation.)

In addition, At-Tirmidhi said that `Amin' means, "Do not disappoint our hope", while the majority of scholars said that it means. "Answer our invocation."

Also, in his Musnad, Imam Ahmad recorded that `A'ishah said that when the Jews were mentioned to him, the Messenger of Allah said,

«إِنَّهُمْ لَنْ يَحْسُدُونَا عَلَى شَيْءٍ كَمَا يَحْسُدُونَا عَلَى الْجُمُعَةِ الَّتِي هَدَانَا اللهُ لَهَا وَضَلُّوا عَنْهَا، وَعَلَى الْقِبْلَةِ الَّتِي هَدَانَا اللهُ لَهَا وَضَلُّوا عَنْهَا وَعَلَى قَوْلِنَا خَلْفَ الْإِمَامِ: آمِينَ»

(They will not envy us for anything more than they envy us for Friday which we have been guided to, while they were led astray from it, and for the Qiblah which we were guided to, while they were led astray from it, and for our saying `Amin' behind the Imam.)

Also, Ibn Majah recorded this Hadith with the wording,

«مَا حَسَدَتْكُمُ الْيَهُودُ عَلَى شَيْءٍ مَا حَسَدَتْكُمْ عَلَى السَّلَامِ وَالتَّأْمِينِ»

(The Jews have never envied you more than for your saying the Salam (Islamic greeting) and for saying Amin.)

INTRODUCTION TO CHAPTER (SURAH) 2: AL-BAQARAH (THE COW)

Ibn Kathir's Introduction

The Virtues of Surat Al-Baqarah

The Virtues of Surat Al-Baqarah

In Musnad Ahmad, Sahih Muslim, At-Tirmidhi and An-Nasa'i, it is recorded that Abu Hurayrah said that the Prophet said,

«لَا تَجْعَلُوا بُيُوتَكُمْ قُبُورًا فَإِنَّ الْبَيْتَ الَّذِي تُقْرَأُ فِيهِ سُورَةُ الْبَقَرَةِ لَا يَدْخُلُهُ الشَّيْطَانُ»

(Do not turn your houses into graves. Verily, Shaytan does not enter the house where Surat Al-Baqarah is recited.) At-Tirmidhi said, "Hasan Sahih.

Also, `Abdullah bin Mas`ud said, "Shaytan flees from the house where Surat Al-Baqarah is heard." This Hadith was collected by An-Nasa'i in Al-Yawm wal-Laylah, and Al-Hakim recorded it in his Mustadrak, and then said that its chain of narration is authentic, although the Two Sahihs did not collect it. In his Musnad, Ad-Darimi recorded that Ibn Mas`ud said, "Shaytan departs the house where Surat Al-Baqarah is being recited, and as he leaves, he passes gas." Ad-Darimi also recorded that Ash-Sha`bi said that `Abdullah bin Mas`ud said, "Whoever recites ten Ayat from Surat Al-Baqarah in a night, then Shaytan will not enter his house that night. (These ten Ayat are) four from the beginning, Ayat Al-Kursi (255), the following two Ayat (256-257) and the last three Ayat." In another narration, Ibn Mas`ud said, "Then Shaytan will not come near him or his family, nor will he be touched by anything that he dislikes. Also, if these Ayat were to be recited over a senile person, they would wake him up."

Further, Sahl bin Sa`d said that the Messenger of Allah said,

«إِنَّ لِكُلِّ شَيْءٍ سَنَامًا، وَإِنَّ سَنَامَ الْقُرْآنِ الْبَقَرَةُ، وَإِنَّ مَنْ قَرَأَهَا فِي بَيْتِهِ لَيْلَةً لَمْ يَدْخُلْهُ الشَّيْطَانُ ثَلَاثَ لَيَالٍ، وَمَنْ قَرَأَهَا فِي بَيْتِهِ نَهَارًا لَمْ يَدْخُلْهُ الشَّيْطَانُ ثَلَاثَةَ أَيَّامٍ»

(Everything has a hump (or, high peek), and Al-Baqarah is the high peek of the Qur'an. Whoever recites Al-Baqarah at night in his house, then Shaytan will not enter that house for three nights. Whoever recites it during a day in his house, then Shaytan will not enter that house for three days.) This Hadith was collected by Abu Al-Qasim At-Tabarani, Abu Hatim Ibn Hibban in his Sahih and Ibn Marduwyah.

At-Tirmidhi, An-Nasa'i and Ibn Majah recorded that Abu Hurayrah said, "The Messenger of Allah sent an expedition force comprising of many men and asked each about what they memorized of the Qur'an. The Prophet came to one of the youngest men among them and asked him, `What have you memorized (of the Qur'an) young man' He said, `I memorized such and such Surahs and also Al-Baqarah.' The Prophet said, `You memorized Surat Al-Baqarah' He said, `Yes.' The Prophet said, `Then you are their commander.' One of the noted men (or chiefs) commented, `By Allah! I did not learn Surat Al-Baqarah, for fear that I would not be able to implement it. The Messenger of Allah said,

«تَعَلَّمُوا الْقُرْآنَ وَاقْرَءُوهُ، فَإِنَّ مَثَلَ الْقُرْآنِ لِمَنْ تَعَلَّمَهُ فَقَرَأَ وَقَامَ بِهِ كَمَثَلِ جِرَابٍ مَحْشُوٍّ مِسْكًا يَفُوحُ رِيحُهُ فِي كُلِّ مَكَانٍ، وَمَثَلُ مَنْ تَعَلَّمَهُ فَيَرْقُدُ وَهُوَ فِي جَوْفِهِ كَمَثَلِ جِرَابٍ أُوكِيَ عَلَى مِسْكٍ»

(Learn Al-Qur'an and recite it, for the example of whoever learns the Qur'an, recites it and adheres to it, is the example of a bag that is full of musk whose scent fills the air. The example of whoever learns the Qur'an and then sleeps (i.e. lazy) while the Qur'an is in his memory, is the example of a bag that has musk, but is closed tight.)

This is the wording collected by At-Tirmidhi, who said that this Hadith is Hasan. In another narration, At-Tirmidhi recorded this same Hadith in a Mursal manner, so Allah knows best.

Also, Al-Bukhari recorded that Usayd bin Hudayr said that he was once reciting Surat Al-Baqarah while his horse was tied next to him. The horse started to make some noise. When Usayd stopped reciting, the horse stopped moving about. When he resumed reading, the horse started moving about again. When he stopped reciting, the horse stopped moving, and when he resumed reading, the horse started to move again. Meanwhile, his son Yahya was close to the horse, and he feared that the horse might step on him. When he moved his son back, he looked up to the sky and saw a cloud radiating with light that looked like lamps. In the morning, he went to the Prophet and told him what had happened and then said, "O Messenger of Allah! My son Yahya was close to the horse and I feared that she might step on him. When I attended to him and raised my head to the sky, I saw a cloud with lights like lamps. So I went, but I couldn't see it." The Prophet said, "Do you know what that was" He said, "No." The Prophet said,

»تِلْكَ الْمَلَائِكَةُ دَنَتْ لِصَوْتِكَ وَلَو قَرَأْتَ لَأَصْبَحْتَ يَنْظُرُ النَّاسُ إِلَيْهَا، لَا تَتَوَارَى مِنْهُم«

(They were the angels, they came close hearing your voice (reciting Surat Al-Baqarah), and if you had kept reading, the people would have been able to see the angels when the morning came, and the angels would not be hidden from their eyes.)

This is the narration reported by Imam Abu Ubayd Al-Qasim bin Salam in his book Fada'il Al-Qur'an.

Virtues of Surat Al-Baqarah and Surat Al `Imran

Imam Ahmad said that Abu Nu`aym narrated to them that Bishr bin Muhajir said that `Abdullah bin Buraydah narrated to him from his father, "I was sitting with the Prophet and I heard him say,

»تَعَلَّمُوا سُورَةَ الْبَقَرَةِ فَإِنَّ أَخْذَهَا بَرَكَةٌ، وَتَرْكَهَا حَسْرَةٌ، وَلَا تَسْتَطِيعُهَا الْبَطَلَة«

(Learn Surat Al-Baqarah, because in learning it there is blessing, in ignoring it there is sorrow, and the sorceresses cannot memorize it.)

He kept silent for a while and then said,

«تَعَلَّمُوا سُورَةَ الْبَقَرَةِ وَآلَ عِمْرَانَ فَإِنَّهُمَا الزَّهْرَاوَانِ، يُظِلَّانِ صَاحِبَهُمَا يَوْمَ الْقِيَامَةِ كَأَنَّهُمَا غَمَامَتَانِ أَوْ غَيَايَتَانِ أَوْ فِرْقَانِ مِنْ طَيْرٍ صَوَافَّ، وَإِنَّ الْقُرْآنَ يَلْقَى صَاحِبَهُ يَوْمَ الْقِيَامَةِ حِينَ يَنْشَقُّ عَنْهُ قَبْرُهُ كَالرَّجُلِ الشَّاحِبِ فَيَقُولُ لَهُ: هَلْ تَعْرِفُنِي؟ فَيَقُولُ: مَا أَعْرِفُكَ. فَيَقُولُ: أَنَا صَاحِبُكَ الْقُرْآنُ الَّذِي أَظْمَأْتُكَ فِي الْهَوَاجِرِ وَأَسْهَرْتُ لَيْلَكَ وَإِنَّ كُلَّ تَاجِرٍ مِنْ وَرَاءِ تِجَارَتِهِ، وَإِنَّكَ الْيَوْمَ مِنْ وَرَاءِ كُلِّ تِجَارَةٍ فَيُعْطَى الْمُلْكَ بِيَمِينِهِ وَالْخُلْدَ بِشِمَالِهِ وَيُوضَعُ عَلَى رَأْسِهِ تَاجُ الْوَقَارِ، وَيُكْسَى وَالِدَاهُ حُلَّتَانِ لَا يَقُومُ لَهُمَا أَهْلُ الدُّنْيَا، فَيَقُولَانِ: بِمَا كُسِينَا هَذَا؟ فَيُقَالُ: بِأَخْذِ وَلَدِكُمَا الْقُرْآنَ ثُمَّ يُقَالُ: اقْرَأْ وَاصْعَدْ فِي دَرَجِ الْجَنَّةِ وَغُرَفِهَا، فَهُوَ فِي صُعُودٍ مَا دَامَ يَقْرَأُ هَذَا كَانَ أَوْ تَرْتِيلًا»

(Learn Surat Al-Baqarah and Al `Imran because they are two lights and they shade their people on the Day of Resurrection, just as two clouds, two spaces of shade or two lines of (flying) birds. The Qur'an will meet its companion in the shape of a pale-faced man on the Day of Resurrection when his grave is opened. The Qur'an will ask him, 'Do you know me' The man will say, 'I do not know you.' The Qur'an will say, 'I am your companion, the Qur'an, which has brought you thirst during the heat and made you stay up during the night. Every merchant has his certain trade. But, this Day, you are behind all types of trade.' Kingship will then be given to him in his right hand, eternal life in his left hand and the crown of grace will be placed on his head. His parents will also be granted two garments that the people of this life could never afford. They will say, 'Why were we granted these garments' It will be said, 'Because your son was carrying the Qur'an.' It will be said (to the reader of the Qur'an), 'Read and ascend through the levels of Paradise.' He will go on ascending as long as he recites, whether reciting slowly or quickly.)"

Ibn Majah also recorded part of this Hadith from Bishr bin Al-Muhajir, and this chain of narrators is Hasan, according to the criteria of Imam Muslim.

A part of this Hadith is also supported by other Hadiths. For instance, Imam Ahmad recorded that Abu Umamah Al-Bahili said that he heard the Messenger of Allah say,

«اقْرَأُوا الْقُرْآنَ فَإِنَّهُ شَافِعٌ لِأَهْلِهِ يَوْمَ الْقِيَامَةِ اقْرَأُوا الزَّهْرَاوَيْنِ، الْبَقَرَةَ وَآلَ عِمْرَانَ، فَإِنَّهُمَا يَأْتِيَانِ يَوْمَ الْقِيَامَةِ كَأَنَّهُمَا غَمَامَتَانِ، أَوْ كَأَنَّهُمَا غَيَايَتَانِ أَوْ كَأَنَّهُمَا فِرْقَانِ مِنْ طَيْرٍ صَوَافَّ، يُحَاجَّانِ عَنْ أَهْلِهِمَا يَوْمَ الْقِيَامَةِ»

(Read the Qur'an, because it will intercede on behalf of its people on the Day of Resurrection. Read the two lights, Al-Baqarah and Al `Imran, because they will come in the shape of two clouds, two shades or two lines of birds on the Day of Resurrection and will argue on behalf of their people on that Day.)

The Prophet then said,

«اقْرَأُوا الْبَقَرَةَ فَإِنَّ أَخْذَهَا بَرَكَةٌ وَتَرْكَهَا حَسْرَةٌ وَلَا تَسْتَطِيعُهَا الْبَطَلَةُ»

(Read Al-Baqarah, because in having it there is blessing, and in ignoring there is a sorrow and the sorceresses cannot memorize it.)

Also, Imam Muslim narrated this Hadith in the Book of Prayer

Imam Ahmad narrated that An-Nawwas bin Sam`an said that the Prophet said,

«يُؤْتَى بِالْقُرْآنِ يَوْمَ الْقِيَامَةِ وَأَهْلِهِ الَّذِينَ كَانُوا يَعْمَلُونَ بِهِ تَقْدَمُهُمْ سُورَةُ الْبَقَرَةِ وَآلُ عِمْرَانَ»

(On the Day of Resurrection the Qur'an and its people who used to implement it will be brought forth, preceded by Surat Al-Baqarah and Al `Imran.)

An-Nawwas said, "The Prophet set three examples for these two Surahs and I did not forget these examples ever since. He said,

«كَأَنَّهُمَا غَمَامَتَانِ، أَوْ ظُلَّتَانِ سَوْدَاوَانِ بَيْنَهُمَا شَرْقٌ، أَوْ كَأَنَّهُمَا فِرْقَانِ

$$\text{«مِنْ طَيْرٍ صَوَافَّ، يُحَاجَّانِ عَنْ صَاحِبِهِمَا»}$$

(They will come like two clouds, two dark shades or two lines of birds arguing on behalf of their people.)

It was also recorded in Sahih Muslim and At-Tirmidhi narrated this Hadith, which he rendered Hasan Gharib.

Surat Al-Baqarah was revealed in Al-Madinah

There is no disagreement over the view that Surat Al-Baqarah was revealed in its entirety in Al-Madinah. Moreover, Al-Baqarah was one of the first Surahs to be revealed in Al-Madinah, while, Allah's statement,

(And be afraid of the Day when you shall be brought back to Allah.) (2:281) was the last Ayah to be revealed from the Qur'an. Also, the Ayat about usury were among the last Ayat to be revealed. Khalid bin Ma`dan used to call Al-Baqarah the Fustat (tent) of the Qur'an. Some of the scholars said that it contains a thousand news incidents, a thousand commands and a thousand prohibitions. Those who count said that the number of Al-Baqarah's Ayat is two hundred and eighty-seven, and its words are six thousand two hundred and twenty-one words. Further, its letters are twenty-five thousand five hundred. Allah knows best.

Ibn Jurayj narrated that `Ata' said that Ibn `Abbas said, "Surat Al-Baqarah was revealed in Al-Madinah." Also, Khasif said from Mujahid that `Abdullah bin Az-Zubayr said; "Surat Al-Baqarah was revealed in Al-Madinah." Several Imams and scholars of Tafsir issued similar statements, and there is no difference of opinion over this as we have stated.

The Two Sahihs recorded that Ibn Mas`ud kept the Ka`bah on his left side and Mina on his right side and threw seven pebbles (at the Jamrah) and said, "The one to whom Surat Al-Baqarah was revealed (i.e. the Prophet) performed Rami (the Hajj rite of throwing pebbles) similarly." The Two Sahihs recorded this Hadith.

Further, Ibn Marduwyah reported a Hadith of Shu`bah from `Aqil bin Talhah from `Utbah bin Marthad; "The Prophet saw that his Companions were not in the first lines and he said,

$$\text{«يَا أَصْحَابَ سُورَةِ الْبَقَرَةِ»}$$

(O Companions of Surat Al-Baqarah.) I Think that this incident occurred during the battle of Hunayn when the Companions retreated. Then, the Prophet commanded Al-`Abbas (his uncle) to yell out,

«يَا أَصْحَابَ الشَّجَرَةِ»

(O Companions of the tree!) meaning the Companions who participated in the pledge of Ar-Ridwan (under the tree). In another narration, Al-`Abbas cried, "O Companions of Surat Al-Baqarah!" encouraging them to come back, so they returned from every direction. Also, during the battle of Al-Yamamah, against the army of Musaylimah the Liar, the Companions first retreated because of the huge number of soldiers in Musaylimah's army. The Muhajirun and the Ansar called out for each other, saying; "O people of Surat Al-Baqarah!" Allah then gave them victory over their enemy, may Allah be pleased with all of the companions of all the Messengers of Allah.

CHAPTER (SURAH) 2: AL-BQARAH (THE COW), VERSES 001-141

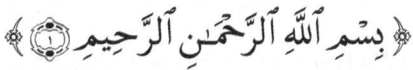

In the Name of Allâh, the Most Gracious, the Most Merciful.

Surah: 2 Ayah: 1

1. Alif-Lâm-Mîm. (These letters are one of the miracles of the Qur'ân and none but Allâh (Alone) knows their meanings.)

Transliteration

1. Alif-lam-meem

Tafsir Ibn Kathir

The Discussion of the Individual Letters

(In the Name of Allah, the Most Gracious, the Most Merciful) (1. Alif Lam Mim).

The individual letters in the beginning of some Surahs are **among** those things whose knowledge Allah has kept only for Himself. This was reported from Abu Bakr, 'Umar, 'Uthman, 'Ali and Ibn Mas'ud. It was said that these letters are the names of some of the Surahs. It was also said that they are the beginnings that Allah chose to start the Surahs of the Qur'an with. Khasif stated that Mujahid said, "The beginnings of the Surahs, such as Qaf, Sad, Ta Sin Mim and Alif Lam Ra, are just some letters of the alphabet." Some linguists also stated that they are letters of the alphabet and that Allah simply did not cite the entire alphabet of twenty-eight letters. For instance, they said, one might say, "My son recites Alif, Ba, Ta, Tha... " he means the entire alphabet although he stops before mentioning the rest of it. This opinion was mentioned by Ibn Jarir.

The Letters at the Beginning of Surahs

If one removes the repetitive letters, then the number of letters mentioned at the beginning of the Surahs is fourteen: Alif, Lam, Mim, Sad, Ra, Kaf, Ha, Ya, 'Ayn, Ta, Sin, Ha, Qaf, Nun.

So glorious is He Who made everything subtly reflect His wisdom.

Moreover, the scholars said, "There is no doubt that Allah did not reveal these letters for jest and play." Some ignorant people said that some of the Qur'an does not mean anything, (meaning, such as these letters) thus committing a major mistake. On the contrary, these letters carry a specific meaning. Further, if we find an authentic narration leading to the Prophet that explains these letters, we will embrace the Prophet's statement. Otherwise, we will stop where we were made to stop and will proclaim,

(We believe in it; all of it (clear and unclear verses) is from our Lord) (3:7).

The scholars did not agree on one opinion or explanation regarding this subject. Therefore, whoever thinks that one scholar's opinion is correct, he is obliged to follow it, otherwise it is better to refrain from making any judgment on this matter. Allah knows best.

These Letters testify to the Miraculous Qur'an

The wisdom behind mentioning these letters in the beginning of the Surahs, regardless of the exact meanings of these letters, is that they testify to the miracle of the Qur'an. Indeed, the servants are unable to produce something like the Qur'an, although it is comprised of the same letters with which they speak to each other. This opinion was mentioned by Ar-Razi in his Tafsir who related it to Al-Mubarrid and several other scholars. Al-Qurtubi also related this opinion to Al-Farra' and Qutrub. Az-Zamakhshari agreed with this opinion in his book, Al-Kashshaf. In addition, the Imam and scholar Abu Al-'Abbas Ibn Taymiyyah and our Shaykh Al-Hafiz Abu Al-Hajjaj Al-Mizzi agreed with this opinion. Al-Mizzi told me that it is also the opinion of Shaykh Al-Islam Ibn Taymiyyah. KAz-Zamakhshari said that these letters, "Were not all mentioned once in the beginning of the Qur'an. Rather, they were repeated so that the challenge (against the creation) is more daring. Similarly, several stories were mentioned repeatedly in the Qur'an, and also the challenge was repeated in various areas (i.e., to produce something like the Qur'an). Sometimes, one letter at a time was mentioned, such as Sad, Nun and Qaf. Sometimes two letters were mentioned, such as

(Ha Mim) (44:1) Sometimes, three letters were mentioned, such as,

(Alif Lam Mim (2: 1)) and four letters, such as,

('Alif Lam Mim Ra) (13:1), and

(Alif Lam Mim Sad) (7:1).

Sometimes, five letters were mentioned, such as,

(Kaf Ha Ya 'Ayn Sad) (19:1), and;

(Ha Mim. 'Ayn Sin Qaf) (42:1-2).

This is because the words that are used in speech are usually comprised of one, two, three, four, or five letters."

Every Surah that begins with these letters demonstrates the Qur'an's miracle and magnificence, and this fact is known by those well-versed in such matters. The count of these Surahs is twenty-nine. For instance, Allah said,

(Alif Lam Mim) This is the Book (the Qur'an), wherein there is no doubt (2:1-2),

(Alif Lam Mim. Allah! La ilaha illa Huwa (none has the right to be worshipped but He), Al-Hayyul-Qayyuum (the Ever Living, the One Who sustains and protects all that exists). It is He Who has sent down the Book (the Qur'an) to you (Muhammad) with truth, confirming what came before it.) (3:1-3), and,

(Alif Lam Mim Sad. (This is the) Book (the Qur'an) sent down unto you (O Muhammad), so let not your breast be narrow therefrom) (7:1-2).

Also, Allah said,

(Alif Lam Ra. (This is) a Book which We have revealed unto you (O Muhammad) in order that you might lead mankind out of darkness (of disbelief and polytheism) into the light (of belief in the Oneness of Allah and Islamic Monotheism) by their Lord's leave) (14:1),

(Alif Lam Mim. The revelation of the Book (this Qur'an) in which there is no doubt, is from the Lord of the 'Alamin (mankind, Jinn and all that exists)!) (32:1-2),

(Ha Mim. A revelation from (Allah) the Most Gracious, the Most Merciful) (41:1-2), and,

(Ha Mim. 'Ain Sin Qaf. Likewise Allah, the Almighty, the Wise sends revelation to you (O Muhammad) as (He sent revelation to) those before you.) (42:1-3).

There are several other Ayat that testify to what we have mentioned above, and Allah knows best.

Surah: 2 Ayah: 2

﴿ ذَٰلِكَ ٱلْكِتَـٰبُ لَا رَيْبَ ۛ فِيهِ ۛ هُدًى لِّلْمُتَّقِينَ ۝ ﴾

2. This is the Book (the Qur'ân), whereof there is no doubt, a guidance to those who are Al-Muttaqûn (the pious and righteous persons who fear Allâh much (abstain from all kinds of sins and evil deeds which He has forbidden) and love Allâh much (perform all kinds of good deeds which He has ordained))

Transliteration

2. Thalika alkitabu la rayba feehi hudan lilmuttaqeena

Tafsir Ibn Kathir

(2. This is the Book (the Qur'ân), whereof there is no doubt, a guidance to those who are *Al-Muttaqûn*).

There is no Doubt in the Qur'an

The Book, is the Qur'an, and Rayb means doubt. As-Suddi said that Abu Malik and Abu Salih narrated from Ibn 'Abbas, and Murrah Al-Hamadani narrated from Ibn Mas'ud and several other Companions of the Messenger of Allah that,

(In which there is no Rayb), means about which there is no doubt. Abu Ad-Darda', Ibn 'Abbas, Mujahid, Sa'id bin Jubayr, Abu Malik, Nafi' 'Ata', Abu Al-'Aliyah, Ar-Rabi' bin Anas, Muqatil bin Hayyan, As-Suddi, Qatadah and Isma'il bin Abi Khalid said similarly. In addition, Ibn Abi Hatim said, "I do not know of any disagreement over this explanation." The meaning of this is that the Book, the Qur'an, is without a doubt revealed from Allah. Similarly, Allah said in Surat As- Sajdah,

(Alif Lam Mim). The revelation of the Book (this Qur'an) in which there is no doubt, is from the Lord of all that exists) (32:1-2).

Some scholars stated that this Ayah - 2:2 - contains a prohibition meaning, "Do not doubt the Qur'an." Furthermore, some of the reciters of the Qur'an pause upon reading,

(there is no doubt) and they then continue;

(in which there is guidance for the Muttaqin (the pious and righteous persons)). However, it is better to pause at,

(in which there is no doubt) because in this case,

(guidance) becomes an attribute of the Qur'an and carries a better meaning than,

(in which there is guidance)

Guidance is granted to Those Who have Taqwa

Hidayah - correct guidance - is only granted to those who have Taqwa - fear of Allah. Allah said,

(Say: It is for those who believe, a guide and a healing. And as for those who disbelieve, there is heaviness (deafness) in their ears, and it (the Qur'an) is blindness for them. They are those who are called from a place far away (so they neither listen nor understand)) (41:44), and,

(And We send down of the Qur'an that which is a healing and a mercy to those who believe (in Islamic Monotheism and act on it), and it increases the Zalimin (wrongdoers) in nothing but loss) (17:82).

This is a sample of the numerous Ayat indicating that the believers, in particular, benefit from the Qur'an. That is because the Qur'an is itself a form of guidance, but the guidance in it is only granted to the righteous, just as Allah said,

(O mankind! There has come to you a good advice from your Lord (i. e. the Qur'an, enjoining all that is good and forbidding all that is evil), and a healing for that (disease of ignorance, doubt, hypocrisy and differences) which is in your breasts,— a guidance and a mercy (explaining lawful and unlawful things) for the believers) (10:57).

Ibn 'Abbas and Ibn Mas'ud and other Companions of the Messenger of Allah said,

(guidance for the Muttaqin (the pious and righteous persons), means, a light for those who have Taqwa.

The Meaning of Al-Muttaqin

Ibn 'Abbas said about,

(guidance for the Muttaqin) that it means, "They are the believers who avoid Shirk with Allah and who work in His obedience." Ibn 'Abbas also said that Al-Muttaqin means, "Those who fear Allah's punishment, which would result if they abandoned the true guidance that they recognize and know. They also hope in Allah's mercy by believing in what He revealed." Further, Qatadah said that, (Al-Muttaqin), are those whom Allah has described in His statement; (Who believe in the Ghayb and perform the Salah) (2:3), and the following Ayat. Ibn Jarir stated that the Ayah (2:2) includes all of these meanings that the scholars have mentioned, and this is the correct view. Also, At-Tirmidhi and Ibn Majah narrated that 'Atiyah As-Sa'di said that the Messenger of Allah said,

«لَا يَبْلُغُ الْعَبْدُ أَنْ يَكُونَ مِنَ الْمُتَّقِينَ حَتَّى يَدَعَ مَا لَا بَأْسَ بِهِ حَذَرًا مِمَّا بِهِ بَأْسٌ»

(The servant will not acquire the status of the Muttaqin until he abandons what is harmless out of fear of falling into that which is harmful.) At-Tirmidhi then said "Hasan Gharib."

There are Two Types of Hidayah (Guidance)

Huda here means the faith that resides in the heart, and only Allah is able to create it in the heart of the servants. Allah said,

(Verily, you (O Muhammad) guide not whom you like) (28:56),

(Not upon you (Muhammad) is their guidance) (2:272),

(Whomsoever Allah sends astray, none can guide him) (7:186), and,

(He whom Allah guides, he is the rightly guided; but he whom He sends astray, for him you will find no Wali (guiding friend) to lead him (to the right path)) (18:17).

Huda also means to explain the truth, give direction and lead to it. Allah, the Exalted, said,

(And verily, you (O Muhammad) are indeed guiding (mankind) to the straight path (i.e. Allah's religion of Islamic Monotheism)) (42: 52),

(You are only a warner, and to every people there is a guide) (13:7), and,

(And as for Thamud, We showed and made clear to them the path of truth (Islamic Monotheism) through Our Messenger (i.e. showed them the way of success), but they preferred blindness to guidance) (41:17).

testifying to this meaning.

Also, Allah said,

(And shown him the two ways (good and evil).) (90:10)

This is the view of the scholars who said that the two ways refer to the paths of righteousness and evil, which is also the correct explanation. And Allah knows best.

Meaning of Taqwa

The root meaning of Taqwa is to avoid what one dislikes. It was reported that 'Umar bin Al-Khattab asked Ubayy bin Ka'b about Taqwa. Ubayy said, "Have you ever walked on a path that has thorns on it" 'Umar said, "Yes." Ubayy said, "What did you do then" He said, "I rolled up my sleeves and struggled." Ubayy said, "That is Taqwa."

Surah: 2 Ayah: 3

﴿ ٱلَّذِينَ يُؤْمِنُونَ بِٱلْغَيْبِ وَيُقِيمُونَ ٱلصَّلَوٰةَ وَمِمَّا رَزَقْنَـٰهُمْ يُنفِقُونَ ۞ ﴾

3. Who believe in the Ghaib and perform As-Salât (Iqâmat-as-Salât), and spend out of what We have provided for them (i.e. give Zakât, spend on themselves, their parents, their children, their wives, etc., and also give charity to the poor and also in Allâh's Cause - Jihâd).

Transliteration

3. Allatheena yu/minoona bialghaybi wayuqeemoona alssalata wamimma razaqnahum yunfiqoona

Tafsir Ibn Kathir

(3.Who believe in the Ghayb).

The Meaning of Iman (Belief, Faith)

Abu Ja'far Ar-Razi said that Al-'Ala' bin Al-Musayyib bin Rafi' narrated from Abu Ishaq that Abu Al-Ahwas said that 'Abdullah said, "Iman is to trust.". 'Ali bin Abi Talhah reported that Ibn 'Abbas said,

(who have faith) means they trust. Also, Ma'mar said that Az-Zuhri said, "Iman is the deeds." In addition, Abu Ja'far Ar-Razi said that Ar-Rabi' bin Anas said that, 'They have faith', means, they fear (Allah).

Ibn Jarir (At-Tabari) commented, "The prefered view is that they be described as having faith in the Unseen by the tongue, deed and creed. In this case, fear of Allah is included in the general meaning of Iman, which necessitates following deeds of the tongue by implementation. Hence, Iman is a general term that includes affirming and believing in Allah, His Books and His Messengers, and realizing this affirmation through adhering to the implications of what the tongue utters and affirms."

Linguistically, in the absolute sense, Iman merely means trust, and it is used to mean that sometimes in the Qur'an, for instance, Allah the Exalted said,

(He trusts (yu'minu) in Allah, and trusts (yu'minu) in the believers.) (9: 61)

Prophet Yusuf's brothers said to their father,

(But you will never believe us even when we speak the truth) (12:17).

Further, the word Iman is sometimes mentioned along with deeds, such as Allah said,

(Save those who believe (in Islamic Monotheism) and do righteous deeds) (95:6).

However, when Iman is used in an unrestricted manner, it includes beliefs, deeds, and statements of the tongue. We should state here that Iman increases and decreases.

There are many narrations and Hadiths on this subject, and we discussed them in the beginning of our explanation of Sahih Al-Bukhari, all favors are from Allah. Some scholars explained that Iman means Khashyah (fear of Allah). For instance, Allah said;

(Verily, those who fear their Lord unseen (i.e. they do not see Him, nor His punishment in the Hereafter)) (67:12), and,

(Who feared the Most Gracious (Allah) in the Ghayb (unseen) and brought a heart turned in repentance (to Him and absolutely free from every kind of polytheism)) (50: 33).

Fear is the core of Iman and knowledge, just as Allah the Exalted said,

(It is only those who have knowledge among His servants that fear Allah) (35:28).

The Meaning of Al-Ghayb

As for the meaning of Ghayb here, the Salaf have different explanations of it, all of which are correct, indicating the same general meaning. For instance, Abu Ja'far Ar-Razi quoted Ar-Rabi' bin Anas, reporting from Abu Al-'Aliyah about Allah's statement,

((Those who) have faith in the Ghayb), "They believe in Allah, His angels, Books, Messengers, the Last Day, His Paradise, Fire and in the meeting with Him. They also believe in life after death and in Resurrection. All of this is the Ghayb." Qatadah bin Di`amah said similarly.

Sa'id bin Mansur reported from 'Abdur-Rahman bin Yazid who said, "We were sitting with 'Abdullah bin Mas'ud when we mentioned the Companions of the Prophet and their deeds being superior to our deeds. 'Abdullah said, 'The matter of Muhammad was clear for those who saw him. By He other than Whom there is no God, no person will ever acquire a better type of faith than believing in Al-Ghayb.' He then recited,

(Alif Lam Mim. This is the Book, wherein there is no doubt, a guidance for the Muttaqin. Those who believe in the Ghayb), until,

(the successful). '' Ibn Abi Hatim, Ibn Marduwyah and Al-Hakim, in his Mustadrak, recorded this Hadith. Al-Hakim commented that this Hadith is authentic and that the Two Shaykhs - Al-Bukhari and Muslim - did not collect it, although it meets their criteria.

Ahmad recorded a Hadith with similar meaning from Ibn Muhayriz who said: I said to Abu Jumu'ah, "Narrate a Hadith for us that you heard from the Messenger of Allah." He said, "Yes. I will narrate a good Hadith for you. Once we had lunch with the Messenger of Allah . Abu 'Ubaydah, who was with us, said, 'O Messenger of Allah! Are people better than us We embraced Islam with you and performed Jihad with you.' He said,

«نَعَمْ قَوْمٌ مِنْ بَعْدِكُمْ يُؤْمِنُونَ بِي وَلَمْ يَرَوْنِي»

(Yes, those who will come after you, who will believe in me although they did not see me.)"

This Hadith has another route collected by Abu Bakr bin Marduwyah in his Tafsir, from Salih bin Jubayr who said: 'Abu Jumu'ah Al-Ansari, the Companion of the Messenger of Allah , came to Bayt Al-Maqdis (Jerusalem) to perform the prayer. Raja' bin Haywah was with us, so when Abu Jumu'ah finished, we went out to greet him. When he was about to leave, he said, "You have a gift and a right. I will narrate a Hadith for you that I heard from the Messenger of Allah. " We said, "Do so, and may Allah grant you mercy." He said, "We were with the Messenger of Allah, ten people including Mu'adh bin Jabal. We said, "O Messenger of Allah! Are there people who will acquire greater rewards than us We believed in Allah and followed you.' He said,

«مَا يَمْنَعُكُمْ مِنْ ذَلِكَ وَرَسُولُ اللهِ بَيْنَ أَظْهُرِكُمْ يَأْتِيكُمْ بِالْوَحْيِ مِنَ السَّمَاءِ، بَلْ قَوْمٌ بَعْدَكُمْ يَأْتِيهِمْ كِتَابٌ مِنْ بَيْنِ لَوْحَيْنِ يُؤْمِنُونَ بِهِ وَيَعْمَلُونَ بِمَا فِيهِ، أُولَئِكَ أَعْظَمُ مِنْكُمْ أَجْرًا مَرَّتَيْنِ»

(What prevents you from doing so, while the Messenger of Allah is among you, bringing you the revelation from heaven There are people who will come after you and who will be given a book between two covers (the Qur'an), and they will believe in it and implement its commands. They have a greater reward than you, even twice as much.)"

(And perform Salah, and spend out of what we have provided for them)

Meaning of Iqamat As-Salah

Ibn 'Abbas said that,

(And perform the Salah), means, "Perform the prayer with all of the obligations that accompany it." Ad-Dahhak said that Ibn `Abbas said, "Iqamat As-Salah means to complete the bowings, prostrations, recitation, humbleness and attendance for the prayer." Qatadah said, "Iqamat As-Salah means to preserve punctuality, and the ablution, bowings, and prostrations of the prayer."

Muqatil bin Hayyan said Iqamat As-Salah means

"To preserve punctuality for it, as well as completing ones purity for it, and completing the bowings, prostrations, recitation of the Qur'an, Tashahhud and blessings for the Prophet . This is Iqamat As-Salah."

The Meaning of "Spending" in this Ayah

'Ali bin Abi Talhah reported that Ibn 'Abbas said,

(And spend out of what We have provided for them) means,

"The Zakah due on their wealth." As-Suddi said that Abu Malik and Abu Salih narrated from Ibn `Abbas, as well as Murrah from Ibn Mas`ud and other Companions of the Messenger of Allah , that, (And spend out of what We have provided for them) means,

"A man's spending on his family. This was before the obligation of Zakah was revealed."

Juwaybir narrated from Ad-Dahhak,

"General spending (in charity) was a means of drawing nearer to Allah, according to one's discretion and capability. Until the obligation of charity was revealed in the seven Ayat of Surat Bara'ah (chapter 9), were revealed. These abrogated the previous case."

In many instances, Allah mentioned prayer and spending wealth together. Prayer is a right of Allah as well as a form of worshipping Him. It includes singling Him out for one's devotion, praising Him, glorifying Him, supplicating to Him, invoking Him, and it displays one's dependence upon Him. Spending is form of kindness towards creatures by giving them what will benefit them, and those people most deserving of this charity are the relatives, the wife, the servants and then the rest of the people. So all types of required charity and required spending are included in Allah's saying, (And spend out of what we have provided for them).

The Two Sahihs recorded that Ibn 'Umar said that the Messenger of Allah said,

«بُنِيَ الْإِسْلَامُ عَلَى خَمْسٍ: شَهَادَةِ أَنْ لَا إِلَهَ إِلَّا اللهُ وَأَنَّ مُحَمَّدًا رَسُولُ اللهِ، وَإِقَامِ الصَّلَاةِ، وَإِيتَاءِ الزَّكَاةِ، وَصَوْمِ رَمَضَانَ، وَحَجِّ الْبَيْتِ»

(Islam is built upon five (pillars): Testifying that there is no deity worthy of worship except Allah and that Muhammad is the Messenger of Allah, establishing the prayer, giving Zakah, fasting Ramadan and Hajj to the House.)

There are many other Hadiths on this subject.

The Meaning of Salah

In the Arabic language, the basic meaing of Salah is supplication. In religious terminology, Salah is used to refer to the acts of bowing and prostration, the remaining specified acts associated with it, specificed at certain times, with those known conditions, and the characteristics, and requirements that are well-known about it.

Surah: 2 Ayah: 4

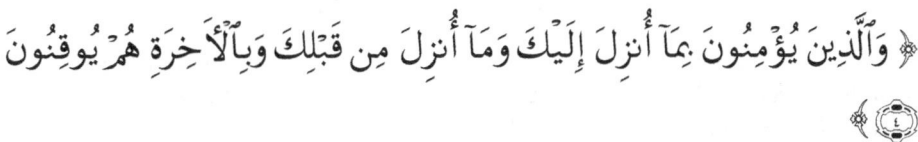

4. And who believe in (the Qur'ân and the Sunnah) which has been sent down (revealed) to you (Muhammad (peace be upon him)) and in that which were sent down before you (the Taurât (Torah) and the Injeel (Gospel), etc.) and they believe with certainty in the Hereafter. (Resurrection, recompense of their good and bad deeds, Paradise and Hell).

Transliteration

4. Waallatheena yu/minoona bima onzila ilayka wama onzila min qablika wabial-akhirati hum yooqinoona

Tafsir Ibn Kathir

Ibn 'Abbas said that,

And who believe in (the Qur'ân and the *Sunnah*) which has been sent down (revealed) to you (Muhammad Peace be upon him) and in [the Taurât (Torah) and the Injeel (Gospel), etc.] which were sent down before you "means, "They believe in what Allah sent you with, and in what the previous Messengers were sent with, they do not distinguish between (believing) them, nor do they reject what they brought from their Lord."''' (And in the Hereafter they are certain) that is the resurrection, the standing (on the Day of Resurrection), Paradise, the Fire, the reckoning and the the Scale that weighs the deeds (the Mizan). The Hereafter is so named because it comes after this earthly life.

Attributes of the Believers

The people described here (2:4) are those whom Allah described in the preceding Ayah,

(3. Who believe in the *Ghaib* and perform *As-Salât* (*Iqâmat-as-Salât*), and spend out of what we have provided for them [i.e. give *Zakât*, spend on themselves, their parents, their children, their wives, etc., and also give charity to the poor and also in Allâh's Cause - *Jihâd*, etc.].)

Mujahid once stated, "Four Ayat at the beginning of Surat Al-Baqarah describe the believers, two describe the disbelievers, and thirteen describe the hypocrites." The four Ayat mentioned in this statement are general and include every believer, whether an Arab, non-Arab, or a person of a previous Scripture, whether they are Jinns or humans. All of these attributes complement each other and require the existence of the other attributes. For instance, it is not possible that one believes in the Unseen, performs the prayer and gives Zakah without believing in what the Messenger of Allah and the previous Messengers were sent with. The same with certainty in the Hereafter, this is not correct without that, for Allah has commanded the believers,

(O you who believe! Believe in Allah, and His Messenger, and the Book (the Qur'an) which He has revealed to the Messenger, and the Book which He sent own to those before (him)) (4:136),

(And argue not with the People of the Book, unless it be in (a way) that is better, except with such of them as do wrong; and say (to them): "We believe in that which has been revealed to us and revealed to you; our Ilah (God) and your Ilah (God) is One (i.e. Allah)') (29:46),

(O you who have been given the Book (Jews and Christians)! Believe in what We have revealed (to Muhammad) confirming what is (already) with you) (4:47), and,

(Say (O Muhammad): "O People of the Book (Jews and Christians)! You have nothing until you act according to the Tawrah (Torah), the Injil (Gospel), and what has (now) been revealed to you from your Lord (the Qur'an).") (5:68).

Also, Allah the Exalted described the believers;

(The Messenger (Muhammad) believes in what has been revealed to him from his Lord, and (so do) the believers. Each one believes in Allah, His Angels, His Books, and His Messengers. (They say,) "We make no distinction between any of His Messengers") (2: 285), and,

(And those who believe in Allah and His Messengers and make no distinction between any of them (Messengers)) (4:152),

This is a sample of the Ayat that indicate that the true believers all believe in Allah, His Messengers and His Books.

The faithful among the People of the Book, have a special significance here, since they believe in their Books and in all of the details related to that, so when such people embrace Islam and sincerely believe in the details of the religion, then they will get two rewards. As for the others, they can only believe in the previous religious teachings in a general way. For instance, the Prophet stated,

»إِذَا حَدَّثَكُمْ أَهْلُ الْكِتَابِ فَلَا تُكَذِّبُوهُمْ وَلَا تُصَدِّقُوهُمْ وَلَكِنْ قُولُوا: آمَنَّا بِالَّذِي أُنْزِلَ إِلَيْنَا وَأُنْزِلَ إِلَيْكُم«

(When the People of the Book narrate to you, neither reject nor affirm what they say. Rather, say, 'We believe in what was revealed to us and what was revealed to you.')

However, the faith that many Arabs have in the religion of Islam as it was revealed to Muhammad might be more complete, encompassing and firmer than the faith of the People of the Book who embraced Islam. Therefore, if the believers in Islam among the People of the Book gain two rewards, other Muslims who have firmer Islamic faith might gain an equal reward that compares to the two the People of the Book gain (upon embracing Islam). And Allah knows best.

Surah: 2 Ayah: 5

﴿ أُولَٰئِكَ عَلَىٰ هُدًى مِّن رَّبِّهِمْ ۖ وَأُولَٰئِكَ هُمُ ٱلْمُفْلِحُونَ ۝ ﴾

5. They are on (true) guidance from their Lord, and they are the successful.

Transliteration

5. Ola-ika AAala hudan min rabbihim waola-ika humu almuflihoona

Tafsir Ibn Kathir

Guidance and Success are awarded to the Believers

Allah said,

(They are) refers to those who believe in the Unseen, establish the prayer, spend from what Allah has granted them, believe in what Allah has revealed to the Messenger and the Messengers before him, believe in the Hereafter with certainty, and prepare the necessary requirements for the Hereafter by performing good deeds and avoiding the prohibitions. Allah then said,

(On guidance) meaning, they are (following) a light, guidance, and have insight from Allah,

(And they are the successful) meaning, in this world and the Hereafter. They shall have what they seek and be saved from the evil that they tried to avoid.

Therefore, they will have rewards, eternal life in Paradise, and safety from the torment that Allah has prepared for His enemies.

Surah: 2 Ayah: 6

﴿إِنَّ ٱلَّذِينَ كَفَرُواْ سَوَآءٌ عَلَيْهِمْ ءَأَنذَرْتَهُمْ أَمْ لَمْ تُنذِرْهُمْ لَا يُؤْمِنُونَ﴾

6. Verily, those who disbelieve, it is the same to them whether you (O Muhammad (peace be upon him)) warn them or do not warn them, they will not believe.

Transliteration

6. Inna allatheena kafaroo sawaon AAalayhim aanthartahum am lam tunthirhum la yu/minoona

Tafsir Ibn Kathir

(6. Verily, those who disbelieve, it is the same to them whether you (O Muhammad Peace be uponm him) warn them or do not warn them, they will not believe.)

Allah said,

(Verily, those who disbelieve) meaning, covered the truth and hid it. Since Allah has written that they would do so, it does not matter if you (O Muhammad) warn them or not, they would still have disbelieved in what you were sent with.

Similarly, Allah said,

(Truly, those against whom the Word (wrath) of your Lord has been justified, will not believe. Even if every sign should come to them, until they see the painful torment) (10:96-97).

About the rebellious People of the Book, Allah said,

(And even if you were to bring to the People of the Book (Jews and Christians) all the Ayat, they would not follow your Qiblah (prayer direction)) (2:5).

These Ayat indicate that whomever Allah has written to be miserable, they shall never find anyone to guide them to happiness, and whomever Allah directs to misguidance, he shall never find anyone to guide him. So do not pity them - O Muhammad - deliver the Message to them. Certainly, whoever among them accepts the Message, then he shall gain the best rewards. As for those who turn away in rejection, do not feel sad for them or concerned about them, for

(Your duty is only to convey (the Message) and on Us is the reckoning) (13: 40), and,

(But you are only a warner. And Allah is a Wakil (Disposer of affairs, Trustee, Guardian) over all things) (11:12).

'Ali bin Abi Talhah reported that Ibn 'Abbas said about Allah's statement,

(Verily, those who disbelieve, it is the same to them whether you (O Muhammad) warn them or do not warn them, they will not believe) "That the Messenger of Allah was eager for all the people to believe and follow the guidance he was sent with. Allah informed him that none would believe except for those whom He decreed happiness for in the first place, and none would stray except those who Allah has decreed to do so in the first place."

Surah: 2 Ayah: 7

﴿ خَتَمَ ٱللَّهُ عَلَىٰ قُلُوبِهِمْ وَعَلَىٰ سَمْعِهِمْ ۖ وَعَلَىٰ أَبْصَـٰرِهِمْ غِشَـٰوَةٌ ۖ وَلَهُمْ عَذَابٌ عَظِيمٌ ۝ ﴾

7. Allâh has set a seal on their hearts and on their hearing, (i.e. they are closed from accepting Allâh's Guidance), and on their eyes there is a covering. Theirs will be a great torment.

Transliteration

7. Khatama Allahu AAala quloobihim waAAala samAAihim waAAala absarihim ghishawatun walahum AAathabun AAa*th*eemun

Tafsir Ibn Kathir

Meaning of Khatama

As-Suddi said that,

(Khatama Allah) means, "Allah has sealed." Qatadah said that this Ayah means, "Shaytan controlled them when they obeyed him. Therefore, Allah sealed their hearts, hearing and sight, and they could neither see the guidance nor hear, comprehend or understand." Ibn Jurayj said that Mujahid said,

(Allah has set a seal on their hearts), "A stamp. It occurs when sin resides in the heart and surrounds it from all sides, and this submersion of the heart in sin constitutes a stamp, meaning a seal." Ibn Jurayj also said that the seal is placed on the heart and the hearing. In addition, Ibn Jurayj said, that `Abdullah bin Kathir narrated that Mujahid said, "The stain is not as bad as the stamp, the stamp is not as bad as the lock which is the worst type." Al-A`mash said, "Mujahid demonstrated with his hand while saying, `They used to say that the heart is just like this - meaning the open palm. When the servant commits a sin, a part of the heart will be rolled up - and he rolled up his index finger. When the servant commits another sin, a part of the heart will be rolled up' - and he rolled up another finger, until he rolled up all of his fingers. Then he said, `Then, the heart will be sealed.' Mujahid also said that this is the description of the Ran (refer to 83:14)."

Al-Qurtubi said, "The Ummah has agreed that Allah has described Himself with sealing and closing the hearts of the disbelievers, as a punishment for their disbelief. Similarly, Allah said,

(Nay, Allah has set a seal upon their hearts because of their disbelief) (4:155)."

He then mentioned the Hadith about changing the hearts, (in which the Prophet supplicated),

«يَا مُقَلِّبَ الْقُلُوبِ ثَبِّتْ قُلُوبَنَا عَلَى دِينِكَ»

(O You Who changes the hearts, make our hearts firm on Your religion.)

He also mentioned the Hadith by Hudhayfah recorded in the Sahih, in which the Messenger of Allah said,

«تُعْرَضُ الْفِتَنُ عَلَى الْقُلُوبِ كَالْحَصِيرِ عُودًا عُودًا، فَأَيُّ قَلْبٍ أُشْرِبَهَا نُكِتَ فِيهِ نُكْتَةٌ سَوْدَاءُ وَأَيُّ قَلْبٍ أَنْكَرَهَا نُكِتَ فِيهِ نُكْتَةٌ بَيْضَاءُ حَتَّى تَصِيرَ عَلَى قَلْبَيْنِ: عَلَى أَبْيَضَ مِثْلِ الصَّفَا، فَلَا تَضُرُّهُ فِتْنَةٌ مَا دَامَتِ السَّمَوَاتُ وَالْأَرْضُ وَالْآخَرُ أَسْوَدُ مُرْبَادًّا كَالْكُوزِ مُجَخِّيًا لَا يَعْرِفُ مَعْرُوفًا وَلَا يُنْكِرُ مُنْكَرًا»

(The Fitan (trials, tests) are offered to the hearts, just as the straws that are sewn into a woven mat, one after another. Any heart that accepts the Fitan, then a black dot will be engraved on it. Any heart that rejects the Fitan, then a white dot will be engraved on it. The hearts will therefore become two categories: white, just like the barren rock; no Fitnah shall ever harm this category as long as the heavens and earth still exist. Another category is black, just as the cup that is turned upside down, for this heart does not recognize righteousness or renounce evil.)

Ibn Jarir said, "The truth regarding this subject is what the authentic Hadith from the Messenger of Allah stated. Abu Hurayrah narrated that the Messenger of Allah said,

«إِنَّ الْمُؤْمِنَ إِذَا أَذْنَبَ ذَنْبًا كَانَتْ نُكْتَةً سَوْدَاءَ فِي قَلْبِهِ، فَإِنْ تَابَ وَنَزَعَ وَاسْتَغْتَبَ صَقِلَ قَلْبُهُ وَإِنْ زَادَ زَادَتْ حَتَّى تَعْلُوَ قَلْبَهُ، فَذلِكَ الرَّانُ الَّذِي قَالَ اللهُ تَعَالى:

[كَلَّا بَلْ رَانَ عَلَى قُلُوبِهِم مَّا كَانُواْ يَكْسِبُونَ]

(When the believer commits a sin, a black dot will be engraved on his heart. If he repents, refrains and regrets, his heart will be polished again. If he commits more errors, the dots will increase until they cover his heart. This is the Ran (stain) that Allah described,

(Nay! But on their hearts is the Ran (stain) which they used to earn)" (83:14).

At-Tirmidhi, An-Nasa'i and Ibn Majah recorded this Hadith, and At-Tirmidhi said that it is Hasan Sahih.

The Meaning of Ghishawah

Reciting the Ayah,

(Allah has set a seal on their hearts and on their hearing), then pausing, then continuing with,

(And on their eyes there is a Ghishawah (covering)) is accurate, for the stamp is placed on the heart and the hearing while the Ghishawah, the covering, is appropriately placed on the eyes. In his Tafsir, As-Suddi said that Ibn 'Abbas and Ibn Mas'ud said about Allah's statement,

(Allah has set a seal on their hearts and on their hearing), "So that they neither understand nor hear. Allah also said that He placed a covering on their sight, meaning eyes, and so, they do not see."

Surah: 2 Ayahs: 8 & 9

﴿ وَمِنَ ٱلنَّاسِ مَن يَقُولُ ءَامَنَّا بِٱللَّهِ وَبِٱلْيَوْمِ ٱلْأَخِرِ وَمَا هُم بِمُؤْمِنِينَ ۝ ﴾

8. And of mankind, there are some (hypocrites) who say: "We believe in Allâh and the Last Day" while in fact they believe not.

﴿ يُخَٰدِعُونَ ٱللَّهَ وَٱلَّذِينَ ءَامَنُوا۟ وَمَا يَخْدَعُونَ إِلَّآ أَنفُسَهُمْ وَمَا يَشْعُرُونَ ۝ ﴾

9. They (think to) deceive Allâh and those who believe, while they only deceive themselves, and perceive (it) not!

Transliteration

8. Wamina alnnasi man yaqoolu amanna biAllahi wabialyawmi al-akhiri wama hum bimu/mineena 9. YukhadiAAoona Allaha waallatheena amanoo wama yakhdaAAoona illa anfusahum wama yashAAuroona

Tafsir Ibn Kathir

The Hypocrites

We mentioned that four Ayat in the beginning of Surat Al-Baqarah described the believers. The two last Ayat (2:6-7) describe the disbelievers. Afterwards, Allah begins to describe the hypocrites who show belief and hide disbelief. Since the matter of the hypocrites is vague and many people do not realize their true reality, Allah mentioned their description in detail. Each of the characteristics that Allah used to described them with is a type of hypocrisy itself. Allah revealed Surat Bara'ah (chapter 9) and Surat Al-Munafiqun (chapter 63) about the hypocrites. He also mentioned the hypocrites in Surat An-Nur (24) and other Surahs, so that their description would be known and their ways and errors could be avoided. Allah said,

(8. And of mankind, there are some (hypocrites) who say: "We believe in Allâh and the Last Day" while in fact they believe not). (9. They (think to) deceive Allâh and those who believe, while they only deceive themselves, and perceive (it) not!)

Meaning of Nifaq

Nifaq means to show conformity - or agreement - and to conceal evil. Nifaq has several types: Nifaq in the creed that causes its people to reside in Hell for eternity, and Nifaq in deed, which is one of the major sins, as we will explain soon, Allah willing. Ibn Jurayj said of the hypocrite that, "His actual deeds are different from what he publicizes, what he conceals is different from what he utters, his entrance and presence are not the same as his exit and absence."

The Beginning of Hypocrisy

The revelations about the characteristics of the hypocrites were revealed in Al-Madinah, this is because there were no hypocrites in Makkah. Rather the opposite was the situation in Makkah, since some people were forced to pretend that they were disbelievers, while their hearts concealed their faith. Afterwards, the Messenger of Allah migrated to Al-Madinah, where the Ansar from the tribes of Aws and Khazraj resided. They used to worship idols during the pre-Islamic period of ignorance, just as the rest of the Arab idolators. Three Jewish tribes resided in Al-Madinah, Banu Qaynuqa'-allies of Al-Khazraj, Banu An-Nadir and Banu Qurayzah-allies of the Aws. Many members of the Aws and Khazraj tribes embraced Islam. However, only a few Jews embraced

Islam, such as 'Abdullah bin Salam. During the early stage in Al-Madinah, there weren't any hypocrites because the Muslims were not strong enough to be feared yet. On the contrary, the Messenger of Allah conducted peace treaties with the Jews and several other Arab tribes around Al-Madinah. Soon after, the battle of Badr occurred and Allah gave victory to Islam and its people. 'Abdullah bin Ubayy bin Salul was a leader in Al-Madinah. He was Al-Khazraj's chief, and during the period of Jahiliyyah he was the master of both tribes - Aws and Khazraj. They were about to appoint him their king when the Message reached Al-Madinah, and many in Al-Madinah embraced Islam. Ibn Salul's heart was filled with hatred against Islam and its people. When the battle of Badr took place, he said, "Allah's religion has become apparent." So he pretended to be Muslim, along with many of those who were just like him, as well as many among the People of the Book. It was then that hypocrisy began in Al-Madinah and among the surrounding nomad tribes. As for the Emigrants, none of them were hypocrites, since they emigrated willingly (seeking the pleasure of Allah). Rather, when a Muslim would emigrate from Makkah, he would be forced to abandon all of his wealth, offspring and land; he would do so seeking Allah's reward in the Hereafter.

The Tafsir of Aya 2:8 (& Aya 2:9)

Muhammad bin Ishaq narrated that Ibn 'Abbas said that,

(And of mankind, there are some who say: "We believe in Allah and the Last Day" while in fact they do not believe) "This refers to the hypocrites among the Aws and Khazraj and those who behaved as they did."

This is how Abu Al-'Aliyah, Al-Hasan, Qatadah and As-Suddi explained this Ayah. Allah revealed the characteristics of the hypocrites, so that the believers would not be deceived by their outer appearance, thus saving the believers from a great evil. Otherwise, the believers might think that the hypocrites were believers, when in reality they are disbelievers. To consider the sinners as righteous people is extremely dangerous, Allah said,

(And of mankind, there are some who say: "We believe in Allah and the Last Day" while in fact they do not believe) meaning, they utter these false statements only with their tongues, just as Allah said,

(When the hypocrites come to you (O Muhammad), they say: "We bear witness that you are indeed the Messenger of Allah." Allah knows that you are indeed His Messenger) (63:1).

This Ayah means that the hypocrites utter these statements only when they meet you, not because they actually believe what they are saying. The hypocrites emphasize their belief in Allah and the Last Day with their words, when that is not the case in reality. Therefore, Allah stated that the hypocrites lie in their testimony of creed, when He said,

(And Allah bears witness that the hypocrites are indeed liars.) (63:1), and,

(while in fact they believe not)

Allah said,

(They try to deceive Allah and those who believe). The hypocrites show belief outwardly while concealing disbelief. They think that by doing this, they will mislead Allah, or that the statements they utter will help them with Allah, and this is an indication of their total ignorance. They think that such behavior will deceive Allah, just as it might deceive some of the believers. Similarly, Allah said,

(On the Day when Allah will resurrect them all together; then they will swear to Him as they swear to you. And they think that they have something (to stand upon). Verily, they are liars!) (58:18). aHence, Allah refuted their way by saying,

(While they only deceive themselves, and perceive (it) not!) Allah stated that the hypocrites only deceive themselves by this behavior, although they are unaware of this fact. Allah also said,

(Verily, the hypocrites try to deceive Allah, but it is He Who deceives them) (4:142).

Also, Ibn Abi Hatim narrated that Ibn Jurayj commented on Allah's statement,

(Verily, the hypocrites seek to deceive Allah, but it is He Who deceives them), "The hypocrites pronounce, `There is no deity worthy of worship except Allah' seeking to ensure the sanctity of their blood and money, all the while concealing disbelief."Sa`id said that Qatadah said, (And of mankind, there are some who say: "We believe in Allah and the Last Day" while in fact they believe not. They try to deceive Allah and those who believe, while they only deceive themselves, and perceive (it) not!) "This is the description of a hypocrite. He is devious, he says the truth with his tongue and defies it with his heart and deeds. He wakes up in a condition other than the one he goes to sleep in, and goes to sleep in a different condition than the one he wakes up in. He changes his mind just like a ship that moves about whenever a wind blows."

Surah: 2 Ayah: 10

﴿ فِى قُلُوبِهِم مَّرَضٌ فَزَادَهُمُ ٱللَّهُ مَرَضًا ۖ وَلَهُمْ عَذَابٌ أَلِيمٌۢ بِمَا كَانُوا۟ يَكْذِبُونَ ۞ ﴾

10. In their hearts is a disease (of doubt and hypocrisy) and Allâh has increased their disease. A painful torment is theirs because they used to tell lies.

Transliteration

10. Fee quloobihim maradun fazadahumu Allahu maradan walahum AAathabun aleemun bima kanoo yakthiboona

Tafsir Ibn Kathir

The Meaning of 'Disease' in this Ayah

As-Suddi narrated from Abu Malik and (also) from Abu Salih, from Ibn 'Abbas, and (also) Murrah Al-Hamdani from Ibn Mas'ud and other Companions that this Ayah,

(In their hearts is a disease) means, 'doubt', and,

(And Allah has increased their disease) also means 'doubt'. Mujahid, 'Ikrimah, Al-Hasan Al-Basri, Abu Al-'Aliyah, Ar-Rabi' bin Anas and Qatadah also said similarly. 'Abdur-Rahman bin Zayd bin Aslam commented on,

(In their hearts is a disease), "A disease in the religion, not a physical disease. They are the hypocrites and the disease is the doubt that they brought to Islam.

(And Allah has increased their disease) meaning, increased them in shameful behavior." He also recited,

(As for those who believe, it has increased their faith, and they rejoice. But as for those in whose hearts is a disease, it will add disgrace to their disgrace.) (9:124-125) and commented, "Evil to their evil and deviation to their deviation." This statement by `Abdur-Rahman is true, and it constitutes a punishment that is compatible to the sin, just as the earlier scholars stated. Similarly, Allah said,

(While as for those who accept guidance, He increases their guidance and grants them their piety) (47:17).

Allah said next,

(Because they used to tell lies). The hypocrites have two characteristics, they lie and they deny the Unseen.

The scholars who stated that the Prophet knew the hypocrites of his time have only the Hadith of Hudhayfah bin Al-Yaman as evidence. In it the Prophet gave him the names of fourteen hypocrites during the battle of Tabuk. These hypocrites plotted to assassinate the Prophet during the night on a hill in that area. They planned to excite the Prophet's camel, so that she would throw him down the hill. Allah informed the Prophet about their plot, and the Prophet told Hudhayfah their names.

As for the other hypocrites, Allah said about them,

(And among the bedouins around you, some are hypocrites, and so are some among the people of Al-Madinah who persist in hypocrisy; you (O Muhammad) know them not, We know them) (9:101), and,

(If the hypocrites, and those in whose hearts is a disease, and those who spread false news among the people in Al-Madinah do not cease, We shall certainly let you overpower them, then they will not be able to stay in it as your neighbors but a little while. Accursed, they shall be seized wherever found, and killed with a (terrible) slaughter) (33:60-61).

These Ayat prove that the Prophet was not informed about each and everyone among the hypocrites of his time. Rather, the Prophet was only informed about their characteristics, and he used to assume that some people possessed these characteristics. Similarly, Allah said,

(Had We willed, We could have shown them to you, and you should have known them by their marks; but surely, you will know them by the tone of their speech!) (47:30).

The most notorious hypocrite at that time was 'Abdullah bin Ubayy bin Salul; Zayd bin Arqam - the Companion - gave truthful testimony to that effect. In addition, 'Umar bin Al-Khattab once mentioned the matter of Ibn Salul to the Prophet , who said,

«إِنِّي أَكْرَهُ أَنْ تَتَحَدَّثَ الْعَرَبُ أَنَّ مُحَمَّدًا يَقْتُلُ أَصْحَابَهُ»

(I would not like the Arabs to say to each other that Muhammad is killing his Companions.)

Yet, when Ibn Salul died, the Prophet performed the funeral prayer for him and attended his funeral just as he used to do with other Muslims. It was recorded in the Sahih that the Prophet said,

«إِنِّي خُيِّرْتُ فَاخْتَرْتُ»

(I was given the choice (to pray for him or not), so I chose.)

In another narration, the Prophet said,

«لَوْ أَعْلَمُ أَنِّي لَوْ زِدْتُ عَلَى السَّبْعِينَ يُغْفَرُ لَهُ لَزِدْتُ»

(If I knew that by asking (Allah to forgive Ibn Salul) more than seventy times that He would forgive him, then I would do that.)

Surah: 2 Ayah: 11 & Ayah: 12

﴿ وَإِذَا قِيلَ لَهُمْ لَا تُفْسِدُوا۟ فِى ٱلْأَرْضِ قَالُوٓا۟ إِنَّمَا نَحْنُ مُصْلِحُونَ ۞ ﴾

11. And when it is said to them: "Make not mischief on the earth," they say: "We are only peace-makers."

﴿ أَلَآ إِنَّهُمْ هُمُ ٱلْمُفْسِدُونَ وَلَـٰكِن لَّا يَشْعُرُونَ ۞ ﴾

12. Verily! They are the ones who make mischief, but they perceive not.

Transliteration

11. Wa-itha qeela lahum la tufsidoo fee al-ardi qaloo innama nahnu muslihoona
12. Ala innahum humu almufsidoona walakin la yashAAuroona

Tafsir Ibn Kathir

Meaning of Mischief

In his Tafsir, As-Suddi said that Ibn 'Abbas and Ibn Mas'ud commented,

(And when it is said to them: "Do not make mischief on the earth," they say: "We are only peacemakers.") "They are the hypocrites. As for,

("Do not make mischief on the earth"), that is disbelief and acts of disobedience." Abu Ja`far said that Ar-Rabi` bin Anas said that Abu Al-`Aliyah said that Allah's statement,

(And when it is said to them: "Do not make mischief on the earth,"), means, "Do not commit acts of disobedience on the earth. Their mischief is disobeying Allah, because whoever disobeys Allah on the earth, or commands that Allah be disobeyed, he has committed mischief on the earth. Peace on both the earth and in the heavens is ensured (and earned) through obedience (to Allah)." Ar-Rabi` bin Anas and Qatadah said similarly.

Types of Mischief that the Hypocrites commit

Ibn Jarir said, "The hypocrites commit mischief on earth by disobeying their Lord on it and continuing in the prohibited acts. They also abandon what Allah made obligatory and doubt His religion, even though He does not accept a deed from anyone except with faith in His religion and certainty of its truth. The hypocrites also lie to the believers by saying contrary to the doubt and hesitation their hearts harbor. They give as much aid as they can, against Allah's loyal friends, and support those who deny Allah, His Books and His Messengers. This is how the hypocrites commit mischief on earth, while thinking that they are doing righteous work on earth."

The statement by Ibn Jarir is true, taking the disbelievers as friends is one of the categories of mischief on the earth. Allah said,

(And those who disbelieve are allies of one another, if you do not do this (help each other), there will be turmoil and oppression on the earth, and great mischief.) (8:73), In this way Allah severed the loyalty between the believers and the disbelievers. Similarly, Allah said,

(O you who believe! Do not take disbelievers as Awliya' (protectors or helpers or friends) instead of believers. Do you wish to offer Allah a manifest proof against yourselves) (4: 144).

Allah then said,

(Verily, the hyprocrites will be in the lowest depth of the Fire; no helper will you find for them) (4:145).

Since the outward appearance of the hypocrite displays belief, he confuses the true believers. Hence, the deceitful behavior of the hypocrites is an act of mischief, because they deceive the believers by claiming what they do not believe in, and because they give support and loyalty to the disbelievers against the believers.

If the hypocrite remains a disbeliever (rather than pretending to be Muslim), the evil that results from him would be less. Even better, if the hypocrite becomes sincere with Allah and makes the statements that he utters conform to his deeds, he will gain success. Allah said,

(And when it is said to them: "Do not make mischief on the earth," they say: "We are only peacemakers.") meaning, "We seek to be friends with both parties, the believers and the disbelievers, and to have peace with both parties." Similarly, Muhammad bin Ishaq reported that Ibn `Abbas said,

(And when it is said to them: "Do not make mischief on the earth," they say: "We are only peacemakers.") means, "We seek to make amends between the believers and the People of the Book. '' Allah said,

(Verily, they are the ones who make mischief, but they perceive not.). This Ayah means that the hypocrites' behavior, and their claim that it is for peace, is itself mischief, although in their ignorance, they do not see it to be mischief.

Surah: 2 Ayah: 13

﴿ وَإِذَا قِيلَ لَهُمْ ءَامِنُوا۟ كَمَآ ءَامَنَ ٱلنَّاسُ قَالُوٓا۟ أَنُؤْمِنُ كَمَآ ءَامَنَ ٱلسُّفَهَآءُ ۗ أَلَآ إِنَّهُمْ هُمُ ٱلسُّفَهَآءُ وَلَٰكِن لَّا يَعْلَمُونَ ﴾

13. And when it is said to them (hypocrites): "Believe as the people (followers of Muhammad (peace be upon him) Al-Ansâr and Al-Muhajirûn) have believed," they say: "Shall we believe as the fools have believed?" Verily, they are the fools, but they know not.

Transliteration

13. Wa-itha qeela lahum aminoo kama amana alnnasu qaloo anu/minu kama amana alssufahao ala innahum humu alssufahao walakin la yaAAlamoona

Tafsir Ibn Kathir

Types of Mischief that the Hypocrites commit (Continued)

Allah said that if the hypocrites are told,

("Believe as the people believe,"), meaning, `Believe just as the believers believe in Allah, His angels, His Books, His Messengers, Resurrection after death, Paradise and Hellfire, etc. And obey Allah and His Messenger by heeding the commandments and avoiding the prohibitions.' Yet the hypocrites answer by saying, ("Shall we believe as the fools have believed") they meant (may Allah curse the hypocrites) the Companions of the Messenger of Allah . This is the same Tafsir given by Abu Al-`Aliyah and As-Suddi in his Tafsir, with a chain of narration to Ibn `Abbas, Ibn Mas`ud and other Companions. This is also the Tafsir of Ar-Rabi` bin Anas and `Abdur-Rahman bin Zayd bin Aslam. The hypocrites said, "Us and them having the same status, following the same path, while they are fools!" `The fool' is the ignorant, simple-minded person who has little knowledge in areas of benefit and harm. This is why, according to the majority of the scholars, Allah used the term foolish to include children, when He said, (And do not give your property, which Allah has made a means of support for you, to the foolish) (4:5).

Allah answered the hypocrites in all of these instances. For instance, Allah said here, (Verily, they are the fools). Allah thus affirmed that the hypocrites are indeed the fools, yet, (But they know not). Since they are so thoroughly ignorant, the hypocrites are unaware of their degree of deviation and ignorance, and such situation is more dangerous, a severer case of blindness, and further from the truth than one who is aware.

Surah: 2 Ayah: 14 & Ayah: 15

﴿ وَإِذَا لَقُوا۟ ٱلَّذِينَ ءَامَنُوا۟ قَالُوٓا۟ ءَامَنَّا وَإِذَا خَلَوْا۟ إِلَىٰ شَيَٰطِينِهِمْ قَالُوٓا۟ إِنَّا مَعَكُمْ إِنَّمَا نَحْنُ مُسْتَهْزِءُونَ ﴾

14. And when they meet those who believe, they say: "We believe," but when they are alone with their Shayâtin (devils - polytheists, hypocrites), they say: "Truly, we are with you; verily, we were but mocking."

﴿ ٱللَّهُ يَسْتَهْزِئُ بِهِمْ وَيَمُدُّهُمْ فِى طُغْيَٰنِهِمْ يَعْمَهُونَ ﴾

15. Allâh mocks at them and gives them increase in their wrong-doings to wander blindly.

Transliteration

14. Wa-itha laqoo allatheena amanoo qaloo amanna wa-itha khalaw ila shayateenihim qaloo inna maAAakum innama nahnu mustahzi-oona 15. Allahu yastahzi-o bihim wayamudduhum fee tughyanihim yaAAmahoona

Tafsir Ibn Kathir

The Hypocrites' Cunning and Deceit

Allah said that when the hypocrites meet the believers, they proclaim their faith and pretend to be believers, loyalists and friends. They do this to misdirect, mislead and deceive the believers. The hypocrites also want to have a share of the benefits and gains that the believers might possibly acquire. Yet,

(But when they are alone with their Shayatin), meaning, if they are alone with their devils, such as their leaders and masters among the rabbis of the Jews, hypocrites and idolators.

Human and Jinn Devils

Ibn Jarir said, "The devils of every creation are the mischievous among them. There are both human devils and Jinn devils. Allah said,

(And so We have appointed for every Prophet enemies — Shayatin (devils) among mankind and Jinn, inspiring one another with adorned speech as a delusion (or by way of deception)) (6:112).

The Meaning of 'Mocking

Allah said,

(They say: "Truly, we are with you"). Muhammad bin Ishaq reported that Ibn `Abbas said that the Ayah means, "We are with you,

(Verily, we were but mocking), meaning, we only mock people (the believers) and deceive them." Ad-Dahhak said that Ibn `Abbas said that the Ayah,

(Verily, we were but mocking), means, "We (meaning the hypocrites) were mocking the Companions of Muhammad." Also, Ar-Rabi` bin Anas and Qatadah said similarly. Allah's statement,

(Allah mocks at them and leaves them increasing in their deviation to wander blindly) answers the hypocrites and punishes them for their behavior. Ibn Jarir commented, "Allah mentioned what He will do to them on the Day of Resurrection, when He said,

(On the Day when the hypocrites @— men and women @— will say to the believers: "Wait for us! Let us get something from your light!" It will be said: "Go back to your rear! Then seek a light!" So a wall will be put up between them, with a gate therein. Inside it will be mercy, and outside it will be torment.) (57:13), and,

(And let not the disbelievers think that Our postponing of their punishment is good for them. We postpone the punishment only so that they may increase in sinfulness.) (3:178)."

He then said, "This, and its like, is Allah's mockery of the hypocrites and the people of Shirk."

The Hypocrites suffering for their Plots

Allah stated that He will punish the hypocrites for their mockery, using the same terms to describe both the deed and its punishment, although the meaning is different. Similarly, Allah said,

(The recompense for an offense is an offense equal to it; but whoever forgives and makes reconciliation, his reward is with Allah) (42:40), and, (Then whoever transgresses (the prohibition) against you, transgress likewise against him) (2:194).

The first act is an act of injustice, while the second act is an act of justice. So both actions carry the same name, while being different in reality. This is how the scholars explain deceit, cunning and mocking when attributed to Allah in the Qur'an. Surely, Allah exacts revenge for certain evil acts with a punishment that is similar in nature to the act itself. We should affirm here that Allah does not do these things out of joyful play, according to the consensus of the scholars, but as a just form of punishment for certain evil acts.

Meaning of 'Leaves them increasing in their deviation to wander blindly

Allah said,

(Allah mocks at them and leaves them increasing in their deviation to wander blindly). As-Suddi reported that Ibn 'Abbas, Ibn Mas'ud and several other Companions of the Messenger of Allah said that,

(and leaves them increasing) means, He gives them respite. Also, Mujahid said, "He (causes their deviation) to increase." Allah said;

(Do they think that by the wealth and the children with which We augment them. (That) We hasten to give them with good things. Nay, but they perceive not.) (23:55-56).

Ibn Jarir commented, "The correct meaning of this Ayah is 'We give them increase from the view of giving them respite and leaving them in their deviation and rebellion.' Similarly, Allah said,

(And We shall turn their hearts and their eyes away (from guidance), as they refused to believe in it the first time, and We shall leave them in their trespass to wander blindly)." (6:110).

Tughyan used in this Ayah means to transgress the limits, just as Allah said in another Ayah,

(Verily, when the water Tagha (rose) beyond its limits, We carried you in the ship) (69:11).

Also, Ibn Jarir said that the term 'Amah, in the Ayah means, 'deviation'. He also said about Allah's statement,

(in their deviation to wander), "In the misguidance and disbelief that has encompassed them, causing them to be confused and unable to find a way out of it. This is because Allah has stamped their hearts, sealed them, and blinded their vision. Therefore, they do not recognize guidance or find the way out of their deviation."

Surah: 2 Ayah: 16

﴿ أُو۟لَـٰٓئِكَ ٱلَّذِينَ ٱشْتَرَوُا۟ ٱلضَّلَـٰلَةَ بِٱلْهُدَىٰ فَمَا رَبِحَت تِّجَـٰرَتُهُمْ وَمَا كَانُوا۟ مُهْتَدِينَ ﴾

16. These are they who have purchased error for guidance, so their commerce was profitless. And they were not guided.

Transliteration

16. Ola-ika allatheena ishtarawoo alddalalata bialhuda fama rabihat tijaratuhum wama kanoo muhtadeena

Tafsir Ibn Kathir

In his Tafsir, As-Suddi reported that Ibn 'Abbas and Ibn Mas'ud commented on;

(These are they who have purchased error for guidance) saying it means, "They pursued misguidance and abandoned guidance." Mujahid said, "They believed and then disbelieved," while Qatadah said, "They preferred deviation to guidance." Qatadah's statement is similar in meaning to Allah's statement about Thamud,

(And as for Thamud, We granted them guidance, but they preferred blindness to guidance) (41:17).

In summary, the statements that we have mentioned from the scholars of Tafsir indicate that the hypocrites deviate from the true guidance and prefer misguidance, substituting wickedness in place of righteousness. This meaning explains Allah's statement,

(These are they who have purchased error with guidance), meaning, they exchanged guidance to buy misguidance. This meaning includes those who first believed, then later disbelieved, whom Allah described,

(That is because they believed, and then disbelieved; therefore their hearts are sealed) (63:3).

The Ayah also includes those who preferred deviation over guidance. The hypocrites fall into several categories. This is why Allah said,

(So their commerce was profitless. And they were not guided), meaning their trade did not succeed nor were they righteous or rightly guided throughout all this. In addition, Ibn Jarir narrated that Qatadah commented on the Ayah,

(So their commerce was profitless. And they were not guided), "By Allah! I have seen them leaving guidance for deviation, leaving the Jama`ah (the community of the believers) for the sects, leaving safety for fear, and the Sunnah for innovation." Ibn Abi Hatim also reported other similar statements.

Surah: 2 Ayah: 17 & Ayah: 18

﴿ مَثَلُهُمْ كَمَثَلِ ٱلَّذِى ٱسْتَوْقَدَ نَارًا فَلَمَّآ أَضَآءَتْ مَا حَوْلَهُۥ ذَهَبَ ٱللَّهُ بِنُورِهِمْ وَتَرَكَهُمْ فِى ظُلُمَٰتٍ لَّا يُبْصِرُونَ ۝ ﴾

17. Their likeness is as the likeness of one who kindled a fire; then, when it lighted all around him, Allâh took away their light and left them in darkness. (So) they could not see.

﴿ صُمٌّۢ بُكْمٌ عُمْىٌ فَهُمْ لَا يَرْجِعُونَ ۝ ﴾

18. They are deaf, dumb, and blind, so they return not (to the Right Path).

Transliteration

17. Mathaluhum kamathali allathee istawqada naran falamma adaat ma hawlahu thahaba Allahu binoorihim watarakahum fee *th*ulumatin la yubsiroona
18. Summun bukmun AAumyun fahum la yarjiAAoona

Tafsir Ibn Kathir

The Example of the Hypocrites

Allah likened the hypocrites when they bought deviation with guidance, thus acquiring utter blindness, to the example of a person who started a fire. When the fire was lit, and illumnitated the surrounding area, the person benefited from it and felt safe. Then the fire was suddenly extinguished. Therefore, total darkness covered this person, and he became unable to see anything or find his way out of it. Further, this person could not hear or speak and became so blind that even if there were light, he would not be able to see. This is why he cannot return to the state that he was in before this happened to him. Such is the case with the hypocrites who preferred misguidance over guidance, deviation over righteousness. This parable indicates that the hypocrites first believed, then disbelieved, just as Allah stated in other parts of the Qur'an.

Allah's statement, (Allah removed their light) means, Allah removed what benefits them, and this is the light, and He left them with what harms them, that is, the darkness and smoke. Allah said, (And left them in darkness), that is their doubts, disbelief and hypocrisy.

((So) they could not see) meaning, they are unable to find the correct path or find its direction. In addition, they are, (deaf) and thus cannot hear the guidance, (dumb) and cannot utter the words that might benefit them, (and blind) in total darkness and deviation. Similarly, Allah said, (Verily, it is not the eyes that grow blind, but it is the hearts which are in the breasts that grow blind) (22:46) and this why they cannot get back to the state of guidance that they were in, since they sold it for misguidance.

Surah: 2 Ayah: 19 & Ayah: 20

﴿ أَوْ كَصَيِّبٍ مِّنَ ٱلسَّمَآءِ فِيهِ ظُلُمَـٰتٌ وَرَعْدٌ وَبَرْقٌ يَجْعَلُونَ أَصَـٰبِعَهُمْ فِىٓ ءَاذَانِهِم مِّنَ ٱلصَّوَٰعِقِ حَذَرَ ٱلْمَوْتِ وَٱللَّهُ مُحِيطٌۢ بِٱلْكَـٰفِرِينَ ﴾

19. Or like a rainstorm from the sky, wherein is darkness, thunder, and lightning. They thrust their fingers in their ears to keep out the stunning thunder-clap for fear of death. But Allâh ever encompasses the disbelievers (i.e. Allâh will gather them all together).

﴿ يَكَادُ ٱلْبَرْقُ يَخْطَفُ أَبْصَـٰرَهُمْ كُلَّمَآ أَضَآءَ لَهُم مَّشَوْاْ فِيهِ وَإِذَآ أَظْلَمَ عَلَيْهِمْ قَامُواْ وَلَوْ شَآءَ ٱللَّهُ لَذَهَبَ بِسَمْعِهِمْ وَأَبْصَـٰرِهِمْ إِنَّ ٱللَّهَ عَلَىٰ كُلِّ شَىْءٍ قَدِيرٌ ﴾

20. The lightning almost snatches away their sight, whenever it flashes for them, they walk therein, and when darkness covers them, they stand still. And if Allâh willed, He could have taken away their hearing and their sight. Certainly, Allâh has power over all things.

Transliteration

19. Aw kasayyibin mina alssama-i feehi thulumatun waraAAdun wabarqun yajAAaloona asabiAAahum fee athanihim mina alssawaAAiqi hathara almawti waAllahu muheetun bialkafireena 20. Yakadu albarqu yakhtafu absarahum

kullama adaa lahum mashaw feehi wa-itha a*th*lama AAalayhim qamoo walaw shaa Allahu lathahaba bisamAAihim waabsarihim inna Allaha AAala kulli shay-in qadeerun

Tafsir Ibn Kathir

Another Parable of the Hypocrites

This is another parable which Allah gave about the hypocrites who sometimes know the truth and doubt it at other times. When they suffer from doubt, confusion and disbelief, their hearts are,

(Like a Sayyib), meaning, "The rain", as Ibn Mas`ud, Ibn `Abbas, and several other Companions have confirmed as well as Abu Al-`Aliyah, Mujahid, Sa`id bin Jubayr, `Ata', Al-Hasan Al-Basri, Qatadah, `Atiyah Al-`Awfi, `Ata' Al-Khurasani, As-Suddi and Ar-Rabi` bin Anas. Ad-Dahhak said "It is the clouds." However, the most accepted opinion is that it means the rain that comes down during,

(darkness), meaning, here, the doubts, disbelief and hypocrisy.

(thunder) that shocks the hearts with fear. The hypocrites are usually full of fear and anxiety, just as Allah described them,

(They think that every cry is against them) (63: 4), and, (They swear by Allah that they are truly of you while they are not of you, but they are a people who are afraid. Should they find refuge, or caves, or a place of concealment, they would turn straightway thereto in a swift rush) (9:56-57).

(The lightning), is in reference to the light of faith that is sometimes felt in the hearts of the hypocrites,

(They thrust their fingers in their ears to keep out the stunning thunderclap for fear of death. But Allah ever encompasses the disbelievers), meaning, their cautiousness does not benefit them because they are bound by Allah's all-encompassing will and decision. Similarly, Allah said,

(Has the story reached you of two hosts. Of Fir`awn (Pharaoh) and Thamud Nay! The disbelievers (persisted) in denying. And Allah encompasses them from behind!) (85:17-20).

Allah then said,

F(The lightning almost snatches away their sight) meaning, because the lightning is strong itself, and because their comprehension is weak and does not allow them to embrace the faith. Also, `Ali bin Abi Talhah reported that Ibn `Abbas commented on the Ayah,

(The lightning almost snatches away their sight), "The Qur'an mentioned almost all of the secrets of the hypocrites." `Ali bin Abi Talhah also narrated that Ibn `Abbas said,

(Whenever it flashes for them, they walk therein), "Whenever the hypocrites acquire a share in the victories of Islam, they are content with this share. Whenever Islam suffers a calamity, they are ready to revert to disbelief.". Similarly, Allah said,

(And among mankind is he who worships Allah on the edge: If good befalls him, he is content with that.) (22:11). Also, Muhammad bin Ishaq reported that Ibn 'Abbas said,

(Whenever it flashes for them, they walk therein, and when darkness covers them, they stand still), "They recognize the truth and speak about it. So their speech is upright, but when they revert to disbeleif, they again fall into confusion." This was also said by Abu Al-`Aliyah, Al-Hasan Al-Basri, Qatadah, Ar-Rabi` bin Anas and As-Suddi, who narrated it from the Companions, and it is the most obvious and most correct view, and Allah knows best.

Consequently, on the Day of Judgment, the believers will be given a light according to the degree of their faith. Some of them will gain light that illuminates over a distance of several miles, some more, some less. Some people's light will glow sometimes and be extinguished at other times. They will, therefore, walk on the Sirat (the bridge over the Fire) in the light, stopping when it is extinguished. Some people will have no light at all, these are the hypocrites whom Allah described when He said,

(On the Day when the hypocrites— men and women— will say to the believers: "Wait for us! Let us get something from your light!" It will be said to them; "Go back to you rear! Then seek a light!") (57:13).

Allah described the believers,

(On the Day you shall see the believing men and the believing women @— their light running forward before them and by their right hands. Glad tidings for you this Day! Gardens under which rivers flow (Paradise)) (57:12), and,

(The Day that Allah will not disgrace the Prophet (Muhammad) and those who believe with him. Their Light will run forward before them and (with their Records @— Books of deeds) in their right hands. They will say: "Our Lord! Keep perfect our Light for us ?and do not put it off till we cross over the Sirat (a slippery bridge over the Hell) safely> and grant us forgiveness. Verily, You are Able to do all things") (66:8).

Ibn Abi Hatim narrated that 'Abdullah bin Mas'ud commented on,

(Their Light will run forward before them), "They will pass on the Sirat. according to their deeds. The light that some people have will be as big as a mountain, while the light of others will be as big as a date tree. The people who will have the least light are those whose index fingers will sometimes be lit and extinguished at other times." Ibn Abi Hatim also reported that Ibn `Abbas said, "Every person among the people of Tawhid (Islamic Monotheism) will gain a light on the Day of Resurrection. As for the hypocrite, his light will be extinguished. When the believers witness the hypocrite's light being extinguished, they will feel anxious. Hence, they will supplicate,

(Our Lord! Keep perfect our Light for us)." Ad-Dahhak bin Muzahim said, "On the Day of Resurrection, everyone who has embraced the faith will be given a light. When they arrive at the Sirat, the light of the hypocrites will be extinguished. When the believers see this, they will feel anxious and supplicate,

(Our Lord! Keep perfect our Light for us)."

Types of Believers and Types of Disbelievers

Consequently, there are several types of people. There are the believers whom the first four Ayat (2:2-5) in Surat Al-Baqarah describe. There are the disbelievers who were described in the next two Ayat. And there are two categories of hypocrites: the complete hypocrites who were mentioned in the parable of the fire, and the hesitant hypocrites, whose light of faith is sometimes lit and sometimes extinguished. The parable of the rain was revealed about this category, which is not as evil as the first category.

This is similar to the parables that were given in Surat An-Nur (chapter 24). Like the example of the believer and the faith that Allah put in his heart, compared to a brightly illuminated lamp, just like a rising star. This is the believer, whose heart is built on faith and receiving its support from the divine legislation that was revealed to it, without any impurities or imperfections, as we will come to know, Allah willing.

Allah gave a parable of the disbelievers who think that they have something, while in reality they have nothing; such people are those who have compounded ignorance. Allah said,

(As for those who disbelieved, their deeds are like a mirage in a desert. The thirsty one thinks it to be water, until he comes up to it, he finds it to be nothing) (24:39).

Allah then gave the example of ignorant disbelievers, simple in their ignorance. He said;

(Or (the state of a disbeliever) is like the darkness in a vast deep sea, overwhelmed by waves, topped by dark clouds, (layers of) darkness upon darkness: if a man stretches out his hand, he can hardly see it! And he for whom Allah has not appointed light, for him there is no light) (24:40).

Therefore, Allah divided the camp of the disbelievers into two groups, advocates and followers. Allah mentioned these two groups in the beginning of Surat Al-Hajj,

(And among mankind is he who disputes about Allah, without knowledge, and follows every rebellious (disobedient to Allah) Shaytan (devil) (devoid of every kind of good)) (22:3), and, (And among men is he who disputes about Allah, without knowledge or guidance, or a Book giving light (from Allah)) (22:8).

Furthermore, Allah has divided the group of the believers in the beginning of Surat Al-Waqi'ah (56) and at the end. He also divided them in Surat Al-Insan (76) into two groups, the Sabiqun (those who preceded), they are the "near ones" (Muqaribun) and Ashab Al-Yamin (the companions of the right), and they are righteous (Abrar).

In summary, these Ayat divide the believers into two categories, the near ones and righteous. Also, the disbelievers are of two types, advocates and followers. In addition, the hypocrites are divided into two types, pure hypocrites and those who have some hypocrisy in them. The Two Sahihs record that 'Abdullah bin 'Amr said that the Prophet said,

«ثَلَاثٌ مَنْ كُنَّ فِيهِ كَانَ مُنَافِقًا خَالِصًا، وَمَنْ كَانَتْ فِيهِ وَاحِدَةٌ مِنْهُنَّ كَانَتْ فِيهِ خَصْلَةٌ مِنَ النِّفَاقِ حَتَّى يَدَعَهَا: مَنْ إِذَا حَدَّثَ كَذَبَ، وَإِذَا وَعَدَ أَخْلَفَ، وَإِذَا ائْتُمِنَ خَانَ»

(Whoever has the following three (characteristics) will be a pure hypocrite, and whoever has one of the following three characteristics will have one characteristic of hypocrisy, unless and until he gives it up. Whenever he speaks, he tells a lie. Whenever he makes a covenant, he proves treacherous. Whenever he is entrusted, he breaches the trust)

Hence, man might have both a part of faith and a part of hypocrisy, whether in deed, as this Hadith stipulates, or in the creed, as the Ayah (2:20) stipulates.

Types of Hearts

Imam Ahmad recorded Abu Sa'id saying that the Messenger of Allah said

«الْقُلُوبُ أَرْبَعَةٌ: قَلْبٌ أَجْرَدُ فِيهِ مِثْلُ السِّرَاجِ يَزْهَرُ وَقَلْبٌ أَغْلَفُ مَرْبُوطٌ عَلَى غِلَافِهِ وَقَلْبٌ مَنْكُوسٌ وَقَلْبٌ مُصْفَحٌ، فَأَمَّا الْقَلْبُ الْأَجْرَدُ فَقَلْبُ

الْمُؤْمِنِ فَسِرَاجُهُ فِيهِ نُورُهُ، وَأَمَّا الْقَلْبُ الْأَغْلَفُ فَقَلْبُ الْكَافِرِ، وَأَمَّا الْقَلْبُ الْمَنْكُوسُ فَقَلْبُ الْمُنَافِقِ الْخَالِصِ عَرَفَ ثُمَّ أَنْكَرَ وَأَمَّا الْقَلْبُ الْمُصْفَحُ فَقَلْبٌ فِيهِ إِيمَانٌ وَنِفَاقٌ وَمَثَلُ الْإِيمَانِ فِيهِ كَمَثَلِ الْبَقْلَةِ يَمُدُّهَا الْمَاءُ الطَّيِّبُ وَمَثَلُ النِّفَاقِ فِيهِ كَمَثَلِ الْقُرْحَةِ يَمُدُّهَا الْقَيْحُ وَالدَّمُ فَأَيُّ الْمَادَّتَيْنِ غَلَبَتْ عَلَى الْأُخْرَى غَلَبَتْ عَلَيْهِ»

(The hearts are four (types): polished as shiny as the radiating lamp, a sealed heart with a knot tied around its seal, a heart that is turned upside down and a wrapped heart. As for the polished heart, it is the heart of the believer and the lamp is the light of faith. The sealed heart is the heart of the disbeliever. The heart that is turned upside down is the heart of the pure hypocrite, because he had knowledge but denied it. As for the wrapped heart, it is a heart that contains belief and hypocrisy. The example of faith in this heart, is the example of the herb that is sustained by pure water. The example of hypocrisy in it, is the example of an ulcer that thrives on puss and blood. Whichever of the two substances has the upper hand, it will have the upper hand on that heart). This Hadith has a Jayid Hasan (good) chain of narration.

Allah said,

(And if Allah willed, He would have taken away their hearing and their sight. Certainly, Allah has power over all things). Muhammad bin Ishaq reported that Ibn 'Abbas commented on Allah's statement,

(And if Allah willed, He would have taken away their hearing and their sight), "Because they abandoned the truth after they had knowledge in it."

(Certainly, Allah has power over all things). Ibn 'Abbas said, "Allah is able to punish or pardon His servants as He wills." Ibn Jarir commented, "Allah only described Himself with the ability to do everything in this Ayah as a warning to the hypocrites of His control over everything, and to inform them that His ability completely encompasses them and that He is able to take away their hearing and sight."

Ibn Jarir and several other scholars of Tafsir stated that these two parables are about the same kind of hypocrite. So the 'or' mentioned in, (Or like a rainstorm from the sky) means 'and', just as the Ayah, (And obey neither a sinner or a disbeliever among them). Therefore, 'or' in the Ayah includes a choice of using either example for the hypocrites. Also, Al-Qurtubi said that 'or' means, "To show compatibility of the two choices, just as when one says, 'Sit with Al-Hasan or Ibn Sirin.' According to the view of Az-Zamakhshari, 'so it means each of these persons is the same as the other, so you may sit with either one of them.' The meaning of 'or' thus becomes 'either.' Allah gave these two examples of the hypocrites, because they both perfectly describe them."

I (Ibn Kathir) say, these descriptions are related to the type of hypocrite, because there is a difference between them as we stated. For instance, Allah mentioned these types in Surat Bara'ah (chapter 9) when He repeated the statement, "And among them" three times, describing their types, characteristics, statements and deeds. So the two examples mentioned here describe two types of hypocrites whose characteristics are similar. For instance, Allah gave two examples in Surat An-Nur, one for the advocates of disbelief and one for the followers of disbelief, He said, (As for those who disbelieved, their deeds are like a mirage in a desert) (24:39), until, (Or (the state of a disbeliever) is like the darkness in a vast deep sea) (24:40). The first example is of the advocates of disbelief who have complex ignorance, while the second is about the followers who have simple ignorance. Allah knows best.

Surah: 2 Ayah: 21 & Ayah: 22

﴿ يَـٰٓأَيُّهَا ٱلنَّاسُ ٱعْبُدُوا۟ رَبَّكُمُ ٱلَّذِى خَلَقَكُمْ وَٱلَّذِينَ مِن قَبْلِكُمْ لَعَلَّكُمْ تَتَّقُونَ ﴾

21. O mankind! Worship your Lord (Allâh), Who created you and those who were before you so that you may become Al-Muttaqûn (the pious - see V.2:2).

﴿ ٱلَّذِى جَعَلَ لَكُمُ ٱلْأَرْضَ فِرَٰشًا وَٱلسَّمَآءَ بِنَآءً وَأَنزَلَ مِنَ ٱلسَّمَآءِ مَآءً فَأَخْرَجَ بِهِۦ مِنَ ٱلثَّمَرَٰتِ رِزْقًا لَّكُمْ ۖ فَلَا تَجْعَلُوا۟ لِلَّهِ أَندَادًا وَأَنتُمْ تَعْلَمُونَ ﴾

22. Who has made the earth a resting place for you, and the sky as a canopy, and sent down water (rain) from the sky and brought forth therewith fruits as a provision for you. Then do not set up rivals unto Allâh (in worship) while you know (that He Alone has the right to be and made them seven heavens and He is the All-Knower of everything.

Transliteration

21. Ya ayyuha alnnasu oAAbudoo rabbakumu allathee khalaqakum waallatheena min qablikum laAAallakum tattaqoona 22. Allathee jaAAala lakumu al-arda firashan waalssamaa binaan waanzala mina alssama-i maan faakhraja bihi mina alththamarati rizqan lakum fala tajAAaloo lillahi andadan waantum taAAlamoona

Tafsir Ibn Kathir

Tawhid Al-Uluhiyyah

Allah next mentioned His Oneness in divinity and stated that He has favored His servants by bringing them to life after they did not exist. He also surrounded them with blessings, both hidden and apparent. He made the earth a resting place for them, just like the bed, stable with the firm mountains.

(And the sky as a canopy) meaning, 'a ceiling'. Similarly, Allah said in another Ayah,

(And We have made the heaven a roof, safe and well-guarded. Yet they turn away from its signs (i.e. sun, moon, winds, clouds)) (21:32).

(And sends down for you water (rain) from the sky) meaning, through the clouds, when they need the rain. Hence, Allah caused the various types of vegetation and fruits to grow as a means of sustenance for people and their cattle. Allah reiterated this bounty in various parts of the Qur'an.

There is another Ayah that is similar to this Ayah (2:22), that is, Allah's statement,

(It is He Who has made for you the earth as a dwelling place and the sky as a canopy, and has given you shape and made your shapes good (looking) and has provided you with good things. That is Allah, your Lord, so Blessed be Allah, the Lord of all that exists) (40:64).

The meaning that is reiterated here is that Allah is the Creator, the Sustainer, the Owner and Provider of this life, all that is in and on it. Hence, He alone deserves to be worshipped, and no one and nothing is to be associated with Him. This is why Allah said next,

(Then do not set up rivals unto Allah (in worship) while you know (that He alone has the right to be worshipped)) (2:22).

The Two Sahihs record that Ibn Mas'ud said, "I said to the Messenger of Allah, 'Which evil deed is the worst with Allah' He said,

«أَنْ تَجْعَلَ لِلَّهِ نِدًّا وَهُوَ خَلَقَكَ»

(To take an equal with Allah, while He alone created you.)"

Also, Mu'adh narrated the Prophet's statement,

«أَتَدْرِي مَا حَقُّ اللَّهِ عَلَى عِبَادِهِ؟ أَنْ يَعْبُدُوهُ وَلَا يُشْرِكُوا بِهِ شَيْئًا»

(Do you know Allah's right on His servants They must worship Him alone and refrain from associating anything with Him in worship.) Another Hadith states,

«لَا يَقُولَنَّ أَحَدُكُمْ مَا شَاءَ اللهُ وَشَاءَ فُلَانٌ، وَلَكِنْ لِيَقُلْ: مَا شَاءَ اللهُ ثُمَّ شَاءَ فُلَانٌ»

(None of you should say, 'What Allah and so-and-so person wills. Rather, let him say, 'What Allah wills, and then what so-and-so person wills.)

A Hadith with the same Meaning

Imam Ahmad narrated that Al-Harith Al-Ash`ari said that the Prophet of Allah said,

«إِنَّ اللهَ عَزَّوَجَلَّ أَمَرَ يَحْيَى بْنَ زَكَرِيَّا عَلَيْهِ السَّلَامُ بِخَمْسِ كَلِمَاتٍ أَنْ يَعْمَلَ بِهِنَّ، وَأَنْ يَأْمُرَ بَنِي إِسْرَائِيلَ أَنْ يَعْمَلُوا بِهِنَّ وَأَنَّهُ كَادَ أَنْ يُبْطِىءَ بِهَا، فَقَالَ لَهُ عِيسَى عَلَيْهِ السَّلَامُ: إِنَّكَ قَدْ أُمِرْتَ بِخَمْسِ كَلِمَاتٍ أَنْ تَعْمَلَ بِهِنَّ وَتَأْمُرَ بَنِي إِسْرَائِيلَ أَنْ يَعْمَلُوا بِهِنَّ فَإِمَّا أَنْ تُبَلِّغَهُمْ وَإِمَّا أَنْ أُبَلِّغَهُنَّ، فَقَالَ: يَا أَخِي إِنِّي أَخْشَى إِنْ سَبَقْتَنِي أَنْ أُعَذَّبَ أَوْ يُخْسَفَ بِي قَالَ: فَجَمَعَ يَحْيَى بْنُ زَكَرِيَّا بَنِي إِسْرَائِيلَ فِي بَيْتِ الْمَقْدِسِ حَتَّى امْتَلَأَ الْمَسْجِدُ، فَقَعَدَ عَلَى الشَّرَفِ فَحَمِدَ اللهَ وَأَثْنَى عَلَيْهِ ثُمَّ قَالَ: إِنَّ اللهَ أَمَرَنِي بِخَمْسِ كَلِمَاتٍ أَنْ أَعْمَلَ بِهِنَّ وَآمُرَكُمْ أَنْ تَعْمَلُوا بِهِنَّ أَوَّلُهُنَّ: أَنْ تَعْبُدُوا اللهَ وَلَا تُشْرِكُوا بِهِ شَيْئًا، فَإِنَّ مَثَلَ ذَلِكَ كَمَثَلِ رَجُلٍ اشْتَرَى عَبْدًا مِنْ خَالِصِ مَالِهِ بِوَرِقٍ أَوْ ذَهَبٍ فَجَعَلَ يَعْمَلُ وَيُؤَدِّي غَلَّتَهُ إِلَى غَيْرِ سَيِّدِهِ، فَأَيُّكُمْ يَسُرُّهُ أَنْ يَكُونَ عَبْدُهُ كَذَلِكَ، وَإِنَّ اللهَ خَلَقَكُمْ وَرَزَقَكُمْ فَاعْبُدُوهُ وَلَا تُشْرِكُوا بِهِ شَيْئًا. وَآمُرُكُمْ بِالصَّلَاةِ فَإِنَّ اللهَ يَنْصِبُ وَجْهَهُ

لِوَجْهِ عَبْدِهِ مَا لَمْ يَلْتَفِتْ فَإِذَا صَلَّيْتُمْ فَلَا تَلْتَفِتُوا. وَآمُرُكُمْ بِالصِّيَامِ فَإِنَّ مَثَلَ ذَلِكَ كَمَثَلِ رَجُلٍ مَعَهُ صُرَّةٌ مِنْ مِسْكٍ فِي عِصَابَةٍ كُلُّهُمْ يَجِدُ رِيحَ الْمِسْكِ وَإِنَّ خَلُوفَ فَمِ الصَّائِمِ أَطْيَبُ عِنْدَ اللهِ مِنْ رِيحِ الْمِسْكِ. وَآمُرُكُمْ بِالصَّدَقَةِ فَإِنَّ مَثَلَ ذَلِكَ كَمَثَلِ رَجُلٍ أَسَرَهُ الْعَدُوُّ فَشَدُّوا يَدَيْهِ إِلَى عُنُقِهِ وَقَدَّمُوهُ لِيَضْرِبُوا عُنُقَهُ فَقَالَ لَهُمْ: هَلْ لَكُمْ أَنْ أَفْتَدِيَ نَفْسِي مِنْكُمْ فَجَعَلَ يَفْتَدِي نَفْسَهُ مِنْهُمْ بِالْقَلِيلِ وَالْكَثِيرِ حَتَّى فَكَّ نَفْسَهُ. وَآمُرُكُمْ بِذِكْرِ اللهِ كَثِيرًا وَإِنَّ مَثَلَ ذَلِكَ كَمَثَلِ رَجُلٍ طَلَبَهُ الْعَدُوُّ سِرَاعًا فِي أَثَرِهِ فَأَتَى حِصْنًا حَصِينًا فَتَحَصَّنَ فِيهِ وَإِنَّ الْعَبْدَ أَحْصَنَ مَا يَكُونُ مِنَ الشَّيْطَانِ إِذَا كَانَ فِي ذِكْرِ اللهِ»

(Allah commanded Yahya bin Zakariya to implement five commands and to order the Children of Israel to implement them, but Yahya was slow in carrying out these commands. `Isa said to Yahya, `You were ordered to implement five commands and to order the Children of Israel to implement them. So either order, or I will do it.' Yahya said, 'My brother! I fear that if you do it before me, I will be punished or the earth will be shaken under my feet.' Hence, Yahya bin Zakariya called the Children of Israel to Bayt Al-Maqdis (Jerusalem), until they filled the Masjid. He sat on the balcony, thanked Allah and praised him and then said, `Allah ordered me to implement five commandments and that I should order you to adhere to them. The first is that you worship Allah alone and not associate any with Him. The example of this command is the example of a man who bought a servant from his money with paper or gold. The servant started to work for the master, but was paying the profits to another person. Who among you would like his servant to do that Allah created you and sustains you. Therefore, worship Him alone and do not associate anything with Him. I also command you to pray, for Allah directs His Face towards His servant's face, as long as the servant does not turn away. So when you pray, do not turn your heads to and fro. I also command you to fast. The example of it is the example of a man in a group of men and he has some musk wrapped in a piece of cloth, and consequently, all of the group smells the scent of the wrapped musk. Verily, the odor of the mouth of a fasting person is better before Allah than the scent of musk. I also command you to give charity. The example of this is the example of a man who was captured by the enemy. They tied his hands to his neck and brought him forth to cut off his neck. He said to them, 'Can I pay a ransom for myself' He kept ransoming himself with small and large amounts until he liberated himself. I also command you to always remember Allah. The example of this deed is that of a man who the enemy is tirelessly pursuing. He takes refuge in a fortified fort. When the servant remembers Allah, he will be resorting to the best refuge from Satan.)

Al-Harith then narrated that the Messenger of Allah said,

«وَأَنَا آمُرُكُمْ بِخَمْسٍ اللهُ أَمَرَنِي بِهِنَّ: الْجَمَاعَةِ وَالسَّمْعِ وَالطَّاعَةِ وَالْهِجْرَةِ وَالْجِهَادِ فِي سَبِيلِ اللهِ. فَإِنَّهُ مَنْ خَرَجَ مِنَ الْجَمَاعَةِ قِيدَ شِبْرٍ فَقَدْ خَلَعَ رِبْقَةَ الْإِسْلَامِ مِنْ عُنُقِهِ إِلَّا أَنْ يُرَاجِعَ وَمَنْ دَعَا بِدَعْوَى جَاهِلِيَّةٍ فَهُوَ مِنْ جُثَى جَهَنَّم»

(And I order you with five commandments that Allah has ordered me. Stick to the Jama`ah (community of the faithful), listen and obey (your leaders) and perform Hijrah (migration) and Jihad for the sake of Allah. Whoever abandons the Jama`ah, even the distance of a hand span, will have removed the tie of Islam from his neck, unless he returns. Whoever uses the slogans of Jahiliyah (the pre-Islamic period of ignorance) he will be among those kneeling in Jahannam (Hellfire).)

They said, "O Messenger of Allah! Even if he prays and fasts" He said,

«وَإِنْ صَلَّى وَصَامَ وَزَعَمَ أَنَّهُ مُسْلِمٌ، فَادْعُوا الْمُسْلِمِينَ بِأَسْمَائِهِمْ عَلَى مَا سَمَّاهُمُ اللهُ عَزَّ وَجَلَّ الْمُسْلِمِينَ الْمُؤْمِنِينَ عِبَادَ الله»

(Even if he prays, fasts and claims to be Muslim. So call the Muslims with their names that Allah has called them: `The Muslims, the believing servants of Allah.')

This is a Hasan Hadith, and it contains the statement, "Allah has created and sustains you, so worship Him and do not associate anything with Him in worship." This statement is relevant in the Ayat (2:21-22) we are discussing here and supports singling Allah in worship, without partners.

Signs of Allah's Existence

Several scholars of Tafsir, like Ar-Razi and others, used these Ayat as an argument for the existence of the Creator, and it is a most worthy method of argument. Indeed, whoever ponders over the things that exist, the higher and lower creatures, their various shapes, colors, behavior, benefits and ecological roles, then he will realize the ability, wisdom, knowledge, perfection and majesty of their Creator.

Once a bedouin was asked about the evidence to Allah's existence, he responded,

"All praise is due to Allah! The camel's dung testifies to the existence of the camel, and the track testifies to the fact that someone was walking. A sky that holds the giant stars, a land that has fairways and a sea that has waves, does not all of this testify that the Most Kind, Most Knowledgeable exists"

Hence, whoever gazes at the sky in its immensity, its expanse, and the various kinds of planets in it, some of which appear stationary in the sky - whoever gazes at the seas that surround the land from all sides, and the mountains that were placed on the earth to stabilize it, so that whoever lives on land, whatever their shape and color, are able to live and thrive - whoever reads Allah's statement, (And among the mountains are streaks white and red, of varying colours and (others) very black. And likewise, men and Ad-Dawabb (moving (living) creatures, beasts) and cattle are of various colours. It is only those who have knowledge among His servants that fear Allah) (35: 27-28).

Whoever thinks about the running rivers that travel from area to area bringing benefit, whoever ponders over what Allah has created on earth; various animals and plants of different tastes, scents, shapes and colors that are a result of unity between land and water, whoever thinks about all of this then he will realize that these facts testify to the existence of the Creator, His perfect ability, wisdom, mercy, kindness, generosity and His overall compassion for His creation.

There is no deity worthy of worship except Allah, nor is there a Lord besides Him, upon Him we rely and to Him we turn in repentance.

There are numerous Ayat in the Qur'an on this subject.

Surah: 2 Ayah: 23 & Ayah: 24

﴿ وَإِن كُنتُمْ فِى رَيْبٍ مِّمَّا نَزَّلْنَا عَلَىٰ عَبْدِنَا فَأْتُوا۟ بِسُورَةٍ مِّن مِّثْلِهِۦ وَٱدْعُوا۟ شُهَدَآءَكُم مِّن دُونِ ٱللَّهِ إِنْ كُنتُمْ صَٰدِقِينَ ﴿٢٣﴾ ﴾

23. And if you (Arab pagans, Jews, and Christians) are in doubt concerning that which We have sent down (i.e. the Qur'ân) to Our slave (Muhammad (peace be upon him) then produce a Sûrah (Chapter) of the like thereof and call your witnesses (supporters and helpers) besides Allâh, if you are truthful.

﴿ فَإِن لَّمْ تَفْعَلُواْ وَلَن تَفْعَلُواْ فَٱتَّقُواْ ٱلنَّارَ ٱلَّتِى وَقُودُهَا ٱلنَّاسُ وَٱلْحِجَارَةُ أُعِدَّتْ لِلْكَٰفِرِينَ ﴿٢٤﴾ ﴾

24. But if you do it not, and you can never do it, then fear the Fire (Hell) whose fuel is men and stones, prepared for the disbelievers.

Transliteration

23. Wa-in kuntum fee raybin mimma nazzalna AAala AAabdina fa/too bisooratin min mithlihi waodAAoo shuhadaakum min dooni Allahi in kuntum sadiqeena
24. Fa-in lam tafAAaloo walan tafAAaloo faittaqoo alnnara allatee waqooduha alnnasu waalhijaratu oAAiddat lilkafireena

Tafsir Ibn Kathir

The Message of Messenger of Allah is True

Allah begins to prove the truth of prophethood after He stated that there is no deity worthy of worship except Him. Allah said to the disbelievers,

(And if you (Arab pagans, Jews, and Christians) are in doubt concerning that which We have sent down (i.e. the Qur'an) to Our servant) meaning, Muhammad ,

(then produce a Surah (chapter)) meaning, similar to what he brought to you. Hence, if you claim that what he was sent with did not come from Allah, then produce something similar to what he has brought to you, using the help of anyone you wish instead of Allah. However, you will not be able to succeed in this quest. Ibn 'Abbas said that,

(your witnesses) means "Aids." Also, As-Suddi reported that Abu Malik said the Ayah means, "Your partners, meaning, some other people to help you in that. Meaning then go and seek the help of your deities to support and aid you." Also, Mujahid said that,

(and call your witnesses) means, "People, meaning, wise and eloquent men who will provide the testimony that you seek."

The Challenge

Allah challenged the disbelievers in various parts of the Qur'an. For instance, Allah said in Surat Al-Qasas (28:49), (Say (to them, O Muhammad): "Then bring a Book from Allah, which is a better guide than these two (the Tawrah (Torah) and the Qur'an), that I may follow it, if you are truthful"). Also, Allah said in Surat Al-Isra' (17:88),

(Say: "If mankind and the Jinn were together to produce the like of this Qur'an, they could not produce the like thereof, even if they helped one another.") Allah said in Surat Hud (11:13),

(Or they say, "He (Prophet Muhammad) forged it (the Qur'an)." Say: "Bring you then ten forged Surahs (chapters) like it, and call whomsoever you can, other than Allah (to your help), if you speak the truth!"), and in Surat Yunus (10:37-38),

(And this Qur'an is not such as could ever be produced by other than Allah (Lord of the heavens and the earth), but it is a confirmation of (the revelation) which was before it (i.e. the Tawrah, and the Injil), and a full explanation of the Book (i.e. Laws decreed for mankind) — wherein there is no doubt — from the Lord of all that exists.) (Or do they say: "He (Muhammad) has forged it" Say: "Bring then a Surah (chapter) like it, and call upon whomsoever you can besides Allah, if you are truthful!"). All of these Ayat were revealed in Makkah.

Allah also challenged the disbelievers in the Ayat that were revealed in Al-Madinah. In this Ayah, Allah said,

(And if you (Arab pagans, Jews, and Christians) are in Rayb) meaning, doubt.

(Concerning that which We have sent down (i.e. the Qur'an) to Our servant) meaning, Muhammad ,

(then produce a Surah (chapter) the like thereof) meaning, similar to the Qur'an. This is the Tafsir of Mujahid, Qatadah, Ibn Jarir At-Tabari, Az-Zamakhshari and Ar-Razi. Ar-Razi said that this is the Tafsir of 'Umar, Ibn Mas'ud, Ibn 'Abbas, Al-Hasan Al-Basri and the majority of the scholars. And he gave preference to this view and mentioned the fact that Allah has challenged the disbelievers as individuals and as groups, whether literate or illiterate, thus making the challenge truly complete. This type of challenge is more daring than simply challenging the disbelievers who might not be literate or knowledgeable.

This is why Allah said,

(Bring you then ten forged Surahs (chapters) like it) (11:13), and, (They could not produce the like thereof) (17:88).

Therefore, this is a general challenge to the Arab disbelievers, the most eloquent among all nations. Allah challenged the Arab disbelievers both in Makkah and Al-Madinah several times, especially since they had tremendous hatred and enmity for the Prophet and his religion. Yet, they were unable to succeed in answering the challenge, and this is why Allah said,

(But if you do it not, and you can never do it), indicating that they will never be able to answer the challenge. This is another miracle, in that, Allah clearly stated without doubt that the Qur'an will never be opposed or challenged by anything similar to it, for eternity. This is a true statement that has not been changed until the present and shall never change. How can anyone be able to produce something like the Qur'an, when the Qur'an is the Word of Allah Who created everything How can the words of the created ever be similar to the Words of the Creator

Examples of the Miracle of the Qur'an

Whoever reads through the Qur'an will realize that it contains various levels of superiority through both the apparent and hidden meanings that it mentions. Allah said,

(Alif Lam Ra. (This is) a Book, the verses whereof are perfect (in every sphere of knowledge, etc.), and then explained in detail from One (Allah), Who is Wise and well-acquainted (with all things)) (11:1)

So the expressions in the Qur'an are perfect and its meanings are explained. Further, every word and meaning in the Qur'an is eloquent and cannot be surpassed. The Qur'an also mentioned the stories of the people of the past; and these accounts and stories occurred exactly as the Qur'an stated. Also, the Qur'an commanded every type of righteousness and forbade every type of evil, just as Allah stated,

(And the Word of your Lord has been fulfilled in truth and in justice) (6:115). meaning, true in the stories it narrates and just in its Laws. The Qur'an is true, just and full of guidance. It does not contain exaggerations, lies or falsehood, unlike Arabic and other types of poems that contained lies. These poems, conform with the popular statement, "The most eloquent speech is the one that contains the most lies!" Sometimes, one would find a long poem that mainly contains descriptions of women, horses or alcohol. Or, the poem might contain praise or the description of a certain person, horse, camel, war, incident, fear, lion, or other types of items and objects. Such praise or descriptions do not bring any benefit, except shed light on the poet's ability to clearly and eloquently describe such items. Yet, one will only be able to find one or two sentences in many long poems that elaborate on the main theme of the poem, while the rest of the poem contains insignificant descriptions and repetitions.

As for the Qur'an, it is entirely eloquent in the most perfect manner, as those who have knowledge in such matters and understand Arabic methods of speech and expressions concur. When one reads through the stories in the Qur'an, he will find them fruitful, whether they were in extended or short forms, repeated or not. The more these stories are repeated, the more fruitful and beautiful they become. The Qur'an does not become old when one repeats reciting it, nor do the scholars ever get bored with it. When the Qur'an mentions the subject of warning and promises, it presents truths that would make solid, firm mountains shake, so what about the comprehending, understanding hearts When the Qur'an promises, it opens the hearts and the ears, making them eager to attain the abode of peace - Paradise - and to be the neighbors of the Throne of the Most Beneficent. For instance, on the subject of promises and encouragement, the Qur'an said,

(No person knows what is kept hidden for them of joy as a reward for what they used to do) (32:17), and,

((There will be) therein all that inner selves could desire, and all that eyes could delight in and you will abide therein forever) (43:71).

On the subject of warning and discouragement;

(Do you then feel secure that He will not cause a side of the land to swallow you up) (17:68), and,

(Do you feel secure that He, Who is over the heaven (Allah), will not cause the earth to sink with you, and then it should quake Or do you feel secure that He, Who is over the heaven (Allah), will not send against you a violent whirlwind Then you shall know how (terrible) has been My warning) (67:16-17).

On the subject of threats, the Qur'an said,

(So We punished each (of them) for his sins) (29:40). Also, on the subject of soft advice, the Qur'an said,

(Tell Me, (even) if We do let them enjoy for years. And afterwards comes to them that (punishment) which they had been promised. All that with which they used to enjoy shall not avail them) (26:205-207).

There are many other examples of the eloquence, beauty, and benefits of the Qur'an.

When the Qur'an is discussing Laws, commandments and prohibitions, it commands every type of righteous, good, pleasing and beneficial act. It also forbids every type of evil, disliked and amoral act. Ibn Mas'ud and other scholars of the Salaf said, "When you hear what Allah said in the Qur'an, such as,

(O you who believe!), then listen with full attention, for it either contains a type of righteousness that Allah is enjoining, or an evil that He is forbidding." For instance, Allah said,

(He (Muhammad) commands them for Al-Ma'ruf (i.e. Islamic Monotheism and all that Islam has ordained); and forbids them from Al-Munkar (i.e. disbelief, polytheism of all kinds, and all that Islam has forbidden); he allows them as lawful At-Tayyibat(i.e. all good and lawful things), and prohibits them as unlawful Al-Khaba'ith (i.e. all evil and unlawful things), he releases them from their heavy burdens and from the fetters (bindings) that were upon them) (7:157).

When the Ayat mention Resurrection and the horrors that will occur on that Day, and Paradise and the Fire and the joys and safe refuge that Allah prepared for His loyal friends, or torment and Hell for His enemies, these Ayat contain glad tidings or warnings. The Ayat then call to perform good deeds and avoid evil deeds, making the life of this world less favorable and the Hereafter more favorable. They also establish the correct methods and guide to Allah's straight path and just legislation, all the while ridding the hearts of the evil of the cursed devil.

The Qur'an is the Greatest Miracle given to the Prophet

The Two Sahihs record that Abu Hurayrah said that the Prophet said,

«مَا مِنْ نَبِيٍّ مِنَ الْأَنْبِيَاءِ إِلَّا قَدْ أُعْطِيَ مِنَ الْآيَاتِ مَا آمَنَ عَلَى مِثْلِهِ الْبَشَرُ، وَإِنَّمَا كَانَ الَّذِي أُوتِيتُهُ وَحْيًا أَوْحَاهُ اللهُ إِلَيَّ فَأَرْجُو أَنْ أَكُونَ أَكْثَرَهُمْ تَابِعًا يَوْمَ الْقِيَامَةِ»

(Every Prophet was given a miracle, the type of which brings mankind to faith. What I was given is a revelation that Allah sent down to me. Yet, I hope that I will have the most following on the Day of Resurrection.)

This is the wording narrated by Muslim. The Prophet stated that among the Prophets he was given a revelation, meaning, he was especially entrusted with the miraculous Qur'an that challenged mankind to produce something similar to it. As for the rest of the divinely revealed Books, they were not miraculous according to many scholars. Allah knows best. The Prophet was also aided with innumerable signs and indications that testify to the truth of his prophethood and what he was sent with, all thanks and praise is due to Allah.

Meaning of 'Stones'

Allah said,

(Then fear the Fire (Hell) whose fuel is men and stones, prepared for the disbelievers) (2:24).

'Fuel' is wood, or similar substances, used to start and feed a fire. Similarly, Allah said,

(And as for the Qasitun (disbelievers who deviated from the right path), they shall be firewood for Hell) (72:15), and,

(Certainly you (disbelievers) and that which you are worshipping now besides Allah, are (but) fuel for Hell! (Surely) you enter it. Had these (idols) been alihah (gods), they would not have entered there (Hell), and all of them will abide therein) (21:98-99).

The stones mentioned here are the giant, rotten, black, sulfuric stones that become the hottest when heated, may Allah save us from this evil end. It was also reported that the stones mentioned here are the idols and rivals that were worshipped instead of Allah, just as Allah said,

(Certainly you (disbelievers) and that which you are worshipping now besides Allah, are (but) fuel for Hell!) (21:28).

Allah's statement,

(prepared for the disbelievers)

It appears most obvious that it refers to the Fire that is fueled by men and stones, and it also may refer to the stones themselves. There is no contradiction between these two views, because they are dependent upon each other. 'Prepared' means, it is 'kept' and will surely touch those who disbelieve in Allah and His Messenger . Ibn Ishaq narrated that Muhammad said that 'Ikrimah or Sa'id bin Jubayr said that Ibn 'Abbas said,

(prepared for the disbelievers),

"For those who embrace the disbelief that you (disbelievers) have embraced."

Jahannam (Hellfire) exists now

Many of the Imams of the Sunnah used this Ayah to prove that the Fire exists now. This is because Allah said,

(prepared) meaning, prepared and kept. There are many Hadiths on this subject. For instance, the Prophet said,

«تَحَاجَّتِ الْجَنَّةُ وَالنَّارِ»

(Paradise and the Fire had an argument..)

Also, the Prophet said,

«اسْتَأْذَنَتِ النَّارُ رَبَّهَا فَقَالَتْ: رَبِّ أَكَلَ بَعْضِي بَعْضًا فَأَذِنَ لَهَا بِنَفَسَيْنِ: نَفَسٍ فِي الشِّتَاءِ وَنَفَسٍ فِي الصَّيْفِ»

(The Fire sought the permission of her Lord. She said, 'O my Lord! Some parts of me consumed the other parts.' And Allah allowed her two periods to exhale, one in winter and one in summer.)

Also, there is a Hadith recorded from Ibn Mas'ud that the Companions heard the sound of a falling object. When they asked about it, the Messenger of Allah said,

«هَذَا حَجَرٌ أُلْقِيَ بِهِ مِنْ شَفِيرِ جَهَنَّمَ مُنْذُ سَبْعِينَ سَنَةً، الْآنَ وَصَلَ إِلَى قَعْرِهَا»

(This is a stone that was thrown from the top of Jahannam seventy years ago, but only now reached its bottom.) This Hadith is in Sahih Muslim.

There are many Hadiths that are Mutawatir (narrated by many different chains of narrations) on this subject, such as the Hadiths about the eclipse prayer, the night of Isra' etc.

Allah's statements, (Then produce a Surah (chapter) of the like thereof) (2:23), and,

(A Surah (chapter) like it) (10:38) this includes the short and long Surahs of the Qur'an. Therefore, the challenge to creation stands with regards to both the long and short Surahs, and there is no disagreement that I know of on this fact between the scholars of old and new. Before he became Muslim, 'Amr bin Al-'As met Musaylimah the Liar who asked him, "What has recently been revealed to your fellow (meaning Muhammad) in Makkah" 'Amr said, "A short, yet eloquent Surah." He asked, "What is it" He said, (By Al-'Asr (the time). Verily, man is in loss,) (103:1-2)

Musaylimah thought for a while and said, "A similar Surah was also revealed to me." 'Amr asked, "What is it" He said, "O Wabr, O Wabr (i.e. a wild cat), you are but two ears and a chest, and the rest of you is unworthy and thin." 'Amr said, "By Allah! You know that I know that you are lying."

Surah: 2 Ayah: 25

﴿ وَبَشِّرِ ٱلَّذِينَ ءَامَنُواْ وَعَمِلُواْ ٱلصَّٰلِحَٰتِ أَنَّ لَهُمْ جَنَّٰتٍ تَجْرِى مِن تَحْتِهَا ٱلْأَنْهَٰرُ ۖ كُلَّمَا رُزِقُواْ مِنْهَا مِن ثَمَرَةٍ رِّزْقًا ۙ قَالُواْ هَٰذَا ٱلَّذِى رُزِقْنَا مِن قَبْلُ ۖ وَأُتُواْ بِهِ مُتَشَٰبِهًا ۖ وَلَهُمْ فِيهَآ أَزْوَٰجٌ مُّطَهَّرَةٌ ۖ وَهُمْ فِيهَا خَٰلِدُونَ ﴿٢٥﴾ ﴾

25. And give glad tidings to those who believe and do righteous good deeds, that for them will be Gardens under which rivers flow (Paradise). Every time they will be provided with a fruit therefrom, they will say: "This is what we were provided with before," and they will be given things in

resemblance (i.e. in the same form but different in taste) and they shall have therein Azwâjun Mutahharatun (purified mates or wives) and they will abide therein forever.

Transliteration

25. Wabashshiri allatheena amanoo waAAamiloo alssalihati anna lahum jannatin tajree min tahtiha alanharu kullama ruziqoo minha min thamaratin rizqan qaloo hatha allathee ruziqna min qablu waotoo bihi mutashabihan walahum feeha azwajun mutahharatun wahum feeha khalidoona

Translation

25. And give glad tidings to those who believe and do righteous good deeds, that for them will be Gardens under which rivers flow (Paradise). Every time they will be provided with a fruit therefrom, they will say: "This is what we were provided with before," and they will be given things in resemblance (i.e. in the same form but different in taste) and they shall have therein *Azwâjun Mutahharatun* (purified mates or wives), (having no menses, stools, urine, etc.) and they will abide therein forever.

Tafsir Ibn Kathir

Rewards of Righteous Believers

After mentioning the torment that Allah has prepared for His miserable enemies who disbelieve in Him and in His Messengers, He mentions the condition of His happy, loyal friends who believe in Him and in His Messengers, adhere to the faith and perform the good deeds. This is the reason why the Qur'an was called Mathani, based on the correct opinion of the scholars. We will elaborate upon this subject later. Mathani means to mention faith and then disbelief, or vice versa. Or, Allah mentions the miserable and then the happy, or vice versa. As for mentioning similar things, it is called Tashabbuh, as we will come to know, Allah willing. Allah said,

(And give glad tidings to those who believe and do righteous good deeds, that for them will be Gardens under which rivers flow (Paradise)). Consequently, Allah stated that Paradise has rivers that run beneath it, meaning, underneath its trees and rooms. From Hadiths it is learned that the rivers of Paradise do not run in valleys, and that the banks of Al-Kawthar (the Prophet's lake in Paradise) are made of domes of hollow pearls, the sand of Paradise is made of scented musk while its stones are made from pearls and jewels. We ask Allah to grant Paradise to us, for verily, He is the Most Beneficent, Most Gracious.

Ibn Abi Hatim reported that Abu Hurayrah said that the Messenger of Allah said,

«أَنْهَارُ الْجَنَّةِ تَفَجَّرُ تَحْتَ تِلَالٍ أَوْ مِنْ تَحْتِ جِبَالِ الْمِسْكِ»

(The rivers of Paradise spring from beneath hills, or mountains of musk.)

He also reported from Masruq that 'Abdullah said, "The rivers of Paradise spring from beneath mountains of musk."

The similarity between the Fruits of Paradise

Allah said next,

(Every time they will be provided with a fruit therefrom, they will say: "This is what we were provided with before").

Ibn Abi Hatim reported that Yahya bin Abi Kathir said, "The grass of Paradise is made of saffron, its hills from musk and the boys of everlasting youth will serve the believers with fruits which they will eat. They will then be brought similar fruits, and the people of Paradise will comment, `This is the same as what you have just brought us.' The boys will say to them, `Eat, for the color is the same, but the taste is different. Hence Allah's statement,

(and they will be given things in resemblance). Abu Ja'far Ar-Razi narrated that Ar-Rabi' bin Anas said that Abu Al-'Aliyah said that, (and they will be given things in resemblance) means, "They look like each other, but the taste is different." Also, `Ikrimah said, (and they will be given things in resemblance) "They are similar to the fruits of this life, but the fruits of Paradise taste better. '' Sufyan Ath-Thawri reported from Al-A`mash, from Abu Thubyan, that Ibn `Abbas said, "Nothing in Paradise resembles anything in the life of this world, except in name." In another narration, Ibn `Abbas said, "Only the names are similar between what is in this life and what is in Paradise."

The Wives of the People of Paradise are Pure

Allah said, (and they shall have therein Azwajun Mutahharatun). Ibn Abi Talhah reported that Ibn 'Abbas said, "Purified from filth and impurity." Also, Mujahid said, "From menstruation, relieving the call of nature, urine, spit, semen and pregnancies." Also, Qatadah said, "Purified from impurity and sin." In another narration, he said, "From menstruation and pregnancies." Further, 'Ata', Al-Hasan, Ad-Dahhak, Abu Salih, 'Atiyah and As-Suddi were reported to have said similarly.

Allah's statement, (and they will abide therein forever) meaning ultimate happiness, for the believers will enjoy everlasting delight, safe from death and disruption of their bliss, for it never ends or ceases. We ask Allah to make us among these believers, for He is the Most Generous, Most Kind and Most merciful.

Surah: 2 Ayah: 26 & Ayah: 27

﴿ ۞ إِنَّ ٱللَّهَ لَا يَسْتَحْىِۦٓ أَن يَضْرِبَ مَثَلًا مَّا بَعُوضَةً فَمَا فَوْقَهَا ۚ فَأَمَّا ٱلَّذِينَ ءَامَنُوا۟ فَيَعْلَمُونَ أَنَّهُ ٱلْحَقُّ مِن رَّبِّهِمْ ۖ وَأَمَّا ٱلَّذِينَ كَفَرُوا۟ فَيَقُولُونَ مَاذَآ أَرَادَ ٱللَّهُ بِهَـٰذَا مَثَلًا ۘ يُضِلُّ بِهِۦ كَثِيرًا وَيَهْدِى بِهِۦ كَثِيرًا ۚ وَمَا يُضِلُّ بِهِۦٓ إِلَّا ٱلْفَـٰسِقِينَ ﴿٢٦﴾ ﴾

26. Verily, Allâh is not ashamed to set forth a parable even of a mosquito or so much more when it is bigger (or less when it is smaller) than it. And as for those who believe, they know that it is the Truth from their Lord, but as for those who disbelieve, they say: "What did Allâh intend by this parable?" By it He misleads many, and many He guides thereby. And He misleads thereby only those who are Al-Fâsiqûn (the rebellious, disobedient to Allâh).

﴿ ٱلَّذِينَ يَنقُضُونَ عَهْدَ ٱللَّهِ مِنۢ بَعْدِ مِيثَـٰقِهِۦ وَيَقْطَعُونَ مَآ أَمَرَ ٱللَّهُ بِهِۦٓ أَن يُوصَلَ وَيُفْسِدُونَ فِى ٱلْأَرْضِ ۚ أُو۟لَـٰٓئِكَ هُمُ ٱلْخَـٰسِرُونَ ﴿٢٧﴾ ﴾

27. Those who break Allah's Covenant after ratifying it, and sever what Allâh has ordered to be joined (as regards Allâh's religion of Islamic Monotheism, and to practice its laws on the earth and also as regards keeping good relations with kith and kin), and do mischief on earth, it is they who are the losers.

Transliteration

26. Inna Allaha la yastahyee an yadriba mathalan ma baAAoodatan fama fawqaha faamma allatheena amanoo fayaAAlamoona annahu alhaqqu min rabbihim waamma allatheena kafaroo fayaqooloona matha arada Allahu bihatha mathalan yudillu bihi katheeran wayahdee bihi katheeran wama yudillu bihi illa alfasiqeena 27. Allatheena yanqudoona AAahda Allahi min baAAdi meethaqihi wayaqtaAAoona ma amara Allahu bihi an yoosala wayufsidoona fee al-ardi ola-ika humu alkhasiroona

Tafsir Ibn Kathir

In his Tafsir, As-Suddi reported that Ibn 'Abbas, Ibn Mas'ud, and some Companions said; "When Allah gave these two examples of the hypocrites" meaning Allah's statements,

(Their likeness is as the likeness of one who kindled a fire), and,

(Or like a rainstorm from the sky), "The hypocrites said, `Allah's far more exalted than for Him to make such examples.' So Allah revealed these Ayat (2:26-27) up to:

(Who are the losers)". Sa'id said that Qatadah said, "Allah does not shy away from the truth when He mentions a matter as a parable, whether this matter is significant or not. When Allah mentioned the flies and the spider in His Book, the people of misguidance said, `Why did Allah mention these things.' So Allah revealed;

(Verily, Allah is not ashamed to set forth a parable even of a mosquito or so much more when it is bigger (or less when it is smaller) than it)."

A Parable about the Life of This World

Abu Ja'far Ar-Razi reported that Ar-Rabi` bin Anas commented on this Ayah (2:26); "This is an example that Allah has given for the life of this world. The mosquito lives as long as it needs food, but when it gets fat, it dies. This is also the example of people whom Allah mentioned in the Qur'an: when they acquire (and collect the delights of) the life of this world, Allah then takes them away." Afterwards, he recited,

(So, when they forgot (the warning) with which they had been reminded, We opened for them the gates of every (pleasant) thing) (6:44)

In this Ayah (2:26) Allah stated that He does not shy away or hesitate in making an example or parable of anything, whether the example involves a significant or an insignificant matter.

Allah's statement,

(Or so much more when it is bigger than it) Fama fawqaha means, something bigger than the mosquito, which is one of the most insignificant and tiniest of creatures. Muslim narrated that Aishah said that the Messenger of Allah said,

«مَا مِنْ مُسْلِمٍ يُشَاكُ شَوْكَةً فَمَا فَوْقَهَا إِلَّا كُتِبَتْ لَهُ بِهَا دَرَجَةٌ، وَمُحِيَتْ عَنْهُ بِهَا خَطِيئَةٌ»

(No Muslim is harmed by a thorn, Fama fawqaha (or something larger), but a good deed will be written for him and an evil deed will be erased from his record.)

So Allah has informed us that there is no matter that is too small that is exempt from being used as an example, even if it was as insignificant as a mosquito or a spider. Allah said,

(O mankind! A similitude has been coined, so listen to it (carefully): Verily, those on whom you call besides Allah, cannot create (even) a fly, even though they combine together for the purpose. And if the fly snatches away a thing from them, they will have no power to release it from the fly. So weak are (both) the seeker and the sought.) (22:73),

(The likeness of those who take (false deities as) Awliya' (protectors, helpers) other than Allah is the likeness of a spider who builds (for itself) a house; but verily, the frailest (weakest) of houses is the spider's house @— if they but knew.) (29:41), and,

(See you not how Allah sets forth a parable A goodly word as a goodly tree, whose root is firmly fixed, and its branches (reach) to the sky (i.e. very high). Giving its fruit at all times, by the leave of its Lord, and Allah sets forth parables for mankind in order that they may remember. And the parable of an evil word is that of an evil tree uprooted from the surface of earth, having no stability. Allah will keep firm those who believe, with the word that stands firm in life of this world (i.e. they will keep on worshipping Allah alone and none else), and in the Hereafter. And Allah will cause the Zalimin (polytheists and wrongdoers) to go astray those and Allah does what He wills.) (14:24-27).

Allah said,

(Allah puts forward the example of (two men @— a believer and a disbeliever); a servant under the possession of another, he has no power of any sort) (16:75). He then said,

(And Allah puts forward (another) example of two men, one of them dumb, who has no power over anything, and he is a burden on his master; whichever way he directs him, he brings no good. Is such a man equal to one who commands justice) (16:76). Also, Allah said,

(He sets forth for you a parable from your own selves: Do you have partners among those whom your right hands possess (i.e. your servants) to share as equals in the wealth we have bestowed on you) (30:28).

Mujahid commented on Allah's statement,

(Verily, Allah is not ashamed to set forth a parable even of a mosquito or so much more when it is bigger than it.) "The believers believe in these parables, whether they involve large matters or small, because they know that they are the truth from their Lord, and Allah guides the believers by these parables."

In his Tafsir, As-Suddi reported that Ibn 'Abbas, Ibn Mas'ud and other people among the Companions said,

(By it He misleads many), "Meaning the hypocrites. Allah guides the believers with these parables, and the straying of the hypocrites increases when they reject the parables that Allah mentioned for them which they know are true. This is how Allah misleads them."

(And He guides thereby) meaning, with the parables,

(many) from among the people of faith and conviction. Allah adds guidance to their guidance, and faith to their faith, because they firmly believe in what they know to be true, that is, the parables that Allah has mentioned. This is guidance that Allah grants them;

(And He misleads thereby only the Fasiqin (the rebellious, disobedient to Allah)), meaning, the hypocrites. The Arabs say that the date has Fasaqat, when it comes out of its skin, and they call the mouse a Fuwaysiqah, because it leaves its den to cause mischief. The Two Sahihs recorded 'A'ishah saying that the Messenger of Allah said,

«خَمْسٌ فَوَاسِقُ يُقْتَلْنَ فِي الْحِلِّ وَالْحَرَمِ: الْغُرَابُ وَالْحِدَأَةُ وَالْعَقْرَبُ وَالْفَأْرَةُ وَالْكَلْبُ الْعَقُورِ»

(Five animals are Fawasiq, and they must be killed during Ihram and otherwise: the crow, the kite, the scorpion, the mouse and the rabid dog.) eFasiq, includes the disbeliever and the disobedient. However, the Fisq of the disbeliever is worse, and this is the type of Fasiq that the Ayah is describing here, because Allah described them as,

(Those who break Allah's covenant after ratifying it, and sever what Allah has ordered to be joined and do mischief on earth, it is they who are the losers.)

These are the characteristics of the disbelievers and they contradict the qualities of the believers. Similarly, Allah said in Surat Ar-Ra'd,

(Shall he then, who knows that what has been revealed unto you (O Muhammad) from your Lord is the truth, be like him who is blind But it is only the men of understanding that pay heed. Those who fulfill the covenant of Allah and break not the Mithaq (bond, treaty, covenant). And those who join that which Allah has commanded to be joined (i.e. they are good to their relatives and do not sever the bond of kinship), and fear their Lord, and dread the terrible reckoning.) (13:19-21)) until,

(And those who break the covenant of Allah, after its ratification, and sever that which Allah has commanded to be joined (i.e. they sever the bond of kinship and are not good to their relatives), and work mischief in the land, on them is the curse (i.e. they will be far away from Allah's mercy), and for them is the unhappy (evil) home (i.e. Hell).) (13:25)

The covenant that these deviant people broke is Allah's covenant with His creation, that is, to obey Him and avoid the sins that He prohibited. This covenant was reiterated in Allah's Books and by the words of His Messengers. Ignoring this covenant constitutes breaking it. It was said that the Ayah (2:27) is about the disbelievers and the hypocrites among the People of the Book. In this case, the covenant that they broke is the pledge that Allah took from them in the Tawrah to follow Muhammad when he is sent as a Prophet, and to believe in him, and in what he was sent with. Breaking Allah's covenant in this case occured when the People of the Book rejected the Prophet after they knew the truth about him, and they hid this truth from people, even though they swore to Allah that they would do otherwise. Allah informed us that they threw the covenant behind their backs and sold it for a miserable price.

It was also reported that the Ayah (2:27) refers to all disbelievers, idol worshippers and hypocrites. Allah took their pledge to believe in His Oneness, showing them the signs that testify to His Lordship. He also took a covenant from them to obey His commands and refrain from His prohibitions, knowing that His Messengers would bring proofs and miracles that none among the creation could ever produce. These miracles testified to the truth of Allah's Messengers. The covenant was broken when the disbelievers denied what was proven to them to be authentic and rejected Allah's Prophets and Books, although they knew that they were the truth. This Tafsir was reported from Muqatil bin Hayyan, and it is very good. It is also the view that Az-Zamakhshari held.

Allah's statement next,

(And sever what Allah has ordered to be joined) is in reference to keeping the relations with the relatives, as Qatadah asserted. This Ayah is similar to Allah's statement, (Would you then, if you were given the authority, do mischief in the land, and sever your ties of kinship) (47:22)

Ibn Jarir At-Tabari preferred this opinion. However, it has been said that the meaning of the Ayah (2:27) here is more general. Hence, everything that Allah has commanded to nurture, and the people severed, is included in its meaning.

The Meaning of 'Loss'

Muqatil bin Hayyan commented on Allah's statement,

(It is they who are the losers) "In the Hereafter." Similarly, Allah said,

(On them is the curse (i.e. they will be far away from Allah's mercy), and for them is the unhappy (evil) home (i.e. Hell)) (13:25).

Also, Ad-Dahhak said that Ibn 'Abbas said,

"Every characteristic that Allah describes those other than the people of Islam - such as being losers - then it refers to disbelief. However, when they are attributed to the people of Islam, then these terms refer to sin."

Ibn Jarir commented on Allah's statement,

(It is they who are the losers,) "`

Losers is plural for loser, this word refers to whoever decreased his own share of Allah's mercy by disobeying Him, just as the merchant loses in his trade by sustaining capital loss. Such is the case with the hypocrite and the disbeliever who lose their share of the mercy that Allah has in store for His servants on the Day of Resurrection. And that is when the disbeliever and the hypocrite most desperately need Allah's mercy."

Surah: 2 Ayah: 28

﴿ كَيْفَ تَكْفُرُونَ بِٱللَّهِ وَكُنتُمْ أَمْوَٰتًا فَأَحْيَـٰكُمْ ثُمَّ يُمِيتُكُمْ ثُمَّ يُحْيِيكُمْ ثُمَّ إِلَيْهِ تُرْجَعُونَ ﴾ ﴿٢٨﴾

28. How can you disbelieve in Allâh? Seeing that you were dead and He gave you life. Then He will give you death, then again will bring you to life (on the Day of Resurrection) and then unto Him you will return (See V.40:11)

Transliteration

28. Kayfa takfuroona biAllahi wakuntum amwatan faahyakum thumma yumeetukum thumma yuhyeekum thumma ilayhi turjaAAoona

Tafsir Ibn Kathir

Allah testifies to the fact that He exists and that He is the Creator and the Sustainer Who has full authority over His servants, (How can you disbelieve in Allah)

How can anyone deny Allah's existence or worship others with Him while;

(You were dead and He gave you life) meaning, He brought them from the state of non-existence to life. Similarly, Allah said, (Were they created by nothing Or were they themselves the creators Or did they create the heavens and the earth Nay, but they have no firm belief) (52:35-36) and,

(Has there not been over man a period of time, when he was not a thing worth mentioning) (76:1).

There are many other Ayat on this subject. Ibn Jarir reported from 'Ata' that Ibn 'Abbas said that, (Seeing that you were dead and He gave you life) means, "You did not exist beforehand. You were nothing until Allah created you; He will bring death to you and then bring you back to life during Resurrection."

Ibn `Abbas then said, "This is similar to Allah's statement; (They will say: "Our Lord! You have made us to die twice and You have given us life twice.") (40:11)"

Surah: 2 Ayah: 29

﴿ هُوَ ٱلَّذِى خَلَقَ لَكُم مَّا فِى ٱلْأَرْضِ جَمِيعًا ثُمَّ ٱسْتَوَىٰٓ إِلَى ٱلسَّمَآءِ فَسَوَّىٰهُنَّ سَبْعَ سَمَـٰوَٰتٍ وَهُوَ بِكُلِّ شَىْءٍ عَلِيمٌ ﴾

29. He it is Who created for you all that is on earth. Then He rose over (Istawâ) towards the heaven and made them seven heavens and He is the All-Knower of everything.

Transliteration

29. Huwa allathee khalaqa lakum ma fee al-ardi jameeAAan thumma istawa ila alssama-i fasawwahunna sabAAa samawatin wahuwa bikulli shay-in AAaleemun

Tafsir Ibn Kathir

Evidence of Allah's Ability

After Allah mentioned the proofs of His creating them, and what they can witness in themselves as proof of that, He mentioned another proof that they can witness, that is, the creation of the heavens and earth. Allah said,

(He it is Who created for you all that is on earth. Then He Istawa ila the heaven and made them seven heavens) meaning, He turned towards the heaven,

(And made them) meaning, that He made the heaven, seven heavens. Allah said,

(And made them seven heavens and He is the Knower of everything) meaning, His knowledge encompasses all His creation, just as He said in another Ayah,

(Should not He Who has created know) (67:14).

The Beginning of the Creation

This Ayah (2:29) is explained in detail in Surat As-Sajdah where Allah said;

(Say (O Muhammad): "Do you verily disbelieve in Him Who created the earth in two Days And you set up rivals (in worship) with Him That is the Lord of all that exists. He placed therein (i.e. the earth) firm mountains from above it, and He blessed it, and measured therein its sustenance (for its dwellers) in four Days equal (i.e. all these four `days' were equal in the length of time) for all those who ask (about its creation). Then He Istawa ila the heaven when it was smoke, and said to it and to the earth: "Come both of you willingly or unwillingly." They both said: "We come willingly." Then He finished them (as) seven heavens in two Days and He made in each heaven its affair. And We adorned the nearest (lowest) heaven with lamps (stars) to be an adornment as well as to guard (from the devils by using them as missiles against the devils). Such is the decree of the Almighty, the Knower) (41:9-12).

These Ayat indicate that Allah started creation by creating earth, then He made heaven into seven heavens. This is how building usually starts, with the lower floors first and then the top floors, as the scholars of Tafsir reiterated, as we will come to know, Allah willing. Allah also said,

(Are you more difficult to create or is the heaven that He constructed He raised its height, and has perfected it. Its night He covers with darkness and its forenoon He brings out (with light). And the earth, after that, He spread it out. And brought forth therefrom its water and its pasture. And the mountains He has fixed firmly. (To be) a provision and benefit for you and your cattle) (79:27-33).

It is said that "Then" in the Ayah (2:29) relates only to the order of reciting the information being given, it does not relate to the order that the events being mentioned took place, this was reported from Ibn `Abbas by `Ali bin Abi Talhah.

The Earth was created before Heaven

Mujahid commented on Allah's statement,

(He it is Who created for you all that is on earth) "Allah created the earth before heaven, and when He created the earth, smoke burst out of it. This is why Allah said,

(Then He Istawa ila (turned towards) the heaven when it was smoke.) (41:11)

(And made them seven heavens) means, one above the other, while the 'seven earths' means, one below the other."

This Ayah testifies to the fact that the earth was created before heaven, as Allah has indicated in the Ayat in Surat As-Sajdah.

Spreading the Earth out after the Heavens were created

Sahih Al-Bukhari records that when Ibn `Abbas was question about this matter, he said that the earth was created before heaven, and the earth was spread out only after the creation of the heaven. Several Tafsir scholars of old and recent times also said similarly, as we have elaborated on in the Tafsir of Surat An-Nazi`at (chapter 79). The result of that discussion is that the word Daha (translated above as "spread") is mentioned and explained in Allah's statement,

(And the earth, after that, He spread it out. And brought forth therefrom its water and its pasture. And the mountains He has fixed firmly.) (79:30-32)

Therefore, Daha means that the earth's treasures were brought to its surface after finishing the job of creating whatever will reside on earth and heaven. When the earth became Daha, the water burst out to its surface and the various types, colors, shapes and kinds of plants grew. The stars started rotating along with the planets that rotate around them. And Allah knows best.

Surah: 2 Ayah: 30

﴿ وَإِذْ قَالَ رَبُّكَ لِلْمَلَـٰئِكَةِ إِنِّى جَاعِلٌ فِى ٱلْأَرْضِ خَلِيفَةً قَالُوٓاْ أَتَجْعَلُ فِيهَا مَن يُفْسِدُ فِيهَا وَيَسْفِكُ ٱلدِّمَآءَ وَنَحْنُ نُسَبِّحُ بِحَمْدِكَ وَنُقَدِّسُ لَكَ قَالَ إِنِّىٓ أَعْلَمُ مَا لَا تَعْلَمُونَ ۝ ﴾

30. And (remember) when your Lord said to the angels: "Verily, I am going to place (mankind) generations after generations on earth." They said: "Will You place therein those who will make mischief therein and shed blood, - while we glorify You with praises and thanks (Exalted be You above all that they associate with You as partners) and sanctify You." He (Allâh) said: "I know that which you do not know."

Transliteration

30. Wa-ith qala rabbuka lilmala-ikati innee jaAAilun fee al-ardi khaleefatan qaloo atajAAalu feeha man yufsidu feeha wayasfiku alddimaa wanahnu nusabbihu bihamdika wanuqaddisu laka qala innee aAAlamu ma la taAAlamoona

Tafsir Ibn Kathir

Adam and His Children inhabited the Earth, Generation after Generation

Allah reiterated His favor on the Children of Adam when He stated that He mentioned them in the highest of heights before He created them. Allah said,

(And (remember) when your Lord said to the angels.)

This Ayah means, "O Muhammad ! Mention to your people what Allah said to the angels,

(Verily, I am going to place a Khalifah on earth).

Meaning people reproducing generation after generation, century after century, just as Allah said,

(And it is He Who has made you (Khala'if) generations coming after generations, replacing each other on the earth) (6:165),

(And makes you (Khulafa') inheritors of the earth) (27:62),

(And if it were Our will, We would have (destroyed you (mankind all, and) made angels to replace you (Yakhlufun) on the earth.) (43: 60) and,

(Then after them succeeded an (evil) generation (Khalf)) (7:169). It appears that Allah was not refering to Adam specifically as Khalifah, otherwise he would not have allowed the angels' statement,

(Will You place therein those who will make mischief therein and shed blood).

The angels meant that this type of creature usually commits the atrocities they mentioned. The angels knew of this fact, according to their understanding of human nature, for Allah stated that He would create man from clay. Or, the angels understood this fact from the word Khalifah, which also means the person who judges disputes that occur between people, forbidding them from injustice and sin, as Al-Qurtubi said.

The statement the angels uttered was not a form of disputing with Allah's, nor out of envy for the Children of Adam, as some mistakenly thought. Allah has described them as those who do not precede Him in speaking, meaning that they do not ask Allah anything without His permission. When Allah informed them that He was going to create a creation on the earth, and they had knowledge that this creation would commit mischief on it, as Qatadah mentioned, they said,

(Will You place therein those who will make mischief therein and shed blood)

This is only a question for the sake of learning about the wisdom of that, as if they said, Our Lord! What is the wisdom of creating such creatures since they will cause trouble in the earth and spill blood "If the wisdom behind this action is that You be worshipped, we praise and glorify You (meaning we pray to You) we never indulge in mischief, so why create other creatures"

Allah said to the angels in answer to their inquiry, (I know that which you do not know.) meaning, "I know that the benefit of creating this type of creature outweighs the harm that you mentioned, that which you have no knowledge of. I will create among them Prophets and send Messengers. I will also create among them truthful, martyrs, righteous believers, worshippers, the modest, the pious, the scholars who implement their knowledge, humble people and those who love Allah and follow His Messengers."

The Sahih recorded that when the angels ascend to Allah with the records of the servant's deeds, Allah asks them, while having better knowledge, "How did you leave My servants" They will say, "We came to them while they were praying and left them while they were praying." This is because the angels work in shifts with mankind, and they change shifts during the Fajr and `Asr prayers. The angels who descended will remain with us, while the angels who have remained with us ascend with our deeds. The Messenger of Allah said,

«يُرْفَعُ إِلَيْهِ عَمَلُ اللَّيْلِ قَبْلَ النَّهَارِ وَعَمَلُ النَّهَارِ قَبْلَ اللَّيْلِ»

(The deeds of the night are elevated to Allah before the morning, and the deeds of the morning before the night falls.)

Hence, the angels' statement, "We came to them while they were praying and left them while they were praying," explains Allah's statement,

(I know that which you do not know.)

It was said that the meaning of Allah's statement,

(I know that which you do not know.) is, "I have a specific wisdom in creating them, which you do not have knowledge of." It was also said that it is in answer to,

(While we glorify You with praises and thanks and sanctify You) after which Allah said,

(I know that which you do not know). Meaning, "I know that Iblis is not as you are, although he is among you." Others said,

"(Will You place therein those who will make mischief therein and shed blood, @— while we glorify you with praises and thanks and sanctify You.) is their request that they should be allowed to inhabit the earth, instead of the Children of Adam. So Allah said to them,

(I know that which you do not know) if your inhabiting the heavens is better, or worse for you." Ar-Razi as well as others said this.

Allah knows best.

The Obligation of appointing a Khalifah and some related Issues

Al-Qurtubi, as well as other scholars, said that this Ayah (2:30) proves the obligation of appointing a Khalifah to pass judgements on matters of dispute between people, to aid the oppressed against the oppressor, to implement the Islamic penal code and to forbid evil. There are many other tasks that can only be fulfilled by appointing the Imam, and what is necessary in performing an obligation, is an obligation itself. We should state here that Imamah occurs by either naming a successor, as a group among Ahl As-Sunnah scholars said occurred - by the Prophet - in the case of Abu Bakr, or hinting to a successor. Or, the current Khalifah names a certain person as Khalifah after him, as Abu Bakr did with 'Umar. Or, the Khalifah might leave the matter in the hands of the Muslim consultative council, or a group of righteous men, just as 'Umar did. Or, the people of authority could gather around a certain person to whom they give the pledge of allegiance, or they could select one among them to choose the candidate, according to the majority of the scholars.

The Khalifah must be a responsible adult Muslim male, able to perform Ijtihad (independent legal judgments), bodily able, righteous, with knowledge of warfare, politics. He also must be from the tribe of Quraysh, according to the correct view, but it is not necessary that he be from the tribe of Bani Hashim, or that he be immune from error, as the Rafidah (Shiites) falsely claim.

When the Khalifah becomes an immoral person (Fasiq), should he be impeached There is disagreement over this matter, but the correct view is that he is not to be removed, because the Messenger of Allah said,

«إِلَّا أَنْ تَرَوْا كُفْرًا بَوَاحًا عِنْدَكُمْ مِنَ اللهِ فِيهِ بُرْهَانٌ»

(Unless you witness a clear Kufr regarding which you have clear proof from Allah.)

Does the Khalifah have the right to resign from his post There is a difference on this issue. It is a fact that Al-Hasan bin 'Ali removed himself from the position of Khalifah and surrendered it to Mu'awiyah. However, this occurred because of a necessity, and Al-Hasan was praised for this action.

It is not permissible to appoint two Imams for the world or more at the same time. This is not allowed because the Messenger of Allah said,

«مَنْ جَاءَكُمْ وَأَمْرُكُمْ جَمِيعٌ يُرِيدُ أَنْ يُفَرِّقَ بَيْنَكُمْ فَاقْتُلُوهُ كَائِنًا مَنْ كَانَ»

(Whoever came to you while you are united and tried to divide you, then execute him, no matter who he is.) This is the view of the majority of scholars.

Imam Al-Haramayn stated that Abu Ishaq allowed the appointment of two or more Imams when the various provinces are far away from each other.

However, Imam Al-Haramayn himself was indecisive about this view.

Surah: 2 Ayah: 31, Ayah: 32 & Ayah: 33

﴿ وَعَلَّمَ ءَادَمَ ٱلْأَسْمَآءَ كُلَّهَا ثُمَّ عَرَضَهُمْ عَلَى ٱلْمَلَٰٓئِكَةِ فَقَالَ أَنۢبِـُٔونِى بِأَسْمَآءِ هَٰٓؤُلَآءِ إِن كُنتُمْ صَٰدِقِينَ ﴾

31. And He taught Adam all the names (of everything), then He showed them to the angels and said, "Tell Me the names of these if you are truthful."

﴿ قَالُواْ سُبْحَٰنَكَ لَا عِلْمَ لَنَآ إِلَّا مَا عَلَّمْتَنَآ إِنَّكَ أَنتَ ٱلْعَلِيمُ ٱلْحَكِيمُ ﴾

32. They (angels) said: "Glory be to You, we have no knowledge except what You have taught us. Verily, it is You, the All-Knower, the All-Wise."

Chapter 2: Al-Baqarah, Verses 001-141

﴿ قَالَ يَٰٓـَٔادَمُ أَنۢبِئۡهُم بِأَسۡمَآئِهِمۡۖ فَلَمَّآ أَنۢبَأَهُم بِأَسۡمَآئِهِمۡ قَالَ أَلَمۡ أَقُل لَّكُمۡ إِنِّيٓ أَعۡلَمُ غَيۡبَ ٱلسَّمَٰوَٰتِ وَٱلۡأَرۡضِ وَأَعۡلَمُ مَا تُبۡدُونَ وَمَا كُنتُمۡ تَكۡتُمُونَ ۝ ﴾

33. He said: "O Adam! Inform them of their names," and when he had informed them of their names, He said: "Did I not tell you that I know the Ghaib (Unseen) in the heavens and the earth, and I know what you reveal and what you have been concealing?"

Transliteration

31. WaAAallama adama al-asmaa kullaha thumma AAaradahum AAala almala-ikati faqala anbi-oonee bi-asma-i haola-i in kuntum sadiqeena 32. Qaloo subhanaka la AAilma lana illa ma AAallamtana innaka anta alAAaleemu alhakeemu 33. Qala ya adamu anbi/hum bi-asma-ihim falamma anbaahum bi-asma-ihim qala alam aqul lakum innee aAAlamu ghayba alssamawati waal-ardi waaAAlamu ma tubdoona wama kuntum taktumoona

Tafsir Ibn Kathir

The Virtue of Adam over the Angels

Allah stated the virtue of Adam above the angels, because He taught Adam, rather than them, the names of everything. This occurred after they prostrated to him. This discussion precedes that event here, only to show the importance of his position, and the absence of the angels' knowledge about creating the Khalifah when they asked about it. So Allah informed the angels that He knows what they do not know, and then He mentioned this to show them Adam's superiority over them in knowledge. Allah said,

(And He taught Adam all the names (of everything)).

Ad-Dahhak said that Ibn 'Abbas commented on the Ayah;

(And He taught Adam all the names (of everything)) "Meaning, the names that people use, such as human, animal, sky, earth, land, sea, horse, donkey, and so forth, including the names of the other species." Ibn Abi Hatim and Ibn Jarir reported that `Asim bin Kulayb narrated from Sa`id bin Ma`bad that Ibn `Abbas was questioned,

(And He taught Adam all the names (of everything)) "Did Allah teach him the names of the plate and the pot" He said, "Yes, and even the terms for breaking wind!"

Allah taught Adam the names of everything, their proper names, the names of their characteristics, and what they do, just as Ibn 'Abbas stated about the terms for passing gas.

In his Sahih, Al-Bukhari explained this Ayah in the Book of Tafsir with a report from Anas bin Malik who said that the Messenger of Allah said,

«يَجْتَمِعُ الْمُؤْمِنُونَ يَوْمَ الْقِيَامَةِ فَيَقُولُونَ: لَوِ اسْتَشْفَعْنَا إِلَى رَبِّنَا فَيَأْتُونَ آدَمَ فَيَقُولُونَ: أَنْتَ أَبُو النَّاسِ خَلَقَكَ اللهُ بِيَدِهِ وَأَسْجَدَ لَكَ مَلَائِكَتَهُ وَعَلَّمَكَ أَسْمَاءَ كُلِّ شَيْءٍ، فَاشْفَعْ لَنَا عِنْدَ رَبِّكَ حَتَّى يُرِيحَنَا مِنْ مَكَانِنَا هَذَا، فَيَقُولُ: لَسْتُ هُنَاكُمْ وَيَذْكُرُ ذَنْبَهُ فَيَسْتَحْيِي ائْتُوا نُوحًا فَإِنَّهُ أَوَّلُ رَسُولٍ بَعَثَهُ اللهُ إِلَى أَهْلِ الْأَرْضِ، فَيَأْتُونَهُ، فَيَقُولُ: لَسْتُ هُنَاكُمْ وَيَذْكُرُ سُؤَالَهُ رَبَّهُ مَا لَيْسَ لَهُ بِهِ عِلْمٌ فَيَسْتَحْيِي فَيَقُولُ: ائْتُوا خَلِيلَ الرَّحْمَنِ فَيَأْتُونَهُ فَيَقُولُ: لَسْتُ هُنَاكُمْ فَيَقُولُ: ائْتُوا مُوسَى عَبْدًا كَلَّمَهُ اللهُ وَأَعْطَاهُ التَّوْرَاةَ، فَيَقُولُ: لَسْتُ هُنَاكُمْ فَيَذْكُرُ قَتْلَ النَّفْسِ بِغَيْرِ نَفْسٍ فَيَسْتَحْيِي مِنْ رَبِّهِ فَيَقُولُ: ائْتُوا عِيسَى عَبْدَاللهِ وَرَسُولَهُ وَكَلِمَةَ اللهِ وَرُوحَهُ، فَيَأْتُونَهُ فَيَقُولُ: لَسْتُ هُنَاكُمْ ائْتُوا مُحَمَّدًا عَبْدًا غُفِرَ لَهُ مَا تَقَدَّمَ مِنْ ذَنْبِهِ وَمَا تَأَخَّرَ، فَيَأْتُونِي فَأَنْطَلِقُ حَتَّى أَسْتَأْذِنَ عَلَى رَبِّي فَيَأْذَنُ لِي، فَإِذَا رَأَيْتُ رَبِّي وَقَعْتُ سَاجِدًا فَيَدَعُنِي مَا شَاءَ اللهُ ثُمَّ يُقَالُ: ارْفَعْ رَأْسَكَ وَسَلْ تُعْطَهْ وَقُلْ يُسْمَعْ وَاشْفَعْ تُشَفَّعْ، فَأَرْفَعُ رَأْسِي فَأَحْمَدُهُ بِتَحْمِيدٍ يُعَلِّمُنِيهِ ثُمَّ أَشْفَعُ فَيَحُدُّ لِي حَدًّا فَأُدْخِلُهُمُ الْجَنَّةَ ثُمَّ أَعُودُ إِلَيْهِ فَإِذَا رَأَيْتُ رَبِّي مِثْلَهُ ثُمَّ أَشْفَعُ فَيَحُدُّ لِي حَدًّا فَأُدْخِلُهُمُ الْجَنَّةَ ثُمَّ أَعُودُ الثَّالِثَةَ ثُمَّ أَعُودُ الرَّابِعَةَ فَأَقُولُ: مَا بَقِيَ فِي النَّارِ إِلَّا مَنْ حَبَسَهُ الْقُرْآنُ وَوَجَبَ عَلَيْهِ الْخُلُودُ»

(The believers will gather on the Day of Resurrection and will say, 'We should seek a means of intercession with our Lord' They will go to Adam and say, 'O Adam! You are the father of all mankind, Allah created you with His Own Hand, ordered the angels to prostrate for you and taught you the names of everything. Will you not intercede for us with your Lord, so that he relieve us from this gathering place' On that Adam will reply, 'I cannot do what you have asked'. He will have remembered his error and will be embarrassed, saying, 'Go to Nuh, for he is the first of Allah's Messengers whom Allah sent to the people of the earth.' They will go to Nuh and ask him. He will say, 'I cannot do what you have asked.' He will recall asking Allah what he was not to know, and will also be embarrassed. He will say, 'Go to Khalil Ar-Rahman.' They will go to Ibrahim and he will also say, 'I cannot do what you have asked.' He will say, 'Go to Musa, a servant to whom Allah spoke directly and gave the Tawrah.' Musa will say, 'I cannot do what you have asked.' He will remember that he killed a person without justification and will be embarrassed before his Lord. He will say, 'Go to 'Isa, Allah's servant and Messenger and His Word and a spirit of His.' They will go to 'Isa and he will say, 'I will not do what you asked. Go to Muhammad, a servant whose previous and latter errors were forgiven.' They will come to me, and I will go to Allah and seek His permission and He will give me His permission. When I gaze at my Lord, I will prostrate myself and Allah will allow me to remain like that as much as He will. Then I will be addressed, 'O Muhammad! Raise your head; ask, for you will be given what you ask, and intercede, for your intercession will be accepted.' I will raise my head and thank and praise Allah with such praise as He will inspire me. I will intercede and He will grant me a quantity of people that He will admit into Paradise. I will go back to Him, and when I see my Lord, I will intercede and He will allow me a quantity that He will admit into Paradise. I will do that for a third and then a fourth time. I will say, 'There are no more people left in Hell except those whom the Qur'an has incarcerated and have thus acquired eternity in Hell.') This Hadith was collected by Muslim, An-Nasa'i and Ibn Majah. fThe reason why we mentioned this Hadith here is the Prophet's statement,

«فَيَأْتُونَ آدَمَ فَيَقُولُونَ: أَنْتَ أَبُو النَّاسِ خَلَقَكَ اللهُ بِيَدِهِ وَأَسْجَدَ لَكَ مَلَائِكَتَهُ وَعَلَّمَكَ أَسْمَاءَ كُلِّ شَيْءٍ»

(They will go to Adam and say, 'O Adam! You are the father of all mankind, and Allah created you with His Own Hand, ordered the angels to prostrate for you, and taught you the names of everything). This part of the Hadith testifies to the fact that Allah taught Adam the names of all creatures.

This is why Allah said,

(Then He showed them to the angels) meaning, the objects or creations. 'Abdur-Razzaq narrated that Ma'mar said that Qatadah said, "Allah paraded the objects before the angels,

(And said, "Tell Me the names of these if you are truthful")."

Allah's statement means, "Tell Me the names of what I paraded before you, O angels who said,

(Will You place therein those who will make mischief therein and shed blood).

You asked, 'Are You appointing a Khalifah from us or from other creations We praise and glorify You.

Therefore, Allah said, "If you say the truth, that if I appoint a non-angel Khalifah on the earth, he and his offspring will disobey Me, commit mischief and shed blood, but if I designate you the Khalifahs you will obey Me, follow My command and honor and glorify Me. However, since you do not know the names of the objects I paraded before you, then you have even less knowledge of what will occur on the earth that does not exist yet."

(They (angels) said: "Glory is to You, we have no knowledge except what you have taught us. Verily, it is You, the Knower, the Wise.").

Here the angels are praising Allah's holiness, and perfection above every kind of deficiency, affirming that no creature could ever acquire any part of Allah's knowledge, except by His permission, nor could anyone know anything except what Allah teaches them. This is why they said,

("Glory is to You, we have no knowledge except what you have taught us. Verily You are the Knower, the Wise) meaning, Allah is knowledgeable of everything, Most Wise about His creation, and He makes the wisest decisions, and He teaches and deprives whom He wills from knowledge. Verily, Allah's wisdom and justice in all matters is perfect.

Adam's Virtue of Knowledge is demonstrated

Allah said,

(He said: "O Adam! Inform them of their names," and when he had informed them of their names, He said: "Did I not tell you that I know the Ghayb (unseen) in the heavens and the earth, and I know what you reveal and what you have been concealing")

Zayd bin Aslam said, "You are Jibril, you are Mika'il, you are Israfil, until he mentioned the name of the crow." Mujahid said that Allah's statement,

(He said: "O Adam! Inform them of their names,") "The name of the pigeon, the crow and everything." Statements of a similar meaning were reported from Sa`id bin Jubayr, Al-Hasan, and Qatadah. When Adam's virtue over the angels became apparent, as he mentioned the names that Allah taught him, Allah said to the angels,

(Did I not tell you that I know the Ghayb (unseen) in the heavens and the earth, and I know what you reveal and what you have been concealing)

This means, "Did I not state that I know the seen and unseen matters." Similarly, Allah said,

(And if you (O Muhammad) speak (the invocation) aloud, then verily, He knows the secret and that which is yet more hidden) (20:7).

Also, Allah said about the hoopoe, that it said to Sulayman; (As Shaytan (Satan) has barred them from Allah's way> so they do not prostrate before Allah, Who brings to light what is hidden in the heavens and the earth, and knows what you conceal and what you reveal. Allah, La ilaha illa Huwa (none has the right to be worshipped but He), the Lord of the Supreme Throne!) (27:25-26).

They also have comments other than what we have said about the meaning of Allah's statement,

(And I know what you reveal and what you have been concealing).

It is reported from Ad-Dahhak that Ibn 'Abbas said that,

(And I know what you reveal and what you have been concealing) means, "`I know the secrets, just as I know the apparent things, such as, what Iblis concealed in his heart of arrogance and pride." Abu Ja`far Ar-Razi narrated that Ar-Rabi` bin Anas said that,

(And I know what you reveal and what you have been concealing) means, "The apparent part of what they said was: `Do you create in it that which would commit mischief and shed blood' The hidden meaning was: `We have more knowledge and honor than any creation our Lord would create.' But they came to know that Allah favored Adam above them regarding knowledge and honor."

Surah: 2 Ayah: 34

﴿ وَإِذْ قُلْنَا لِلْمَلَٰٓئِكَةِ ٱسْجُدُوا۟ لِءَادَمَ فَسَجَدُوٓا۟ إِلَّآ إِبْلِيسَ أَبَىٰ وَٱسْتَكْبَرَ وَكَانَ مِنَ ٱلْكَٰفِرِينَ ﴾

34. And (remember) when We said to the angels: "Prostrate yourselves before Adam." And they prostrated except Iblîs (Satan), he refused and was proud and was one of the disbelievers (disobedient to Allâh).

Transliteration

34. Wa-ith qulna lilmala-ikati osjudoo li-adama fasajadoo illa ibleesa aba waistakbara wakana mina alkafireena

Tafsir Ibn Kathir

Honoring Adam when the Angels prostrated before Him

This Ayah mentions the great honor that Allah granted Adam, and Allah reminded Adam's offspring of this fact. Allah commanded the angels to prostrate before Adam, as this Ayah and many Hadiths testify, such as the Hadith about the intercession that we discussed. There is a Hadith about the supplication of Musa, "O my Lord! Show me Adam who caused us and himself to be thrown out of Paradise." When Musa met Adam, he said to him, "Are you Adam whom Allah created with His Own Hands, blew life into and commanded the angels to prostrate before" Iblis was among Those ordered to prostrate before Adam, although He was not an Angel

When Allah commanded the angels to prostrate before Adam, Iblis was included in this command. Although Iblis was not an angel, he was trying - and pretending - to imitate the angels' behavior and deeds, and this is why he was also included in the command to the angels to prostrate before Adam. Satan was criticized for defying that command, as we will explain with detail, Allah willing, when we mention the Tafsir of Allah's statement,

(Except Iblis (Satan). He was one of the Jinn; he disobeyed the command of his Lord.) (18:50)

Similarly, Muhammad bin Ishaq reported that Ibn 'Abbas said, "Before he undertook the path of sin, Iblis was with the angels and was called 'Azazil.' He was among the residents of the earth and was one of the most active worshippers and knowledgeable persons among the angels. This fact caused him to be arrogant. Iblis was from a genus called Jinn."

The Prostration was before Adam but the Obedience was to Allah

Qatadah commented on Allah's statement,

(And (remember) when We said to the angels: "Prostrate yourselves before Adam.")

"The obedience was for Allah and the prostration was before Adam. Allah honored Adam and commanded the angels to prostrate before him." Some people said that this prostration was just a prostration of greeting, peace and honor, hence Allah's statement,

(And he (Prophet Yusuf) raised his parents to the throne and they fell down before him prostrate. And he said: "O my father! This is the interpretation of my dream aforetime! My Lord has made it come true!") (12:100)

The practice of prostrating was allowed for previous nations, but was repealed for ours.

Mu'adh said to the Prophet ,

"I visited Ash-Sham and found that they used to prostate before their priests and scholars. You, O Messenger of Allah, are more deserving of prostration." The Prophet said,

«لَا لَوْ كُنْتُ آمِرًا بَشَرًا أَنْ يَسْجُدَ لِبَشَرٍ لَأَمَرْتُ الْمَرْأَةَ أَنْ تَسْجُدَ لِزَوْجِهَا مِنْ عِظَمِ حَقِّهِ عَلَيْهَا»

(No. If I was to command any human to prostrate before another human, I would command the wife to prostrate before her husband because of the enormity of his right on her.)

Ar-Razi agreed with this view. Also, Qatadah said about Allah's statement,

(And they prostrated except Iblis (Shaytan), he refused and was proud and was one of the disbelievers (disobedient to Allah).)

"Iblis, the enemy of Allah, envied Adam because Allah honored Adam. He said, `I was created from fire, and he was created from clay.' Therefore, the first error ever committed was arrogance, for the enemy of Allah was too arrogant to prostrate before Adam." I - Ibn Kathir - say, the following is recorded in the Sahih,

«لَا يَدْخُلُ الْجَنَّةَ مَنْ كَانَ فِي قَلْبِهِ مِثْقَالُ حَبَّةٍ مِنْ خَرْدَلٍ مِنْ كِبْرٍ»

(No person who has the weight of a mustard seed of arrogance in his heart shall enter Paradise.)

Iblis had disbelief, arrogance, and rebellion, all of which caused him to be expelled from the holy presence of Allah, and His mercy.

Surah: 2 Ayah: 35 & Ayah: 36

﴿ وَقُلْنَا يَـٰٓـَٔادَمُ ٱسْكُنْ أَنتَ وَزَوْجُكَ ٱلْجَنَّةَ وَكُلَا مِنْهَا رَغَدًا حَيْثُ شِئْتُمَا وَلَا تَقْرَبَا هَـٰذِهِ ٱلشَّجَرَةَ فَتَكُونَا مِنَ ٱلظَّـٰلِمِينَ ۝ ﴾

35. And We said: "O Adam! Dwell you and your wife in the Paradise and eat both of you freely with pleasure and delight, of things therein as wherever you will, but come not near this tree or you both will be of the Zâlimûn (wrong-doers)."

$$\textarabic{﴿ فَأَزَلَّهُمَا ٱلشَّيْطَانُ عَنْهَا فَأَخْرَجَهُمَا مِمَّا كَانَا فِيهِ ۖ وَقُلْنَا ٱهْبِطُوا۟ بَعْضُكُمْ لِبَعْضٍ عَدُوٌّ ۖ وَلَكُمْ فِى ٱلْأَرْضِ مُسْتَقَرٌّ وَمَتَاعٌ إِلَىٰ حِينٍ ﴾}$$

36. Then the Shaitân (Satan) made them slip therefrom (the Paradise), and got them out from that in which they were. We said: "Get you down, all, with enmity between yourselves. On earth will be a dwelling place for you and an enjoyment for a time."

Transliteration

35. Waqulna ya adamu oskun anta wazawjuka aljannata wakula minha raghadan haythu shi/tuma wala taqraba hathihi alshshajarata fatakoona mina alth*th*alimeena 36. Faazallahuma alshshaytanu AAanha faakhrajahuma mimma kana feehi waqulna ihbitoo baAAdukum libaAAdin AAaduwwun walakum fee al-ardi mustaqarrun wamataAAun ila heenin

Tafsir Ibn Kathir

Adam was honored again

Allah honored Adam by commanding the angels to prostrate before him, so they all complied except for Iblis. Allah then allowed Adam to live and eat wherever and whatever he wished in Paradise.

Al-Hafiz Abu Bakr bin Marduwyah reported Abu Dharr saying, "I said, `O Messenger of Allah! Was Adam a Prophet' He said,

$$\textarabic{«نَعَمْ نَبِيًّا رَسُولًا كَلَّمَهُ اللَّهُ قُبُلًا»}$$

(Yes. He was a Prophet and a Messenger to whom Allah spoke directly), meaning

((O Adam!) Dwell you and your wife in the Paradise.)"

Hawwa' was created before Adam entered Paradise

The Ayah (2:35) indicates that Hawwa' was created before Adam entered Paradise, as Muhammad bin Ishaq stated. Ibn Ishaq said, "After Allah finished criticizing Iblis, and after teaching Adam the names of everything, He said,

(O Adam! Inform them of their names) until,

(Verily, You are the Knower, the Wise.)

Then Adam fell asleep, as the People of the Book and other scholars such as Ibn 'Abbas have stated, Allah took one of Adam's left ribs and made flesh grow in its place, while Adam was asleep and unaware. Allah then created Adam's wife, Hawwa', from his rib and made her a woman, so that she could be a comfort for him. When Adam woke up and saw Hawwa' next to him, it was claimed, he said, 'My flesh and blood, my wife.' Hence, Adam reclined with Hawwa'. When Allah married Adam to Hawwa' and gave him comfort, Allah said to him directly,

("O Adam! Dwell you and your wife in the Paradise and eat both of you freely with pleasure and delight, of things therein wherever you will, but come not near this tree or you both will be of the Zalimin (wrongdoers).")."

Allah tests Adam

Allah's statement to Adam,

(but come not near this tree) is a test for Adam. There are conflicting opinions over the nature of the tree mentioned here. Some said that it was the grape tree, barley, date tree, fig tree, and so forth. Some said that it was a certain tree, and whoever eats from it will be relieved of the call of nature. It was also said that it was a tree from which the angels eat so that they live for eternity. Imam Abu Ja'far bin Jarir said, "The correct opinion is that Allah forbade Adam and his wife from eating from a certain tree in Paradise, but they ate from it. We do not know which tree that was, because Allah has not mentioned anything in the Qur'an or the authentic Sunnah about the nature of this tree. It was said that it was barley, grape, or a fig tree. It is possible that it was one of those trees. Yet, this is knowledge that does not bring any benefit, just as being ignorant in its nature does no harm. Allah knows best." This is similar to what Ar-Razi stated in his Tafsir, and this is the correct opinion. Allah's statement,

(Then the Shaytan made them slip therefrom) either refers to Paradise, and in this case, it means that Shaytan led Adam and Hawwa' away from it, as 'Asim bin Abi An-Najud recited it. It is also possible that this Ayah refers to the forbidden tree. In this case, the Ayah would mean, as Al-Hasan and Qatadah stated, "He tripped them." In this case,

(Then the Shaytan made them slip therefrom)

means, "Because of the tree", just as Allah said,

(Turned aside therefrom (i.e. from Muhammad and the Qur'an) is he who is turned aside (by the decree and preordainment of Allah)) (51:9) meaning, the deviant person becomes turned aside - or slips - from the truth because of so and so reason.

This is why then Allah said,

(And got them out from that in which they were) meaning, the clothes, spacious dwelling and comfortable sustenance.

(We said: "Get you down, all, with enmity between yourselves. On earth will be a dwelling place for you and an enjoyment for a time.") meaning, dwelling, sustenance and limited life, until the commencement of the Day of Resurrection

Adam was very Tall

Ibn Abi Hatim narrated that Ubayy bin Ka'b said that the Messenger of Allah said,

»إِنَّ اللهَ خَلَقَ آدَمَ رَجُلًا طُوَالًا كَثِيرَ شَعْرِ الرَّأْسِ كَأَنَّهُ نَخْلَةٌ سَحُوقٌ، فَلَمَّا ذَاقَ الشَّجَرَةَ سَقَطَ عَنْهُ لِبَاسُهُ فَأَوَّلُ مَا بَدَا مِنْهُ عَوْرَتُهُ، فَلَمَّا نَظَرَ إِلَى عَوْرَتِهِ جَعَلَ يَشْتَدُّ فِي الْجَنَّةِ فَأَخَذَتْ شَعْرَهُ شَجَرَةٌ فَنَازَعَهَا، فَنَادَاهُ الرَّحْمَنُ: يَا آدَمُ مِنِّي تَفِرُّ؟ فَلَمَّا سَمِعَ كَلَامَ الرَّحْمَنِ قَالَ: يَا رَبِّ لَا وَلَكِنِ اسْتِحْيَاءً«

(Allah created Adam tall, with thick hair, just as a date tree with full branches. When Adam ate from the forbidden tree, his cover fell off, and the first thing that appeared was his private area. When he saw his private area, he ran away in Paradise and his hair got caught in a tree. He tried to free himself and Ar-Rahman called him, 'O Adam! Are you running away from Me' When Adam heard the words of Ar-Rahman (Allah), he said, 'No, O my Lord! But I am shy.')

Adam remained in Paradise for an Hour

Al-Hakim recorded that Ibn 'Abbas said, "Adam was allowed to reside in Paradise during the time period between the 'Asr (Afternoon) prayer until sunset." Al-Hakim then commented this is "Sahih according to the Two Shaykhs (Al-Bukhari and Muslim), but they did not include it in their collections." Also, Ibn Abi Hatim recorded Ibn 'Abbas saying, "Allah sent Adam to earth to an area called, Dahna, between Makkah and At-Ta'if." Al-Hasan Al-Basri said that Adam was sent down to India, while Hawwa' was sent to Jeddah. Iblis was sent down to Dustumaysan, several miles from Basra. Further, the snake was sent down to Asbahan. This was reported by Ibn Abi Hatim. Also, Muslim and An-Nasa'i recorded that Abu Hurayrah said that the Messenger of Allah said,

»خَيْرُ يَوْمٍ طَلَعَتْ فِيهِ الشَّمْسُ يَوْمُ الْجُمُعَةِ فِيهِ خُلِقَ آدَمُ وَفِيهِ أُدْخِلَ الْجَنَّةَ وَفِيهِ أُخْرِجَ مِنْهَا«

(Friday is the best day on which the sun has risen. On Friday, Allah created Adam, admitted him into Paradise, and expelled him from it.)

A Doubt and a Rebuttal

If one asks, "If the Paradise that Adam was thrown out of was in heaven, as the majority of the scholars assert, then is it possible for Iblis to enter Paradise, although he was expelled from it by Allah's decision (when he refused to prostrate before Adam)"

Basically, the response to this would be that the Paradise which Adam was in, was in the heavens, not on the earth, as we explained in the beginning of our book Al-Bidayah wan-Nihayah.

The majority of scholars said that Shaytan was originally prohibited from entering Paradise, but there were times when he sneaked into it in secret. For instance, the Tawrah stated that Iblis hid inside the snake's mouth and entered Paradise. Some scholars said that it is possible that Shaytan led Adam and Hawwa' astray on his way out of Paradise. Some scholars said that he led Adam and Hawwa' astray when he was on earth, while they were still in heaven, as stated by Az-Zamakhshari. Al-Qurtubi mentioned several beneficial Hadiths here about snakes and the ruling on killing them.

Surah: 2 Ayah: 37

﴿ فَتَلَقَّىٰٓ ءَادَمُ مِن رَّبِّهِۦ كَلِمَٰتٍ فَتَابَ عَلَيْهِ ۚ إِنَّهُۥ هُوَ ٱلتَّوَّابُ ٱلرَّحِيمُ ﴾

37. Then Adam received from his Lord Words. And his Lord pardoned him (accepted his repentance). Verily, He is the One Who forgives (accepts repentance), the Most Merciful.

Transliteration

37. Fatalaqqa adamu min rabbihi kalimatin fataba AAalayhi innahu huwa alttawwabu alrraheemu

Tafsir Ibn Kathir

Adam repents and supplicates to Allah

It was reported that the above Ayah is explained by Allah's statement,

(They said: "Our Lord! We have wronged ourselves. If You forgive us not, and bestow not upon us Your mercy, we shall certainly be of the losers.") (7:23) as Mujahid, Sa`id bin Jubayr, Abu Al-`Aliyah, Ar-Rabi` bin Anas, Al-Hasan, Qatadah, Muhammad bin Ka`b Al-Qurazi, KhaD—lid bin Ma`dan, `Ata' Al-Khurasani and `Abdur-Rahman bin Zayd bin Aslam have stated.

As-Suddi said that Ibn `Abbas commented on,

(Then Adam received from his Lord Words) "Adam said, `O Lord! Did You not created me with Your Own Hands' He said, `Yes.' He said, `And blow life into me' He said, `Yes.' He said, `And when I sneezed, You said, `May Allah grant you His mercy.' Does not Your mercy precede Your anger' He was told, `Yes.' Adam said, `And You destined me to commit this evil act' He was told, `Yes.' He said, `If I repent, will You send me back to Paradise' Allah said, `Yes.'"

Similar is reported from Al-`Awfi, Sa`id bin Jubayr, Sa`id bin Ma`bad, and Ibn `Abbas. Al-Hakim recorded this Hadith in his Mustadrak from Ibn Jubayr, who narrated it from Ibn `Abbas. Al-Hakim said, "Its chain is Sahih and they (Al-Bukhari and Muslim) did not record it."

Allah's statement, (Verily, He is the One Who forgives (accepts repentance), the Most Merciful) (2:37) means that Allah forgives whoever regrets his error and returns to Him in repentance. This meaning is similar to Allah's statements,

(Know they not that Allah accepts repentance from His servants) (9:104),

(And whoever does evil or wrongs himself) (4:110) and

(And whosoever repents and does righteous good deeds) (25:71).

The Ayat mentioned above, testify to the fact that Allah forgives the sins of whoever repents, demonstrating His kindness and mercy towards His creation and servants. There is no deity worthy of worship except Allah, the Most Forgiving, the Most Merciful.

Surah: 2 Ayah: 38 & Ayah: 39

﴿ قُلْنَا ٱهْبِطُوا۟ مِنْهَا جَمِيعًا ۖ فَإِمَّا يَأْتِيَنَّكُم مِّنِّى هُدًى فَمَن تَبِعَ هُدَاىَ فَلَا خَوْفٌ عَلَيْهِمْ وَلَا هُمْ يَحْزَنُونَ ﴾ ٣٨

38. We said: "Get down all of you from this place (the Paradise), then whenever there comes to you Guidance from Me, and whoever follows My Guidance, there shall be no fear on them, nor shall they grieve.

﴿ وَٱلَّذِينَ كَفَرُوا۟ وَكَذَّبُوا۟ بِـَٔايَـٰتِنَآ أُو۟لَـٰٓئِكَ أَصْحَـٰبُ ٱلنَّارِ ۖ هُمْ فِيهَا خَـٰلِدُونَ ﴾ ٣٩

39. But those who disbelieve and belie Our Ayât (proofs, evidences, verses, lessons, signs, revelations, etc.) - such are the dwellers of the Fire. They shall abide therein forever.

Transliteration

38. Qulna ihbitoo minha jameeAAan fa-imma ya/tiyannakum minnee hudan faman tabiAAa hudaya fala khawfun AAalayhim wala hum yahzanoona 39. Waallatheena kafaroo wakaththaboo bi-ayatina ola-ika as-habu alnnari hum feeha khalidoona

Tafsir Ibn Kathir

Allah stated that when He sent Adam, Hawwa', and Shaytan to earth from Paradise, He warned them that He will reveal Books and send Prophets and Messengers to them, i.e., to their offspring. Abu Al-'Aliyah said, "Al-Huda, refers to the Prophets, Messengers, the clear signs and plain explanation."

(And whoever follows My guidance) meaning, whoever accepts what is contained in My Books and what I send the Messengers with,

(There shall be no fear on them) regarding the Hereafter,

(nor shall they grieve) regarding the life of this world. Similarly, in Surat Ta Ha, Allah said,

(He (Allah) said: "Get you down (from the Paradise to the earth), both of you, together, some of you are an enemy to some others. Then if there comes to you guidance from Me, then whoever follows My guidance, he shall neither go astray, nor shall he be distressed.) (20:123)

Ibn 'Abbas commented, "He will not be misguided in this life or miserable in the Hereafter." The Ayah,

(But whosoever turns away from My Reminder (i.e. neither believes in this Qur'an nor acts on its teachings) verily, for him is a life of hardship, and We shall raise him up blind on the Day of Resurrection.) (20:124) is similar to what Allah stated here,

(But those who disbelieve and belie Our Ayat @— such are the dwellers of the Fire. They shall abide therein forever), meaning, they will remain in Hell for eternity and will not find a way out of it.

Surah: 2 Ayah: 40 & Ayah: 41

﴿ يَـٰبَنِىٓ إِسْرَٰٓءِيلَ ٱذْكُرُواْ نِعْمَتِىَ ٱلَّتِىٓ أَنْعَمْتُ عَلَيْكُمْ وَأَوْفُواْ بِعَهْدِىٓ أُوفِ بِعَهْدِكُمْ وَإِيَّـٰىَ فَٱرْهَبُونِ ﴾

40. O Children of Israel! Remember My Favor which I bestowed upon you, and fulfil (your obligations to) My Covenant (with you) so that I fulfil (My Obligations to) your covenant (with Me), and fear none but Me.

﴿ وَءَامِنُواْ بِمَآ أَنزَلْتُ مُصَدِّقًا لِّمَا مَعَكُمْ وَلَا تَكُونُوٓاْ أَوَّلَ كَافِرٍۭ بِهِۦ ۖ وَلَا تَشْتَرُواْ بِـَٔايَـٰتِى ثَمَنًا قَلِيلًا وَإِيَّـٰىَ فَٱتَّقُونِ ۞ ﴾

41. And believe in what I have sent down (this Qur'ân), confirming that which is with you, (the Taurât (Torah) and the Injeel (Gospel)) and be not the first to disbelieve therein, and buy (get) not with My Verses (the Taurât (Torah) and the Injeel (Gospel)) a small price (i.e. getting a small gain by selling My Verses), and fear Me and Me Alone. (Tafsir At-Tabarî).

Transliteration

40. Ya banee isra-eela othkuroo niAAmatiya allatee anAAamtu AAalaykum waawfoo biAAahdee oofi biAAahdikum wa-iyyaya fairhabooni 41. Waaminoo bima anzaltu musaddiqan lima maAAakum wala takoonoo awwala kafirin bihi wala tashtaroo bi-ayatee thamanan qaleelan wa-iyyaya faittaqooni

Tafsir Ibn Kathir

Encouraging the Children of Israel to embrace Islam

Allah commanded the Children of Israel to embrace Islam and to follow Muhammad . He also reminded them with the example of their father Israel, Allah's Prophet Ya'qub, as if saying, "O children of the pious, righteous servant of Allah who obeyed Allah! Be like your father, following the truth." This statement is similar to one's saying, "O you son of that generous man! Do this or that" or, "O son of the brave man, engage the strong fighters," or "O son of the scholar, seek the knowledge," and so forth. Similarly, Allah said,

(O offspring of those whom We carried (in the ship) with Nuh (Noah)! Verily, he was a grateful servant) (17:3).

Israel is Prophet Ya'qub (Jacob)

Israel is Prophet Ya'qub, for Abu Dawud At-Tayalisi recorded that 'Abdullah Ibn 'Abbas said, "A group of Jews came to the Prophet and he said to them,

«هَلْ تَعْلَمُونَ أَنَّ إِسْرَائِيلَ يَعْقُوبُ؟»

(Do you know that Israel is Jacob) They said, "Yes, by Allah." He said,

«اللَّهُمَّ اشْهَدْ»

(O Allah! Be witness.)"

At-Tabari recorded that 'Abdullah Ibn 'Abbas said that 'Israel' means, 'the servant of Allah.'

Allah's Blessings for the Children of Israel

Allah said, (Remember My favor which I bestowed upon you). Mujahid commented, "Allah's favor that He granted the Jews is that He made water gush from stones, sent down manna and quails for them, and saved them from being enslaved by Pharaoh." Abu Al-`Aliyah also said, "Allah's favor mentioned here is His sending Prophets and Messengers among them, and revealing Books to them." I - Ibn Kathir - say that this Ayah is similar to what Musa said to the Children of Israel,

(O my people! Remember the favor of Allah to you: when He made Prophets among you, made you kings, and gave you what He had not given to any other among the nations (of their time) (5:20) meaning, during their time. Also, Muhammad bin Ishaq said that Ibn `Abbas said, (Remember My favor which I bestowed upon you,) means, "My support for you and your fathers," that is saving them from Pharaoh and his people.

Reminding the Children of Israel of Allah's Covenant with Them

Allah's statement,

(And fulfill (your obligations to) My covenant (with you) so that I fulfill (My obligations to) your covenant (with Me),) means, 'My covenant that I took from you concerning Prophet Muhammad , when he is sent to you, so that I grant you what I promised you if you believe in him and follow him. I will then remove the chains and restrictions that were placed around your necks, because of the errors that you committed.' Also, Al-Hasan Al-Basri said, "The 'covenant' is in reference to Allah's statement, i

(Indeed, Allah took the covenant from the Children of Israel (Jews), and We appointed twelve leaders among them. And Allah said: "I am with you if you perform As-Salah and give Zakah and believe in My Messengers; honor and assist them, and lend a good loan to Allah, verily, I will expiate your sins and admit you to Gardens under which rivers flow (in Paradise)) (5:12)."

Other scholars said, "The covenant is what Allah took from them in the Tawrah, in that, He will send a great Prophet - meaning Muhammad - from among the offspring of Isma`il, who will be obeyed by all peoples. Therefore, whoever obeys him, then Allah will forgive his sins, enter him into Paradise and award him two rewards." We should mention here that Ar-Razi mentioned several cases of information brought by the earlier Prophets regarding the coming of Muhammad . Further, Abu Al-`Aliyah said that, (And fulfill (your obligations to) My covenant (with you)) means, "His covenant with His servants is to embrace Islam and to adhere to it." Ad-Dahhak said that Ibn `Abbas said, "`I fulfill My obligations to you' means, `I (Allah) will be pleased with you and admit you into Paradise.'" As-Suddi, Ad-Dahhak, Abu Al-`Aliyah and Ar-Rabi` bin Anas said similarly.

Ibn `Abbas said that Allah's statement,

(And fear Me and Me alone.) means, "Fear the torment that I might exert on you, just as I did with your fathers, like the mutation, etc." This Ayah contains encouragement, followed by warning. Allah first called the Children of Israel, using encouragement, then He warned them, so that they might return to the Truth, follow the Messenger , heed the Qur'an's prohibitions and commands and believe in its content. Surely, Allah guides whom He wills to the straight path.

Allah said next,

(And believe in what I have sent down, confirming that which is with you (the Tawrah and the Injil)) meaning, the Qur'an that Allah sent down to Muhammad , the unlettered Arab Prophet, as bringer of glad tidings, a warner and a light. The Qur'an contains the Truth from Allah and affirms what was revealed beforehand in the Tawrah and the Injil (the Gospel). Abu Al-'Aliyah said that Allah's statement,

(And believe in what I have sent down (this Qur'an), confirming that which is with you (the Tawrah and the Injil)) "means, `O People of the Book! Believe in what I sent down that conforms to what you have.' This is because they find the description of Muhammad recorded in the Tawrah and the Injil." Similar statements were attributed to Mujahid, Ar-Rabi` bin Anas and Qatadah.

Allah said, (and be not the first to disbelieve therein).

Ibn 'Abbas commented, "Do not become the first to disbelieve in the Qur'an (or Muhammad), while you have more knowledge in it than other people." Abu Al-'Aliyah commented, "'Do not become the first to disbelieve in Muhammad, ` meaning from among the People of the Book, 'after you hear that he was sent as a Prophet.'" Similar statements were attributed to Al-Hasan, As-Suddi and Ar-Rabi` bin Anas. Ibn Jarir stated that the Ayah (disbelieve therein 2:41) refers to the Qur'an, mentioned earlier in the Ayah, (in what I have sent down (this Qur'an),)

Both statements are correct because they are inter-related. For instance, whoever disbelieves in the Qur'an will have disbelieved in Muhammad , and whoever disbelieves in Muhammad will have disbelieved in the Qur'an. Allah's statement,

(the first to disbelieve therein) means, do not become the first among the Children of Israel to disbelieve in it, for there were people from Quraysh and the Arabs in general who rejected Muhammad before the People of the Book disbelieved in him. We should state here that the Ayah is talking about the Children of Israel in specific, because the Jews in Al-Madinah were the first among the Children of Israel to be addressed by the Qur'an. Hence, their disbelief in the Qur'an means that they were the first among the People of the Book to disbelieve in it.

Allah's statement, (and buy not with My verses a small price,) means, "Do not substitute faith in My Ayat and belief in My Prophet with the life of this world and its lusts which are minute and bound to end." Allah said, (and have Taqwa of Me and Me alone).

Ibn Abi Hatim reported that Talq bin Habib said, "Taqwa is to work in Allah's obedience, on a light from Allah, hoping in Allah's mercy, and to avoid Allah's disobedience, on a light from Allah, fearing Allah's punishment." Allah's statement,

(and fear Me and Me alone) means, that Allah warns the People of the Book against intentionally hiding the truth and spreading the opposite of it, as well as, against defying the Messenger .

Surah: 2 Ayah: 42 & Ayah: 43

﴿ وَلَا تَلْبِسُوا۟ ٱلْحَقَّ بِٱلْبَٰطِلِ وَتَكْتُمُوا۟ ٱلْحَقَّ وَأَنتُمْ تَعْلَمُونَ ۝ ﴾

42. And mix not truth with falsehood, nor conceal the truth (i.e. Muhammad (peace be upon him) is Allâh's Messenger and his qualities are written in your Scriptures, the Taurât (Torah) and the Injeel (Gospel)) while you know (the truth).

﴿ وَأَقِيمُوا۟ ٱلصَّلَوٰةَ وَءَاتُوا۟ ٱلزَّكَوٰةَ وَٱرْكَعُوا۟ مَعَ ٱلرَّٰكِعِينَ ۝ ﴾

43. And perform As-Salât (Iqâmat-as-Salât), and give Zakât, and bow down (or submit yourselves with obedience to Allâh) along with Ar-Raki'ûn.

Transliteration

42. Wala talbisoo alhaqqa bialbatili wataktumoo alhaqqa waantum taAAlamoona 43. Waaqeemoo alssalata waatoo alzzakata wairkaAAoo maAAa alrrakiAAeena

Tafsir Ibn Kathir

The Prohibition of hiding the Truth and distorting It with Falsehood

Allah forbade the Jews from intentionally distorting the truth with falsehood and from hiding the truth and spreading falsehood,

(And mix not truth with falsehood, nor conceal the truth while you know (the truth)).

So Allah forbade them from two things; He ordered them to make the truth known, as well as explaining it. Ad-Dahhak said that Ibn 'Abbas mentioned the Ayah,

(And mix not truth with falsehood) and said; "Do not mix the truth with falsehood and the facts with lies." Qatadah said that,

(And mix not truth with falsehood) means, "Do not mix Judaism and Christianity with Islam,

(while you know (the truth).) that the religion of Allah is Islam, and that Judaism and Christianity are innovations that did not come from Allah." It was reported that Al-Hasan Al-Basri said similarly.

Also, Muhammad bin Ishaq narrated that Ibn 'Abbas said that, (nor conceal the truth while you know (the truth).) means, "Do not hide the knowledge that you have of My Messenger and what he was sent with. His description, which you know about, can be found written in the Books that you have."

It is possible that it means, "..although you know the tremendous harm that this evil will cause people, misguiding them and leading them to the Fire, because they will follow the falsehood that you mixed with the truth in your claims."

(And perform As-Salat and give Zakah, and bow down along with Ar-Raki'in.)

Muqatil said, "Allah's statement to the People of the Book,

(And perform As-Salah) commands them to perform the prayer behind the Prophet ,

(and give Zakah) commands them to pay the Zakah to the Prophet , and

(and bow down along with Ar-Raki'in) commands them to bow down with those who bow down among the Ummah of Muhammad . Allah therefore commands the People of the Book to be with, and among the Ummah of Muhammad ." In addition, Allah's statement,

(And bow down along with Ar-Raki'in) means, "And be among the believers performing the best deeds they perform, such as, and foremost, the prayer." Many scholars said that this Ayah (2:43) is proof for the obligation of performing the prayer in congregation (for men only). I will explain this ruling in detail in Kitab Al-Ahkam Al-Kabir, Allah willing.

Surah: 2 Ayah: 44

﴿ ۞ أَتَأْمُرُونَ ٱلنَّاسَ بِٱلْبِرِّ وَتَنسَوْنَ أَنفُسَكُمْ وَأَنتُمْ تَتْلُونَ ٱلْكِتَـٰبَ أَفَلَا تَعْقِلُونَ ﴿٤٤﴾ ﴾

44. Enjoin you Al-Birr (piety and righteousness and each and every act of obedience to Allâh) on the people and you forget (to practise it)

yourselves, while you recite the Scripture (the Taurât (Torah))! Have you then no sense?

Transliteration

44. Ata/muroona alnnasa bialbirri watansawna anfusakum waantum tatloona alkitaba afala taAAqiloona

Tafsir Ibn Kathir

The Condemnation of commanding Others to observe Righteousness while ignoring Righteousness

Allah said, "How is it, O People of the Book, that you command people to perform Al-Birr, which encompasses all types of righteousness, yet forget yourselves and do not heed what you call others to And you read Allah's Book (the Tawrah) and know what it promises to those who do not fulfill Allah's commandments.

(Have you then no sense) of what you are doing to yourselves, so that you might become aware of your slumber and restore your sight from blindness" 'Abdur-Razzaq said that Ma'mar stated that Qatadah commented on Allah's statement,

(Enjoin you Al-Birr (piety and righteousness and every act of obedience to Allah) on the people and you forget (to practise it) yourselves,) "The Children of Israel used to command people to obey Allah, fear Him and perform Al-Birr. Yet, they contradicted these orders, so Allah reminded them of this fact." As-Suddi said similarly. Ibn Jurayj said that the Ayah:

(Enjoin you Al-Birr on the people) "Is about the People of the Book and the hypocrites. They used to command people to pray and fast. However, they did not practice what they commanded others. Allah reminded them of this behavior. So whoever commands people to do righteousness, let him be among the first of them to implement that command." Also, Muhammad bin Ishaq narrated that Ibn `Abbas said that,

(And you forget yourselves,) means, "You forget to practice it yourselves,

(While you recite the Scripture (Tawrah)! Have you then no sense) You forbid the people from rejecting the prophethood and the covenant that you have mentioned with you in the Tawrah, while you yourselves have forgotten it, meaning that 'you have forgotten the covenant that I made with you that you will accept My Messenger. You have breeched My covenant, and rejected what you know is in My Book.' "

Therefore, Allah admonished the Jews for this behavior and alerted them to the wrongs that they were perpetrating against themselves by ordering righteousness, yet refraining themselves from righteousness. We should state that Allah is not criticizing the People of the Book for ordering righteousness, because enjoining good is a part of righteousness and is an obligation for the scholars. However, the scholar is himself required to heed, and adhere to, what he invites others to. For instance, Prophet Shu'ayb said,

(I wish not, in contradiction to you, to do that which I forbid you. I only desire reform to the best of my power. And my guidance cannot come except from Allah, in Him I trust and unto Him I repent) (11:88).

Therefore, enjoining righteousness and performing righteousness are both required. Neither category is rendered not necessary by the practice of the other, according to the most correct view of the scholars among the Salaf (predecessors) and the Khalaf.

Imam Ahmad reported that Abu Wa'il said, "While I was riding behind Usamah, he was asked, `Why not advise `Uthman' He said, `Do you think that if I advise him I should allow you to hear it I advise him in secret, and I will not start something that I would hate to be the first to start. I will not say to a man, `You are the best man,' even if he was my leader, after what I heard from the Messenger of Allah .' They said, `What did he say' He said, `I heard him say,

«يُجَاءُ بِالرَّجُلِ يَوْمَ الْقِيَامَةِ فَيُلْقَى فِي النَّارِ فَتَنْدَلِقُ بِهِ أَقْتَابُهُ فَيَدُورُ بِهَا فِي النَّارِ كَمَا يَدُورُ الْحِمَارُ بِرَحَاهُ فَيُطِيفُ بِهِ أَهْلُ النَّارِ فَيَقُولُونَ: يَا فُلَانُ مَا أَصَابَكَ؟ أَلَمْ تَكُنْ تَأْمُرُنَا بِالْمَعْرُوفِ وَتَنْهَانَا عَنِ الْمُنْكَرِ؟ فَيَقُولُ: كُنْتُ آمُرُكُمْ بِالْمَعْرُوفِ وَلَا آتِيهِ وَأَنْهَاكُمْ عَنِ الْمُنْكَرِ وَآتِيهِ»

(A man will be brought on the Day of Resurrection and thrown in the Fire. His intestines will fall out and he will continue circling pulling them behind him, just as the donkey goes around the pole. The people of the Fire will go to that man and ask him, 'What happened to you Did you not used to command us to do righteous acts and forbid us from committing evil' He will say, 'Yes. I used to enjoin righteousness, but refrained from performing righteousness, and I used to forbid you to perform from evil while I myself did it.').'"

This Hadith was also recorded by Al-Bukhari and Muslim. eAlso, Ibrahim An-Nakha'i said,

"I hesitate in advising people because of three Ayat: (Enjoin you Al-Birr on the people and you forget (to practise it) yourselves). (O you who believe! Why do you say that which you do not do Most hateful it is to Allah that you say that which you do not do) (61:2-3)."

And Allah informed us that the Prophet Shu'ayb said, (I wish not, in contradiction to you, to do that which I forbid you. I only desire reform to the best of my power. And my guidance cannot come except from Allah, in Him I trust and unto Him I repent) (11:88).

Surah: 2 Ayah: 45 & Ayah: 46

﴿ وَٱسْتَعِينُوا۟ بِٱلصَّبْرِ وَٱلصَّلَوٰةِ ۚ وَإِنَّهَا لَكَبِيرَةٌ إِلَّا عَلَى ٱلْخَٰشِعِينَ ۝ ﴾

45. And seek help in patience and As-Salât (the prayer) and truly it is extremely heavy and hard except for Al-Khâshi'ûn (i.e. the true believers in Allâh - those who obey Allâh with full submission, fear much from His Punishment, and believe in His Promise (Paradise) and in His Warnings (Hell))

﴿ ٱلَّذِينَ يَظُنُّونَ أَنَّهُم مُّلَٰقُوا۟ رَبِّهِمْ وَأَنَّهُمْ إِلَيْهِ رَٰجِعُونَ ۝ ﴾

46. (They are those) who are certain that they are going to meet their Lord, and that unto Him they are going to return.

Transliteration

45. WaistaAAeenoo bialssabri waalssalati wa-innaha lakabeeratun illa AAala alkhashiAAeena 46. Allatheena ya*th*unnoona annahum mulaqoo rabbihim waannahum ilayhi rajiAAoona

Tafsir Ibn Kathir

The Support that comes with Patience and Prayer

Allah commanded His servants to use patience and prayer to acquire the good of this life and the Hereafter. Muqatil bin Hayan said that this Ayah means, "Utilize patience and the obligatory prayer in seeking the Hereafter. As for patience (here), they say that it means fasting." There are similar texts reported from Mujahid. Al-Qurtubi and other scholars commented, "This is why Ramadan is called the month of patience," as is mentioned in the Hadith literature. It was also said that `patience' in the Ayah means, refraining from evil, and this is why `patience' was mentioned along with practicing acts of worship, especially and foremost, the prayer. Also, Ibn Abi Hatim narrated that `Umar bin Al-Khattab said, "There are two types of patience: good patience when the disaster strikes, and a better patience while avoiding the prohibitions of Allah." Ibn Abi Hatim said that Al-Hasan Al-Basri was reported to have said similarly.

Allah then said,

(And As-Salah (the prayer).)

The prayer is one of the best means of assistance for firmly adhering to Allah's orders, just as Allah said;

(Recite (O Muhammad) what has been revealed to you of the Book (the Qur'an), and perform As-Salah. Verily, As-Salah (the prayer) prevents from Al-Fahsha' (i.e. great sins of every kind), and Al-Munkar and the remembrance of (praising) of (you by) Allah is greater indeed) (29:45).

The personal pronoun in the Ayah,

(And truly, it is extremely heavy and hard) refers to prayer, as Mujahid is reported to have said, and it was also the choice of Ibn Jarir. It is possible that the pronoun might be referring to the advice - to observe patience and the prayer - mentioned in the same Ayah. Similarly, Allah said about Qarun (Korah),

(But those who had been given (religious) knowledge said: "Woe to you! The reward of Allah (in the Hereafter) is better for those who believe and do righteous good deeds, and this, none shall attain except As-Sabirun (the patient).") (28:80).

Also, Allah said,

(The good deed and the evil deed cannot be equal. Repel (the evil) with one which is better then verily he, between whom and you there was enmity, (will become) as though he was a close friend. But none is granted it (the above quality) except those who are patient @— and none is granted it except the owner of the great portion (of happiness in the Hereafter and) in this world.) (41:34-35) meaning, this advice is only implemented by those who are patient and the fortunate. In any case, Allah's statement here means, prayer is 'heavy and burdensome', (except for Al-Khashi'in.)

Ibn Abi Talhah reported that Ibn 'Abbas commented on this Ayah, "They (Al-Khashi'in) are those who believe in what Allah has revealed."

Allah's statement, (They are those who are certain that they are going to meet their Lord, and that unto Him they are going to return.) continues the subject that was started in the previous Ayah. Therefore, the prayer, or the advice to observe it is heavy, (except for Al-Khashi'in. (They are those) who are certain (Yazunnuna) that they are going to meet their Lord,) meaning, they know that they will be gathered and face their Lord on the Day of Resurrection, (and that unto Him they are going to return.) meaning, their affairs are all subject to His will and He justly decides what He wills. Since they are certain that they will be returned to Allah and be reckoned, it is easy for them to perform the acts of obedience and refrain from the prohibitions. Ibn Jarir commented on Allah's statement;

(Yazunnuna that they are going to meet their Lord)

Ibn Jarir said; "The Arabs call certainty as well as doubt, Zann. There are similar instances in the Arabic language where a subject as well as its opposite share the same name. For instance, Allah said, (And the Mujrimun (criminals, polytheists, sinners), shall see the Fire and Zannu (apprehend) that they have to fall therein)"(18:53).

It is recorded in the Sahih that on the Day of Resurrection, Allah will say to a servant, "Have I not allowed you to marry, honored you, made the horses and camels subservient to you and allowed you to become a chief and a master" He will say, "Yes." Allah will say, "Did you have Zann (think) that you will meet Me" He will say, "No." Allah will say, "This Day, I will forget you, just as you forgot Me." If Allah wills, we will further elaborate on this subject when we explain Allah's statement, (They have forgotten Allah, so He has forgotten them) (9:67).

Surah: 2 Ayah: 47

﴿ يَٰبَنِىٓ إِسْرَٰٓءِيلَ ٱذْكُرُواْ نِعْمَتِىَ ٱلَّتِىٓ أَنْعَمْتُ عَلَيْكُمْ وَأَنِّى فَضَّلْتُكُمْ عَلَى ٱلْعَٰلَمِينَ ﴿٤٧﴾ ﴾

47. O Children of Israel! Remember My Favor which I bestowed upon you and that I preferred you to the 'Alamîn (mankind and jinn (of your time period, in the past))

Transliteration

47. Ya banee isra-eela othkuroo niAAmatiya allatee anAAamtu AAalaykum waannee faddaltukum AAala alAAalameena

Tafsir Ibn Kathir

Reminding the Children of Israel that They were preferred above the Other Nations

Allah reminds the Children of Israel of the favors that He granted their fathers and grandfathers, how He showed preference to them by sending them Messengers from among them and revealing Books to them, more so than any of the other previous nations. Similarly, Allah said,

(And We chose them (the Children of Israel) over the 'Alamin, (nations) with knowledge.) (44:32) and,

(And (remember) when Musa (Moses) said to his people: "O my people! Remember the favor of Allah to you: when He made Prophets among you, made you kings, honored you above the `Alamin (nations).") (5:20).

Abu Ja'far Ar-Razi reported that Ar-Rabi` bin Anas said that Abu Al-'Aliyah said that Allah's statement, (and that I preferred you over the 'Alamin) means, "The kingship, Messengers and Books that were granted to them, instead of granting such to the other kingdoms that existed during their time, for every period there is a nation." It was also reported that Mujahid, Ar-Rabi' bin Anas, Qatadah and Isma'il bin Abi Khalid said similarly.

The Ummah of Muhammad is Better than the Children of Israel

This is the only way the Ayah can be understood, because this Ummah is better than theirs, as Allah said;

(You are the best of people ever raised up for mankind; you enjoin good and forbid evil, and you believe in Allah. And had the People of the Book (Jews and Christians) believed, it would have been better for them) (3:110).

Also, the Musnad and Sunan Collections of Hadith recorded that Mu'awiyah bin Haydah Al-Qushayri said that the Messenger of Allah said,

«أَنْتُمْ تُوَفُّونَ سَبْعِينَ أُمَّةً أَنْتُمْ خَيْرُهَا وَأَكْرَمُهَا عَلَى اللهِ»

(You (Muslims) are the seventieth nation, but you are the best and most honored of them according to Allah.)

There are many Hadiths on this subject, and they will be mentioned when we discuss Allah's statement,

(You are the best of peoples ever raised up for mankind) (3:110).

Surah: 2 Ayah: 48

﴿ وَاتَّقُواْ يَوْمًا لاَّ تَجْزِى نَفْسٌ عَن نَّفْسٍ شَيْئًا وَلاَ يُقْبَلُ مِنْهَا شَفَـعَةٌ وَلاَ يُؤْخَذُ مِنْهَا عَدْلٌ وَلاَ هُمْ يُنصَرُونَ ﴾

48. And fear a Day (of Judgement) when a person shall not avail another, nor will intercession be accepted from him nor will compensation be taken from him nor will they be helped.

Transliteration

48. Waittaqoo yawman la tajzee nafsun AAan nafsin shay-an wala yuqbalu minha shafaAAatun wala yu/khathu minha AAadlun wala hum yunsaroona

Tafsir Ibn Kathir

After Allah reminded the Children of Israel of the favors that He has granted them, He warned them about the duration of the torment which He will punish them with on the Day of Resurrection. He said,

(And fear a Day) meaning, the Day of Resurrection,

(When a person shall not avail another) meaning, on that Day, no person shall be of any help to another. Similarly, Allah said,

(And no bearer of burdens shall bear another's burden) (35:18)

(Every man that Day will have enough to make him careless of others.) (80:37) and,

(O mankind! Have Taqwa of your Lord (by keeping your duty to Him and avoiding all evil), and fear a Day when no father can avail aught for his son, nor a son avail aught for his father) (31: 33).

This indeed should serve as a great warning that both the father and the son will not be of help to each other on that Day.

Neither Intercession, Ransom, or Assistance will be accepted on behalf of the Disbelievers

Allah said,

(nor will intercession be accepted from him)

meaning, from the disbelievers. Similarly, Allah said,

(So no intercession of intercessors will be of any use to them) (74:48) and described the people of the Fire saying,

(Now we have no intercessors. Nor a close friend (to help us)) (26:100-101).

Allah's statement here (2:48)

(nor will compensation be taken from him) means, that Allah does not accept the disbelievers to ransom themselves.

Similarly, Allah said,

(Verily, those who disbelieved, and died while they were disbelievers, the (whole) earth full of gold will not be accepted from anyone of them even if they offered it as a ransom) (3:91)

(Verily, those who disbelieve, if they had all that is in the earth, and as much again therewith to ransom themselves from the torment on the Day of Resurrection, it would never be accepted of them, and theirs would be a painful torment) (5:36)

(And even if he offers every ransom, it will not be accepted from him) (6:70) and, (So this Day no ransom shall be taken from you (hypocrites), nor of those who disbelieved. Your abode is the Fire. That is your Mawla (friend— proper place)) (57:15).

Allah stated that if the people do not believe in His Messenger and follow what He sent him with, then when they meet Him on the Day of Resurrection, after remaining on the path of disbelief, their family lineage and/or the intercession of their masters will not help them at all. It will not be accepted of them, even if they paid the earth's fill of gold as ransom. Similarly, Allah said, (Before a Day comes when there will be no bargaining, nor friendship, nor intercession) (2:254) and,

(On which there will be neither mutual bargaining nor befriending) (19:31). Allah's statement next,

(nor will they be helped.) means, "no person shall get angry - or anxious - on their behalf and offer them any help, or try to save them from Allah's punishment." As stated earlier on that Day, neither the relative, nor persons of authority will feel pity for the disbelievers, nor will any ransom be accepted for them. Consequently, they will receive no help from others and they will be helpless themsleves. Allah said,

(While He (Allah) grants refuge (or protection), but none grants refuge from Him) (23:88)

(So on that Day none will punish as He will punish. And none will bind (the wicked, disbelievers and polytheists) as He will bind) (89:25-26)

("What is the matter with you Why do you not help one another (as you used to do in the world)" Nay, but that Day they shall surrender) (37:25-26) and,

(Then why did those whom they had taken for alihah (gods) besides Allah, as a way of approach (to Allah) not help them Nay, but they vanished completely from them) (46:28).

Also, Ad-Dahhak said that Ibn 'Abbas said that Allah's statement,

("What is the matter with you Why do you not help one another") (37:25) means, "This Day, you shall not have a refuge from Us. Not this Day." Ibn Jarir said that Allah's statement,

(nor will they be helped.) meaning, on that Day, they shall neither be helped by any helper, nor shall anyone intercede on their behalf. No repeal or ransom will be accepted for them, all courtesy towards them will have ceased, along with any helpful intercession. No type of help or cooperation will be available for them on that Day. The judgment will, on that Day, be up to the Most Great, the Most Just, against whom no intercessor or helper can ever assist. He will then award the evil deed its kind and will multiply the good deeds.

This is similar to Allah's statement,

(But stop them, verily, they are to be questioned. "What is the matter with you Why do you not help one another" Nay, but that Day they shall surrender) (37:24-26).

Surah: 2 Ayah: 49 & Ayah: 50

﴿ وَإِذْ نَجَّيْنَٰكُم مِّنْ ءَالِ فِرْعَوْنَ يَسُومُونَكُمْ سُوٓءَ ٱلْعَذَابِ يُذَبِّحُونَ أَبْنَآءَكُمْ وَيَسْتَحْيُونَ نِسَآءَكُمْ ۚ وَفِى ذَٰلِكُم بَلَآءٌ مِّن رَّبِّكُمْ عَظِيمٌ ﴾

49. And (remember) when We delivered you from Fir'aun's (Pharaoh) people, who were afflicting you with a horrible torment, killing your sons and sparing your women, and therein was a mighty trial from your Lord.

﴿ وَإِذْ فَرَقْنَا بِكُمُ ٱلْبَحْرَ فَأَنجَيْنَٰكُمْ وَأَغْرَقْنَآ ءَالَ فِرْعَوْنَ وَأَنتُمْ تَنظُرُونَ ﴾

50. And (remember) when We separated the sea for you and saved you and drowned Fir'aun's (Pharaoh) people while you were looking (at them, when the sea-water covered them).

Transliteration

49. Wa-ith najjaynakum min ali firAAawna yasoomoonakum soo-a alAAathabi yuthabbihoona abnaakum wayastahyoona nisaakum wafee thalikum balaon min rabbikum AAa*th*eemun 50. Wa-ith faraqna bikumu albahra faanjaynakum waaghraqna ala firAAawna waantum tan*th*uroona

Tafsir Ibn Kathir

The Children of Israel were saved from Pharaoh and His Army Who drowned

Allah said to the Children of Israel, "Remember My favor on you

(And (remember) when We delivered you from Fir'awn's (Pharaoh) people, who were afflicting you with a horrible torment,) meaning, 'I - Allah - saved you from them and delivered you from their hands in the company of Musa, after they subjected you to horrible torture.' This favor came after the cursed Pharaoh had a dream in which he saw a fire emerge from Bayt Al-Maqdis (Jerusalem), and then the fire entered the houses of the Coptics in Egypt, with the exception of the Children of Israel. Its purport was that his kingship would be toppled by a man among the Children of Israel. It was also said that some of Pharaoh's entourage said that the Children of Israel were expecting a man among them to arise who would establish a state for them. We will mention the Hadith on this subject when we explain Surat Ta Ha (20), Allah willing. After the dream, Pharaoh ordered that every newborn male among the Children of Israel be killed and that the girls be left alone. He also commanded that the Children of Israel be given tasks of hard labor and assigned the most humiliating jobs.

The torment here refers to killing the male infants. In Surat Ibrahim (14) this meaning is clearly mentioned,

(Who were afflicting you with horrible torment, and were slaughtering your sons and letting your women live.) (14:6).

We will explain this Ayah in the beginning of Surat Al-Qasas (28), Allah willing, and our reliance and trust are with Him.

The meaning of, (who were afflicting you) is, "They humiliated you," as Abu `Ubaydah stated. It was also said that it means, "They used to exaggerate in tormenting you" according to Al-Qurtubi. As for Allah saying,

(killing your sons and sparing your women) that explains His statement,

(who were afflicting you with horrible torment) then it explains the meaning of the favor He gave them, as mentioned in His statement,

(Remember My favor which I bestowed upon you). As for what Allah said in Surat Ibrahim,

(And remind them of the annals of Allah) (14:5) meaning, the favors and blessing He granted them, He then said,

(Who were afflicting you with horrible torment, and were slaughtering your sons and letting your women live.) (14:6)

So Allah mentioned saving their children from being slaughtered in order to remind them of the many favors that He granted them.

We should state here that 'Pharaoh' (Fir`awn) is a title that was given to every disbelieving king who ruled Egypt, whether from the `Amaliq (Canaanites) or otherwise, just as Caesar (Qaysar) is the title of the disbelieving kings who ruled Rome and Damascus. Also, Khosrau (Kisra) is the title of the kings who ruled Persia, while Tubb`a is the title of the kings of Yemen, and the kings of Abyssinia (Ethiopia) were called Negus (An-Najashi).

Allah said,

(And therein was a mighty trial from your Lord.)

Ibn Jarir commented that this part of the Ayah means, "Our saving your fathers from the torment that they suffered by the hand of Pharaoh, is a great blessing from your Lord." We should mention that in the blessing there a is test, the same as with hardship, for Allah said,

(And We shall make a trial of you with evil and with good) (21:35) and,

(And We tried them with good (blessings) and evil (calamities) in order that they might turn (to obey Allah.)) (7:168).

Allah's statement next, (And (remember) when We separated the sea for you and saved you and drowned Fir'awn's (Pharaoh) people while you were watching) means, 'After We saved you from Fir'awn and you escaped with Musa; Fir'awn went out in your pursuit and We parted the sea for you.' Allah mentioned this story in detail, as we will come to know, Allah willing.

One of the shortest references to this story is Allah's statement,

(And saved you) meaning, "We saved you from them, drowning them while you watched, bringing relief to your hearts and humiliation to your enemy."

Fasting the Day of 'Ashura

It was reported that the day the Children of Israel were saved from Fir'awn was called the day of 'Ashura'. Imam Ahmad reported that Ibn 'Abbas said that the Messenger of Allah came to Al-Madinah and found that the Jews were fasting the day of 'Ashura'. He asked them, "What is this day that you fast" They said, "This is a good day during which Allah saved the Children of Israel from their enemy, and Musa used to fast this day." The Messenger of Allah said,

》أَنَا أَحَقُّ بِمُوسَى مِنْكُمْ《

(I have more right to Musa than you have.)

So the Messenger of Allah fasted that day and ordered that it be fasted. This Hadith was collected by Al-Bukhari, Muslim, An-Nasa'i and Ibn Majah.

Surah: 2 Ayah: 51, Ayah: 52 & Ayah: 53

﴿ وَإِذْ وَاعَدْنَا مُوسَىٰ أَرْبَعِينَ لَيْلَةً ثُمَّ اتَّخَذْتُمُ الْعِجْلَ مِنْ بَعْدِهِ وَأَنْتُمْ ظَالِمُونَ ﴾

51. And (remember) when We appointed for Mûsâ (Moses) forty nights, and (in his absence) you took the calf (for worship), and you were Zâlimûn (polytheists and wrong-doers).

﴿ ثُمَّ عَفَوْنَا عَنْكُمْ مِنْ بَعْدِ ذَٰلِكَ لَعَلَّكُمْ تَشْكُرُونَ ﴾

52. Then after that We forgave you so that you might be grateful.

$$\left\{ \text{وَإِذْ ءَاتَيْنَا مُوسَى ٱلْكِتَٰبَ وَٱلْفُرْقَانَ لَعَلَّكُمْ تَهْتَدُونَ} \right\}$$

53. And (remember) when We gave Mûsâ (Moses) the Scripture (the Taurât (Torah)) and the criterion (of right and wrong) so that you may be guided aright.

Transliteration

51. Wa-ith waAAadna moosa arbaAAeena laylatan thumma ittakhathtumu alAAijla min baAAdihi waantum *th*alimoona 52. Thumma AAafawna AAankum min baAAdi thalika laAAallakum tashkuroona 53. Wa-ith atayna moosa alkitaba waalfurqana laAAallakum tahtadoona

Tafsir Ibn Kathir

The Children of Israel worshipped the Calf

Allah then said, "Remember My favor on you when I forgave you for worshipping the calf." This happened after Musa went to the meeting place with his Lord at the end of that period which was forty days. These forty days were mentioned in Surat Al-A`raf, when Allah said,

(And We appointed for Musa thirty nights and added (to the period) ten (more)) (7:142).

It was said that these days were during the month of Dhul-Qa'dah plus the first ten days in Dhul-Hijjah, after the Children of Israel were delivered from Fir'awn and they safely crossed the sea. Allah's statement,

(And (remember) when We gave Musa the Scripture) means, the Tawrah,

(And the criterion) that is that which differentiates between truth and falsehood, guidance and deviation.

(So that you may be guided aright), after escaping the sea, as another Ayah in Surat Al-A'raf clearly stated, (And indeed We gave Musa — after We had destroyed the generations of old — the Scripture (the Tawrah) as an enlightenment for mankind, and a guidance and a mercy, that they might remember (or receive admonition)) (28:43).

Surah: 2 Ayah: 54

$$\left\{ \text{وَإِذْ قَالَ مُوسَىٰ لِقَوْمِهِۦ يَٰقَوْمِ إِنَّكُمْ ظَلَمْتُمْ أَنفُسَكُم بِٱتِّخَاذِكُمُ ٱلْعِجْلَ فَتُوبُوٓا۟ إِلَىٰ بَارِئِكُمْ فَٱقْتُلُوٓا۟ أَنفُسَكُمْ ذَٰلِكُمْ خَيْرٌ لَّكُمْ عِندَ بَارِئِكُمْ فَتَابَ عَلَيْكُمْ إِنَّهُۥ هُوَ ٱلتَّوَّابُ ٱلرَّحِيمُ} \right\}$$

54. And (remember) when Mûsâ (Moses) said to his people: "O my people! Verily, you have wronged yourselves by worshipping the calf. So turn in repentance to your Creator and kill yourselves (the innocent kill the wrongdoers among you), that will be better for you with your Creator." Then He accepted your repentance. Truly, He is the One Who accepts repentance, the Most Merciful.

Transliteration

54. Wa-ith qala moosa liqawmihi ya qawmi innakum thalamtum anfusakum biittikhathikumu alAAijla fatooboo ila bari-ikum faoqtuloo anfusakum thalikum khayrun lakum AAinda bari-ikum fataba AAalaykum innahu huwa alttawwabu alrraheemu

Tafsir Ibn Kathir

The Children of Israel kill each other in Repentance

This was the repentance required from the Children of Israel for worshipping the calf. Commenting on Allah's statement;

(And (remember) when Musa said to his people: "O my people! Verily, you have wronged yourselves by worshipping the calf..."), Al-Hasan Al-Basri said, "When their hearts thought of worshipping the calf,

(And when they regretted and saw that they had gone astray, they (repented and) said: "If our Lord does not have mercy upon us and forgive us") (7:149). This is when Musa said to them,

(O my people! Verily, you have wronged yourselves by worshipping the calf...)." Abu 'Al-'Aliyah, Sa'id bin Jubayr and Ar-Rabi' bin Anas commented on,

(So turn in repentance to your Bari') that it means, "To your Creator." Allah's statement,

(to your Bari' (Creator)) alerts the Children of Israel to the enormity of their error and means, "Repent to He Who created you after you associated others with Him in worship."

An-Nasa'i, Ibn Jarir and Ibn Abi Hatim recorded Ibn 'Abbas saying,

"Allah told the Children of Israel that their repentance would be to slay by the sword every person they meet, be he father or son. They should not care whom they kill. Those were guilty whom Musa and Harun were not aware of their guilt, they admitted their sin and did as they were ordered. So Allah forgave both the killer and the one killed."

This is part of the Hadith about the trials that we will mention in Surat Ta Ha, (20) Allah willing.

Ibn Jarir narrated that Ibn 'Abbas said, "Musa said to his people,

("So turn in repentance to your Creator and kill each other (the innocent kill the wrongdoers among you), that will be better for you with your Creator." Then He accepted your repentance. Truly, He is the One Who accepts repentance, the Most Merciful.)

Allah ordered Musa to command his people to kill each other. He ordered those who worshipped the calf to sit down and those who did not worship the calf to stand holding knives in their hands. When they started killing them, a great darkness suddenly overcame them. After the darkness lifted, they had killed seventy thousand of them. Those who were killed among them were forgiven, and those who remained alive were also forgiven."

Surah: 2 Ayah: 55 & Ayah: 56

﴿ وَإِذْ قُلْتُمْ يَٰمُوسَىٰ لَن نُّؤْمِنَ لَكَ حَتَّىٰ نَرَى ٱللَّهَ جَهْرَةً فَأَخَذَتْكُمُ ٱلصَّٰعِقَةُ وَأَنتُمْ تَنظُرُونَ ﴿٥٥﴾ ﴾

55. And (remember) when you said: "O Mûsâ (Moses)! We shall never believe in you until we see Allâh plainly." But you were seized with a thunder-bolt (lightning) while you were looking.

﴿ ثُمَّ بَعَثْنَٰكُم مِّنۢ بَعْدِ مَوْتِكُمْ لَعَلَّكُمْ تَشْكُرُونَ ﴿٥٦﴾ ﴾

56. Then We raised you up after your death, so that you might be grateful.

Transliteration

55. Wa-ith qultum ya moosa lan nu/mina laka hatta nara Allaha jahratan faakhathatkumu alssaAAiqatu waantum tan*th*uroona 56. Thumma baAAathnakum min baAAdi mawtikum laAAallakum tashkuroona

Tafsir Ibn Kathir

The Best among the Children of Israel ask to see Allah; their subsequent Death and Resurrection

Allah said, 'Remember My favor on you for resurrecting you after you were seized with lightning when you asked to see Me directly, which neither you nor anyone else can bear or attain.' This was said by Ibn Jurayj. Ibn 'Abbas said that the Ayah

(And (remember) when you said: "O Musa ! We shall never believe in you until we see Allah plainly.") means, "Publicly", "So that we gaze at Allah." Also, `Urwah bin Ruwaym said that Allah's statement,

(While you were looking) means, "Some of them were struck with lightning while others were watching." Allah resurrected those, and struck the others with lightning. As-Suddi commented on,

(But you were seized with a bolt of lightning) saying; "They died, and Musa stood up crying and supplicating to Allah, `O Lord! What should I say to the Children of Israel when I go back to them after You destroyed the best of them,

(If it had been Your will, You could have destroyed them and me before; would You destroy us for the deeds of the foolish ones among us)' Allah revealed to Musa that these seventy men were among those who worshipped the calf. Afterwards, Allah brought them back to life one man at a time, while the rest of them were watching how Allah was bringing them back to life. That is why Allah's said,

(Then We raised you up after your death, so that you might be grateful.)"

Ar-Rabi' bin Anas said, "Death was their punishment, and they were resurrected after they died so they could finish out their lives." Qatadah said similarly.

'Abdur-Rahman bin Zayd bin Aslam commented on this Ayah,

"Musa returned from meeting with his Lord carrying the Tablets on which He wrote the Tawrah. He found that they had worshipped the calf in his absence. Consequently, he commanded them to kill themselves, and they complied, and Allah forgave them. He said to them, 'These Tablets have Allah's Book, containing what He commanded you and what He forbade for you.' They said, 'Should we believe this statement because you said it By Allah, we will not believe until we see Allah in the open, until He shows us Himself and says: This is My Book, therefore, adhere to it. Why does He not talk to us as He talked to you, O, Musa'"

Then he ('Abdur-Rahman bin Zayd) recited Allah's statement,

(We shall never believe in you until we see Allah plainly)

and said, "So Allah's wrath fell upon them, a thunderbolt struck them, and they all died. Then Allah brought them back to life after He killed them."

Then he (`Abdur-Rahman) recited Allah's statement,

(Then We raised you up after your death, so that you might be grateful), and said, "Musa said to them, `Take the Book of Allah.' They said, `No.' He said, `What is the matter with you' They said, `The problem is that we died and came back to life.' He said, `Take the Book of Allah.' They said, `No.' So Allah sent some angels who made the mountain topple over them." This shows that the Children of Israel were required to fulfill the commandments after they were brought back to life.

However, Al-Mawardy said that there are two opinions about this matter. The first opinion is that since the Children of Israel witnessed these miracles, they were compelled to believe, so they did not have to fulfill the commandments. The second opinion states that they were required to adhere to the commandments, so that no responsible adult is free of such responsibilities. Al-Qurtubi said that this is what is correct, because, he said, although the Children of Israel witnessed these tremendous calamities and incidents, that did not mean that they were not responsible for fulfilling the commandments any more. Rather they are responsible for that, and this is clear. Allah knows best.

Surah: 2 Ayah: 57

﴿ وَظَلَّلْنَا عَلَيْكُمُ ٱلْغَمَامَ وَأَنزَلْنَا عَلَيْكُمُ ٱلْمَنَّ وَٱلسَّلْوَىٰ كُلُواْ مِن طَيِّبَـٰتِ مَا رَزَقْنَـٰكُمْ وَمَا ظَلَمُونَا وَلَـٰكِن كَانُوٓاْ أَنفُسَهُمْ يَظْلِمُونَ ۝ ﴾

57. And We shaded you with clouds and sent down on you Al-Manna and the quails, (saying): "Eat of the good lawful things We have provided for you," (but they rebelled). And they did not wrong Us but they wronged themselves.

Translation

57. And We shaded you with clouds and sent down on you *Al-Manna* and the quails, (saying): "Eat of the good lawful things We have provided for you," (but they rebelled). And they did not wrong Us but they wronged themselves.

Tafsir Ibn Kathir

The Shade, the Manna and the Quail

After Allah mentioned the calamities that He saved the Children of Israel from, He mentioned the favors that He granted them, saying,

And We shaded you with clouds. This Ayah mentions the white clouds that provided shade for the Children of Israel, protecting them from the sun's heat during their years of wandering. In the Haadith about the trials, An-Nasai recorded Ibn Abbas saying, Allah shaded the Children of Israel with clouds during the years of wandering. Ibn Abi Hatim said, Narrations similar to that of Ibn Abbas were reported from Ibn Umar, Ar-Rabi bin Anas, Abu Milaz, Ad-Dahhak, and As-Suddi. Al-Hasan and Qatadah said that,

(And We shaded you with clouds) "This happened when they were in the desert and the clouds shielded them from the sun." Ibn Jarir said that several scholars said that the type of cloud the Ayah mentioned, "was cooler and better than the type we know."

'Ali bin Abi Talhah reported that Ibn 'Abbas commented on Allah's statement,

And sent down on you Al-Manna, The manna used to descend to them to the trees, and they used to eat whatever they wished of it. Also, Qatadah said, The manna, which was whiter than milk and sweeter than honey, used to rain down on the Children of Israel, just as the snow falls, from dawn until sunrise. One of them would collect enough for that particular day, for if it remained more than that, it would spoil. On the sixth day, Friday, one would collect enough for the sixth and the seventh day, which was the Sabbath during which one would not leave home to seek his livelihood, or for anything else. All this occurred in the wilderness. The type of manna that we know provides sufficient food when eaten alone, because it is nutritious and sweet. When manna is mixed with water, it becomes a sweet drink. It also changes composition when mixed with other types of food. However, this is not the only type. The evidence to this fact is that Al-Bukhari narrated, that Sa 'd bin Zayd said that the Messenger of Allah said,

«الْكَمْأَةُ مِنَ الْمَنِّ وَمَاؤُهَا شِفَاءٌ لِلْعَيْنِ»

(Kam'ah (truffles) is a type of manna, and its liquid is a remedy for the eyes.)

This Hadith was also collected by Imam Ahmad. The group of Hadith compilers, with the exception of Abu Dawud, also collected it, and At-Tirmidhi graded it Hasan Sahih. At-Tirmidhi recorded Abu Hurayrah saying that the Messenger of Allah said,

«الْعَجْوَةُ مِنَ الْجَنَّةِ وَفِيهَا شِفَاءٌ مِنَ السُّمِّ وَالْكَمْأَةُ مِنَ الْمَنِّ وَمَاؤُهَا شِفَاءٌ لِلْعَيْنِ»

(The 'Ajwah (pressed, dried date) is from Paradise and it cures poison, Al-Kam'ah (truffles) is a form of manna, and its liquid heals the eye.") At-Tirmidhi is the only one of them who recorded this Hadith.

As for the quail (Salwa) in question, 'Ali bin Abi Talhah reported that Ibn 'Abbas said, "The (Salwa) is a bird that looks like the quail." This is the same opinion reported from Mujahid, Ash-Sha'bi, Ad-Dahhak, Al-Hasan, 'Ikrimah and Ar-Rabi' bin Anas, may Allah have mercy upon them. Also, 'Ikrimah said that the Salwa is a bird in Paradise about the size of a sparrow. Qatadah said "The Salwa is a bird that is similar to a sparrow. During that time, an Israelite could catch as many quails as was sufficient for that particular day, otherwise the meat would spoil. On the sixth day, Friday, he would collect what is enough for the sixth and the seventh day, the Sabbath, during which one was not allowed to depart his home to seek anything."

Allah said, (Eat of the good lawful things We have provided for you,) (7:160) this form of command is a simple order of allowance, guiding to what is good. Allah said,

(And they did not wrong Us but they wronged themselves) means, 'We commanded them to eat from what We gave them, and to perform the acts of worship (but they rebelled).' This Ayah is similar to Allah's statement,

(Eat of the provision of your Lord, and be grateful to Him) (34:15).

Yet, the Children of Israel rebelled, disbelieved and committed injustice against themselves, even though they saw the clear signs, tremendous miracles and extraordinary events.

The Virtue of Muhammad's Companions over the Companions of all Other Prophets

Here it is important to point out the virtue of Muhammad's Companions over the companions of the other Prophets. This includes firmness in the religion, patience and the lack of arrogance, may Allah be pleased with them. Although the Companions accompanied the Prophet in his travels and battles, such as during the battle of Tabuk, in intense heat and hardship, they did not ask for a miracle, though this was easy for the Prophet by Allah's leave. And when the Companions became hungry, they merely asked the Prophet - to invoke Allah - for an increase in the amount of food. They collected whatever food they had and brought it to the Prophet , and he asked Allah to bless it, told each of them to take some food, and they filled every pot they had. Also, when they needed rain, the Prophet asked Allah to send down rain, and a rain cloud came. They drank, gave water to their camels and filled their water skins. When they looked around, they found that the cloud had only rained on their camp. This is the best example of those who were willing to accept Allah's decision and follow the Messenger of Allah.

Surah: 2 Ayah: 58 & Ayah: 59

﴿ وَإِذْ قُلْنَا ٱدْخُلُوا۟ هَـٰذِهِ ٱلْقَرْيَةَ فَكُلُوا۟ مِنْهَا حَيْثُ شِئْتُمْ رَغَدًا وَٱدْخُلُوا۟ ٱلْبَابَ سُجَّدًا وَقُولُوا۟ حِطَّةٌ نَّغْفِرْ لَكُمْ خَطَـٰيَـٰكُمْ ۚ وَسَنَزِيدُ ٱلْمُحْسِنِينَ

58. And (remember) when We said: "Enter this town (Jerusalem) and eat bountifully therein with pleasure and delight wherever you wish, and enter the gate in prostration (or bowing with humility) and say: 'Forgive us,' and

We shall forgive you your sins and shall increase (reward) for the good-doers."

﴿ فَبَدَّلَ ٱلَّذِينَ ظَلَمُواْ قَوْلاً غَيْرَ ٱلَّذِى قِيلَ لَهُمْ فَأَنزَلْنَا عَلَى ٱلَّذِينَ ظَلَمُواْ رِجْزًا مِّنَ ٱلسَّمَآءِ بِمَا كَانُواْ يَفْسُقُونَ ۝ ﴾

59. But those who did wrong changed the word from that which had been told to them for another, so We sent upon the wrong-doers Rijzan (a punishment) from the heaven because of their rebelling against Allâh's Obedience. (Tafsir At-Tabarî).

Transliteration

58. Wa-ith qulna odkhuloo hathihi alqaryata fakuloo minha haythu shi/tum raghadan waodkhuloo albaba sujjadan waqooloo hittatun naghfir lakum khatayakum wasanazeedu almuhsineena 59. Fabaddala allatheena *th*alamoo qawlan ghayra allathee qeela lahum faanzalna AAala allatheena *th*alamoo rijzan mina alssama-i bima kanoo yafsuqoona

Tafsir Ibn Kathir

The Jews were Rebellious instead of Appreciative when They gained Victory

Allah admonished the Jews for avoiding Jihad and not entering the holy land as they had been ordered to do when they came from Egypt with Musa. They were also commanded to fight the disbelieving 'Amaliq (Canaanites) dwelling in the holy land at that time. But they did not want to fight, because they were weak and exhausted. Allah punished them by causing them to become lost, and to continue wandering, as Allah has stated in Surat Al-Ma'idah (5). The correct opinion about the meaning of, 'the holy land' mentioned here is that it was Bayt Al-Maqdis (Jerusalem), as As-Suddi, Ar-Rabi' bin Anas, Qatadah and Abu Muslim Al-Asfahani, as well as others have stated. Musa said,

(O people! Enter the holy land which Allah has assigned to you and turn not back (in flight).) (5:21)

However, some scholars said that the holy land is Jericho, (Ariha') and this opinion was mentioned from Ibn 'Abbas and 'Abdur-Rahman bin Zayd.

After the years of wandering ended forty years later, in the company of Yuwsha' (Joshua) bin Nun, Allah allowed the Children of Israel to conquer the holy land on the eve of a Friday. On that day, the sun was kept from setting for a little more time, until victory was achieved. When the Children of Israel conquered the holy land, they were commanded to enter its gate while, (prostrating) in appreciation to Allah for making them victorious, triumphant, returning them to their land and saving them from being lost and wandering. Al-'Awfi said that Ibn 'Abbas said that,

(and enter the gate Sujjadan) means, "While bowing". Ibn Jarir reported Ibn 'Abbas saying,

(and enter the gate in prostration) means, "Through a small door while bowing." Al-Hakim narrated it, and Ibn Abi Hatim added, "And they went through the door backwards!" Al-Hasan Al-Basri said that they were ordered to prostrate on their faces when they entered the city, but Ar-Razi discounted this explanation. It was also said that the Sujud mentioned here means, 'submissiveness', for actually entering while prostrating is not possible.

Khasif said that 'Ikrimah said that Ibn 'Abbas said, "The door mentioned here was facing the Qiblah." Ibn 'Abbas, Mujahid, As-Suddi, Qatadah and Ad-Dahhak said that the door is the door of Hittah in Iylya', which is Jerusalem. Ar-Razi also reported that some of them said that it was a door in the direction of the Qiblah". Khasif said that 'Ikrimah said that Ibn 'Abbas said that the Children of Israel entered the door sideways. As-Suddi said that Abu Sa'id Al-Azdy said that Abu Al-Kanud said that 'Abdullah bin Mas'ud said that they were commanded to, u

(enter the gate in prostration (or bowing with humility)) but instead, they entered while their heads were raised in defiance.

Allah said next,

(and say: 'Hittah'). Ibn 'Abbas commented, "Seek Allah's forgiveness." Al-Hasan and Qatadah said that it means, "Say, 'Relieve us from our errors.'"

(and We shall forgive you your sins and shall increase (reward) for the good-doers) Here is the reward for fulfilling Allah's commandment. This Ayah means, "If you implement what We commanded you, We will forgive your sins and multiply your good deeds." In summary, upon achieving victory, the Children of Israel were commanded to submit to Allah in tongue and deed and, to admit to their sins and seek forgiveness for them, to be grateful to Allah for the blessings He gave them, hastening to do the deeds that Allah loves, as He said,

(When there comes the help of Allah (to you, O Muhammad against your enemies) and the conquest (of Makkah). And you see that the people enter Allah's religion (Islam) in crowds. So glorify the praises of your Lord, and ask His forgiveness. Verily, He is the One Who accepts the repentance.) (110).

Allah said,

(But those who did wrong changed the word from that which had been told to them for another).

Al-Bukhari recorded Abu Hurayrah saying that the Prophet said,

»قِيلَ لِبَنِي إِسْرَائِيلَ ادْخُلُوا الْبَابَ سُجَّدًا وَقُولُوا: حِطَّةٌ، فَدَخَلُوا يَزْحَفُونَ عَلَى أَسْتَاهِهِم فَبَدَّلُوا وَقَالُوا، حَبَّةٌ فِي شَعْرَة«

(The Children of Israel were commanded to enter the door while bowing and to say 'Hittah'. Yet, they entered the door on their behinds, distorting the words. They said; 'Habbah (seed), in Sha'rah (a hair).')

An-Nasa'i recorded this part of it from Abu Hurayrah only, but he has a chain from the Prophet , explaining Allah's statement,

('Hittah'), saying, "So they deviated and said 'Habbah.'" Similar was recorded by 'Abdur-Razzaq, and his route was also collected by Al-Bukhari. Muslim and At-Tirmidhi narrated similar versions of this Hadith, At-Tirmidhi said, "Hasan Sahih."

The summary of what the scholars have said about this subject is that the Children of Israel distorted Allah's command to them to submit to Him in tongue and deed. They were commanded to enter the city while bowing down, but they entered while sliding on their rear ends and raising their heads! They were commanded to say, 'Hittah' meaning, "Relieve us from our errors and sins." However, they mocked this command and said, "Hintah (grain seed) in Sha'irah (barley)." This demonstrates the worst type of rebellion and disobedience, and it is why Allah released His anger and punishment upon them, all because of their sinning and defying His commands.

Allah said,

(So We sent upon the wrongdoers Rijz (a punishment) from the heaven because of their rebellion.)

Ad-Dahhak said that Ibn 'Abbas said, "Every word in Allah's Book that says Rijz means, 'a punishment.'" Mujahid, Abu Malik, As-Suddi, Al-Hasan and Qatadah were reported to have said that Rijz means 'Torment.' Ibn Abi Hatim narrated that Sa'd bin Malik, Usamah bin Zayd and Khuzaymah bin Thabit said that the Messenger of Allah said,

»الطَّاعُونُ رِجْزٌ.عَذَابٌ عُذِّبَ بِهِ مَنْ كَانَ قَبْلَكُم«

(The plague is a Rijz, a punishment with which Allah punished those before you.)

This is also how An-Nasa'i recorded this Hadith. In addition, the basis of this Hadith was collected in the Two Sahihs,

$$\text{«إِذَا سَمِعْتُمُ الطَّاعُونَ بِأَرْضٍ فَلَا تَدْخُلُوهَا»}$$

(If you hear of the plague in a land, then do not enter it.)

Ibn Jarir recorded Usamah bin Zayd saying that the Messenger of Allah said,

$$\text{«إِنَّ هَذَا الْوَجَعَ وَالسَّقَمَ رِجْزٌ عُذِّبَ بِهِ بَعْضُ الْأُمَمِ قَبْلَكُمْ»}$$

(This calamity and sickness (i.e. the plague) is a Rijz, a punishment with which some nations who were before you were punished.)

The basis of this Hadith was also collected in the Two Sahihs.

Surah: 2 Ayah: 60

$$\text{﴿ ۞ وَإِذِ اسْتَسْقَىٰ مُوسَىٰ لِقَوْمِهِ فَقُلْنَا اضْرِب بِّعَصَاكَ الْحَجَرَ ۖ فَانفَجَرَتْ مِنْهُ اثْنَتَا عَشْرَةَ عَيْنًا ۖ قَدْ عَلِمَ كُلُّ أُنَاسٍ مَّشْرَبَهُمْ ۖ كُلُوا وَاشْرَبُوا مِن رِّزْقِ اللَّهِ وَلَا تَعْثَوْا فِي الْأَرْضِ مُفْسِدِينَ ﴾}$$

60. And (remember) when Mûsâ (Moses) asked for water for his people, We said: "Strike the stone with your stick." Then gushed forth therefrom twelve springs. Each (group of) people knew its own place for water. "Eat and drink of that which Allâh has provided and do not act corruptly, making mischief on the earth."

Transliteration

60. Wa-ithi istasqa moosa liqawmihi faqulna idrib biAAasaka alhajara fainfajarat minhu ithnata AAashrata AAaynan qad AAalima kullu onasin mashrabahum kuloo waishraboo min rizqi Allahi wala taAAthaw fee al-ardi mufsideena

Tafsir Ibn Kathir

Twelve Springs gush forth

Allah said, "Remember My favor on you when I answered the supplication of your Prophet, Musa, when he asked Me to provide you with water. I made the water available for you, making it gush out through a stone. Twelve springs burst out of that stone, a designated spring for each of your tribes. You eat from the manna and the quails and drink from the water that I provided for you, without any effort or hardship for you. So worship the One Who did this for you.

(And do not act corruptly, making mischief on the earth) meaning, "Do not return the favor by committing acts of disobedience that cause favors to disappear."

Ibn 'Abbas said that the Children of Israel, "Had a square stone that Musa was commanded to strike with his staff and, as a result, twelve springs burst out of that stone, three on each side. Each tribe was, therefore, designated a certain spring, and they used to drink from their springs. They never had to travel from their area, they would find the same bounty in the same manner they had in the first area."This narration is part of the long Hadith that An-Nasa'i, Ibn Jarir and Ibn Abi Hatim recorded about the trials.

This story is similar to the story in Surat Al-'Araf (Chapter 7) although the latter was revealed in Makkah. In Surat Al-A'raf, Allah used the third person when He mentioned the Children of Israel to the Prophet and narrated what He favored them with.

In this Surat Al-Baqarah, which was revealed in Al-Madinah, Allah directed His Speech at the Children of Israel. Further, Allah said in Surat Al-A'raf,

(And there gushed forth out of it twelve springs) (7:160), describing what first occurred when the water begins to gush out. In the Ayah in Surat Al-Baqarah, Allah described what happened later on, meaning when the water burst out in full force. Allah knows best.

Surah: 2 Ayah: 61

﴿ وَإِذْ قُلْتُمْ يَـٰمُوسَىٰ لَن نَّصْبِرَ عَلَىٰ طَعَامٍ وَاحِدٍ فَادْعُ لَنَا رَبَّكَ يُخْرِجْ لَنَا مِمَّا تُنبِتُ ٱلْأَرْضُ مِنْ بَقْلِهَا وَقِثَّآئِهَا وَفُومِهَا وَعَدَسِهَا وَبَصَلِهَا ۖ قَالَ أَتَسْتَبْدِلُونَ ٱلَّذِى هُوَ أَدْنَىٰ بِٱلَّذِى هُوَ خَيْرٌ ۚ ٱهْبِطُوا۟ مِصْرًا فَإِنَّ لَكُم مَّا سَأَلْتُمْ ۗ وَضُرِبَتْ عَلَيْهِمُ ٱلذِّلَّةُ وَٱلْمَسْكَنَةُ وَبَآءُو بِغَضَبٍ مِّنَ ٱللَّهِ ۗ ذَٰلِكَ بِأَنَّهُمْ كَانُوا۟ يَكْفُرُونَ بِـَٔايَـٰتِ ٱللَّهِ وَيَقْتُلُونَ ٱلنَّبِيِّـۧنَ بِغَيْرِ ٱلْحَقِّ ۗ ذَٰلِكَ بِمَا عَصَوا۟ وَّكَانُوا۟ يَعْتَدُونَ ﴾

61. And (remember) when you said, "O Mûsâ (Moses)! We cannot endure one kind of food. So invoke your Lord for us to bring forth for us of what the earth grows, its herbs, its cucumbers, its Fûm (wheat or garlic), its lentils and its onions." He said, "Would you exchange that which is better for that which is lower? Go you down to any town and you shall find what you want!" And they were covered with humiliation and misery, and they drew on themselves the Wrath of Allâh. That was because they used to disbelieve the Ayât (proofs, evidences, verses, lessons, signs, revelations,

etc.) of Allâh and killed the Prophets wrongfully. That was because they disobeyed and used to transgress the bounds (in their disobedience to Allâh, i.e. commit crimes and sins).

Transliteration

61. Wa-ith qultum ya moosa lan nasbira AAala taAAamin wahidin faodAAu lana rabbaka yukhrij lana mimma tunbitu al-ardu min baqliha waqiththa-iha wafoomiha waAAadasiha wabasaliha qala atastabdiloona allathee huwa adna biallathee huwa khayrun ihbitoo misran fa-inna lakum ma saaltum waduribat AAalayhimu alththillatu waalmaskanatu wabaoo bighadabin mina Allahi thalika biannahum kanoo yakfuroona bi-ayati Allahi wayaqtuloona alnnabiyyeena bighayri alhaqqi thalika bima AAasaw wakanoo yaAAtadoona

Tafsir Ibn Kathir

The Children of Israel preferred Foods inferior to Manna and Quails

Allah said, "And remember My favor on you when I sent down the manna and quails to you, a good, pure, beneficial, easily acquired food. And remember your ungratefulness for what We granted you. Remember how you asked Musa to exchange this type of food for an inferior type that consists of vegetation, and so forth." Al-Hasan Al-Basri said about the Children of Israel, "They were bored and impatient with the type of food they were provided. They also remembered the life they used to live, when their diet consisted of lentils, onions, garlic and herbs." They said,

(O Musa ! We cannot endure one kind of food. So invoke your Lord for us to bring forth for us of what the earth grows, its herbs, its cucumbers, its Fum, its lentils and its onions). They said,

(One kind of food) meaning, the manna and quails, because they ate the same food day after day. The Ayah mentioned lentils, onions and herbs, which are all known types of foods. As for the Fum, Ibn Mas'ud read it, Thum (garlic). Also, Ibn Abi Hatim narrated that Al-Hasan said about the Ayah, (Its Fum), "Ibn `Abbas said that Fum means, garlic."

He also said that the expression, 'Fumu-lanna' means, 'bake for us', according to the languages of old. Ibn Jarir commented, "If this is true, then 'Fum' is one of the words whose pronounciation were altered, the letter 'fa' was replaced by the letter 'tha', since they are similar in sound." And Allah knows best. Others said that Fum is wheat, the kind used for bread. Al-Bukhari said, "Some of them said that Fum includes all grains or seeds that are eaten."

Allah's statement,

(He said, "Would you exchange that which is better for that which is lower") criticized the Jews for asking for inferior foods, although they were living an easy life, eating tasty, beneficial and pure food. Allah's statement,

(Go you down to any Misr) means, 'any city', as Ibn 'Abbas said. Ibn Jarir also reported that Abu Al-'Aliyah and Ar-Rabi' bin Anas said that the Ayah refers to Misr, the Egypt of Fir'awn. The truth is that the Ayah means any city, as Ibn 'Abbas and other scholars stated. Therefore, the meaning of Musa's statement to the Children of Israel becomes, "What you are asking for is easy, for it is available in abundance in any city that you might enter. So since what you asked for is available in all of the villages and cities, I will not ask Allah to provide us with it, especially when it is an inferior type of food. " This is why Musa said to them,

(Would you exchange that which is better for that which is lower Go you down to any town and you shall find what you want!)

Since their request was the result of boredom and arrogance and since fulfilling it was unnecessary, their request was denied. Allah knows best.

Covering the Jews in Humiliation and Misery

Allah said, (And they were covered with humiliation and misery). This Ayah indicates that the Children of Israel were plagued with humiliation, and that this will continue, meaning that it will never cease. They will continue to suffer humiliation at the hands of all who interact with them, along with the disgrace that they feel inwardly. Al-Hasan commented, "Allah humiliated them, and they shall have no protector. Allah put them under the feet of the Muslims, who appeared at a time when the Majus (Zoroastrians) were taking the Jizyah (tax) from the Jews." Also, Abu Al-'Aliyah, Ar-Rabi' bin Anas and As-Suddi said that `misery' used in the Ayah means, `poverty.' `Atiyah Al-`Awfi said that `misery' means, `paying the tilth (tax).'

In addition, Ad-Dahhak commented on Allah's statement, (and they drew on themselves the wrath of Allah), "They deserved Allah's anger." Also, Ibn Jarir said that,

(and they drew on themselves the wrath of Allah) means, "They went back with the wrath. Similarly, Allah said, (Verily, I intend to let you draw my sin on yourself as well as yours) (Al-Ma'idah 5:29) meaning, 'You will end up carrying my, and your, mistakes instead of me'. Thus, the meaning of the Ayah becomes, 'They went back carrying Allah's anger; Allah's wrath descended on them; they deserved Allah's anger.'"

Allah's statement, (That was because they used to disbelieve in the Ayat (proofs, evidences, etc.) of Allah and killed the Prophets wrongfully.) means, "This is what We rewarded the Children of Israel with: humiliation and misery." Allah's anger that descended on the Children of Israel was a part of the humiliation they earned, because of their defiance of the truth, disbelief in Allah's Ayat and belittling the carriers of Allah's Law i.e. the Prophets and their following. The Children of Israel rejected the Messengers and even killed them. Surely, there is no form of disbelief worse than disbelieving in Allah's Ayat and murdering the Prophets of Allah.

Meaning of Kibr

Similarly, in a Hadith recorded in the Two Sahihs the Messenger of Allah said,

«الْكِبْرُ بَطَرُ الْحَقِّ وَغَمْطُ النَّاسِ»

('Kibr, is refusing the truth and degrading (belittling) people.)

Imam Ahmad recorded, 'Abdullah bin Mas'ud saying that the Messenger of Allah said,

«أَشَدُّ النَّاسِ عَذَابًا يَوْمَ الْقِيَامَةِ رَجُلٌ قَتَلَهُ نَبِيٌّ أَوْ قَتَلَ نَبِيًّا، وَإِمَامُ ضَلَالَةٍ وَمُمَثِّلٌ مِنَ الْمُمَثِّلِينَ»

(The people who will receive the most torment on the Day of Resurrection are: a man who was killed by a Prophet or who killed a Prophet, an unjust ruler and one who mutilates (the dead).)

Allah's statement,

(That was because they disobeyed and used to transgress the bounds) mentions another reason why the Children of Israel were punished in this manner, for they used to disobey and transgress the limits. Disobedience is to do what is prohibited, while transgression entails overstepping the set limits of what is allowed and what is prohibited. Allah knows best.

Surah: 2 Ayah: 62

﴿ إِنَّ ٱلَّذِينَ ءَامَنُواْ وَٱلَّذِينَ هَادُواْ وَٱلنَّصَٰرَىٰ وَٱلصَّٰبِـِٔينَ مَنْ ءَامَنَ بِٱللَّهِ وَٱلْيَوْمِ ٱلْءَاخِرِ وَعَمِلَ صَٰلِحًا فَلَهُمْ أَجْرُهُمْ عِندَ رَبِّهِمْ وَلَا خَوْفٌ عَلَيْهِمْ وَلَا هُمْ يَحْزَنُونَ ۝ ﴾

62. Verily! Those who believe and those who are Jews and Christians, and Sabians, whoever believes in Allâh and the Last Day and does righteous good deeds shall have their reward with their Lord, on them shall be no fear, nor they grieve.

Transliteration

62. Inna allatheena amanoo waallatheena hadoo waalnnasara waalssabi-eena man amana biAllahi waalyawmi al-akhiri waAAamila salihan falahum ajruhum AAinda rabbihim wala khawfun AAalayhim wala hum yahzanoona

Tafsir Ibn Kathir

Faith and doing Righteous Deeds equals Salvation in all Times

After Allah described the condition - and punishment - of those who defy His commands, fall into His prohibitions and transgress set limits by committing prohibited acts, He stated that the earlier nations who were righteous and obedient received the rewards for their good deeds. This shall be the case, until the Day of Judgment. Therefore, whoever follows the unlettered Messenger and Prophet shall acquire eternal happiness and shall neither fear from what will happen in the future nor become sad for what has been lost in the past. Similarly, Allah said,

(No doubt! Verily, the Awliya' of Allah, no fear shall come upon them nor shall they grieve) (10:62).

The angels will proclaim to the dying believers, as mentioned, (Verily, those who say: "Our Lord is Allah (alone)," and then they stand firm, on them the angels will descend (at the time of their death) (saying): "Fear not, nor grieve! But receive the glad tidings of Paradise which you have been promised!"). (41:30)

The Meaning of Mu'min, or Believer

'Ali bin Abi Talhah narrated from Ibn 'Abbas, about,

(Verily, those who believe and those who are Jews and Christians, and Sabians, whoever believes in Allah and the Last Day) that Allah revealed the following Ayah afterwards,

(And whoever seeks religion other than Islam, it will never be accepted of him, and in the Hereafter he will be one of the losers) (3:85).

This statement by Ibn 'Abbas indicates that Allah does not accept any deed or work from anyone, unless it conforms to the Law of Muhammad that is, after Allah sent Muhammad . Before that, every person who followed the guidance of his own Prophet was on the correct path, following the correct guidance and was saved.

Why the Jews were called 'Yahud

The Jews are the followers of Prophet Musa, who used to refer to the Tawrah for judgment. Yahud is a word that means, 'repenting', just as Musa said, "We repent to You".

why the christians were called nasara

("Who will be my helpers in Allah's cause" Al-Hawariyyun said: "We are the helpers of Allah.") (61:14)

It was said that they were called 'Nasara', because they inhabited a land called An-Nasirah (Nazareth), as Qatadah, Ibn Jurayj and Ibn 'Abbas were reported to have said, Allah knows best. Nasara is certainly plural for Nasran.

When Allah sent Muhammad as the Last and Final Prophet and Messenger to all of the Children of Adam, mankind was required to believe in him, obey him and refrain from what he prohibited them; those who do this are true believers. The Ummah of Muhammad was called 'Mu'minin' (believers), because of the depth of their faith and certainty, and because they believe in all of the previous Prophets and matters of the Unseen.

The Sabi'un or Sabians

There is a difference of opinion over the identity of the Sabians. Sufyan Ath-Thawri said that Layth bin Abu Sulaym said that Mujahid said that, "The Sabians are between the Majus, the Jews and the Christians. They do not have a specific religion." Similar is reported from Ibn Abi Najih. Similar statements were attributed to `Ata' and Sa`id bin Jubayr. They (others) say that the Sabians are a sect among the People of the Book who used to read the Zabur (Psalms), others say that they are a people who worshipped the angels or the stars. It appears that the closest opinion to the truth, and Allah knows best, is Mujahid's statement and those who agree with him like Wahb bin Munabbih, that the Sabians are neither Jews nor Christians nor Majus nor polytheists. Rather, they did not have a specific religion that they followed and enforced, because they remained living according to their Fitrah (instinctual nature). This is why the idolators used to call whoever embraced Islam a `Sabi', meaning, that he abandoned all religions that existed on the earth. Some scholars stated that the Sabians are those who never received a message by any Prophet.

And Allah knows best.

Surah: 2 Ayah: 63 & Ayah: 64

﴿ وَإِذْ أَخَذْنَا مِيثَـٰقَكُمْ وَرَفَعْنَا فَوْقَكُمُ ٱلطُّورَ خُذُوا۟ مَآ ءَاتَيْنَـٰكُم بِقُوَّةٍ وَٱذْكُرُوا۟ مَا فِيهِ لَعَلَّكُمْ تَتَّقُونَ ﴾

63. And (O Children of Israel, remember) when We took your covenant and We raised above you the Mount (saying): "Hold fast to that which We have given you, and remember that which is therein so that you may become Al-Muttaqûn (the pious - See V.2:2).

﴿ ثُمَّ تَوَلَّيْتُم مِّنۢ بَعْدِ ذَٰلِكَ ۖ فَلَوْلَا فَضْلُ ٱللَّهِ عَلَيْكُمْ وَرَحْمَتُهُۥ لَكُنتُم مِّنَ ٱلْخَـٰسِرِينَ ﴾

64. Then after that you turned away. Had it not been for the Grace and Mercy of Allâh upon you, indeed you would have been among the losers.

Transliteration

63. Wa-ith akhathna meethaqakum warafaAAna fawqakumu alttoora khuthoo ma ataynakum biquwwatin waothkuroo ma feehi laAAallakum tattaqoona 64. Thumma tawallaytum min baAAdi thalika falawla fadlu Allahi AAalaykum warahmatuhu lakuntum mina alkhasireena

Tafsir Ibn Kathir

Taking the Covenant from the Jews

Allah reminded the Children of Israel of the pledges, covenants and promises that He took from them to believe in Him alone, without a partner, and follow His Messengers. Allah stated that when He took their pledge from them, He raised the mountain above their heads, so that they affirm the pledge that they gave Allah and abide by it with sincerity and seriousness.

Hence, Allah's statement,

(And (remember) when We raised the mountain over them as if it had been a canopy, and they thought that it was going to fall on them. (We said): "Hold firmly to what We have given you (Tawrah), and remember that which is therein (act on its commandments), so that you may fear Allah and obey Him.") (7:171).

The mount mentioned here is At-Tur, just as it was explained in Surat Al-A'raf, according to the Tafsir of Ibn 'Abbas, Mujahid, 'Ata', 'Ikrimah, Al-Hasan, Ad-Dahhak, Ar-Rabi' bin Anas and others. This is more obvious. There is another report from Ibn 'Abbas saying; 'The Tur is a type of mountain that vegetation grows on, if no vegetation grows on it, it is not called Tur.' And in the Hadith about the trials, Ibn 'Abbas said; "When they (the Jews) refused to obey, Allah raised the mountain above their heads so that they would listen."

Al-Hasan said that Allah's statement, (Hold fast to that which We have given you) means, the Tawrah. Mujahid said that the Ayah commanded, "Strictly adhere to it." Abu Al-'Aliyah and Ar-Rabi` said that, (and remember that which is therein) means, "Read the Tawrah and implement it." Allah's statement,

(Then after that you turned away. Had it not been for the grace of Allah) means, "Yet, after the firm pledge that you gave, you still deviated and broke your pledge";

(Had it not been for the grace and mercy of Allah upon you), meaning, by forgiving you and by sending the Prophets and Messengers to you, (Indeed you would have been among the losers) meaning, in this life and the Hereafter due to their breach of the covenant.

Surah: 2 Ayah: 65 & Ayah: 66

﴿ وَلَقَدْ عَلِمْتُمُ ٱلَّذِينَ ٱعْتَدَوْاْ مِنكُمْ فِى ٱلسَّبْتِ فَقُلْنَا لَهُمْ كُونُواْ قِرَدَةً خَـٰسِـِٔينَ ۝ ﴾

65. And indeed you knew those amongst you who transgressed in the matter of the Sabbath (i.e. Saturday). We said to them: "Be you monkeys, despised and rejected."

﴿ فَجَعَلْنَـٰهَا نَكَـٰلاً لِّمَا بَيْنَ يَدَيْهَا وَمَا خَلْفَهَا وَمَوْعِظَةً لِّلْمُتَّقِينَ ۝ ﴾

66. So We made this punishment an example to their own and to succeeding generations and a lesson to those who are Al-Muttaqûn (the pious - See V.2:2).

Transliteration

65. Walaqad AAalimtumu allatheena iAAtadaw minkum fee alssabti faqulna lahum koonoo qiradatan khasi-eena   66. FajaAAalnaha nakalan lima bayna yadayha wama khalfaha wamawAAithatan lilmuttaqeena

Tafsir Ibn Kathir

The Jews breach the Sanctity of the Sabbath

Allah said,

(And indeed you knew). This Ayah means, O Jews! Remember that Allah sent His torment on the village that disobeyed Him and broke their pledge and their covenant to observe the sanctity of the Sabbath. They began using deceitful means to avoid honoring the Sabbath by placing nets, ropes and artificial pools of water for the purpose of fishing before the Sabbath. When the fish came in abundance on Saturday as usual, they were caught in the ropes and nets for the rest of Saturday. During the night, the Jews collected the fish after the Sabbath ended. When they did that, Allah changed them from humans into monkeys, the animals having the form closest to humans. Their evil deeds and deceit appeared lawful on the surface, but they were in reality wicked. This is why their punishment was compatible with their crime. This story is explained in detail in Surat Al-A'raf, where Allah said (7:163),

(And ask them (O Muhammad) about the town that was by the sea; when they transgressed in the matter of the Sabbath (i.e. Saturday): when their fish came to them openly on the Sabbath day, and did not come to them on the day they had no Sabbath. Thus We made a trial of them, for they used to rebel (disobey Allah).)(7:163)

In his Tafsir, Al-'Awfi reported from Ibn 'Abbas that he said,

(We said to them: "Be you monkeys, despised and rejected") means, "Allah changed their bodies into those of monkeys and swines. The young people turned into monkeys while the old people turned into swine." Shayban An-Nahwi reported that Qatadah commented on,

(We said to them: "Be you monkeys, despised and rejected"), "These people were turned into howling monkeys with tails, after being men and women."

The Monkeys and Swine that exist now are not the Descendants of Those that were transformed

Ibn Abi Hatim recorded that Ibn 'Abbas said, "Those who violated the sanctity of the Sabbath were turned into monkeys, then they perished without offspring." Ad-Dahhak said that Ibn 'Abbas said, "Allah turned them into monkeys because of their sins. They only lived on the earth for three days, for no transformed person ever lives more than three days. They did not eat, drink or have offspring. Allah transformed their shapes into monkeys, and He does what He wills, with whom He wills and He changes the shape of whomever He wills. On the other hand, Allah created the monkeys, swines and the rest of the creation in the six days (of creation) that He mentioned in His Book."

Allah's statement,

(So We made this punishment an example) means, Allah made the people of this village, who violated the sanctity of the Sabbath,

(an example) via the way they were punished. Similarly, Allah said about Pharaoh,

(So Allah, seized him with punishing example for his last and first transgression) (79:25). nAllah's statement,

(for those in front of it and those behind it) meaning, for the other villages. Ibn 'Abbas commented, "Meaning, 'We made this village an example for the villages around it by the manner in which We punished its people.'" Similarly, Allah said,

(And indeed We have destroyed towns (populations) round about you, and We have (repeatedly) shown (them) the Ayat (proofs, evidences, verses, lessons, signs, revelations, etc.) in various ways that they might return (to the truth and believe in the Oneness of Allah — Islamic Monotheism)).(46:27)

Therefore, Allah made them an example for those who lived during their time as well as a reminder for those to come, by preserving their story. This is why Allah said, (and a lesson for Al-Muttaqin (the pious)), meaning, a reminder. This Ayah means, "The torment and punishment that this village suffered was a result of indulging in Allah's prohibitions and their deceit. Hence, those who have Taqwa should be aware of their evil behavior, so that what occurred to this village does not befall them as well." Also, Imam Abu `Abdullah bin Battah reported that Abu Hurayrah said that the Messenger of Allah said,

«لَا تَرْتَكِبُوا مَا ارْتَكَبَتِ الْيَهُودُ فَتَسْتَحِلُّوا مَحَارِمَ اللهِ بِأَدْنَى الْحِيَل»

(Do not commit what the Jews committed, breaching what Allah has forbidden, by resorting to the lowest types of deceit.)

This Hadith has a good (Jayid) chain of narration. Allah knows best.

Surah: 2 Ayah: 67

﴿ وَإِذْ قَالَ مُوسَىٰ لِقَوْمِهِ إِنَّ ٱللَّهَ يَأْمُرُكُمْ أَن تَذْبَحُوا۟ بَقَرَةً ۖ قَالُوٓا۟ أَتَتَّخِذُنَا هُزُوًا ۖ قَالَ أَعُوذُ بِٱللَّهِ أَنْ أَكُونَ مِنَ ٱلْجَٰهِلِينَ ﴿٦٧﴾ ﴾

67. And (remember) when Mûsâ (Moses) said to his people: "Verily, Allâh commands you that you slaughter a cow." They said, "Do you make fun of us?" He said, "I take Allâh's Refuge from being among Al-Jâhilûn (the ignorant or the foolish)."

Transliteration

67. Wa-ith qala moosa liqawmihi inna Allaha ya/murukum an tathbahoo baqaratan qaloo atattakhithuna huzuwan qala aAAoothu biAllahi an akoona mina aljahileena

Tafsir Ibn Kathir

The Story of the murdered Israeli Man and the Cow

Allah said, 'O Children of Israel! Remember how I blessed you with miracle of the cow that was the means for discovering the identity of the murderer, when the murdered man was brought back to life.'

Ibn Abi Hatim recorded 'Ubaydah As-Salmani saying, "There was a man from among the Children of Israel who was impotent. He had substantial wealth, and only a nephew who would inherit from him. So his nephew killed him and moved his body at night, placing it at the doorstep of a certain man. The next morning, the nephew cried out for revenge, and the people took up their weapons and almost fought each other. The wise men among them said, 'Why would you kill each other, while the Messenger of Allah is still among you' So they went to Musa and mentioned the matter to him and Musa said, ("Verily, Allah commands you that you slaughter a cow.") They said, "Do you make fun of us" He said, "I take Allah's refuge from being among Al-Jahilin (the ignorant or the foolish))." "Had they not disputed, it would have been sufficient for them to slaughter any cow. However, they disputed, and the matter was made more difficult for them, until they ended up looking for the specific cow that they were later ordered to slaughter. They found the designated cow with a man, only who owned that cow. He said, `By Allah! I will only sell it for its skin's fill of gold.' So they paid the cow's fill of its skin in gold, slaughtered it and touched the dead man with a part of it. He stood up, and they asked him, `Who killed you' He said, `That man,' and pointed to his nephew. He died again, and his nephew was not allowed to inherit him. Thereafter, whoever committed murder for the purpose of gaining inheritance was not allowed to inherit." Ibn Jarir reported something similar to that. Allah knows best.

Surah: 2 Ayah: 68, Ayah: 69, Ayah: 70 & Ayah: 71

﴿ قَالُوا۟ ٱدْعُ لَنَا رَبَّكَ يُبَيِّن لَّنَا مَا هِىَ ۚ قَالَ إِنَّهُۥ يَقُولُ إِنَّهَا بَقَرَةٌ لَّا فَارِضٌ وَلَا بِكْرٌ عَوَانٌۢ بَيْنَ ذَٰلِكَ ۖ فَٱفْعَلُوا۟ مَا تُؤْمَرُونَ ﴾ ۶۸

68. They said, "Call upon your Lord for us that He may make plain to us what it is!" He said, "He says, 'Verily, it is a cow neither too old nor too young, but (it is) between the two conditions', so do what you are commanded."

﴿ قَالُوا۟ ٱدْعُ لَنَا رَبَّكَ يُبَيِّن لَّنَا مَا لَوْنُهَا ۚ قَالَ إِنَّهُۥ يَقُولُ إِنَّهَا بَقَرَةٌ صَفْرَآءُ فَاقِعٌ لَّوْنُهَا تَسُرُّ ٱلنَّٰظِرِينَ ﴾ ۶۹

69. They said, "Call upon your Lord for us to make plain to us its color." He said, "He says, 'It is a yellow cow, bright in its color, pleasing to the beholders.'"

﴿ قَالُوا۟ ٱدْعُ لَنَا رَبَّكَ يُبَيِّن لَّنَا مَا هِىَ إِنَّ ٱلْبَقَرَ تَشَٰبَهَ عَلَيْنَا وَإِنَّآ إِن شَآءَ ٱللَّهُ لَمُهْتَدُونَ ﴾ ۷۰

70. They said, "Call upon your Lord for us to make plain to us what it is. Verily to us all cows are alike, And surely, if Allâh wills, we will be guided."

﴿ قَالَ إِنَّهُۥ يَقُولُ إِنَّهَا بَقَرَةٌ لَّا ذَلُولٌ تُثِيرُ ٱلْأَرْضَ وَلَا تَسْقِى ٱلْحَرْثَ مُسَلَّمَةٌ لَّا شِيَةَ فِيهَا ۚ قَالُوا۟ ٱلْـَٰٔنَ جِئْتَ بِٱلْحَقِّ ۚ فَذَبَحُوهَا وَمَا كَادُوا۟ يَفْعَلُونَ ﴾ ۷۱

﴾

71. He (Mûsâ (Moses)) said, "He says, 'It is a cow neither trained to till the soil nor water the fields, sound, having no other color except bright yellow.'" They said, "Now you have brought the truth." So they slaughtered it though they were near to not doing it.

Transliteration

68. Qaloo odAAu lana rabbaka yubayyin lana ma hiya qala innahu yaqoolu innaha baqaratun la faridun wala bikrun AAawanun bayna thalika faifAAaloo ma tu/maroona 69. Qaloo odAAu lana rabbaka yubayyin lana ma lawnuha qala innahu yaqoolu innaha baqaratun safrao faqiAAun lawnuha tasurru alnna*th*ireena 70. Qaloo odAAu lana rabbaka yubayyin lana ma hiya inna albaqara tashabaha AAalayna wa-inna in shaa Allahu lamuhtadoona 71. Qala innahu yaqoolu innaha baqaratun la thaloolun tutheeru al-arda wala tasqee alhartha musallamatun la shiyata feeha qaloo al-ana ji/ta bialhaqqi fathabahooha wama kadoo yafAAaloona

Tafsir Ibn Kathir

The Stubbornness of the Jews regarding the Cow; Allah made the Matter difficult for Them

Allah mentioned the stubbornness of the Children of Israel and the many unnecessary questions they asked their Messengers. This is why when they were stubborn, Allah made the decisions difficult for them. Had they slaughtered a cow, any cow, it would have been sufficient for them, as Ibn 'Abbas and 'Ubaydah have said. Instead, they made the matter difficult, and this is why Allah made it even more difficult for them. They said,

(Call upon your Lord for us that He may make plain to us what it is!), meaning, "What is this cow and what is its description" Musa said,

(He says, 'Verily, it is a cow neither too old nor too young'), meaning, that it is neither old nor below the age of breeding. This is the opinion of Abu Al-'Aliyah, As-Suddi, Mujahid, 'Ikrimah, 'Atiyah Al-'Awfi, 'Ata', Al-Khurasani, Wahb bin Munabbih, Ad-Dahhak, Al-Hasan, Qatadah and Ibn 'Abbas. Ad-Dahhak reported that Ibn 'Abbas said that,

(But (it is) between the two conditions) means, "Neither old nor young. Rather, she was at the age when the cow is strongest and fittest." In his Tafsir Al-'Awfi reported from Ibn 'Abbas that, (bright in its colour) "A deep yellowish white."

As-Suddi said, (pleasing the beholder) meaning, that it pleases those who see it. This is also the opinion of Abu Al-'Aliyah, Qatadah and Ar-Rabi' bin Anas. Furthermore, Wahb bin Munabbih said, "If you look at the cow's skin, you will think that the sun's rays radiate through its skin." The modern version of the Tawrah mentions that the cow in the Ayah was red, but this is an error. Or, it might be that the cow was so yellow that it appeared blackish or reddish in color. Allah's knows best.

(Verily, to us all cows are alike) this means, that since cows are plentiful, then describe this cow for us further, (And surely, if Allah wills) and if you further describe it to us, (we will be guided.)

(He says, 'It is a cow neither trained to till the soil nor water the fields') meaning, it is not used in farming, or for watering purposes. Rather, it is honorable and fair looking. 'Abdur-Razzaq said that Ma'mar said that Qatadah said that,

(sound) means, "The cow does not suffer from any defects." This is also the opinion of Abu Al-'Aliyah and Ar-Rabi`. Mujahid also said that the Ayah means the cow is free from defects. Further, `Ata' Al-Khurasani said that the Ayah means that its legs and body are free of physical defects.

Also, Ad-Dahhak said that Ibn 'Abbas said that the Ayah,

(So they slaughtered it though they were near to not doing it) means, "They did not want to slaughter it."

This means that even after all the questions and answers about the cow's description, the Jews were still reluctant to slaughter the cow. This part of the Qur'an criticized the Jews for their behavior, because their only goal was to be stubborn, and this is why they nearly did not slaughter the cow. Also, 'Ubaydah, Mujahid, Wahb bin Munabbih, Abu Al-'Aliyah and 'Abdur-Rahman bin Zayd bin Aslam said, "The Jews bought the cow with a large amount of money." There is a difference of opinion over this.

Surah: 2 Ayah: 72 & Ayah: 73

﴿ وَإِذْ قَتَلْتُمْ نَفْسًا فَٱدَّٰرَٰٔتُمْ فِيهَا ۖ وَٱللَّهُ مُخْرِجٌ مَّا كُنتُمْ تَكْتُمُونَ ۝ ﴾

72. And (remember) when you killed a man and fell into dispute among yourselves as to the crime. But Allâh brought forth that which you were hiding.

﴿ فَقُلْنَا ٱضْرِبُوهُ بِبَعْضِهَا ۚ كَذَٰلِكَ يُحْىِ ٱللَّهُ ٱلْمَوْتَىٰ وَيُرِيكُمْ ءَايَٰتِهِۦ لَعَلَّكُمْ تَعْقِلُونَ ۝ ﴾

73. So We said: "Strike him (the dead man) with a piece of it (the cow)." Thus Allâh brings the dead to life and shows you His Ayât (proofs, evidences, verses, lessons, signs, revelations, etc.) so that you may understand.

Transliteration

72. Wa-ith qataltum nafsan faiddara/tum feeha waAllahu mukhrijun ma kuntum taktumoona 73. Faqulna idriboohu bibaAAdiha kathalika yuhyee Allahu almawta wayureekum ayatihi laAAallakum taAAqiloona

Tafsir Ibn Kathir

Bringing the murdered Man back to Life

Al-Bukhari said that,

(And disagreed among yourselves as to the crime) means, "Disputed."

This is also the Tafsir of Mujahid. 'Ata' Al-Khurasani and Ad-Dahhak said, "Disputed about this matter." Also, Ibn Jurayj said that, (And (remember) when you killed a man and disagreed among yourselves as to the crime) means, some of them said, "You killed him," while the others said, "No you killed him."

This is also the Tafsir of `Abdur-Rahman bin Zayd bin Aslam. Mujahid said that,

(But Allah brought forth that which you were Taktumun) means, "what you were hiding." Allah said, (So We said: "Strike him (the dead man) with a piece of it (the cow)") meaning, "any part of the cow will produce the miracle (if they struck the dead man with it)." We were not told which part of the cow they used, as this matter does not benefit us either in matters of life or religion. Otherwise, Allah would have made it clear for us. Instead, Allah made this matter vague, so this is why we should leave it vague. Allah's statement, (Thus Allah brings the dead to life) means, "They struck him with it, and he came back to life." This Ayah demonstrates Allah's ability in bringing the dead back to life. Allah made this incident proof against the Jews that the Resurrection shall occur, and ended their disputing and stubbornness over the dead person.

Allah mentioned His bringing the dead back to life in five instances in Surat Al-Baqarah. First Allah said, (Then We raised you up after your death). He then mentioned the story about the cow. Allah also mentioned the story of those who escaped death in their land, while they were numbering in the thousands. He also mentioned the story of the Prophet who passed by a village that was destroyed, the story of Abraham and the four birds, and the land that comes back to life after it has died. All these incidents and stories alert us to the fact that bodies shall again become whole, after they were rotten. The proof of Resurrection is also reiterated in Allah's statement, (And a sign for them is the dead land. We give it life, and We bring forth from it grains, so that they eat thereof. And We have made therein gardens of date palms and grapes, and We have caused springs of water to gush forth therein. So that they may eat of the fruit thereof and their hands made it not. Will they not then give thanks) (36:33-35).

Surah: 2 Ayah: 74

﴿ ثُمَّ قَسَتْ قُلُوبُكُم مِّنْ بَعْدِ ذَٰلِكَ فَهِىَ كَٱلْحِجَارَةِ أَوْ أَشَدُّ قَسْوَةً وَإِنَّ مِنَ ٱلْحِجَارَةِ لَمَا يَتَفَجَّرُ مِنْهُ ٱلْأَنْهَارُ وَإِنَّ مِنْهَا لَمَا يَشَّقَّقُ فَيَخْرُجُ مِنْهُ ٱلْمَآءُ وَإِنَّ مِنْهَا لَمَا يَهْبِطُ مِنْ خَشْيَةِ ٱللَّهِ وَمَا ٱللَّهُ بِغَـٰفِلٍ عَمَّا تَعْمَلُونَ ۝ ﴾

74. Then, after that, your hearts were hardened and became as stones or even worse in hardness. And indeed, there are stones out of which rivers gush forth, and indeed, there are of them (stones) which split asunder so that water flows from them, and indeed, there are of them (stones) which fall down for fear of Allâh. And Allâh is not unaware of what you do.

Transliteration

74. Thumma qasat quloobukum min baAAdi thalika fahiya kaalhijarati aw ashaddu qaswatan wa-inna mina alhijarati lama yatafajjaru minhu al-anharu wa-inna minha lama yashshaqqaqu fayakhruju minhu almao wa-inna minha lama yahbitu min khashyati Allahi wama Allahu bighafilin AAamma taAAmaloona

Translation

74. Then, after that, your hearts were hardened and became as stones or even worse in hardness. And indeed, there are stones out of which rivers gush forth, and indeed, there are of them (stones) which split asunder so that water flows from them, and indeed, there are of them (stones) which fall down for fear of Allâh. And Allâh is not unaware of what you do.

Tafsir Ibn Kathir

The Harshness of the Jews

Allah criticized the Children of Israel because they witnessed the tremendous signs and the Ayat of Allah, including bringing the dead back to life, yet,

(Then after that your hearts were hardened).

So their hearts were like stones that never become soft. This is why Allah forbade the believers from imitating the Jews when He said,

(Has not the time come for the hearts of those who believe (in the Oneness of Allah @— Islamic Monotheism) to be affected by Allah's Reminder (this Qur'an), and that which has been revealed of the truth, lest they become as those who received the Scripture (the Tawrah) and the Injil (Gospel)) before (i.e. Jews and Christians), and the term was prolonged for them and so their hearts were hardened And many of them were Fasiqun (the rebellious, the disobedient to Allah)) (57:16). v In his Tafsir, Al-'Awfi said that Ibn 'Abbas said, "When the dead man was struck with a part of the cow, he stood up and became more alive than he ever was. He was asked, 'Who killed you' He said, 'My nephews killed me.' He then died again. His nephews said, after Allah took his life away, 'By Allah! We did not kill him' and denied the truth while they knew it. Allah said,

(And became as stones or even worse in hardness)."

And by the passage of time, the hearts of the Children of Israel were unlikely to accept any admonishment, even after the miracles and signs they witnessed. Their hearts became harder than stones, with no hope of ever softening. Sometimes, springs and rivers burst out of stones, some stones split and water comes out of them, even if there are no springs or rivers around them, sometimes stones fall down from mountaintops out of their fear of Allah. Muhammad bin Ishaq narrated that Ibn 'Abbas said that,

(And indeed, there are stones out of which rivers gush forth, and indeed, there are of them (stones) which split asunder so that water flows from them, and indeed, there are of them (stones) which fall down for fear of Allah), means, "Some stones are softer than your hearts, they acknowledge the truth that you are being called to,

(And Allah is not unaware of what you do)."

Solid Inanimate Objects possess a certain Degree of Awareness

Some claimed that the Ayat mentioned the stones being humble as a metaphor. However, Ar-Razi, Al-Qurtubi and other Imams said that there is no need for this explanation, because Allah creates this characteristic - humbleness - in stones. For instance, Allah said,

(Truly, We did offer Al-Amanah (the trust) to the heavens and the earth, and the mountains, but they declined to bear it and were afraid of it (i.e. afraid of Allah's torment)) (33:72),

(The seven heavens and the earth and all that is therein, glorify Him) (17:44),

(And the stars and the trees both prostrate themselves (to Allah)) (55:6),

(Have they not observed things that Allah has created: (how) their shadows incline) (16:48),

(They both said: "We come willingly.") (41:11),

(Had We sent down this Qur'an on a mountain) (59:21), and,

(And they will say to their skins, "Why do you testify against us" They will say: "Allah has caused us to speak.") (41:21).

It is recorded in the Sahih that the Prophet said,

《هَذَا جَبَلٌ يُحِبُّنَا وَنُحِبُّهُ》

(This (Mount Uhud) is a mount that loves us and that we love.)

Similarly, the compassion of the stump of the palm tree for the Prophet as confirmed in authentic narrations. In Sahih Muslim it is recorded that the Prophet said,

《إِنِّي لَأَعْرِفُ حَجَرًا بِمَكَّةَ كَانَ يُسَلِّمُ عَلَيَّ قَبْلَ أَنْ أُبْعَثَ إِنِّي لَأَعْرِفُهُ الْآنَ》

(I know a stone in Makkah that used to greet me with the Salam before I was sent. I recognize this stone now.)

He said about the Black Stone that,

《إِنَّهُ يَشْهَدُ لِمَنِ اسْتَلَمَ بِحَقٍّ يَوْمَ الْقِيَامَةِ》

(On the Day of Resurrection it will testifiy for those who kiss it.)

There are several other texts with this meaning. The scholars of the Arabic language disagreed over the meaning of Allah's statement,

(And became as stones or even worse in hardness) after agreeing that 'or' here is not being used to reflect doubt. Some scholars said that 'or' here means, 'and'. So the meaning becomes, "As hard as stones, and harder." For instance, Allah said,

(And obey not a sinner or a disbeliever among them) (76:24), and,

(To cut off all excuses or to warn) (77:6).

Some other scholars said that 'or' here means, 'rather'. Hence, the meaning becomes, 'As hard as stones. Rather, harder.' For instance, Allah said, (A section of them fear men as they fear Allah or even more) (4:77), (And We sent him to a hundred thousand (people) or even more) (37:147), and, (And was at a distance of two bows' length or (even) nearer) (53:9).

Some other scholars said that this Ayah means their hearts are only of two types, as hard as stone or harder than stone. Further, Ibn Jarir commented that this Tafsir means that some of their hearts are as hard as stone and some hearts are harder than stone. Ibn Jarir said that he favored this last Tafsir, although the others are plausible. I - Ibn Kathir - say that the last Tafsir is similar to Allah's statement,

(Their likeness is as the likeness of one who kindled a fire) (2:17), and then His statement, (Or like a rainstorm from the sky) (2:19).

It is also similar to Allah's statement, (As for those who disbelieved, their deeds are like a mirage in a desert) (24:39), and then His statement, (Or (the state of a disbeliever) is like the darkness in a vast deep sea) (24:40).

This then means that some of them are like the first example, and some others are like the second example.

Allah knows best.

Surah: 2 Ayah: 75, Ayah: 76 & Ayah: 77

﴿ ۞ أَفَتَطْمَعُونَ أَن يُؤْمِنُواْ لَكُمْ وَقَدْ كَانَ فَرِيقٌ مِّنْهُمْ يَسْمَعُونَ كَلَٰمَ ٱللَّهِ ثُمَّ يُحَرِّفُونَهُۥ مِنۢ بَعْدِ مَا عَقَلُوهُ وَهُمْ يَعْلَمُونَ ۝ ﴾

75. Do you (faithful believers) covet that they will believe in your religion in spite of the fact that a party of them (Jewish rabbis) used to hear the Word of Allâh (the Taurât (Torah)) then they used to change it knowingly after they understood it?

﴿ وَإِذَا لَقُواْ ٱلَّذِينَ ءَامَنُواْ قَالُوٓاْ ءَامَنَّا وَإِذَا خَلَا بَعْضُهُمْ إِلَىٰ بَعْضٍ قَالُوٓاْ أَتُحَدِّثُونَهُم بِمَا فَتَحَ ٱللَّهُ عَلَيْكُمْ لِيُحَآجُّوكُم بِهِۦ عِندَ رَبِّكُمْ أَفَلَا تَعْقِلُونَ ۝ ﴾

76. And when they (Jews) meet those who believe (Muslims), they say, "We believe", but when they meet one another in private, they say, "Shall you (Jews) tell them (Muslims) what Allâh has revealed to you (Jews, about the description and the qualities of Prophet Muhammad (peace be upon him), that which are written in the Taurât (Torah)) that they (Muslims) may argue with you (Jews) about it before your Lord?" Have you (Jews) then no understanding?

﴿ أَوَلَا يَعْلَمُونَ أَنَّ ٱللَّهَ يَعْلَمُ مَا يُسِرُّونَ وَمَا يُعْلِنُونَ ۝ ﴾

77. Know they (Jews) not that Allâh knows what they conceal and what they reveal?

Transliteration

75. AfatatmaAAoona an yu/minoo lakum waqad kana fareequn minhum yasmaAAoona kalama Allahi thumma yuharrifoonahu min baAAdi ma AAaqaloohu wahum yaAAlamoona 76. Wa-itha laqoo allatheena amanoo qaloo amanna wa-itha khala baAAduhum ila baAAdin qaloo atuhaddithoonahum bima fataha Allahu AAalaykum liyuhajjookum bihi AAinda rabbikum afala taAAqiloona 77. Awa la yaAAlamoona anna Allaha yaAAlamu ma yusirroona wama yuAAlinoona

Tafsir Ibn Kathir

There was little Hope that the Jews Who lived during the Time of the Prophet could have believed

Allah said,

(Do you covet) O believers, (That they will believe in your religion) meaning, that these people would obey you They are the deviant sect of Jews whose fathers witnessed the clear signs but their hearts became hard afterwards. Allah said next,

(Inspite of the fact that a party of them (Jewish rabbis) used to hear the Word of Allah (the Tawrah), then they used to change it) meaning, distort its meaning,

(after they understood it). They understood well, yet they used to defy the truth,

(knowingly), being fully aware of their erroneous interpretations and corruption. This statement is similar to Allah's statement,

(So, because of their violation of their covenant, We cursed them and made their hearts grow hard. They change the words from their (right) places) (5:13).

Qatadah commented that Allah's statement;

(Then they used to change it knowingly after they understood it) "They are the Jews who used to hear Allah's Words and then alter them after they understood and comprehended them." Also, Mujahid said, "Those who used to alter it and conceal its truths; they were their scholars." Also, Ibn Wahb said that Ibn Zayd commented,

(used to hear the Word of Allah (the Tawrah), then they used to change it) "They altered the Tawrah that Allah revealed to them, making it say that the lawful is unlawful and the prohibited is allowed, and that what is right is false and that what is false is right. So when a person seeking the truth comes to them with a bribe, they judge his case by the Book of Allah, but when a person comes to them seeking to do evil with a bribe, they take out the other (distorted) book, in which it is stated that he is in the right. When someone comes to them who is not seeking what is right, nor offering them bribe, then they enjoin righteousness on him. This is why Allah said to them,

(Enjoin you Al-Birr (piety and righteousness and every act of obedience to Allah) on the people and you forget (to practise it) yourselves, while you recite the Scripture (the Tawrah)! Have you then no sense) (2:44)"

The Jews knew the Truth of the Prophet, but disbelieved in Him

Allah said next,

(And when they (Jews) meet those who believe (Muslims), they say, "We believe", but when they meet one another in private..). Muhammad bin Ishaq reported that Ibn `Abbas commented,

(And when they (Jews) meet those who believe (Muslims), they say, "We believe") "They believe that Muhammad is the Messenger of Allah, `But he was only sent for you (Arabs)'" However, when they meet each other they say, "Do not convey the news about this Prophet to the Arabs, because you used to ask Allah to grant you victory over them when he came, but he was sent to them (not to you)." Allah then revealed,

(And when they (Jews) meet those who believe (Muslims), they say, "We believe," but when they meet one another in private, they say, "Shall you (Jews) tell them (Muslims) what Allah has revealed to you, that they (Muslims) may argue with you (Jews) about it before your Lord") meaning, "If you admit to them that he is a Prophet, knowing that Allah took the covenant from you to follow him, they will know that Muhammad is the Prophet that we were waiting for and whose coming we find foretold of in our Book. Therefore, do not believe in him and deny him." Allah said,

(Know they (Jews) not that Allah knows what they conceal and what they reveal).

Al-Hasan Al-Basri said, "When the Jews met the believers they used to say, `We believe.' When they met each other, some of them would say, `Do not talk to the companions of Muhammad about what Allah has foretold in your Book, so that the news (that Muhammad is the Final Messenger) does not become a proof for them against you with your Lord, and, thus, you will win the dispute.'"

Further, Abu Al-`Aliyah said about Allah's statement,

(Know they (Jews) not that Allah knows what they conceal and what they reveal), "Meaning their secret denial and rejection of Muhammad, although they find his coming recorded in their Book." This is also the Tafsir of Qatadah. Al-Hasan commented on,

(That Allah knows what they conceal), "What they concealed refers to when they were alone with each other away from the Companions of Muhammad . Then they would forbid each other from conveying the news that Allah revealed to them in their Book to the Companions of Muhammad , fearing that the Companions would use this news (about the truth of Muhammad) against them before their Lord."

(And what they reveal) meaning, when they said to the Companions of Muhammad ,

(We believe), as Abu Al-'Aliyah, Ar-Rabi' and Qatadah stated.

Surah: 2 Ayah: 78 & Ayah: 79

﴿ وَمِنْهُمْ أُمِّيُّونَ لَا يَعْلَمُونَ ٱلْكِتَٰبَ إِلَّآ أَمَانِىَّ وَإِنْ هُمْ إِلَّا يَظُنُّونَ ۝ ﴾

78. And there are among them (Jews) unlettered people, who know not the Book, but they trust upon false desires and they but guess.

﴿ فَوَيْلٌ لِّلَّذِينَ يَكْتُبُونَ ٱلْكِتَٰبَ بِأَيْدِيهِمْ ثُمَّ يَقُولُونَ هَٰذَا مِنْ عِندِ ٱللَّهِ لِيَشْتَرُوا۟ بِهِۦ ثَمَنًا قَلِيلًا ۖ فَوَيْلٌ لَّهُم مِّمَّا كَتَبَتْ أَيْدِيهِمْ وَوَيْلٌ لَّهُم مِّمَّا يَكْسِبُونَ ۝ ﴾

79. Then woe to those who write the Book with their own hands and then say, "This is from Allâh," to purchase with it a little price! Woe to them for what their hands have written and woe to them for that they earn thereby.

Transliteration

78. Waminhum ommiyyoona la yaAAlamoona alkitaba illa amaniyya wa-in hum illa ya*th*unnoona 79. Fawaylun lillatheena yaktuboona alkitaba bi-aydeehim thumma yaqooloona hatha min AAindi Allahi liyashtaroo bihi thamanan qaleelan fawaylun lahum mimma katabat aydeehim wawaylun lahum mimma yaksiboona

Tafsir Ibn Kathir

The Meaning of 'Ummi

Allah said,

(And there are among them Ummyyun people) meaning, among the People of the Book, as Mujahid stated. Ummyyun, is plural for Ummi, that is, a person who does not write, as Abu Al-'Aliyah, Ar-Rabi', Qatadah, Ibrahim An-Nakha'i and others said. This meaning is clarified by Allah's statement, (Who know not the Book) meaning, are they not aware of what is in it.

Ummi was one of the descriptions of the Prophet because he was unlettered. For instance, Allah said,

(Neither did you (O Muhammad) read any book before it (this Qur'an) nor did you write any book (whatsoever) with your right hand. In that case, indeed, the followers of falsehood might have doubted) (29:48).

Also, the Prophet said,

«إِنَّا أُمَّةٌ أُمِّيَّةٌ لَا نَكْتُبُ وَلَا نَحْسِبُ، الشَّهْرُ هكَذَا وهكَذَا وهكَذَا»

(We are an Ummi nation, neither writing nor calculating. The (lunar) month is like this, this and this (i.e. thirty or twenty-nine days.)

This Hadith stated that Muslims do not need to rely on books, or calculations to decide the timings of their acts of worship. Allah also said,

(He it is Who sent among the Ummiyyin ones a Messenger (Muhammad) from among themselves) (62:2).

The Explanation of Amani

Ad-Dahhak said that Ibn 'Abbas said that Allah's statement,

(But they trust upon Amani) means, "It is just a false statement that they utter with their tongues." It was also said that Amani means `wishes and hopes'. Mujahid commented, "Allah described the Ummiyyin as not understanding any of the Book that Allah sent down to Musa, yet they create lies and falsehood." Therefore, the word Amani mentioned here refers to lying and falsehood. Mujahid said that Allah's statement, (And they but guess) means, "They lie." Qatadah, Abu Al-`Aliyah and Ar-Rabi` said that it means, "They have evil false ideas about Allah."

Woe unto Those Criminals among the Jews

Allah said, (Then Waylun (woe) to those who write the book with their own hands and then say, "This is from Allah," to purchase with it a little price!).

This is another category of people among the Jews who called to misguidance with falsehood and lies about Allah, thriving on unjustly amassing people's property. 'Waylun (woe)' carries meanings of destruction and perishing, and it is a well-known word in the Arabic language. Az-Zuhri said that 'Ubadydullah bin 'Abdullah narrated that Ibn 'Abbas said, "O Muslims! How could you ask the People of the Book about anything, while the Book of Allah (Qur'an) that He revealed to His Prophet is the most recent Book from Him and you still read it fresh and young Allah told you that the People of the Book altered the Book of Allah, changed it and wrote another book with their own hands. They then said, 'This book is from Allah,' so that they acquired a small profit by it. Hasn't the knowledge that came to you prohibited you from asking them By Allah! We have not seen any of them asking you about what was revealed to you." This Hadith was also collected by Al-Bukhari. Al-Hasan Al-Basri said, "The little amount here means this life and all that it contains."

Allah's statement, (Woe to them for what their hands have written and woe to them for that they earn thereby) means, "Woe to them because of what they have written with their own hands, the lies, falsehood and alterations. Woe to them because of the property that they unjustly acquired." Ad-Dahhak said that Ibn `Abbas commented,

(Woe to them), "Means the torment will be theirs because of the lies that they wrote with their own hands,

(And woe to them for that they earn thereby), which they unjustly acquired from people, be they commoners or otherwise."

Surah: 2 Ayah: 80

﴿ وَقَالُواْ لَن تَمَسَّنَا ٱلنَّارُ إِلَّآ أَيَّامًا مَّعْدُودَةً قُلْ أَتَّخَذْتُمْ عِندَ ٱللَّهِ عَهْدًا فَلَن يُخْلِفَ ٱللَّهُ عَهْدَهُۥٓ أَمْ تَقُولُونَ عَلَى ٱللَّهِ مَا لَا تَعْلَمُونَ ۝ ﴾

80. And they (Jews) say, "The Fire (i.e. Hell-fire on the Day of Resurrection) shall not touch us but for a few numbered days." Say (O Muhammad (peace be upon him) to them): "Have you taken a covenant from Allâh, so that Allâh will not break His Covenant? Or is it that you say of Allâh what you know not?"

Transliteration

80. Waqaloo lan tamassana alnnaru illa ayyaman maAAdoodatan qul attakhathtum AAinda Allahi AAahdan falan yukhlifa Allahu AAahdahu am taqooloona AAala Allahi ma la taAAlamoona

Tafsir Ibn Kathir

The Jews hope They will only remain in the Fire for a Few Days

Allah mentioned the claim of the Jews, that the Fire will only touch them for a few days, and then they will be saved from it. Allah refuted this claim by saying, (Say (O Muhammad to them): "Have you taken a covenant from Allah'). Hence, the Ayah proclaims, `if you had a promise from Allah for that, then Allah will never break His promise. However, such promise never existed. Rather, what you say, about Allah, you have no knowledge of and you thus utter a lie about Him.' Al-`Awfi said that Ibn `Abbas said about the Ayah,

(And they (Jews) say, "The Fire shall not touch us but for a few numbered days.").

"The Jews said, `The Fire will only touch us for forty days.'" Others added that this was the period during which the Jews worshipped the calf.

Also, Al-Hafiz Abu Bakr bin Marduwyah reported Abu Hurayrah saying,

(When Khaybar was conquered, a roasted poisoned sheep was presented to the Prophet as a gift (by the Jews). The Messenger of Allah ordered,

《اجْمَعُوا لِي مَنْ كَانَ مِنَ الْيَهُودِ ههُنَا》

'Assemble before me all the Jews who were here.'

The Jews were summoned and the Prophet said (to them),

《مَنْ أَبُوكُم》

'Who is your father'

They replied, 'So-and-so.' He said,

《كَذَبْتُمْ بَلْ أَبُوكُمْ فُلَان》

'You have lied; your father is so-and-so.'

They said, 'You have uttered the truth.' He said,

《هَلْ أَنْتُمْ صَادِقِيَّ عَنْ شَيْءٍ إِنْ سَأَلْتُكُمْ عَنْه》

'Will you now tell me the truth, if I ask you about something'

They replied, 'Yes, O Abul-Qasim; and if we should tell a lie, you will know our lie as you have about our fathers.' On that he asked,

《مَنْ أَهْلُ النَّارِ》

'Who are the people of the (Hell) Fire'

They said, 'We shall remain in the (Hell) Fire for a short period, and after that you will replace us in it.' The Prophet said,

《اخْسَئُوا وَاللهِ لَا نَخْلُفُكُمْ فِيهَا أَبَدًا》

'May you be cursed and humiliated in it! By Allah, we shall never replace you in it.'

Then he asked,

«هَلْ أَنْتُمْ صَادِقِيَّ عَنْ شَيْءٍ إِنْ سَأَلْتُكُمْ عَنْهُ؟»

'Will you tell me the truth if I ask you a question'

They said, 'Yes, O Abul-Qasim.' He asked,

«هَلْ جَعَلْتُمْ فِي هذِهِ الشَّاةِ سُمًّا؟»

'Have you poisoned this sheep'

They said, 'Yes.' He asked,

«فَمَا حَمَلَكُم عَلى ذلِكَ؟»

'What made you do so'

They said, 'We wanted to know if you were a liar, in which case we would get rid of you, and if you were a Prophet then the poison would not harm you.') Imam Ahmad, Al-Bukhari and An-Nasa'i recorded similarly.

Surah: 2 Ayah: 81 & Ayah: 82

﴿ بَلَىٰ مَن كَسَبَ سَيِّئَةً وَأَحَاطَتْ بِهِۦ خَطِيٓـَٔتُهُۥ فَأُو۟لَـٰٓئِكَ أَصْحَـٰبُ ٱلنَّارِ ۖ هُمْ فِيهَا خَـٰلِدُونَ ﴾

81. Yes! Whosoever earns evil and his sin has surrounded him, they are dwellers of the Fire (i.e. Hell); they will dwell therein forever.

﴿ وَٱلَّذِينَ ءَامَنُوا۟ وَعَمِلُوا۟ ٱلصَّـٰلِحَـٰتِ أُو۟لَـٰٓئِكَ أَصْحَـٰبُ ٱلْجَنَّةِ ۖ هُمْ فِيهَا خَـٰلِدُونَ ﴾

82. And those who believe (in the Oneness of Allâh - Islâmic Monotheism) and do righteous good deeds, they are dwellers of Paradise, they will dwell therein forever. (See V. 2:257)

Transliteration

81. Bala man kasaba sayyi-atan waahatat bihi khatee-atuhu faola-ika as-habu alnnari hum feeha khalidoona 82. Waallatheena amanoo waAAamiloo alssalihati ola-ika as-habu aljannati hum feeha khalidoona

Tafsir Ibn Kathir

Allah says, the matter is not as you have wished and hoped it to be. Rather, whoever does an evil deed and abides purposefully in his error, coming on the Day of Resurrection with no good deeds, only evil deeds, then he will be among the people of the Fire.

(And those who believe and do righteous good deeds) meaning, "They believe in Allah and His Messenger and perform the good deeds that conform with the Islamic Law. They shall be among the people of Paradise." Allah said in a similar statement,

(It will not be in accordance with your desires (Muslims), nor those of the People of the Scripture (Jews and Christians), whosoever works evil, will have the recompense thereof, and he will not find any protector or helper besides Allah. And whoever does righteous good deeds, male or female, and is a (true) believer ?in the Oneness of Allah (Muslim)>, such will enter Paradise and not the least injustice, even the size of a Naqira (speck on the back of a date stone), will be done to them) (4: 123-124).

Also, Abu Hurayrah, Abu Wa'il, 'Ata', and Al-Hasan said that,

(And his sin has surrounded him) means, "His Shirk (polytheism) has surrounded him."

Also, Al-A`mash reported from Abu Razin that Ar-Rabi` bin Khuthaym said, (And his sin has surrounded him), "Whoever dies before repenting from his wrongs." As-Suddi and Abu Razin said similarly. Abu Al-`Aliyah, Mujahid, Al-Hasan, Qatadah and Ar-Rabi` bin Anas said that, (And his sin has surrounded him) refers to major sins. All of these statements carry similar meanings, and Allah knows best.

When Small Sins gather, They bring about Destruction

Here we should mention the Hadith that Imam Ahmad recorded, in which 'Abdullah bin Mas'ud said that the Messenger of Allah said,

«إِيَّاكُمْ وَمُحَقَّرَاتِ الذُّنُوبِ فَإِنَّهُنَّ يَجْتَمِعْنَ عَلَى الرَّجُلِ حَتَّى يُهْلِكْنَهُ»

(Beware of the belittled sins, because they gather on a person until they destroy him.)

He then said that the Messenger of Allah gave them an example,

«كَمَثَلِ قَوْمٍ نَزَلُوا بِأَرْضٍ فَلَاةٍ، فَحَضَرَ صَنِيعُ الْقَوْمِ فَجَعَلَ الرَّجُلُ يَنْطَلِقُ فَيَجِيءُ بِالْعُودِ وَالرَّجُلُ يَجِيءُ بِالْعُودِ، حَتَّى جَمَعُوا سَوَادًا وَأَجَّجُوا نَارًا فَأَنْضَجُوا مَا قَذَفُوا فِيهَا»

(This is the example of people who set up camp on a flat land, and then their servants came. One of them collected some wood and another man collected some wood until they collected a great deal. They then started a fire and cooked what they put on it.)

Muhammad bin Ishaq reported that Ibn 'Abbas said that, (And those who believe and do righteous good deeds, they are dwellers of Paradise, they will dwell therein forever) "Whoever believes in what you (Jews) did not believe in and implements what you refrained from implementing of Muhammad's religion, shall acquire Paradise for eternity. Allah stated that the recompense for good or evil works shall remain with its people for eternity."

Surah: 2 Ayah: 83

﴿ وَإِذْ أَخَذْنَا مِيثَاقَ بَنِى إِسْرَٰٓءِيلَ لَا تَعْبُدُونَ إِلَّا ٱللَّهَ وَبِٱلْوَٰلِدَيْنِ إِحْسَانًا وَذِى ٱلْقُرْبَىٰ وَٱلْيَتَٰمَىٰ وَٱلْمَسَٰكِينِ وَقُولُوا۟ لِلنَّاسِ حُسْنًا وَأَقِيمُوا۟ ٱلصَّلَوٰةَ وَءَاتُوا۟ ٱلزَّكَوٰةَ ثُمَّ تَوَلَّيْتُمْ إِلَّا قَلِيلًا مِّنكُمْ وَأَنتُم مُّعْرِضُونَ ۝ ﴾

83. And (remember) when We took a covenant from the Children of Israel, (saying): Worship none but Allâh (Alone) and be dutiful and good to parents, and to kindred, and to orphans and Al-Masâkîn (the poor), and speak good to people (i.e. enjoin righteousness and forbid evil, and say the truth about Muhammad (peace be upon him)) and perform As-Salât (Iqâmat-as-Salât), and give Zakât. Then you slid back, except a few of you, while you are backsliders. (Tafsir Al-Qurtubî).

Transliteration

83. Wa-ith akhathna meethaqa banee isra-eela la taAAbudoona illa Allaha wabialwalidayni ihsanan wathee alqurba waalyatama waalmasakeeni waqooloo lilnnasi husnan waaqeemoo alssalata waatoo alzzakata thumma tawallaytum illa qaleelan minkum waantum muAAridoona

Tafsir Ibn Kathir

The Covenant that Allah took from the Children of Israel

Allah reminded the Children of Israel of the commandments that He gave them, and the covenants that He took from them to abide by those commands, and how they intentionally and knowingly turned away from all of that. Allah commanded them to worship Him and to associate none with Him in worship, just as He has commanded all of His creatures, for this is why Allah created them. Allah said,

(And We did not send any Messenger before you (O Muhammad) but We revealed to him (saying): La ilaha illa Ana ?ýnone has the right to be worshipped but I (Allah)>, so worship Me (alone and none else)) (21:25), and,

(And verily, We have sent among every Ummah (community, nation) a Messenger (proclaiming): "Worship Allah (alone), and avoid the Taghut (all false deities,)) (16:36).

This is the highest and most important right, that is, Allah's right that He be worshipped alone without partners.

After that comes the right of the creatures, foremost, the right of the parents. Allah usually mentions the rights of the parents along with His rights. For instance, Allah said,

(Give thanks to Me and to your parents. Unto Me is the final destination) (31:14). Also, Allah said,

(And your Lord has decreed that you worship none but Him. And that you be dutiful to your parents) (17:23), until,

(And give to the kinsman his due and to the Miskin (poor) and to the wayfarer) (17:26). The Two Sahihs record that Ibn Mas`ud said,

قُلْتُ:

«يَا رَسُولَ اللهِ أَيُّ الْعَمَلِ أَفْضَلُ؟ قَالَ:

«الصَّلَاةُ عَلى وَقْتِهَا»

قُلْتُ: ثُمَّ أَيٌّ؟ قَالَ:

«بِرُّ الْوَالِدَيْن»

قُلْتُ: ثُمَّ أَيٌّ؟ قَالَ:

«الْجِهَادُ فِي سَبِيلِ اللهِ»

(I said, `O Messenger of Allah! What is the best deed' He said, `Performing the prayer on time.' I said, 'Then what' He said, `Being kind to one's parents.' I said, `Then what' He said, `Jihad in the cause of Allah.')

Allah then said, (and to orphans) meaning, the young who have no fathers to fend for them. (and Al-Masakin (the poor)), plural for Miskin, the one who does not find what he needs to spend on himself and his family. We will discuss these categories when we explain the Ayah of Surat An-Nisa' where Allah said, (Worship Allah and join none with Him (in worship); and do good to parents) (4:36).

Allah's statement, (and speak good to people) meaning, say good words to them and be lenient with them, this includes commanding good and forbidding evil. Al-Hasan Al-Basri commented on Allah's statement, (and speak good to people), ".`The good saying' means commanding good and forbidding evil, and being patient and forgiving. The `good words to people', as Allah commanded, also includes every good type of behavior that Allah is pleased with."

Imam Ahmad narrated that Abu Dharr said that the Prophet said,

«لَا تَحْقِرَنَّ مِنَ الْمَعْرُوفِ شَيْئًا وَإِنْ لَمْ تَجِدْ فَالْقَ أَخَاكَ بِوَجْهٍ مُنْطَلِقٍ»

(Do not belittle any form of righteousness, and even if you did not find any good deed except meeting your brother with a smiling face, then do so.) This Hadith was also collected by Muslim in his Sahih and At-Tirmidhi, who graded it Sahih.

Allah commands the servants to say good words to people, after He commanded them to be kind to them, thereby mentioning two categories of manners: good speech and good actions. He then emphasized the command to worship Him and the command to do good, ordaining the prayer and the Zakah,

(and perform As-Salah and give Zakah). Allah informed us that the People of the Book, except for a few among them, ignored these orders, that is, they knowingly and intentionally abandoned them.

Allah ordered this Ummah similarly in Surat An-Nisa' when He said,

(Worship Allah and join none with Him (in worship); and do good to parents, kinsfolk, orphans, Al-Masakin (the poor), the neighbor who is near of kin, the neighbor who is a stranger, the companion by your side, the wayfarer (you meet), and those (servants) whom your right hands possess. Verily, Allah does not like such as are proud and boastful) (4:36).

Of these orders, this Ummah has practiced what no other nation before it has, and all praise is due to Allah.

Surah: 2 Ayah: 84, Ayah: 85 & Ayah: 86

﴿ وَإِذْ أَخَذْنَا مِيثَـٰقَكُمْ لَا تَسْفِكُونَ دِمَآءَكُمْ وَلَا تُخْرِجُونَ أَنفُسَكُم مِّن دِيَـٰرِكُمْ ثُمَّ أَقْرَرْتُمْ وَأَنتُمْ تَشْهَدُونَ ﴾

84. And (remember) when We took your covenant (saying): Shed not the blood of your (people), nor turn out your own people from their dwellings. Then, (this) you ratified and (to this) you bear witness.

﴿ ثُمَّ أَنتُمْ هَـٰٓؤُلَآءِ تَقْتُلُونَ أَنفُسَكُمْ وَتُخْرِجُونَ فَرِيقًا مِّنكُم مِّن دِيَـٰرِهِم تَظَـٰهَرُونَ عَلَيْهِم بِالْإِثْمِ وَالْعُدْوَٰنِ وَإِن يَأْتُوكُمْ أُسَـٰرَىٰ تُفَـٰدُوهُمْ وَهُوَ مُحَرَّمٌ عَلَيْكُمْ إِخْرَاجُهُمْ ۚ أَفَتُؤْمِنُونَ بِبَعْضِ ٱلْكِتَـٰبِ وَتَكْفُرُونَ بِبَعْضٍ ۚ فَمَا جَزَآءُ مَن يَفْعَلُ ذَٰلِكَ مِنكُمْ إِلَّا خِزْىٌ فِى ٱلْحَيَوٰةِ ٱلدُّنْيَا ۖ وَيَوْمَ ٱلْقِيَـٰمَةِ يُرَدُّونَ إِلَىٰٓ أَشَدِّ ٱلْعَذَابِ ۗ وَمَا ٱللَّهُ بِغَـٰفِلٍ عَمَّا تَعْمَلُونَ ﴾

85. After this, it is you who kill one another and drive out a party of you from their homes, assist (their enemies) against them, in sin and transgression. And if they come to you as captives, you ransom them, although their expulsion was forbidden to you. Then do you believe in a part of the Scripture and reject the rest? Then what is the recompense of those who do so among you, except disgrace in the life of this world, and on the Day of Resurrection they shall be consigned to the most grievous torment. And Allâh is not unaware of what you do.

﴿ أُوْلَـٰٓئِكَ ٱلَّذِينَ ٱشْتَرَوُاْ ٱلْحَيَوٰةَ ٱلدُّنْيَا بِٱلْءَاخِرَةِ ۖ فَلَا يُخَفَّفُ عَنْهُمُ ٱلْعَذَابُ وَلَا هُمْ يُنصَرُونَ ﴾

86. Those are they who have bought the life of this world at the price of the Hereafter. Their torment shall not be lightened nor shall they be helped.

Transliteration

84. Wa-ith akhathna meethaqakum la tasfikoona dimaakum wala tukhrijoona anfusakum min diyarikum thumma aqrartum waantum tashhadoona   85. Thumma antum haola-i taqtuloona anfusakum watukhrijoona fareeqan minkum min diyarihim ta*th*aharoona AAalayhim bial-ithmi waalAAudwani wa-in ya/tookum osara tufadoohum wahuwa muharramun AAalaykum ikhrajuhum afatu/minoona bibaAAdi alkitabi watakfuroona bibaAAdin fama jazao man

yafAAalu thalika minkum illa khizyun fee alhayati alddunya wayawma alqiyamati yuraddoona ila ashaddi alAAathabi wama Allahu bighafilin AAamma taAAmaloona 86. Ola-ika allatheena ishtarawoo alhayata alddunya bial-akhirati fala yukhaffafu AAanhumu alAAathabu wala hum yunsaroona

Tafsir Ibn Kathir

The Terms of the Covenant and their Breach of It

Allah criticized the Jews who lived in Al-Madinah during the time of the Messenger of Allah . They used to suffer, because of the armed conflicts between the tribes of Al-Madinah, Aws and Khazraj. Before Islam, the Aws and Khazraj worshipped idols, and many battles took place between them. There were three Jewish tribes in Al-Madinah at that time, Banu Qaynuqa' and Banu An-Nadir, the allies of the Khazraj, and Banu Qurayzah, who used to be the allies of the Aws. When war erupted between Aws and Khazraj, their Jewish allies would assist them. The Jew would kill his Arab enemy, and sometimes they also killed Jews who were the allies of the other Arab tribe, although the Jews were prohibited from killing each other according to clear religious texts in their Books. They would also drive each other from their homes and loot whatever furniture and money they could. When the war ended, the victorious Jews would release the prisoners from the defeated party, according to the rulings of the Tawrah. This is why Allah said, (Then do you believe in a part of the Scripture and reject the rest) Allah said, (And (remember) when We took your covenant (saying): Shed not the blood of your (people), nor turn out your own people from their dwellings.) meaning, "Do not kill each other, nor expel one another from their homes, nor participate in fighting against them." Allah mentioned the word `your own' here, just as He said in another Ayah. (So turn in repentance to your Creator and kill yourselves, that will be better for you with your Creator) (2:54) because the followers of one religion are just like one soul. Also, the Messenger of Allah said,

«مَثَلُ الْمُؤْمِنِينَ فِي تَوَادِّهِمْ وَتَرَاحُمِهِمْ وَتَوَاصُلِهِمْ بِمَنْزِلَةِ الْجَسَدِ الْوَاحِدِ إِذَا اشْتَكَى مِنْهُ عُضْوٌ تَدَاعَى لَهُ سَائِرُ الْجَسَدِ بِالْحُمَّى وَالسَّهَرِ»

(The example of the believers in their kindness, mercy and sympathy to each other is the example of one body, when an organ of it falls ill, the rest of the body rushes to its aid in fever and sleeplessness.) Allah's statement, (Then, (this) you ratified and (to this) you bore witness.) means, "You testified that you know of the covenant and that you were witnesses to it." (After this, it is you who kill one another and drive out a party of you from their homes). Muhammad bin Ishaq bin Yasar reported that Ibn 'Abbas commented on the Ayah,

(After this, it is you who kill one another and drive out a party of you from their homes) "Allah mentioned what they were doing, and that in the Tawrah He had prohibited them from shedding each other's blood, and required them to free their prisoners. Now they were divided into two camps in Al-Madinah, Banu Qaynuqa`, who were the allies of the Khazraj, and An-Nadir and Qurayzah, who were the allies of the Aws. When fighting erupted between Aws and Khazraj, Banu Qaynuqa` would fight along with the Khazraj, while Banu An-Nadir and Qurayzah would fight along with the Aws. Each Jewish camp would fight against their Jewish brethren from the other camp. They would shed each other's blood, although they had the Tawrah with them, and they knew their rights and dues. Meanwhile, the Aws and Khazraj were polytheists who worshipped idols. They did not know about Paradise, the Fire, Resurrection, Divine Books the lawful and prohibited. When the war would end, the Jews would ransom their prisoners and implement the Tawrah. Consequently, Banu Qaynuqa` would ransom their prisoners who were captured by the Aws, while Banu An-Nadir and Qurayzah would ransom their prisoners who were captured by the Khazraj. They would also ask for blood money. During these wars, they would kill whomever (Jews or Arabs) they could, while helping the polytheists against their brethren. Therefore, Allah reminded them of this when He said, (Then do you believe in a part of the Scripture and reject the rest) This Ayah means, 'Do you ransom them according to the rulings of the Tawrah, yet kill them while the Tawrah forbade you from killing them and from expelling them from their homes The Tawrah also commanded that you should not aid the polytheists and those who associate with Allah in the worship against your brethren. You do all this to acquire the life of this world.' I was informed that the behavior of the Jews regarding the Aws and Khazraj was the reason behind revealing these Ayat."

These noble Ayat criticized the Jews for implementing the Tawrah sometimes and defying it at other times, although they believed in the Tawrah and knew what they were doing was wrong. This is why they should not be trusted to preserve or convey the Tawrah. Further, they should not be believed when it comes to the description of the Messenger of Allah , his coming, his expulsion from his land, and his Hijrah, and the rest of the information that the previous Prophets informed them about him, all of which they hid. The Jews, may they suffer the curse of Allah, hid all of these facts among themselves, and this is why Allah said, (Then what is the recompense of those who do so among you, except disgrace in the life of this world), because they defied Allah's Law and commandments, (And on the Day of Resurrection they shall be consigned to the most grievous torment) as punishment for defying the Book of Allah that they had. (And Allah is not unaware of what you do. Those are they who have bought the life of this world at the price of the Hereafter) meaning, they prefer this life to the Hereafter. Therefore, (Their torment shall not be lightened) not even for an hour, (Nor shall they be helped), and they shall find no helper who will save them from the eternal torment they will suffer, nor shall they find any to grant them refuge from it.

Surah: 2 Ayah: 87

﴿ وَلَقَدْ ءَاتَيْنَا مُوسَى ٱلْكِتَٰبَ وَقَفَّيْنَا مِنۢ بَعْدِهِۦ بِٱلرُّسُلِ ۖ وَءَاتَيْنَا عِيسَى ٱبْنَ مَرْيَمَ ٱلْبَيِّنَٰتِ وَأَيَّدْنَٰهُ بِرُوحِ ٱلْقُدُسِ ۗ أَفَكُلَّمَا جَآءَكُمْ رَسُولٌۢ بِمَا لَا تَهْوَىٰٓ أَنفُسُكُمُ ٱسْتَكْبَرْتُمْ فَفَرِيقًا كَذَّبْتُمْ وَفَرِيقًا تَقْتُلُونَ ۝ ﴾

87. And indeed, We gave Mûsâ (Moses) the Book and followed him up with a succession of Messengers. And We gave 'Isâ (Jesus), the son of Maryam (Mary), clear signs and supported him with Rûh-ul-Qudus (Jibrael (Gabriel)) Is it that whenever there came to you a Messenger with what you yourselves desired not, you grew arrogant? Some, you disbelieved and some you killed.

Transliteration

87. Walaqad atayna moosa alkitaba waqaffayna min baAAdihi bialrrusuli waatayna AAeesa ibna maryama albayyinati waayyadnahu biroohi alqudusi afakullama jaakum rasoolun bima la tahwa anfusukumu istakbartum fafareeqan kaththabtum wafareeqan taqtuloona

Tafsir Ibn Kathir

The Arrogance of the Jews who denied and killed Their Prophets

Allah described the insolence of Children of Israel, their rebelliousness, defiance and arrogance towards the Prophets, following their lusts and desires. Allah mentioned that He gave Musa the Book, the Tawrah, and that the Jews changed, distorted, and defied its commands, as well as altered its meanings.

Allah sent Messengers and Prophets after Musa who followed his law, as Allah stated,

(Verily, We did reveal the Tawrah (to Musa), therein was guidance and light, by which the Prophets, who submitted themselves to Allah's will, judged for the Jews. And the rabbis and the priests (too judged for the Jews by the Tawrah after those Prophets), for to them was entrusted the protection of Allah's Book, and they were witnesses thereto) (5:44). This is why Allah said here,

(And Qaffayna him with Messengers).

As-Suddi said that Abu Malik said that Qaffayna means, "Succeeded", while others said, "Followed". Both meanings are plausible, since Allah said,

(Then We sent Our Messengers in succession) (23:44).

Thereafter, Allah sent the last Prophet among the Children of Israel, 'Isa the son of Mary, who was sent with some laws that differed with some in the Tawrah. This is why Allah also sent miracles to support 'Isa. These included bringing the dead back to life, forming the shape of birds from clay and blowing into them, afterwhich they became living birds by Allah's leave, healing the sick and foretelling the Unseen, as Ibn 'Abbas stated. Allah also aided him with Ruh Al-Qudus, and that refers to Jibril. All of these signs testified to the truthfulness of 'Isa and what he was sent with. Yet, the Children of Israel became more defiant and envious of him and did not want to differ with even one part of the Tawrah, as Allah said about 'Isa,

(And to make lawful to you part of what was forbidden to you, and I have come to you with a proof from your Lord) (3:50).

Hence, the Children of Israel treated the Prophets in the worst manner, rejecting some of them and killing some of them. All of this occurred because the Prophets used to command the Jews with what differed from their desires and opinions. The Prophets also upheld the rulings of the Tawrah that the Jews had changed, and this is why it was difficult for them to believe in these Prophets. Therefore, they rejected the Prophets and killed some of them. Allah said,

(Is it that whenever there came to you a Messenger with what you yourselves desired not, you grew arrogant Some you disbelieved and some you kill).

Jibril is Ruh Al-Qudus

The proof that Jibril is the Ruh Al-Qudus is the statement of Ibn Mas'ud in explanation of this Ayah. This is also the view of Ibn 'Abbas, Muhammad bin Ka'b, Isma'il bin Khalid, As-Suddi, Ar-Rabi' bin Anas, 'Atiyah Al-'Awfi and Qatadah. Additionally, Allah said,

(Which the trustworthy Ruh (Jibril) has brought down. Upon your heart (O Muhammad) that you may be (one) of the warners) (26:193-194).

Al-Bukhari recorded 'A'ishah saying that the Messenger of Allah erected a Minbar in the Masjid on which Hassan bin Thabit (the renowned poet) used to defend the Messenger of Allah (with his poems). The Messenger of Allah said,

«اللَّهُمَّ أَيِّدْ حَسَّانَ بِرُوحِ الْقُدُسِ كَمَا نَافَحَ عَنْ نَبِيِّكَ»

(O Allah! Aid Hassan with Ruh Al-Qudus, for he defended Your Prophet.)

Abu Dawud recorded this Hadith in his Sunan as did At-Tirmidhi who graded it Hasan Sahih. Further, Ibn Hibban recorded in his Sahih that Ibn Mas'ud said that the Prophet said,

«إِنَّ رُوحَ الْقُدُسِ نَفَثَ فِي رُوعِي أَنَّهُ لَنْ تَمُوتَ نَفْسٌ حَتَّى تَسْتَكْمِلَ

$$\text{رِزْقَهَا وَأَجَلَهَا، فَاتَّقُوا اللهَ وَأَجْمِلُوا فِي الطَّلَبِ}$$

(Ruh Al-Qudus informed me that no soul shall die until it finishes its set provisions and term limit. Therefore, have Taqwa of Allah and seek your sustenance in the most suitable way.)

The Jews tried to kill the Prophet

Az-Zamakhshari commented on Allah's statement,

(Some you disbelieved and some you kill), "Allah did not say `killed' here, because the Jews would still try to kill the Prophet in the future, using poison and magic." During the illness that preceded his death, the Prophet said,

$$\text{«مَا زَالَتْ أَكْلَةُ خَيْبَرَ تُعَاوِدُنِي، فَهَذَا أَوَانُ انْقِطَاعِ أَبْهَرِي»}$$

(I kept feeling the effect of what I ate (from the poisoned sheep) during the day of Khaybar, until now, when it is the time that the aorta will be cut off (meaning when death is near).)

This Hadith was collected by Al-Bukhari and others

Surah: 2 Ayah: 88

$$\text{﴿وَقَالُوا قُلُوبُنَا غُلْفٌ ۚ بَل لَّعَنَهُمُ اللَّهُ بِكُفْرِهِمْ فَقَلِيلًا مَّا يُؤْمِنُونَ﴾}$$

88. And they say, "Our hearts are wrapped (i.e. do not hear or understand Allâh's Word)." Nay, Allâh has cursed them for their disbelief, so little is that which they believe.

Transliteration

88. Waqaloo quloobuna ghulfun bal laAAanahumu Allahu bikufrihim faqaleelan ma yu/minoona

Tafsir Ibn Kathir

Muhammad bin Ishaq reported that Ibn `Abbas said that, (And they say, "Our hearts are Ghulf."), means, "Our hearts are screened." Mujahid also said that,

(And they say, "Our hearts are Ghulf."), means, "They are covered."`Ikrimah said, "There is a stamp on them." Abu Al-`Aliyah said, "They do not comprehend." Mujahid and Qatadah said that Ibn `Abbas read the Ayah in a way that means, "Our hearts contain every type of knowledge and do not need the knowledge that you (O Muhammad) have." This is the opinion of `Ata' and Ibn `Abbas. (Nay, Allah has cursed them for their disbelief) meaning, "Allah expelled them and deprived them of every type of righteousness." Qatadah said that the Ayah, (So little is that which they believe.) means, "Only a few of them believe." Allah's statement, (And they say, "Our hearts are Ghulf.") is similar to His statement, (And they say: "Our hearts are under coverings (screened) from that to which you invite us) (41:5).

This is why Allah said here, (Nay, Allah has cursed them for their disbelief, so little is that which they believe.) meaning, "It is not as they claim. Rather, their hearts are cursed and stamped," just as Allah said in Surat An-Nisa' (4:155), (And of their saying: "Our hearts are wrapped (with coverings, i.e. we do not understand what the Messengers say) — nay, Allah has set a seal upon their hearts because of their disbelief, so they believe not but a little.)

There is a difference of opinion regarding the meaning of Allah's statement,

(So little is that which they believe.) and His statement, (So they believe not except a few).

Some scholars said that the Ayat indicate that a few of them would believe, or that their faith is minute, because they believe in Resurrection and in Allah's reward and punishment that Musa foretold. Yet, this faith will not benefit them since it is overshadowed by their disbelief in what Muhammad brought them.

Some scholars said that the Jews did not actually believe in anything and that Allah said,

(So little is that which they believe),

meaning, they do not believe. This meaning is similar to the Arabic expression, "Hardly have I seen anything like this," meaning, "I have never seen anything like this."

Surah: 2 Ayah: 89

﴿ وَلَمَّا جَآءَهُمْ كِتَـٰبٌ مِّنْ عِندِ ٱللَّهِ مُصَدِّقٌ لِّمَا مَعَهُمْ وَكَانُواْ مِن قَبْلُ يَسْتَفْتِحُونَ عَلَى ٱلَّذِينَ كَفَرُواْ فَلَمَّا جَآءَهُم مَّا عَرَفُواْ كَفَرُواْ بِهِۦ ۚ فَلَعْنَةُ ٱللَّهِ عَلَى ٱلْكَـٰفِرِينَ ۞ ﴾

89. And when there came to them (the Jews), a Book (this Qur'ân) from Allâh confirming what is with them (the Taurât (Torah) and the Injeel (Gospel)) although aforetime they had invoked Allâh (for coming of Muhammad (peace be upon him)) in order to gain victory over those who disbelieved, then when there came to them that which they had recognized, they disbelieved in it. So let the Curse of Allâh be on the disbelievers.

Transliteration

89. Walamma jaahum kitabun min AAindi Allahi musaddiqun lima maAAahum wakanoo min qablu yastaftihoona AAala allatheena kafaroo falamma jaahum ma AAarafoo kafaroo bihi falaAAnatu Allahi AAala alkafireena

Tafsir Ibn Kathir

The Jews were awaiting the Prophet's coming, but They disbelieved in Him when He was sent

Allah said,

(And when there came to them) meaning, the Jews, (a Book from Allah) meaning, the Qur'an that Allah sent down to Muhammad,

(confirming what is with them) meaning, the Tawrah.

Further, Allah said,

(although aforetime they had invoked Allah (for coming of Muhammad) in order to gain victory over those who disbelieved) meaning, before this Messenger came to them, they used to ask Allah to aid them by his arrival, against their polytheistic enemies in war.

They used to say to the polytheists, "A Prophet shall be sent just before the end of this world and we, along with him, shall exterminate you, just as the nations of `Ad and Iram were exterminated."

Also, Muhammad bin Ishaq narrated that Ibn `Abbas said,

"The Jews used to invoke Allah (for the coming of Muhammad) in order to gain victory over the Aws and Khazraj, before the Prophet was sent. When Allah sent him to the Arabs, they rejected him and denied what they used to say about him. Hence, Mu`adh bin Jabal and Bishr bin Al-Bara' bin Ma`rur, from Bani Salamah, said to them, `O Jews! Fear Allah and embrace Islam. You used to invoke Allah for the coming of Muhammad when we were still disbelievers and you used to tell us that he would come and describe him to us,' Salam bin Mushkim from Bani An-Nadir replied, `He did not bring anything that we recognize. He is not the Prophet we told you about.'

Allah then revealed this Ayah about their statement,

(And when there came to them (the Jews), a Book (this Qur'an) from Allah confirming what is with them (the Tawrah) and the Injil (Gospel))."'

Abu Al-`Aliyah said,

"The Jews used to ask Allah to send Muhammad so that they would gain victory over the Arab disbelievers. They used to say, `O Allah! Send the Prophet that we read about - in the Tawrah - so that we can torment and kill the disbelievers alongside him.' When Allah sent Muhammad and they saw that he was not one of them, they rejected him and envied the Arabs, even though they knew that he was the Messenger of Allah. Hence, Allah said,

(Then when there came to them that which they had recognized, they disbelieved in it. So let the curse of Allah be on the disbelievers)."

Surah: 2 Ayah: 90

﴿ بِئْسَمَا ٱشْتَرَوْاْ بِهِۦٓ أَنفُسَهُمْ أَن يَكْفُرُواْ بِمَآ أَنزَلَ ٱللَّهُ بَغْيًا أَن يُنَزِّلَ ٱللَّهُ مِن فَضْلِهِۦ عَلَىٰ مَن يَشَآءُ مِنْ عِبَادِهِۦ ۖ فَبَآءُو بِغَضَبٍ عَلَىٰ غَضَبٍ ۚ وَلِلْكَٰفِرِينَ عَذَابٌ مُّهِينٌ ﴾

90. How bad is that for which they have sold their ownselves, that they should disbelieve in that which Allâh has revealed (the Qur'ân), grudging that Allâh should reveal of His Grace unto whom He will of His slaves. So they have drawn on themselves wrath upon wrath. And for the disbelievers, there is disgracing torment.

Transliteration

90. Bi/sama ishtaraw bihi anfusahum an yakfuroo bima anzala Allahu baghyan an yunazzila Allahu min fadlihi AAala man yashao min AAibadihi fabaoo bighadabin AAala ghadabin walilkafireena AAathabun muheenun

Tafsir Ibn Kathir

Mujahid said,

(How bad is that for which they have sold their own selves), "The Jews sold the truth for falsehood and hid the truth about Muhammad ." As-Suddi said that the Ayah,

(How bad is that for which they have sold their own selves) means, "The Jews sold themselves." meaning, what is worse is what they chose for themselves by disbelieving in what Allah revealed to Muhammad instead of believing, aiding and supporting him. This behavior of theirs is the result of their injustice, envy and hatred,

(grudging that Allah should reveal of His grace unto whom He wills of His servants)." There is no envy worse than this. Therefore, (So they have drawn on themselves wrath upon wrath). Ibn 'Abbas commented on this Ayah, "Allah became angry with them because they ignored some of the Tawrah and disbelieved in the Prophet that He sent to them." I (Ibn Kathir) say that the meaning of,

(And they drew on themselves) is that they deserved and acquired multiplied anger. Also, Abu Al-'Aliyah said, "Allah became angry with them, because of their disbelief in the Injil and 'Isa and He became angry with them again, because they disbelieved in Muhammad and the Qur'an." Similar was said by 'Ikrimah and Qatadah. Allah said, (And for the disbelievers, there is disgracing torment). Since their disbelief was a result of their transgression and envy, which was caused by arrogance, they were punished with disgrace and humiliation in this world and the Hereafter. Similarly, Allah said, (Verily, those who scorn My worship (i.e. do not invoke Me, and do not believe in My Oneness) they will surely enter Hell in humiliation!") (40:60) meaning, "Disgraced, degraded and humiliated." Imam Ahmad narrated that `Amr bin Shu`ayb said that his father said that his grandfather said that the Prophet said,

«يُحْشَرُ الْمُتَكَبِّرُونَ يَوْمَ الْقِيَامَةِ أَمْثَالَ الذَّرِّ فِي صُوَرِ النَّاسِ، يَعْلُوهُمْ كُلُّ شَيْءٍ مِنَ الصَّغَارِ حَتَّى يَدْخُلُوا سِجْنًا فِي جَهَنَّمَ يُقَالُ لَهُ. بُولَسُ تَعْلُوهُمْ نَارُ الْأَنْيَارِ يُسْقَوْنَ مِنْ طِينَةِ الْخَبَالِ عُصَارَةِ أَهْلِ النَّارِ»

(The arrogant people will be gathered on the Day of Resurrection in the size of ants, but in the shape of men. Everything shall be above them, because of the humiliation placed on them, until they enter a prison in Jahannam called 'Bawlas' where the fire will surround them from above. They shall drink from the puss of the people of the Fire.)

Surah: 2 Ayah: 91 & Ayah: 92

﴿ وَإِذَا قِيلَ لَهُمْ ءَامِنُوا۟ بِمَآ أَنزَلَ ٱللَّهُ قَالُوا۟ نُؤْمِنُ بِمَآ أُنزِلَ عَلَيْنَا وَيَكْفُرُونَ بِمَا وَرَآءَهُۥ وَهُوَ ٱلْحَقُّ مُصَدِّقًا لِّمَا مَعَهُمْ ۗ قُلْ فَلِمَ تَقْتُلُونَ أَنۢبِيَآءَ ٱللَّهِ مِن قَبْلُ إِن كُنتُم مُّؤْمِنِينَ ﴿٩١﴾ ﴾

91. And when it is said to them (the Jews), "Believe in what Allâh has sent down," they say, "We believe in what was sent down to us." And they disbelieve in that which came after it, while it is the truth confirming what is with them. Say (O Muhammad (peace be upon him) to them): "Why then have you killed the Prophets of Allâh aforetime, if you indeed have been believers?"

$$\textrm{۞ وَلَقَدْ جَآءَكُم مُّوسَىٰ بِٱلْبَيِّنَٰتِ ثُمَّ ٱتَّخَذْتُمُ ٱلْعِجْلَ مِنۢ بَعْدِهِۦ وَأَنتُمْ ظَٰلِمُونَ ۞}$$

92. And indeed Mûsâ (Moses) came to you with clear proofs, yet you worshipped the calf after he left, and you were Zâlimûn (polytheists and wrongdoers).

Transliteration

91. Wa-itha qeela lahum aminoo bima anzala Allahu qaloo nu/minu bima onzila AAalayna wayakfuroona bima waraahu wahuwa alhaqqu musaddiqan lima maAAahum qul falima taqtuloona anbiyaa Allahi min qablu in kuntum mu/mineena 92. Walaqad jaakum moosa bialbayyinati thumma ittakhathtumu alAAijla min baAAdihi waantum *th*alimoona

Tafsir Ibn Kathir

Although The Jews denied the Truth, They claimed to be Believers!

Allah said,

(And when it is said to them), meaning, the Jews and the People of the Book,

(Believe in what Allah has sent down) to Muhammad , believe in and follow him,

(They say, "We believe in what was sent down to us.") meaning, it is enough for us to believe in what was revealed to us in the Tawrah and the Injil, and this is the path that we choose,

(And they disbelieve in that which came after it).

(while it is the truth confirming what is with them) meaning, while knowing that what was revealed to Muhammad ,

(it is the truth confirming what is with them). This means that since what was sent to Muhammad conforms to what was revealed to the People of the Book, then this fact constitutes a proof against them. Similarly, Allah said, (Those to whom We gave the Scripture (Jews and Christians) recognize him (Muhammad) as they recognize their sons) (2:146). Allah said next, ("Why then have you killed the Prophets of Allah aforetime, if you indeed have been believers").

This means, "If your claim that you believe in what was revealed to you is true, then why did you kill the Prophets who came to you affirming the Tawrah's Law, although you knew they were true Prophets You killed them simply out of transgression, stubbornness and injustice with Allah's Messengers. Therefore, you only follow your lusts, opinions and desires." Similarly, Allah said, (Is it that whenever there came to you a Messenger with what you yourselves desired not, you grew arrogant Some you disbelieved and some you killed.)

Also, As-Suddi said,

"In this Ayah, Allah chastised the People of the Book, (Say (O Muhammad to them): "Why then have you killed the Prophets of Allah aforetime, if you indeed have been believers")." (And indeed Musa came to you with clear proofs) meaning, with clear signs and clear proofs that he was the Messenger of Allah and that there is no deity worthy of worship except Allah. The clear signs -or miracles- mentioned here are the flood, the locusts, the lice, the frogs, the blood, the staff and the hand. Musa's miracles also include parting the sea, shading the Jews with clouds, the manna and quails, the gushing stone, etc. (yet you worshipped the calf) meaning, as a deity instead of Allah, during the time of Musa. Allah's statement, (after he left) after Musa went to Mount Tur to speak to Allah. Similarly, Allah said, (And the people of Musa made in his absence, out of their ornaments, the image of a calf (for worship). It had a sound (as if it was mooing)) (7:148). (and you were Zalimun) meaning, you were unjust in this behavior of worshipping the calf, although you knew that there is no deity worthy of worship except Allah. Similarly, Allah said, (And when they regretted and saw that they had gone astray, they (repented and) said: "If our Lord have not mercy upon us and forgive us, we shall certainly be of the losers") (7:149).

Surah: 2 Ayah: 93

﴿ وَإِذْ أَخَذْنَا مِيثَٰقَكُمْ وَرَفَعْنَا فَوْقَكُمُ ٱلطُّورَ خُذُوا۟ مَآ ءَاتَيْنَٰكُم بِقُوَّةٍ وَٱسْمَعُوا۟ قَالُوا۟ سَمِعْنَا وَعَصَيْنَا وَأُشْرِبُوا۟ فِى قُلُوبِهِمُ ٱلْعِجْلَ بِكُفْرِهِمْ قُلْ بِئْسَمَا يَأْمُرُكُم بِهِۦٓ إِيمَٰنُكُمْ إِن كُنتُم مُّؤْمِنِينَ ۝ ﴾

93. And (remember) when We took your covenant and We raised above you the Mount (saying), "Hold firmly to what We have given you and hear (Our Word). They said, "We have heard and disobeyed." And their hearts absorbed (the worship of) the calf because of their disbelief. Say: "Worst indeed is that which your faith enjoins on you if you are believers."

Transliteration

93. Wa-ith akhathna meethaqakum warafaAAna fawqakumu alttoora khuthoo ma ataynakum biquwwatin waismaAAoo qaloo samiAAna waAAasayna waoshriboo fee quloobihimu alAAijla bikufrihim qul bi/sama ya/murukum bihi eemanukum in kuntum mu/mineena

Tafsir Ibn Kathir

The Jews rebel after Allah took Their Covenant and raised the Mountain above Their Heads

Allah reminded the Jews of their errors, breaking His covenant, transgression and defiance, when He raised Mount Tur above them so that they would believe and agree to the terms of the covenant. Yet, they broke it soon afterwards,

(They said,

"We have heard and disobeyed.") We have mentioned the Tafsir of this subject before. `Abdur-Razzaq said that Ma`mar narrated that Qatadah said that,

(And their hearts absorbed (the worship of) the calf) means, "They absorbed its love, until its love resided in their hearts." This is also the opinion of Abu Al-`Aliyah and Ar-Rabi` bin Anas.

Allah's statement,

(Say: "Worst indeed is that which your faith enjoins on you if you are believers.") means, "Worse yet is the manner in which you behaved in the past and even now, disbelieving in Allah's Ayat and defying the Prophets. You also disbelieved in Muhammad , which is the worst of your deeds and the harshest sin that you committed. You disbelieved in the Final Messenger and the master of all Prophets and Messengers, the one who was sent to all mankind. How can you then claim that you believe, while committing the evil of breaking Allah's covenant, disbelieving in Allah's Ayat and worshipping the calf instead of Allah"

Surah: 2 Ayah: 94, Ayah: 95 & Ayah: 96

﴿ قُلْ إِن كَانَتْ لَكُمُ ٱلدَّارُ ٱلْأَخِرَةُ عِندَ ٱللَّهِ خَالِصَةً مِّن دُونِ ٱلنَّاسِ فَتَمَنَّوُاْ ٱلْمَوْتَ إِن كُنتُمْ صَـٰدِقِينَ ۝ ﴾

94. Say to (them): "If the home of the Hereafter with Allâh is indeed for you specially and not for others, of mankind, then long for death if you are truthful."

﴿ وَلَن يَتَمَنَّوْهُ أَبَدًا بِمَا قَدَّمَتْ أَيْدِيهِمْ ۚ وَٱللَّهُ عَلِيمٌۢ بِٱلظَّـٰلِمِينَ ۝ ﴾

95. But they will never long for it because of what their hands have sent before them (i.e. what they have done). And Allâh is All-Aware of the Zâlimûn (polytheists and wrongdoers).

Chapter 2: Al-Baqarah, Verses 001-141

$$\text{﴿ وَلَتَجِدَنَّهُمْ أَحْرَصَ النَّاسِ عَلَىٰ حَيَاةٍ وَمِنَ الَّذِينَ أَشْرَكُوا ۚ يَوَدُّ أَحَدُهُمْ لَوْ يُعَمَّرُ أَلْفَ سَنَةٍ وَمَا هُوَ بِمُزَحْزِحِهِ مِنَ الْعَذَابِ أَن يُعَمَّرَ ۗ وَاللَّهُ بَصِيرٌ بِمَا يَعْمَلُونَ ۞ ﴾}$$

96. And verily, you will find them (the Jews) the greediest of mankind for life and (even greedier) than those who ascribe partners to Allâh (and do not believe in Resurrection - Majûs, pagans, and idolaters). Everyone of them wishes that he could be given a life of a thousand years. But the grant of such life will not save him even a little from (due) punishment. And Allâh is All-Seer of what they do.

Transliteration

94. Qul in kanat lakumu alddaru al-akhiratu AAinda Allahi khalisatan min dooni alnnasi fatamannawoo almawta in kuntum sadiqeena 95. Walan yatamannawhu abadan bima qaddamat aydeehim waAllahu AAaleemun bialththalimeena 96. Walatajidannahum ahrasa alnnasi AAala hayatin wamina allatheena ashrakoo yawaddu ahaduhum law yuAAammaru alfa sanatin wama huwa bimuzahzihihi mina alAAathabi an yuAAammara waAllahu baseerun bima yaAAmaloona

Tafsir Ibn Kathir

Calling the Jews to invoke Allah to destroy the Unjust Party

Muhammad bin Ishaq narrated that Ibn `Abbas said, "Allah said to His Prophet ,

(Say to (them): "If the home of the Hereafter with Allah is indeed for you especially and not for others, of mankind, then long for death if you are truthful.") meaning, `Invoke Allah to bring death to the lying camp among the two (Muslims and Jews).' The Jews declined this offer by the Messenger of Allah ."

(But they will never long for it because of what their hands have sent before them (i.e. what they have done). And Allah is Aware of the Zalimin (polytheists and wrongdoers).) meaning, "Since they know that they recognize you, and yet disbelieve in you." Had they wished death that day, no Jew would have remained alive on the face of the earth. Moreover, Ad-Dahhak said that Ibn `Abbas said that,

(Then long for death), means, "Invoke (Allah) for death." Also, `Abdur-Razzaq narrated that `Ikrimah said that Ibn `Abbas commented,

(Then long for death if you are truthful), "Had the Jews invoked Allah for death, they would have perished." Also, Ibn Abi Hatim recorded Sa`id bin Jubayr saying that Ibn `Abbas said, "Had the Jews asked for death, one of them would have choked on his own saliva." These statements have authentic chains of narration up to Ibn `Abbas. Further, Ibn Jarir said in his Tafsir, "We were told that the Prophet said,

«لَوْ أَنَّ الْيَهُودَ تَمَنَّوُا الْمَوْتَ لَمَاتُوا وَلَرَأَوْا مَقَاعِدَهُمْ مِنَ النَّارِ، وَلَوْ خَرَجَ الَّذِينَ يُبَاهِلُونَ رَسُولَ اللهِ صلى الله عليه وسلّم لَرَجَعُوا لَا يَجِدُونَ أَهْلًا وَلَا مَالًا»

(Had the Jews wished for death, they would have died and seen their seats in the Fire. And, those who invoked such curse against Allah's Messenger would have found no families or property had they returned to their homes)."

Similar to this Ayah is Allah's statement in Surat Al-Jumu'ah,

((Say (O Muhammad): "O you Jews! If you pretend that you are friends of Allah, to the exclusion of (all) other mankind, then long for death if you are truthful. "But they will never long for it (death), because of what (deeds) their hands have sent before them! And Allah knows well the Zalimin. Say (to them): "Verily, the death from which you flee will surely meet you, then you will be sent back to (Allah) the Knower of the unseen and the seen, and He will tell you what you used to do.") (62:6-8).

So they claimed that they are Allah's sons and loved ones and said, "Only those who are Christian or Jews shall enter Paradise." Therefore, they were called to invoke Allah to destroy the lying group, be it them or the Muslims. When the Jews declined, every one was sure of their wrong, for had they been sure of their claims, then they would have accepted the proposal. Their lies were thus exposed after they declined the offer to invoke the curse.

Similarly, the Messenger of Allah called a delegation of Najran's Christians to curse after he refuted them in a debate in which they demonstrated stubbornness and defiance. Allah said,

(Then whoever disputes with you concerning him ('Isa) after (all this) knowledge that has come to you (i.e. 'Isa) being a servant of Allah, and having no share in divinity), say (O Muhammad): "Come, let us call our sons and your sons, our women and your women, ourselves and yourselves @— then we pray and invoke (sincerely) the curse of Allah upon those who lie.") (3:61).

When the Christians heard this challenge, some of them said to each other, "By Allah! If you do such with this Prophet, none of you will have an eye that blinks." This is when they resorted to peace and gave the Jizyah (tax) in disgrace. The Prophet accepted the Jizyah from them and sent Abu `Ubaydah bin Al-Jarrah with them as a trustee. Similar to this meaning is Allah's command to His Prophet to proclaim to the polytheists:

(Say (O Muhammad) whoever is in error, the Most Gracious (Allah) will prolong him (in it).) (19:75) meaning, "Whoever among us has deviated, may Allah increase and prolong his deviation." We will mention this subject later, Allah willing.

The Mubahalah (invocation to Allah to destroy the liars) was called a 'wish' here, because every just person wishes that Allah destroy the unjust opponent who is debating with him, especially when the just person has a clear, apparent proof for the truth he is calling to. Also, the Mubahalah involves invoking Allah for death of the unjust group, because to disbelievers, life is the biggest prize, especially when they know the evil destination they will meet after death.

Disbelievers wish They could live longer

This is why Allah said next,

(But they will never long for it because of what their hands have sent before them (i.e.what they have done). And Allah is Aware of the Zalimin. And verily, you will find them (the Jews) the greediest of mankind for life.) meaning, greedy to live longer, because they know their evil end, and the only reward they will have with Allah is total loss. This life is a prison for the believer and Paradise for the disbeliever. Therefore, the People of the Book wish they could delay the Hereafter, as much as possible. However, they shall certainly meet what they are trying to avoid, even if they are more eager to delay the Hereafter than the polytheists who do not have a divine book.

Muhammad bin Ishaq narrated that Ibn 'Abbas commented on,

(But the grant of such life will not save him even a little from (due) punishment.) "Long life shall not save them from torment. Certainly, the polytheists do not believe in resurrection after death, and they would love to enjoy a long life. The Jews know the humiliation they will suffer in the Hereafter for knowingly ignoring the truth." Also, `Abdur-Rahman bin Zayd bin Aslam said, "The Jews are most eager for this life. They wish they could live for a thousand years. However, living for a thousand years will not save them from torment, just as Iblis' - Satan - long life did not benefit him, due to being a disbeliever." t

(And Allah is Seer of what they do.) meaning, "Allah knows what His servants are doing, whether good or evil, and will compensate each of them accordingly."

Surah: 2 Ayah: 97 & Ayah: 98

﴿ قُلْ مَن كَانَ عَدُوًّا لِّجِبْرِيلَ فَإِنَّهُ نَزَّلَهُ عَلَىٰ قَلْبِكَ بِإِذْنِ ٱللَّهِ مُصَدِّقًا لِّمَا بَيْنَ يَدَيْهِ وَهُدًى وَبُشْرَىٰ لِلْمُؤْمِنِينَ ۝ ﴾

97. Say (O Muhammad (peace be upon him)) "Whoever is an enemy to Jibrael (Gabriel) (let him die in his fury), for indeed he has brought it (this Qur'ân) down to your heart by Allâh's Permission, confirming what came before it (i.e. the Taurât (Torah) and the Injeel (Gospel)) and guidance and glad tidings for the believers.

﴿ مَن كَانَ عَدُوًّا لِّلَّهِ وَمَلَٰٓئِكَتِهِۦ وَرُسُلِهِۦ وَجِبْرِيلَ وَمِيكَىٰلَ فَإِنَّ ٱللَّهَ عَدُوٌّ لِّلْكَٰفِرِينَ ۝ ﴾

98. Whoever is an enemy to Allâh, His Angels, His Messengers, Jibrael (Gabriel) and Mikael (Michael), then verily, Allâh is an enemy to the disbelievers."

Transliteration

97. Qul man kana AAaduwwan lijibreela fa-innahu nazzalahu AAala qalbika bi-ithni Allahi musaddiqan lima bayna yadayhi wahudan wabushra lilmu/mineena
98. Man kana AAaduwwan lillahi wamala-ikatihi warusulihi wajibreela wameekala fa-inna Allaha AAaduwwun lilkafireena

Tafsir Ibn Kathir

The Jews are the Enemies of Jibril

Imam Abu Ja'far bin Jarir At-Tabari said, "The scholars of Tafsir agree that this Ayah (2: 97-98) was revealed in response to the Jews who claimed that Jibril (Gabriel) is an enemy of the Jews and that Mika'il (Michael) is their friend." Al-Bukhari said, "Allah said,

(Whoever is an enemy of Jibril (let him die in his fury)). 'Ikrimah said, "Jibr, Mik and Israf all mean, worshipper, while il means, Allah". Anas bin Malik said, "When 'Abdullah bin Salam heard of the arrival of the Prophet in Al-Madinah, he was working on his land. He came to the Prophet and said, 'I am going to ask you about three things which nobody knows except a Prophet. What will be the first portent of the Hour What will be the first meal taken by the people of Paradise Why does a child resemble its father, and why does it resemble its maternal uncle' Allah's Messenger said, (Jibril has just told me the answers.) 'Abdullah said, 'He (i.e. Jibril), among all the angels, is the enemy of the Jews.' Allah's Messenger recited the Ayah,

(Whoever is an enemy to Jibril (Gabriel) (let him die in his fury), for indeed he has brought it (this Qur'an) down to your heart). Allah's Messenger then said, (The first portent of the Hour will be a fire that will bring together the people from the east to the west; the first meal of the people of Paradise will be the caudate lobe of the liver of fish. As for the child resembling his parents: If a man has sexual intercourse with his wife and his discharge is first, the child will resemble the father. If the woman has a discharge first, the child will resemble her side of the family.) On that 'Abdullah bin Salam said, 'I testify that there is no deity worthy of worship except Allah and you are the Messenger of Allah.' 'Abdullah bin Salam further said, 'O Allah's Messenger! The Jews are liars, and if they should come to know about my conversion to Islam before you ask them (about me), they will tell a lie about me.' The Jews came to Allah's Messenger , and 'Abdullah went inside the house. Allah's Messenger asked (the Jews), ('What kind of man is 'Abdullah bin Salam') They replied, 'He is the best among us, the son of the best among us, our master and the son of our master.' Allah's Messenger said, (What do you think if he would embrace Islam) The Jews said, 'May Allah save him from it.' Then 'Abdullah bin Salam came out in front of them saying, 'I testify that none has the right to be worshipped but Allah and that Muhammad is the Messenger of Allah.' Thereupon they said, 'He is the evilest among us, and the son of the evilest among us.' And they continued talking badly about him. Ibn Salam said, 'This is what I feared, O Messenger of Allah!.'" Only Al-Bukhari recorded this Hadith with this chain of narration. Al-Bukhari and Muslim recorded this Hadith from Anas using another chain of narration.

Some people say that 'il' means worshipper while whatever word that is added to it becomes Allah's Name, because 'il' is a constant in such conjunction. This is similar to the names 'Abdullah, 'Abdur-Rahman, 'Abdul-Malik, 'Abdul-Quddus, 'Abdus-Salam, 'Abdul-Kafi, 'Abdul-Jalil, and so forth. Hence, 'Abd' is constant in these compound names, while the remainder differs from name to name. This is the same case with Jibril, Mika'il, 'Azra'il, Israfil, and so forth. Allah knows best.

Choosing Some Angels to believe in over Others is Disbelief like choosing Some Prophets over Others

Allah said,

(Whoever is an enemy to Jibril (Gabriel) (let him die in his fury), for indeed he has brought it (this Qur'an) down to your heart by Allah's permission,) meaning, whoever becomes an enemy of Jibril, let him know that he is Ruh Al-Qudus who brought down the Glorious Dhikr (Qur'an) to your heart from Allah by His leave. Hence, he is a messenger from Allah. Whoever takes a messenger as an enemy, will have taken all the messengers as enemies. Further, whoever believes in one messenger, is required to believe in all of the messengers. Whoever rejects one messenger, he has rejected all of the messengers. Similarly, Allah said,

(Verily, those who disbelieve in Allah and His Messengers and wish to make distinction between Allah and His Messengers (by believing in Allah and disbelieving in His Messengers) saying, "We believe in some but reject others.") (4:150)

Allah decreed that they are disbelievers, because they believe in some Prophets and reject others. This is the same with those who take Jibril as an enemy, because Jibril did not choose missions on his own, but by the command of his Lord,

(And we (angels) descend not except by the command of your Lord) (19: 64), and,

(And truly, this (the Qur'an) is a revelation from the Lord of all that exists. Which the trustworthy Ruh (Jibril) has brought down. Upon your heart (O Muhammad) that you may be (one) of the warners) (26:192-194).

Al-Bukhari reported that Abu Hurayrah said that the Messenger of Allah said,

«مَنْ عَادَى لِي وَلِيًّا فَقَدْ بَارَزَنِي بِالْحَرْبِ»

(Allah said, 'Whoever takes a friend of Mine as an enemy, will have started a war with Me.)

Therefore, Allah became angry with those who took Jibril as an enemy. Allah said,

(Whoever is an enemy to Jibril (Gabriel) (let him die in his fury), for indeed he has brought it (this Qur'an) down to your heart by Allah's permission, confirming what came before it) meaning, the previous Books,

(and guidance and glad tidings for the believers) meaning, as guidance to their hearts and bringer of the good news of Paradise, which is exclusively for the believers.

Similarly, Allah said,

(Say: "It is for those who believe, a guide and a healing.") (41:44), and,

(And We send down of the Qur'an that which is a healing and a mercy to those who believe) (17:82).

Allah then said,

(Whoever is an enemy to Allah, His Angels, His Messengers, Jibril and Mika'il (Michael), then verily, Allah is an enemy to the disbelievers.)

Allah stated that whoever takes Him, His angels and messengers as enemies, then...Allah's messengers include angels and men, for Allah said,

(Allah chooses Messengers from angels and from men) (22:75).

Allah said,

(Jibril (Gabriel) and Mika'il (Michael)).

Allah mentioned Jibril and Mika'il specifically - although they are included among the angels who were messengers - only because this Ayah was meant to support Jibril the emissary between Allah and His Prophets.

Allah also mentioned Mika'il here, because the Jews claimed that Jibril was their enemy and Mika'il was their friend.

Allah informed them that whoever is an enemy of either of them, then he is also an enemy of the other as well as Allah.

We should state here that Mika'il sometimes descended to some of Allah's Prophets, although to a lesser extent than Jibril, because this was primarily Jibril's task, and Israfil is entrusted with the job of blowing the Trumpet for the commencement of Resurrection on the Day of Judgment.

It is recorded in the Sahih that whenever the Messenger of Allah would wake up at night, he would supplicate,

«اللَّهُمَّ رَبَّ جِبْرَائِيلَ وَمِيكَائِيلَ وَإِسْرَافِيلَ فَاطِرَ السَّمَوَاتِ وَالْأَرْضِ عَالِمَ الْغَيْبِ وَالشَّهَادَةِ، أَنْتَ تَحْكُمُ بَيْنَ عِبَادِكَ فِيمَا كَانُوا فِيهِ يَخْتَلِفُونَ، اهْدِنِي لِمَا اخْتُلِفَ فِيهِ مِنَ الْحَقِّ بِإِذْنِكَ إِنَّكَ تَهْدِي مَنْ تَشَاءُ إِلَى صِرَاطٍ مُسْتَقِيمٍ»

(O Allah, Lord of Jibril, Mika'il and Israfil, Creator of the heavens and earth and Knower of the seen and the unseen! You judge between Your servants regarding what they differ in, so direct me to the truth which they differ on, by Your leave. Verily, You guide whom You will to the straight path.)

Allah's statement,

(then verily, Allah is an enemy to the disbelievers) informed the disbelievers that whoever takes a friend of Allah as an enemy, then he has taken Allah as an enemy, and whoever treats Allah as an enemy, then he shall be Allah's enemy. Indeed, whoever is an enemy of Allah then he will lose in this life and the Hereafter, as stated earlier;

«مَنْ عَادَى لِي وَلِيًّا فَقَدْ آذَنْتُهُ بِالْمُحَارَبَةِ»

(Whoever takes a friend of Mine as an enemy, I shall wage war on him.)

Surah: 2 Ayah: 99, Ayah: 100, Ayah: 101, Ayah: 102 & Ayah: 103

﴿ وَلَقَدْ أَنزَلْنَآ إِلَيْكَ ءَايَـٰتٍۭ بَيِّنَـٰتٍ وَمَا يَكْفُرُ بِهَآ إِلَّا ٱلْفَـٰسِقُونَ ۝ ﴾

99. And indeed We have sent down to you manifest Ayât (these Verses of the Qur'ân which inform in detail about the news of the Jews and their secret intentions, etc.), and none disbelieve in them but Fâsiqûn (those who rebel against Allâh's Command).

﴿ أَوَكُلَّمَا عَـٰهَدُوا۟ عَهْدًا نَّبَذَهُۥ فَرِيقٌ مِّنْهُم ۚ بَلْ أَكْثَرُهُمْ لَا يُؤْمِنُونَ ۝ ﴾

100. Is it not (the case) that every time they make a covenant, some party among them throw it aside? Nay! the truth is most of them believe not.

﴿ وَلَمَّا جَآءَهُمْ رَسُولٌ مِّنْ عِندِ ٱللَّهِ مُصَدِّقٌ لِّمَا مَعَهُمْ نَبَذَ فَرِيقٌ مِّنَ ٱلَّذِينَ أُوتُوا۟ ٱلْكِتَـٰبَ كِتَـٰبَ ٱللَّهِ وَرَآءَ ظُهُورِهِمْ كَأَنَّهُمْ لَا يَعْلَمُونَ ۝ ﴾

101. And when there came to them a Messenger from Allâh (i.e. Muhammad (peace be upon him)) confirming what was with them, a party of those who were given the Scripture threw away the Book of Allâh behind their backs as if they did not know!

﴿ وَٱتَّبَعُوا۟ مَا تَتْلُوا۟ ٱلشَّيَـٰطِينُ عَلَىٰ مُلْكِ سُلَيْمَـٰنَ ۖ وَمَا كَفَرَ سُلَيْمَـٰنُ وَلَـٰكِنَّ ٱلشَّيَـٰطِينَ كَفَرُوا۟ يُعَلِّمُونَ ٱلنَّاسَ ٱلسِّحْرَ وَمَآ أُنزِلَ عَلَى ٱلْمَلَكَيْنِ بِبَابِلَ هَـٰرُوتَ وَمَـٰرُوتَ ۚ وَمَا يُعَلِّمَانِ مِنْ أَحَدٍ حَتَّىٰ يَقُولَآ إِنَّمَا نَحْنُ فِتْنَةٌ فَلَا تَكْفُرْ ۖ فَيَتَعَلَّمُونَ مِنْهُمَا مَا يُفَرِّقُونَ بِهِۦ بَيْنَ ٱلْمَرْءِ وَزَوْجِهِۦ ۚ وَمَا هُم بِضَآرِّينَ بِهِۦ مِنْ أَحَدٍ إِلَّا بِإِذْنِ ٱللَّهِ ۚ وَيَتَعَلَّمُونَ مَا يَضُرُّهُمْ وَلَا يَنفَعُهُمْ ۚ وَلَقَدْ عَلِمُوا۟ لَمَنِ ٱشْتَرَىٰهُ مَا لَهُۥ فِى ٱلْـَٔاخِرَةِ مِنْ خَلَـٰقٍ ۚ وَلَبِئْسَ مَا شَرَوْا۟ بِهِۦٓ أَنفُسَهُمْ ۚ لَوْ كَانُوا۟ يَعْلَمُونَ ۝ ﴾

102. They followed what the Shayâtin (devils) gave out (falsely of the magic) in the lifetime of Sulaimân (Solomon). Sulaimân did not disbelieve, but the Shayâtin (devils) disbelieved, teaching men magic and such things that came down at Babylon to the two angels, Hârût and Mârût, but neither of these two (angels) taught anyone (such things) till they had said, "We are

only for trial, so disbelieve not (by learning this magic from us)." And from these (angels) people learn that by which they cause separation between man and his wife, but they could not thus harm anyone except by Allâh's Leave. And they learn that which harms them and profits them not. And indeed they knew that the buyers of it (magic) would have no share in the Hereafter. And how bad indeed was that for which they sold their ownselves, if they but knew.

﴿ وَلَوْ أَنَّهُمْ ءَامَنُواْ وَاتَّقَوْاْ لَمَثُوبَةٌ مِّنْ عِندِ ٱللَّهِ خَيْرٌ لَّوْ كَانُواْ يَعْلَمُونَ ۝ ﴾

103. And if they had believed, and guarded themselves from evil and kept their duty to Allâh, far better would have been the reward from their Lord, if they but knew!

Transliteration

99. Walaqad anzalna ilayka ayatin bayyinatin wama yakfuru biha illa alfasiqoona 100. Awa kullama AAahadoo AAahdan nabathahu fareequn minhum bal aktharuhum la yu/minoona 101. Walamma jaahum rasoolun min AAindi Allahi musaddiqun lima maAAahum nabatha fareequn mina allatheena ootoo alkitaba kitaba Allahi waraa thuhoorihim kaannahum la yaAAlamoona 102. WaittabaAAoo ma tatloo alshshayateenu AAala mulki sulaymana wama kafara sulaymanu walakinna alshshayateena kafaroo yuAAallimoona alnnasa alssihra wama onzila AAala almalakayni bibabila haroota wamaroota wama yuAAallimani min ahadin hatta yaqoola innama nahnu fitnatun fala takfur fayataAAallamoona minhuma ma yufarriqoona bihi bayna almar-i wazawjihi wama hum bidarreena bihi min ahadin illa bi-ithni Allahi wayataAAallamoona ma yadurruhum wala yanfaAAuhum walaqad AAalimoo lamani ishtarahu ma lahu fee al-akhirati min khalaqin walabi/sa ma sharaw bihi anfusahum law kanoo yaAAlamoona 103. Walaw annahum amanoo waittaqaw lamathoobatun min AAindi Allahi khayrun law kanoo yaAAlamoona

Tafsir Ibn Kathir

Proofs of Muhammad's Prophethood

Imam Abu Ja'far bin Jarir said that Allah's statement,

(And indeed We have sent down to you manifest Ayat) means, "We have sent to you, O Muhammad, clear signs that testify to your prophethood." These Ayat are contained in the Book of Allah (Qur'an) which narrates the secrets of the knowledge that the Jews possess, which they hid, and the stories of their earlier generations. The Book of Allah also mentions the texts in the Books of the Jews that are known to only the rabbis and scholars, and the sections where they altered and distorted the rulings of the Tawrah. Since Allah mentioned all of this in His Book revealed to His Prophet Muhammad , then this fact alone should be enough evidence for those who are truthful with themselves and who wish to avoid bringing themselves to destruction due to envy and transgression. Further human instict testifies to the truth that Muhammad was sent with and the clear signs that he brought which he did not learn or acquire from mankind.

Ad-Dahhak said that Ibn `Abbas said that,

(And indeed We have sent down to you manifest Ayat) means, "You recite and convey this Book to them day and night, although you are an Ummi (unlettered) who never read a book. Yet, you inform them of what they have (in their own Books). Allah stated that this fact should serve as an example, a clear sign and a proof against them, if they but knew."

The Jews break Their Covenants

When the Messenger of Allah was sent and Allah reminded the Jews of the covenant that they had with Him, especially concerning Muhammad , Malik bin As-Sayf said, "By Allah! Allah never made a covenant with us about Muhammad, nor did He take a pledge from us at all." Allah then revealed,

(Is it not (the case) that every time they make a covenant, some party among them throw it aside) Al-Hasan Al-Basri said that Allah's statement,

(Nay! (the truth is:) most of them believe not) means, "There is not a promise that they make, but they break it and abandon it. They make a promise today and break it tomorrow."

The Jews abandoned the Book of Allah and practiced Magic

As-Suddi commented on,

(And when there came to them a Messenger from Allah (i.e. Muhammad) confirming what was with them), "When Muhammad came to them, they wanted to contradict and dispute with him using the Tawrah. However, the Tawrah and the Qur'an affirmed each other. So the Jews gave up on using the Torah, and took to the Book of Asaf, and the magic of Harut and Marut, which indeed did not conform to the Qur'an. Hence Allah's statement,

(As if they did not know!)."

Also, Qatadah said that Allah's statement,

(As if they did not know!) means, "They knew the truth but abandoned it, hid it and denied the fact that they even had it."

Magic existed before Sulayman (Solomon)

As-Suddi said that Allah's statement,

(They followed what the Shayatin (devils) gave out (falsely of the magic) in the lifetime of Sulayman) means, "`During the time of Prophet Solomon.'

Beforehand, the devils used to ascend to heaven and eavesdrop on the conversations of the angels about what will occur on the earth regarding death, other incidents or unseen matters. They would convey this news to the soothsayers, and the soothsayers would in turn convey the news to the people. The people would believe what the soothsayers told them as being true. When the soothsayers trusted the devils, the devils started to lie to them and added other words to the true news that they heard, to the extent of adding seventy false words to each true word. The people recorded these words in some books. Soon after, the Children of Israel said that the Jinns know matters of the Unseen. When Solomon was sent as a Prophet, he collected these books in a box and buried it under his throne; any devil that dared get near the box was burned. Solomon said, `I will not hear of anyone who says that the devils know the Unseen, but I will cut off his head.' When Solomon died and the scholars who knew the truth about Solomon perished, there came another generation. To them, the devil materialized in the shape of a human and said to some of the Children of Israel, `Should I lead you to a treasure that you will never be able to use up' They said. `Yes.' He said, `Dig under this throne,' and he went with them and showed them Solomon's throne. They said to him, `Come closer.' He said, `No. I will wait for you here, and if you do not find the treasure then kill me.' They dug and found the buried books, and Satan said to them, `Solomon only controlled the humans, devils and birds with this magic.' Thereafter, the news that Solomon was a sorcerer spread among the people, and the Children of Israel adopted these books. When Muhammad came, they disputed with him relying on these books. Hence Allah's statement,

(Sulayman did not disbelieve, but the Shayatin (devils) disbelieved).

The Story of Harut and Marut, and the Explanation that They were Angels

Allah said,

(And such things that came down at Babylon to the two angels, Harut and Marut, but neither of these two (angels) taught anyone (such things) till they had said, "We are for trial, so disbelieve not (by learning this magic from us)." And from these (angels) people learn that by which they cause separation between man and his wife).

There is a difference of opinion regarding this story. It was said that this Ayah denies that anything was sent down to the two angels, as Al-Qurtubi stated and then referred to the Ayah,

(Sulayman did not disbelieve) saying, "The negation applies in both cases. Allah then said,

(But the Shayatin (devils) disbelieved, teaching men magic and such things that came down at Babylon to the two angels).

The Jews claimed that Gabriel and Michael brought magic down to the two angels, but Allah refuted this false claim."

Also, Ibn Jarir reported, that Al-'Awfi said that Ibn 'Abbas said about Allah's statement,

(And such things that came down at Babylon to the two angels)

"Allah did not send magic down."

Also, Ibn Jarir narrated that Ar-Rabi' bin Anas said about,

(And such things that came down to the two angels), "Allah did not send magic down to the them." Ibn Jarir commented, "This is the correct explanation for this Ayah.

(They followed what the Shayatin (devils) gave out (falsely) in the lifetime of Sulayman.) meaning, magic. However, neither did Solomon disbelieve nor did Allah send magic with the two angels. The devils, on the other hand, disbelieved and taught magic to the people of the Babylon of Harut and Marut."

Ibn Jarir continued; "If someone asks about explaining this Ayah in this manner, we say that,

(They followed what the Shayatin (devils) gave out (falsely) in the lifetime of Sulayman.) means, magic. Solomon neither disbelieved nor did Allah send magic with the two angels. However, the devils disbelieved and taught magic to the people in the Babylon of Harut and Marut, meaning Gabriel and Michael, for Jewish sorcerers claimed that Allah sent magic by the words of Gabriel and Michael to Solomon, son of David. Allah denied this false claim and stated to His Prophet Muhammad that Gabriel and Michael were not sent with magic. Allah also exonerated Solomon from practicing magic, which the devils taught to the people of Babylon by the hands of two men, Harut and Marut. Hence, Harut and Marut were two ordinary men (not angels or Gabriel or Michael)." These were the words of At-Tabari, and this explanation is not plausible.

Many among the Salaf, said that Harut and Marut were angels who came down from heaven to earth and did what they did as the Ayah stated. To conform this opinion with the fact that the angels are immune from error, we say that Allah had eternal knowledge what these angels would do, just as He had eternal knowledge that Iblis would do as he did, while Allah refered to him being among the angels,

(And (remember) when We said to the angels: "Prostrate yourselves before Adam." And they prostrated except Iblis (Satan), he refused) (20:116) and so forth. However, what Harut and Marut did was less evil than what Iblis, may Allah curse him, did. Al-Qurtubi reported this opinion from `Ali, Ibn Mas`ud, Ibn `Abbas, Ibn `Umar, Ka`b Al-Ahbar, As-Suddi and Al-Kalbi.

Learning Magic is Kufr

Allah said,

(But neither of these two (angels) taught anyone (such things) till they had said, "We are for trial, so disbelieve not (by learning this magic from us).)

Abu Ja'far Ar-Razi said that Ar-Rabi' bin Anas said that Qays bin 'Abbad said that Ibn 'Abbas said, "When someone came to the angels to learn magic, they would discourage him and say to him, 'We are only a test, so do not fall into disbelief.' They had knowledge of what is good and evil and what constitutes belief or disbelief, and they thus knew that magic is a form of disbelief. When the person who came to learn magic still insisted on learning it, they commanded him to go to such and such place, where if he went, Satan would meet him and teach him magic. When this man would learn magic, the light (of faith) would depart him, and he would see it shining (and flying away) in the sky. He would then proclaim, 'O my sorrow! Woe unto me! What should I do." Al-Hasan Al-Basri said that this Ayah means, "The angels were sent with magic, so that the people whom Allah willed would be tried and tested. Allah made them promise that they would not teach anyone until first proclaiming, 'We are a test for you, do not fall into disbelief.'" It was recorded by Ibn Abi Hatim. Also, Qatadah said, "Allah took their covenant to not teach anyone magic until they said, 'We are a test. Therefore, do not fall in disbelief.'"

Also, As-Suddi said, "When a man would come to the two angels they would advise him, `Do not fall into disbelief. We are a test. ' When the man would ignore their advice, they would say, `Go to that pile of ashes and urinate on it.' When he would urinate on the ashes, a light, meaning the light of faith, would depart from him and would shine until it entered heaven. Then something black that appeared to be smoke would descend and enter his ears and the rest of his body, and this is Allah's anger. When he told the angels what happened, they would teach him magic. So Allah's statement,

(But neither of these two (angels) taught anyone (such things) till they had said, "We are for trial, so disbelieve not (by learning this magic from us).)

Sunayd said that Hajjaj said that Ibn Jurayj commented on this Ayah (2:102), "No one dares practice magic except a disbeliever. As for the Fitnah, it involves trials and freedom of choice."The scholars who stated that learning magic is disbelief relied on this Ayah for evidence. They also mentioned the Hadith that Abu Bakr Al-Bazzar recorded from `Abdullah, which states,

«مَنْ أَتَى كَاهِنًا أَوْ سَاحِرًا فَصَدَّقَهُ بِمَا يَقُولُ فَقَدْ كَفَرَ بِمَا أُنْزِلَ عَلى مُحَمَّدٍصلى الله عليه وسلّم»

(Whoever came to a soothsayer or a sorcerer and believed in what he said, will have disbelieved in what Allah revealed to Muhammad .)

This Hadith has an authentic chain of narration and there are other Hadiths which support it.

Causing a Separation between the Spouses is One of the Effects of Magic

Allah said,

(And from these (angels) people learn that by which they cause separation between man and his wife,) This means, "The people learned magic from Harut and Marut and indulged in evil acts that included separating spouses, even though spouses are close to, and intimately associate with each other. This is the devil's work." Muslim recorded that Jabir bin `Abdullah said that the Messenger of Allah said,

«إِنَّ الشَّيْطَانَ لَيَضَعُ عَرْشَهُ عَلَى الْمَاءِ ثُمَّ يَبْعَثُ سَرَايَاهُ فِي النَّاسِ فَأَقْرَبُهُمْ عِنْدَهُ مَنْزِلَةً أَعْظَمُهُمْ عِنْدَهُ فِتْنَةً وَيَجِيءُ أَحَدُهُمْ فَيَقُولُ: مَا زِلْتُ بِفُلَانٍ حَتَّى تَرَكْتُهُ وَهُوَ يَقُولُ كَذَا وَكَذَا، فَيَقُولُ إِبْلِيسُ: لَا وَاللهِ مَا صَنَعْتَ شَيْئًا، وَيَجِيءُ أَحَدُهُمْ فَيَقُولُ: مَا تَرَكْتُهُ حَتَّى فَرَّقْتُ بَيْنَهُ وَبَيْنَ أَهْلِهِ، قَالَ: فَيُقَرِّبُهُ وَيُدْنِيهِ وَيَلْتَزِمُهُ وَيَقُولُ: نِعْمَ أَنْتَ»

(Satan erects his throne on water and sends his emissaries among the people. The closest person to him is the person who causes the most Fitnah. One of them (a devil) would come to him and would say, 'I kept inciting so-and-so, until he said such and such words.' Iblis says, 'No, by Allah, you have not done much.' Another devil would come to him and would say, 'I kept inciting so-and-so, until I separated between him and his wife.' Satan would draw him closer and embrace him, saying, 'Yes, you did well.')

Separation between a man and his wife occurs here because each spouse imagines that the other spouse is ugly or ill-mannered, etc.

Allah's Appointed Term supercedes Everything

Allah said,

(But they could not thus harm anyone except by Allah's leave).

Sufyan Ath-Thawri commented, "Except by Allah's appointed term."

Further, Al-Hasan Al-Basri said that,

(But they could not thus harm anyone except by Allah's leave) means, "Allah allows magicians to adversely affect whomever He wills and saves whomever He wills from them. Sorcerers never bring harm to anyone except by Allah's leave."

Allah's statement, (And they learn that which harms them and profits them not.) means, it harms their religion and does not have a benefit compared to its harm.

(And indeed they knew that the buyers of it (magic) would have no (Khalaq) share in the Hereafter.) meaning, "The Jews who preferred magic over following the Messenger of Allah knew that those who commit the same error shall have no Khalaq in the Hereafter."

Ibn `Abbas, Mujahid and As-Suddi stated that `no Khalaq' means, `no share.'

Allah then said,

(And how bad indeed was that for which they sold their own selves, if they but knew. And if they had believed and guarded themselves from evil and kept their duty to Allah, far better would have been the reward from their Lord, if they but knew!). Allah stated, (And how bad) meaning, what they preferred, magic, instead of faith and following the Messenger, if they but comprehend the advice. (And if they had believed and guarded themselves from evil and kept their duty to Allah, far better would have been the reward from their Lord,) meaning, "Had they believed in Allah and His Messenger and avoided the prohibitions, then Allah's reward for these good deeds would have been better for them than what they chose and preferred for themselves."

Similarly, Allah said, (But those who had been given (religious) knowledge said: "Woe to you! The reward of Allah (in the Hereafter) is better for those who believe and do righteous good deeds, and this none shall attain except As-Sabirun (the patient in following the truth).") (28:80).

Surah: 2 Ayah: 104 & Ayah: 105

﴿ يَـٰٓأَيُّهَا ٱلَّذِينَ ءَامَنُواْ لَا تَقُولُواْ رَٰعِنَا وَقُولُواْ ٱنظُرْنَا وَٱسْمَعُواْ ۗ وَلِلْكَـٰفِرِينَ عَذَابٌ أَلِيمٌ ﴾

104. O you who believe! Say not (to the Messenger (peace be upon him)) Râ'ina but say Unzurna (make us understand) and hear. And for the disbelievers there is a painful torment. (See Verse 4:46)

$$\left\{\text{مَّا يَوَدُّ ٱلَّذِينَ كَفَرُواْ مِنْ أَهْلِ ٱلْكِتَٰبِ وَلَا ٱلْمُشْرِكِينَ أَن يُنَزَّلَ عَلَيْكُم مِّنْ خَيْرٍ مِّن رَّبِّكُمْ ۗ وَٱللَّهُ يَخْتَصُّ بِرَحْمَتِهِۦ مَن يَشَآءُ ۚ وَٱللَّهُ ذُو ٱلْفَضْلِ ٱلْعَظِيمِ ﴿١٠٥﴾}\right\}$$

105. Neither those who disbelieve among the people of the Scripture (Jews and Christians) nor Al-Mushrikûn (the disbelievers in the Oneness of Allâh, idolaters, polytheists, pagans, etc.) like that there should be sent down unto you any good from your Lord. But Allâh chooses for His Mercy whom He wills. And Allâh is the Owner of Great Bounty.

Transliteration

104. Ya ayyuha allatheena amanoo la taqooloo raAAina waqooloo on*th*urna waismaAAoo walilkafireena AAathabun aleemun   105. Ma yawaddu allatheena kafaroo min ahli alkitabi wala almushrikeena an yunazzala AAalaykum min khayrin min rabbikum waAllahu yakhtassu birahmatihi man yashao waAllahu thoo alfadli alAAa*th*eemi

Tafsir Ibn Kathir

Manners in Speech

Allah forbade His believing servants from imitating the behavior and deeds of the disbelievers. The Jews used to use devious words that hide what they really meant. May Allah's curse be upon them. When they wanted to say, 'hear us,' they would use the word Ra'ina, which is an insult (in Hebrew, but means 'hear us' in Arabic). Allah said,

(Among those who are Jews, there are some who displace words from (their) right places and say: "We hear your word (O Muhammad) and disobey," and "Hear and let you (O Muhammad) hear nothing." And Ra`ina with a twist of their tongues and as a mockery of the religion (Islam). And if only they had said: "We hear and obey," and "Do make us understand," it would have been better for them, and more proper; but Allah cursed them for their disbelief, so they believe not except a few) (4:46).

Also, the Hadiths stated that when they would greet Muslims, they would say, 'As-Samu 'alaykum,' meaning, 'death be to you'. This is why we were commanded to answer them by saying, 'Wa 'alaykum,' meaning, 'and to you too', then our supplication against them shall be answered, rather than theirs against us.

Allah forbade the believers from imitating the disbelievers in tongue or deed. Allah said,

(O you who believe! Say not (to the Messenger) Ra'ina but say Unzurna (make us understand) and hear. And for the disbelievers there is a painful torment) (2:104).

Also, Imam Ahmad narrated that Ibn 'Umar said that the Messenger of Allah said,

«بُعِثْتُ بَيْنَ يَدَيِ السَّاعَةِ بِالسَّيْفِ حَتَّى يُعْبَدَاللهُ وَحْدَهُ لَا شَرِيكَ لَهُ، وَجُعِلَ رِزْقِي تَحْتَ ظِلِّ رُمْحِي، وَجُعِلَتِ الذِّلَّةُ وَالصَّغَارُ عَلَى مَنْ خَالَفَ أَمْرِي، وَمَنْ تَشَبَّهَ بِقَوْمٍ فَهُوَ مِنْهُمْ»

(I was sent with the sword just before the Last Hour, so that Allah is worshipped alone without partners. My sustenance was provided for me from under the shadow of my spear. Those who oppose my command were humiliated and made inferior, and whoever imitates a people, he is one of them.)

Abu Dawud narrated that the Prophet said,

«مَنْ تَشَبَّهَ بِقَوْمٍ فَهُوَ مِنْهُمْ»

(Whoever imitates a people is one of them.)

These Hadiths indicate, along with their threats and warnings, that we are not allowed to imitate the disbelievers in their statements, deeds, clothes, feasts, acts of worship, etc., whatever actions of the disbelievers that were not legislated for us.

Ad-Dahhak said that Ibn 'Abbas commented on the Ayah,

(Say not (to the Messenger) Ra'ina) "They used to say to the Prophet , Ar'ina samak (which is an insult)." Ibn Abu Hatim said that it was reported that Abu Al-'Aliyah, Abu Malik, Ar-Rabi' bin Anas, 'Atiyah Al-'Awfi and Qatadah said similarly. Further, Mujahid said, "'Do not say Ra'ina' means, 'Do not dispute'." Mujahid said in another narration, "Do not say, 'We hear from you, and you hear from us.'" Also, 'Ata' said, "Do not say,

(Ra'ina), which was a dialect that the Ansar used and which was forbidden from use by Allah."

Also, As-Suddi said, "Rifa'ah bin Zayd, a Jewish man from the tribe of Qaynuqa`, used to come to the Prophet and say to him, `Hear, Ghayr Musma'in (let you hear nothing).' The Muslims used to think that the Prophets are greeted and honored with this type of speech, and this is why some of them used to say, 'Hear, let you hear nothing,' and so on, as mentioned in Surat An-Nisa." Thereafter, Allah forbade the believers from uttering the word Ra`ina." `Abdur-Rahman bin Zayd bin Aslam also said similarly.

The extreme Enmity that the Disbelievers and the People of the Book have against Muslims

Allah said next (2:105),

(Neither those who disbelieve among the People of the Scripture (Jews and Christians) nor Al-Mushrikin (the idolaters), like that there should be sent down unto you any good from your Lord).

Allah described the deep enmity that the disbelieving polytheists and People of the Scripture, whom Allah warned against imitating, have against the believers, so that Muslims should sever all friendship with them. Also, Allah mentioned what He granted the believers of the perfect Law that He legislated for their Prophet Muhammad . Allah said,

(But Allah chooses for His mercy whom He wills. And Allah is the Owner of great bounty) (2:105).

Surah: 2 Ayah: 106 & Ayah: 107

﴿ ۞ مَا نَنسَخْ مِنْ ءَايَةٍ أَوْ نُنسِهَا نَأْتِ بِخَيْرٍ مِّنْهَا أَوْ مِثْلِهَا ۗ أَلَمْ تَعْلَمْ أَنَّ ٱللَّهَ عَلَىٰ كُلِّ شَىْءٍ قَدِيرٌ ۝ ﴾

106. Whatever a Verse (revelation) do We abrogate or cause to be forgotten, We bring a better one or similar to it. Know you not that Allâh is able to do all things?

﴿ أَلَمْ تَعْلَمْ أَنَّ ٱللَّهَ لَهُۥ مُلْكُ ٱلسَّمَـٰوَٰتِ وَٱلْأَرْضِ ۗ وَمَا لَكُم مِّن دُونِ ٱللَّهِ مِن وَلِىٍّ وَلَا نَصِيرٍ ۝ ﴾

107. Know you not that it is Allâh to Whom belongs the dominion of the heavens and the earth? And besides Allâh you have neither any Walî (protector or guardian) nor any helper.

Transliteration

106. Ma nansakh min ayatin aw nunsiha na/ti bikhayrin minha aw mithliha alam taAAlam anna Allaha AAala kulli shay-in qadeerun   107. Alam taAAlam anna Allaha lahu mulku alssamawati waal-ardi wama lakum min dooni Allahi min waliyyin wala naseerin

Tafsir Ibn Kathir

The Meaning of Naskh

Ibn Abi Talhah said that Ibn `Abbas said that, (Whatever a verse (revelation) do Nansakh) means, "Whatever an Ayah We abrogate." Also, Ibn Jurayj said that Mujahid said that, (Whatever a verse (revelation) do Nansakh) means, "Whatever an Ayah We erase." Also, Ibn Abi Najih said that Mujahid said that,

(Whatever a verse (revelation) do Nansakh) means, "We keep the words, but change the meaning." He related these words to the companions of `Abdullah bin Mas`ud. Ibn Abi Hatim said that similar statements were mentioned by Abu Al-`Aliyah and Muhammad bin Ka`b Al-Qurazi. Also As-Suddi said that,

(Whatever a verse (revelation) do Nansakh) means, "We erase it." Further, Ibn Abi Hatim said that it means, "Erase and raise it, such as erasing the following wordings (from the Qur'an), `The married adulterer and the married adulteress: stone them to death,' and, `If the son of Adam had two valleys of gold, he would seek a third.'"

Ibn Jarir stated that,

(Whatever a verse (revelation) do Nansakh) means, "Whatever ruling we repeal in an Ayah by making the allowed unlawful and the unlawful allowed." The Nasakh only occurs with commandments, prohibitions, permissions, and so forth. As for stories, they do not undergo Nasakh. The word, `Nasakh' literally means, `to copy a book'. The meaning of Nasakh in the case of commandments is removing the commandment and replacing it by another. And whether the Nasakh involves the wordings, the ruling or both, it is still called Nasakh.

Allah said next,

(or Nunsiha (cause it to be forgotten)). `Ali bin Abi Talhah said that Ibn `Abbas said that,

(Whatever a verse (revelation) do Nansakh or Nunsiha) means, "Whatever Ayah We repeal or uphold without change." Also, Mujahid said that the companions of Ibn Mas`ud (who read this word Nansa'ha) said that it means, "We uphold its wording and change its ruling." Further, `Ubayd bin `Umayr, Mujahid and `Ata' said, `Nansa'ha' means, "We delay it (i.e., do not abrogate it)." Further, `Atiyyah Al-`Awfi said that the Ayah means, "We delay repealing it." This is the same Tafsir provided by As-Suddi and Ar-Rabi` bin Anas. `Abdur-Razzaq said that Ma`mar said that Qatadah said about Allah's statement,

(Whatever a verse (revelation) do We abrogate or cause to be forgotten) "Allah made His Prophet forget what He willed and He abrogated what He will."

Allah's said,

(We bring a better one or similar to it), better, relates to the benefit provided for the one it addresses, as reported from 'Ali bin Abi Talhah that Ibn 'Abbas said,

(We bring a better one) means, "We bring forth a more beneficial ruling, that is also easier for you." Also, As-Suddi said that,

(We bring a better one or similar to it) means, "We bring forth a better Ayah, or similar to that which was repealed." Qatadah also said that, (We bring a better one or similar to it) means, "We replace it by an Ayah more facilitating, permitting, commanding, or prohibiting."

Naskh occurs even though the Jews deny it

Allah said,

(Know you not that Allah is Able to do all things Know you not that it is Allah to Whom belongs the dominion of the heavens and the earth And besides Allah you have neither any Wali (protector or guardian) nor any helper).

Allah directed His servants to the fact that He alone is the Owner of His creatures and that He does with them as He wills. Indeed, His is the supreme authority and all creation is His, and just as He created them as He wills, He brings happiness to whom He wills, misery to whom He wills, health to whom He wills and ailment to whom He wills. He also brings success to whom He wills and failure to whom He wills. He judges between His servants as He wills, allows what He wills and disallows what He wills. He decides what He wills, there is no opponent for His judgment, and no one can question Him about what He does, while they shall be questioned. He tests His servants and their obedience to His Messengers by the Naskh. He commands a matter containing a benefit which He knows of, and then He out of His wisdom, prohibits it. Hence, perfect obedience is realized by adhering to His commands, following His Messengers, believing in what ever they convey, implementing their commands and avoiding what they prohibit.

The statements of Allah here contain tremendous benefit, prove that the Jews are disbelievers and refute their claim that Naskh does not occur, may Allah curse the Jews. In ignorance and arrogance they claimed that the sound mind stipulates that Naskh does not occur. Some of them falsely claimed that there are divine texts that dismiss the possibility that Naskh occurred.

Imam Abu Ja'far bin Jarir said, "The Ayah means, 'Do you not know, O Muhammad, that I alone own the heavens and the earth and that I decide whatever I will in them I forbid whatever I will, change and repeal whatever I will of My previous rulings, whenever I will. I also uphold whatever I will."

Ibn Jarir then said, "Although Allah directed His statement indicating His greatness towards His Prophet , He also rejected the lies of the Jews who denied that the rulings of the Torah could undergo Naskh. The Jews also denied the prophethood of Jesus and Muhammad, because of their dislike for what they brought from Allah, such as changing some rulings of the Torah, as Allah commanded. Allah thus proclaimed to the Jews that He owns the heavens and earth and also all authority in them. Further, the subjects in Allah's kingdom are His creation, and they are required to hear and obey His commands and prohibitions. Allah has full authority to command the creation as He wills, forbidding them from what He wills, abrogate what He wills, uphold what He wills, and decide whatever commandments and prohibitions He wills."

I (Ibn Kathir) say that the Jews' dismissal of the occurrence of the Naskh is only a case of their disbelief and rebellion. The sound mind does not deny that there could be a Naskh in Allah's commandments, for He decides what He wills, just as He does what He wills. Further, Naskh occurred in previous Books and Law. For instance, Allah allowed Adam to marry his daughters to his sons and then later forbade this practice. Allah also allowed Nuh to eat from all kinds of animals after they left the ark, then prohibited eating some types of foods. Further, marrying two sisters to one man was allowed for Israel and his children, but Allah prohibited this practice later in the Torah. Allah commanded Abraham to slaughter his son, then repealed that command before it was implemented. Also, Allah commanded the Children of Israel to kill those who worshipped the calf and then repealed that command, so that the Children of Israel were not all exterminated. There are many other instances that the Jews admit have occurred, yet they ignore them. Also, it is a well-known fact that their Books foretold about Muhammad and contained the command to follow him. These texts, in their Books, indicate that the Jews were required to follow the Prophet Muhammad and that no good deed would be accepted from them, unless it conformed to Muhammad's Law. The Prophet brought another Book, - the Qur'an -, which is the last revelation from Allah.

Surah: 2 Ayah: 108

﴿أَمْ تُرِيدُونَ أَن تَسْـَٔلُوا۟ رَسُولَكُمْ كَمَا سُئِلَ مُوسَىٰ مِن قَبْلُ ۗ وَمَن يَتَبَدَّلِ ٱلْكُفْرَ بِٱلْإِيمَٰنِ فَقَدْ ضَلَّ سَوَآءَ ٱلسَّبِيلِ ۝﴾

108. Or do you want to ask your Messenger (Muhammad (peace be upon him)) as Mûsâ (Moses) was asked before (i.e. show us openly our Lord?) And he who changes Faith for disbelief, verily, he has gone astray from the Right Way.

Transliteration

108. Am tureedoona an tas-aloo rasoolakum kama su-ila moosa min qablu waman yatabaddali alkufra bial-eemani faqad dalla sawaa alssabeeli

Tafsir Ibn Kathir

The Prohibition of Unnecessary Questions

In this Ayah, Allah forbade the believers from asking the Prophet numerous questions about matters that did not occur yet. Similarly, Allah said,

(O you who believe! Ask not about things which, if made plain to you, may cause you trouble. But if you ask about them while the Qur'an is being revealed, they will be made plain to you) (5:101).

This Ayah means,

"If you ask about a matter after it is revealed, it shall be duly explained to you. Therefore, do not ask about matters that have not occurred yet, for they might become prohibited, due to your questions."

This is why the Sahih narrated,

«إِنَّ أَعْظَمَ الْمُسْلِمِينَ جُرْمًا مَنْ سَأَلَ عَنْ شَيْءٍ لَمْ يُحَرَّمْ، فَحُرِّمَ مِنْ أَجْلِ مَسْأَلَتِهِ»

(The greatest criminal among the Muslims is the one who asks if a thing is prohibited, which is not prohibited, and it becomes prohibited because of his asking about it.)

This is why when the Messenger of Allah was asked about a husband who finds another man with his wife; if he exposes the adultery, he will be exposing a major incident; if he is quiet about it, he will be quiet about a major matter. The Messenger of Allah did not like such questions. Later on, Allah revealed the ruling of Mula`anah [Refer to Nur 24:6-9 in the Qur'an]. The Two Sahihs recorded that Al-Mughirah bin Shu`bah said that the Messenger of Allah "Forbade saying, `It was said' and `He said,' and wasting money and asking many questions." Muslim recorded that the Prophet said,

«ذَرُونِي مَا تَرَكْتُكُمْ، فَإِنَّمَا هَلَكَ مَنْ كَانَ قَبْلَكُمْ بِكَثْرَةِ سُؤَالِهِمْ وَاخْتِلَافِهِمْ عَلَى أَنْبِيَائِهِمْ، فَإِذَا أَمَرْتُكُمْ بِأَمْرٍ فَأْتُوا مِنْهُ مَا اسْتَطَعْتُمْ وَإِنْ نَهَيْتُكُمْ عَنْ شَيْءٍ فَاجْتَنِبُوه»

(Leave me as I leave you; those before you were only destroyed because of their excessive questioning and disputing with their Prophets. Therefore, when

I command you with a matter, adhere to it as much as you can, and when I forbid from something, avoid it.)

The Prophet only said this after he told the Companions that Allah has ordered them to perform Hajj. A man asked, "Every year, O Messenger of Allah" The Prophet did not answer him, but he repeated his question three times. Then the Prophet said,

»لَا، وَلَوْ قُلْتُ: نَعَمْ، لَوَجَبَتْ وَلَوْ وَجَبَتْ لَمَا اسْتَطَعْتُمْ«

(No. Had I said yes, it would have been ordained, and you would not have been able to implement it.)

This is why Anas bin Malik said, "We were forbidden from asking the Messenger of Allah about things. So we were delighted when a bedouin man would come and ask him while we listened."

Muhammad bin Ishaq said that Muhammad bin Abi Muhammad told him that 'Ikrimah or Sa'id said that Ibn 'Abbas said that Rafi' bin Huraymilah or Wahb bin Zayd said, "O Muhammad! Bring us a Book sent down from heaven and which we could read, and make some rivers flow for us, then we will follow you and believe in you." Allah sent down the answer to this challenge,

(Or do you want to ask your Messenger (Muhammad) as Musa was asked before (i.e. show us openly our Lord) And he who changes faith for disbelief, verily, he has gone astray from the right way).

Allah criticized those who ask the Messenger of Allah about a certain matter just for the purpose of being difficult, just as the Children of Israel asked Musa out of stubbornness, rejection and rebellion. Allah said,

(And he who changes faith for disbelief) meaning, whoever prefers disbelief to faith,

(verily, he has gone astray from the right way) meaning, he has strayed from the straight path, to the path of ignorance and misguidance. This is the case of those who deviated from accepting the Prophets and obeying them and those who kept asking their Prophets unnecessary questions in defiance and disbelief, just as Allah said,

(Have you not seen those who have changed the blessings of Allah into disbelief (by denying Prophet Muhammad and his Message of Islam), and caused their people to dwell in the house of destruction Hell, in which they will burn and what an evil place to settle in!) (14:28-29).

Abu Al-'Aliyah commented, "They exchanged comfort for hardship."

Surah: 2 Ayah: 109 & Ayah: 110

$$ \text{﴿ وَدَّ كَثِيرٌ مِّنْ أَهْلِ ٱلْكِتَـٰبِ لَوْ يَرُدُّونَكُم مِّنۢ بَعْدِ إِيمَـٰنِكُمْ كُفَّارًا حَسَدًا مِّنْ عِندِ أَنفُسِهِم مِّنۢ بَعْدِ مَا تَبَيَّنَ لَهُمُ ٱلْحَقُّ ۖ فَٱعْفُوا۟ وَٱصْفَحُوا۟ حَتَّىٰ يَأْتِىَ ٱللَّهُ بِأَمْرِهِۦٓ ۗ إِنَّ ٱللَّهَ عَلَىٰ كُلِّ شَىْءٍ قَدِيرٌ ﴾ } $$

109. Many of the people of the Scripture (Jews and Christians) wish that if they could turn you away as disbelievers after you have believed, out of envy from their ownselves, even, after the truth (that Muhammad (peace be upon him) is Allâh's Messenger) has become manifest unto them. But forgive and overlook, till Allâh brings His Command. Verily, Allâh is Able to do all things.

$$ \text{﴿ وَأَقِيمُوا۟ ٱلصَّلَوٰةَ وَءَاتُوا۟ ٱلزَّكَوٰةَ ۚ وَمَا تُقَدِّمُوا۟ لِأَنفُسِكُم مِّنْ خَيْرٍ تَجِدُوهُ عِندَ ٱللَّهِ ۗ إِنَّ ٱللَّهَ بِمَا تَعْمَلُونَ بَصِيرٌ ﴾ } $$

110. And perform As-Salât (Iqâmat-as-Salât), and give Zakât, and whatever of good (deeds that Allâh loves) you send forth for yourselves before you, you shall find it with Allâh. Certainly, Allâh is All-Seer of what you do.

Transliteration

109. Wadda katheerun min ahli alkitabi law yaruddoonakum min baAAdi eemanikum kuffaran hasadan min AAindi anfusihim min baAAdi ma tabayyana lahumu alhaqqu faoAAfoo waisfahoo hatta ya/tiya Allahu bi-amrihi inna Allaha AAala kulli shay-in qadeerun   110. Waaqeemoo alssalata waatoo alzzakata wama tuqaddimoo li-anfusikum min khayrin tajidoohu AAinda Allahi inna Allaha bima taAAmaloona baseerun

Tafsir Ibn Kathir

The Prohibition of following the Ways of the People of the Book

Allah warned His believing servants against following the ways of the People of Book, who publicly and secretly harbor emnity and hatred for the believers, and who envy the believers, while they recognize the virtue of the believers and their Prophet . Allah also commanded His believing servants to forgive them and to be patient with them, until Allah delivers His aid and victory to them. Allah commanded the believers to perform the prayer perfectly, to pay the Zakah and He encouraged them to preserve the practice of these righteous deeds.

Ibn Abi Hatim recorded that 'Abdullah bin Ka'b bin Malik said that Ka'b bin Al-Ashraf, who was a Jew and a poet, used to criticize the Prophet in his poems, so Allah revealed,

(Many of the People of the Scripture (Jews and Christians) wish that they could turn you away..) regarding his matter.

Also, Ad-Dahhak said that Ibn 'Abbas said, "An unlettered Messenger came to the People of the Scriptures confirming what they have in their own Books about the Messengers and the Ayat of Allah. He also believes in all of this, just as they believe in it. Yet, they rejected the Prophet out of disbelief, envy and transgression. This is why Allah said,

(out of envy from their own selves, even after the truth (that Muhammad is Allah's Messenger) has become manifest unto them).

Allah said that after He illuminated the truth for them, such that they were not ignorant of any of it, yet their envy made them deny the Prophet . Thus Allah criticized, chastised and denounced them." Allah legislated the characteristics that His Prophet and the believers should adhere to: belief, faith and accepting what Allah revealed to them and to those before them out of His generosity and tremendous kindness.

Ar-Rabi' bin Anas said that,

(from their own selves) means, "of their making." Also, Abu Al-'Aliyah said that,

(even after the truth (that Muhammad is Allah's Messenger) has become manifest unto them) means, "After it became clear that Muhammad is the Messenger of Allah whom they find written of in the Torah and the Injil. They denied him in disbelief and transgression because he was not one of them." Qatadah and Ar-Rabi' bin Anas said similarly. Allah said,

(But forgive and overlook, till Allah brings His command.) this is similar to His saying;

(And you shall certainly hear much that will grieve you from those who received the Scripture before you (Jews and Christians) and from those who ascribe partners to Allah) (3: 186).

'Ali bin Abi Talhah said that Ibn 'Abbas said that Allah's statement,

(But forgive and overlook, till Allah brings His command.) was abrogated by the Ayah,

(Then kill the Mushrikin wherever you find them) (9:5), and,

(Fight against those who believe not in Allah, nor in the Last Day) (9:29) until,

(And feel themselves subdued) (9:29).

Allah's pardon for the disbelievers was repealed." Abu Al-'Aliyah, Ar-Rabi' bin Anas, Qatadah and As-Suddi said similarly: It was abrogated by the Ayah of the sword." (Mentioned above). The Ayah,

(till Allah brings His command.) gives further support for this view.

Ibn Abi Hatim recorded Usamah bin Zayd saying that the Messenger of Allah and his Companions used to forgive the disbelievers and the People of the Book, just as Allah commanded in His statement,

(But forgive and overlook, till Allah brings His command. Verily, Allah is able to do all things).

The Messenger of Allah used to forgive them and was patient with them as Allah ordered him, until Allah allowed fighting them. Then Allah destroyed those who He decreed to be killed among the strong men of Quraysh, by the Prophet's forces. The chain of narration for this text is Sahih, but I did not see its wordings in the six collections of Hadith, although the basis of it is in the Two Sahihs, narrated from Usamah bin Zayd.

The Encouragement to perform Good Deeds

Allah said,

(And perform the Salah and give the Zakah, and whatever of good you send forth for yourselves before you, you shall find it with Allah).

Allah encouraged the believers to busy themselves in performing deeds that would bring them benefit and reward on the Day of Resurrection, such as prayer and paying Zakah. This way, they will gain Allah's aid in this life and on a Day when the witnesses testify,

(The Day when their excuses will be of no profit to the Zalimin (wrongdoers). Theirs will be the curse, and theirs will be the evil abode (i.e. painful torment in Hell-fire)) (40:52).

This is why Allah said,

(Certainly, Allah sees what you do), meaning, that He is never unaware of the deeds of any person, nor will these deeds be lost by Him. Whether deeds are righteous or evil, Allah will award each according to what he or she deserves based on their deeds.

Surah: 2 Ayah: 111, Ayah: 112 & Ayah: 113

﴿ وَقَالُواْ لَن يَدْخُلَ ٱلْجَنَّةَ إِلَّا مَن كَانَ هُودًا أَوْ نَصَـٰرَىٰ ۗ تِلْكَ أَمَانِيُّهُمْ ۗ قُلْ هَاتُواْ بُرْهَـٰنَكُمْ إِن كُنتُمْ صَـٰدِقِينَ ۝ ﴾

111. And they say, "None shall enter Paradise unless he be a Jew or a Christian." These are their own desires. Say (O Muhammad (peace be upon him)) "Produce your proof if you are truthful."

$$\text{﴿ بَلَىٰ مَنْ أَسْلَمَ وَجْهَهُ لِلَّهِ وَهُوَ مُحْسِنٌ فَلَهُ أَجْرُهُ عِندَ رَبِّهِ وَلَا خَوْفٌ عَلَيْهِمْ وَلَا هُمْ يَحْزَنُونَ ﴾}$$

112. Yes, but whoever submits his face (himself) to Allâh (i.e. follows Allâh's Religion of Islâmic Monotheism) and he is a Muhsin (good-doer i.e. performs good deeds totally for Allâh's sake only without any show off or to gain praise or fame, etc., and in accordance with the Sunnah of Allâh's Messenger Muhammad (peace be upon him)) then his reward is with his Lord (Allâh), on such shall be no fear, nor shall they grieve. (See Tafsir Ibn Kathîr).

$$\text{﴿ وَقَالَتِ الْيَهُودُ لَيْسَتِ النَّصَارَىٰ عَلَىٰ شَيْءٍ وَقَالَتِ النَّصَارَىٰ لَيْسَتِ الْيَهُودُ عَلَىٰ شَيْءٍ وَهُمْ يَتْلُونَ الْكِتَابَ كَذَٰلِكَ قَالَ الَّذِينَ لَا يَعْلَمُونَ مِثْلَ قَوْلِهِمْ فَاللَّهُ يَحْكُمُ بَيْنَهُمْ يَوْمَ الْقِيَامَةِ فِيمَا كَانُوا فِيهِ يَخْتَلِفُونَ ﴾}$$

113. The Jews said that the Christians follow nothing (i.e. are not on the right religion); and the Christians said that the Jews follow nothing (i.e. are not on the right religion); though they both recite the Scripture. Like unto their word, said (the pagans) who know not. Allâh will judge between them on the Day of Resurrection about that wherein they have been differing.

Transliteration

111. Waqaloo lan yadkhula aljannata illa man kana hoodan aw nasara tilka amaniyyuhum qul hatoo burhanakum in kuntum sadiqeena 112. Bala man aslama wajhahu lillahi wahuwa muhsinun falahu ajruhu AAinda rabbihi wala khawfun AAalayhim wala hum yahzanoona 113. Waqalati alyahoodu laysati alnnasara AAala shay-in waqalati alnnasara laysati alyahoodu AAala shay-in wahum yatloona alkitaba kathalika qala allatheena la yaAAlamoona mithla qawlihim faAllahu yahkumu baynahum yawma alqiyamati feema kanoo feehi yakhtalifoona

Tafsir Ibn Kathir

The Hopes of the People of the Book

Allah made the confusion of the Jews and the Christians clear, since they claim that no one will enter Paradise, unless he is a Jew or a Christian.

Similarly, Allah mentioned their claims in Surat Al-Ma'idah:

(We are the children of Allah and His loved ones) (5:18).

Allah refuted this false claim and informed them that they will be punished because of their sins. Previously we mentioned their claim that the Fire would not touch them for more than a few days, after which they would be put in Paradise. Allah rebuked this claim, and He said about this baseless claim,

(These are their own desires). Abu Al-'Aliyah commented, "These are wishes that they wished Allah would answer, without basis." Similar was stated by Qatadah and Ar-Rabi' bin Anas. Allah then said,

(Say) meaning, "Say O Muhammad:"

("Produce your Burhan...") meaning, "Your proof", as Abu Al-'Aliyah, Mujahid, As-Suddi and Ar-Rabi' bin Anas stated. Qatadah said that the Ayah means, "Bring the evidence that supports your statement,

(if you are truthful) in your claim."

Allah then said,

(Yes! But whoever submits his face (himself) to Allah (i.e. follows Allah's religion of Islamic Monotheism) and he is a Muhsin) meaning, "Whoever performs deeds in sincerity, for Allah alone without partners." In a similar statement, Allah said,

(So if they dispute with you (Muhammad) say: "I have submitted myself to Allah (in Islam), and (so have) those who follow me.") (3:20)

Abu Al-'Aliyah and Ar-Rabi' said that,

(Yes! But whoever submits his face (himself) to Allah) means, "Whoever is sincere with Allah."

Also, Sa'id bin Jubayr said that,

(Yes! But whoever submits) means, he is sincere,

(his face (himself)) meaning, in his religion.

(and he is a Muhsin) following the Messenger . For there are two conditions for deeds to be accepted; the deed must be performed for Allah's sake alone and conform to the Shari'ah. When the deed is sincere, but does not conform to the Shari'ah, then it will not be accepted. The Messenger of Allah said,

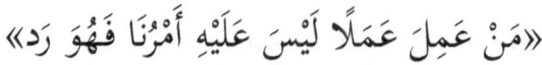

(Whoever performs a deed that does not conform with our matter (religion), then it will be rejected.)

This Hadith was recorded by Muslim. Therefore, the good deeds of the priests and rabbis will not be accepted, even if they are sincerely for Allah alone, because these deeds do not conform with the method of the Messenger, who was sent for all mankind. Allah said regarding such cases,

(And We shall turn to whatever deeds they (disbelievers, polytheists, sinners) did, and We shall make such deeds as scattered floating particles of dust.) (25:23)

(As for those who disbelieved, their deeds are like a mirage in a desert. The thirsty one thinks it to be water, until he comes up to it, he finds it to be nothing.) (24:39) and, (Some faces, that Day will be humiliated. Laboring, weary. They will enter in the hot blazing Fire. They will be given to drink from a boiling spring) (88:2-5).

When the deed conforms to the Shari'ah outwardly, but the person did not perform it sincerely for Allah alone, the deed will also be rejected, as in the case of the hypocrites and those who do their deeds to show off. Similarly, Allah said,

(Verily, the hypocrites seek to deceive Allah, but it is He Who deceives them. And when they stand up for As-Salah (the prayer), they stand with laziness to be seen by people, and they do not remember Allah but little.) (4:142) and,

(So woe unto those performers of Salah (prayers) (hypocrites). Those who delay their Salah (from their stated fixed times). Those who do good deeds only to be seen (of men). And withhold Al-Ma'un (small kindnesses)) (107:4-7).

This is why Allah said,

(So whoever hopes for the meeting with his Lord, let him work righteousness and associate none as a partner in the worship of his Lord) (18:110).

He also said in this Ayah,

(Yes, but whoever submits his face (himself) to Allah (follows Allah's religion of Islamic Monotheism) and he is a Muhsin).

Allah's statement,

(Shall have their reward with their Lord, on them shall be no fear, nor shall they grieve) guaranteed them the rewards and safety from what they fear and should avoid.

(There shall be no fear on them) in the future, (nor shall they grieve) about what they abandoned in the past. Moreover, Sa'id bin Jubayr said, "(There

The Jews and Christians dispute among Themselves out of Disbelief and Stubbornness

Allah said,

(The Jews said that the Christians follow nothing (i.e. are not on the right religion); and the Christians said that the Jews follow nothing (i.e. are not on the right religion); though they both recite the Scripture.)

Allah explained the disputes, hatred and stubbornness that the People of the Book have towards each other. Muhammad bin Ishaq reported that Ibn `Abbas said, "When a delegation of Christians from Najran came to the Messenger of Allah , the Jewish rabbis came and began arguing with them before the Messenger of Allah . Rafi` bin Huraymilah said, 'You do not follow anything,' and he reiterated his disbelief in Jesus and the Injil. Then a Christian man from Najran's delegation said to the Jews, 'Rather, you do not follow anything,' and he reiterated his rejection of Musa's prophethood and his disbelief in the Torah. So Allah revealed the Ayah,

(The Jews said that the Christians follow nothing (i.e. are not on the right religion); and the Christians said that the Jews follow nothing (i.e. are not on the right religion); though they both recite the Scripture.)"

Allah made it clear that each party read the affirmation of what they claimed to reject in their Book. Consequently, the Jews disbelieve in Jesus, even though they have the Torah in which Allah took their Covenant by the tongue of Moses to believe in Jesus. Also, the Gospel contains Jesus' assertion that Moses' prophethood and the Torah came from Allah. Yet, each party disbelieved in what the other party had.

Allah said,

(Like unto their word, said those who know not) thus exposing the ignorance displayed by the Jews and the Christians concerning their statements that we mentioned. There is a difference of opinion regarding the meaning of Allah's statement,

(who know not)

For instance, Ar-Rabi` bin Anas and Qatadah said that,

(Like unto their word, said those said those who know not) means, "The Christians said similar statements to the Jews." Ibn Jurayj asked `Ata' "Who are those `who know not'" `Ata' said, "Nations that existed before the Jews and the Christians and before the Torah and the Gospel." Also, As-Suddi said that, (said those who know not) is in reference to the Arabs who said that

Muhammad was not following anything (i. e. did not follow a true or existing religion). Abu Ja'far bin Jarir chose the view that this Ayah is general and that there is no evidence that specifically supports any of these explanations. So interpreting the Ayah in a general way is better. Allah knows best.

Allah said, (Allah will judge between them on the Day of Resurrection about that wherein they have been differing.) meaning, that Allah will gather them all on the Day of Return. On that Day, Allah will justly judge between them, for He is never unjust with anyone, even as little as the weight of an atom. This Ayah is similar to Allah's statement in Surat Al-Hajj (22:17),

(Verily, those who believe (in Allah and in His Messenger Muhammad), and those who are Jews, and the Sabians, and the Christians, and the Majus, and those who associate partners with Allah; truly, Allah will judge between them on the Day of Resurrection. Verily, Allah is over all things a Witness).

Allah said, (Say: "Our Lord will assemble us all together (on the Day of Resurrection), then He will judge between us with truth. And He is the Just Judge, the Knower of the true state of affairs.") (34:26).

Surah: 2 Ayah: 114

﴿ وَمَنْ أَظْلَمُ مِمَّن مَّنَعَ مَسَـٰجِدَ ٱللَّهِ أَن يُذْكَرَ فِيهَا ٱسْمُهُۥ وَسَعَىٰ فِى خَرَابِهَآ أُوْلَـٰٓئِكَ مَا كَانَ لَهُمْ أَن يَدْخُلُوهَآ إِلَّا خَآئِفِينَ ۚ لَهُمْ فِى ٱلدُّنْيَا خِزْىٌ وَلَهُمْ فِى ٱلْـَٔاخِرَةِ عَذَابٌ عَظِيمٌ ﴾

114. And who are more unjust than those who forbid that Allâh's Name be glorified and mentioned much (i.e. prayers and invocations, etc.) in Allâh's Mosques and strive for their ruin? It was not fitting that such should themselves enter them (Allâh's Mosques) except in fear. For them there is disgrace in this world, and they will have a great torment in the Hereafter.

Transliteration

114. Waman a*th*lamu mimman manaAAa masajida Allahi an yuthkara feeha ismuhu wasaAAa fee kharabiha ola-ika ma kana lahum an yadkhulooha illa kha-ifeena lahum fee alddunya khizyun walahum fee al-akhirati AAathabun AAa*th*eemun

Tafsir Ibn Kathir

Of the Most Unjust are Those Who prevent People from the Masjids and strive for their Ruin

The Quraysh idolators are those who hindered the people from the Masjids of Allah and wanted to destroy them. Ibn Jarir reported that Ibn Zayd said that Allah's statement,

(And who are more unjust than those who forbid that Allah's Name be mentioned (i.e. prayers and invocations) in Allah's Masjids and strive for their ruin) is about the Quraysh idolators who prevented the Prophet from entering Makkah from Al-Hudaybiyyah, until he slaughtered the Hadi (animal for sacrifice) at Dhi-Tuwa. He then agreed to a peace treaty with the idolators and said to them, (No one before has ever prevented people from entering the House. One would even see the killer of his father and brother, but would not prevent him (from entering the House of Allah).) They said, "Whoever killed our fathers at Badr, shall never enter it while there is one of us alive." Allah's statement,

(and strive for their ruin) means those who prevent whoever maintain the Masjids with Allah's remembrance and who visit Allah's House to perform Hajj and 'Umrah. Ibn Abi Hatim recorded that Ibn 'Abbas said that the Quraysh prevented the Prophet from praying at the Ka'bah in Al-Masjid Al-Haram, so Allah revealed,

(And who are more unjust than those who forbid that Allah's Name be mentioned (i.e. prayers and invocations) in Allah's Masjids)"

After Allah chastised the Jews and Christians, He also criticized the idolators who expelled the Messenger of Allah and his Companions from Makkah, preventing them from praying in Al-Masjid Al-Haram, which they kept exclusively for their idols and polytheism. Allah said,

(And why should not Allah punish them while they hinder (men) from Al-Masjid Al-Haram, and they are not its guardians None can be its guardians except Al-Muttaqun (the pious), but most of them know not.) (8:34)

(It is not for the Mushrikin (polytheists), to maintain the Masjids of Allah while they witness against their own selves of disbelief. The works of such are in vain and in Fire shall they abide. The Masjids of Allah shall be maintained only by those who believe in Allah and the Last Day; perform the Salah, and give the Zakah and fear none but Allah. It is they who are on true guidance.) (9:17-18)

and,

(They are the ones who disbelieved and hindered you from Al-Masjid-Al-Haram (at Makkah) and detained the sacrificial animals, from reaching their place of sacrifice. Had there not been believing men and believing women whom you did not know, that you may kill them and on whose account a sin would have been committed by you without (your) knowledge, that Allah might bring into His mercy whom He wills @— if they (the believers and the disbelievers) had been apart, We verily, would have punished those of them who disbelieved with painful torment) (48:25). Therefore, Allah said here,

(The Masjids of Allah shall be maintained only by those who believe in Allah and the Last Day; perform the Salah, and give the Zakah and fear none but Allah). Therefore, if those believers who follow the virtues mentioned in the

Ayah were prevented from attending the Masjid, then what cause for destruction is worse than this Maintaining the Masjids not only means beautifying them, but it involves remembering Allah, establishing His Shari'ah in the Masjids and purifying them from the filth of Shirk.

The Good News that Islam shall prevail

Allah said next,

(It was not fitting that such should themselves enter them (Allah's Masjids) except in fear).

This Ayah means, "Do not allow them - the disbelievers - to enter the Masjids, except to satisfy the terms of an armistice or a treaty." When the Messenger of Allah conquered Makkah in 9 H, he commanded that someone announce at Mina, "After the current year, no idolators shall perform Hajj, and no naked persons shall perform Tawaf around the House, except for those who have a treaty. In this case, the treaty will be carried to the end of its term." This Ayah supports the Ayah,

(O you who believe! (in Allah's Oneness and in His Messenger Muhammad)! Verily, the Mushrikun (idolators) are Najasun (impure). So let them not come near Al-Masjid-Al-Haram (at Makkah) after this year) (9:28).

It was also said that this Ayah (2:114) carries the good news for the Muslims from Allah that He will allow them to take over Al-Masjid Al-Haram and all the Masjids and disgrace the idolators. Soon after, the Ayah indicated, no idolator shall enter the House, except out of fear of being seized or killed, unless he embraces Islam. Allah fulfilled this promise and later decreed that idolators not be allowed to enter Al-Masjid Al-Haram. The Messenger of Allah stated that no two religions should remain in the Arabian Peninsula, and the Jews and Christians should be expelled from it, all praise is due to Allah. All of these rulings ensure maintaining the honor of Al-Masjid Al-Haram and purifying the area where Allah sent His Messenger to warn and bring good news to all of mankind, may Allah's peace and blessings be on him.

This Ayah also described the disgrace that the disbelievers earn in this life, and that the punishment comes in a form comparable to the deed. Just as they prevented the believers from entering Al-Masjid Al-Haram, they were prevented from entering it in turn. Just as they expelled the believers from Makkah, they were in turn expelled from Makkah,

(and they will have a great torment in the Hereafter) because they breached the sanctity of the House and brought filth to it by erecting idols all around it, invoking other than Allah and performing Tawaf around it while naked, etc.

Here it is worth mentioning the Hadith about seeking refuge from disgrace in this life and the torment of the Hereafter. Imam Ahmad recorded that Busr bin Artah said that the Messenger of Allah used to supplicate,

»اللَّهُمَّ أَحْسِنْ عَاقِبَتَنَا فِي الْأُمُورِ كُلِّهَا وَأَجِرْنَا مِنْ خِزْيِ الدُّنْيَا وَعَذَابِ الْآخِرَةِ«

(O Allah! Make our end better in all affairs, and save us from disgrace in this life and the torment of the Hereafter.) This Hadith is Hasan.

Surah: 2 Ayah: 115

﴿ وَلِلَّهِ ٱلْمَشْرِقُ وَٱلْمَغْرِبُ فَأَيْنَمَا تُوَلُّواْ فَثَمَّ وَجْهُ ٱللَّهِ إِنَّ ٱللَّهَ وَٰسِعٌ عَلِيمٌ ﴾

115. And to Allâh belong the east and the west, so wherever you turn (yourselves or your faces) there is the Face of Allâh (and He is High above, over His Throne). Surely! Allâh is All-Sufficient for His creatures' needs, All-Knowing.

Transliteration

115. Walillahi almashriqu waalmaghribu faaynama tuwalloo fathamma wajhu Allahi inna Allaha wasiAAun AAaleemun

Translation

115. And to Allâh belong the east and the west, so wherever you turn yourselves or your faces there is the Face of Allâh (and He is High above, over His Throne). Surely! Allâh is All-Sufficient for His creatures' needs, All-Knowing.

Tafsir Ibn Kathir

Facing the Qiblah (Direction of the Prayer)

This ruling brought comfort to the Messenger of Allah and his Companions, who were driven out of Makkah and had to depart from the area of Al-Masjid Al-Haram. In Makkah, the Messenger of Allah used to pray in the direction of Bayt Al-Maqdis, while the Ka'bah was between him and the Qiblah. When the Messenger migrated to Al-Madinah, he faced Bayt Al-Maqdis for sixteen or seventeen months, and then Allah directed him to face Al-Ka'bah in prayer. This is why Allah said,

(And to Allah belong the east and the west, so wherever you turn (yourselves or your faces) there is the Face of Allah (and He is High above, over His Throne)).

'Ali bin Abi Talhah said that Ibn 'Abbas said, "The first part of the Qur'an that was abrogated was about the Qiblah. When the Messenger of Allah migrated to Al-Madinah, which was inhabited by the Jews, he was at first commanded to face Bayt Al-Maqdis. The Jews were happy, and the Messenger of Allah faced Bayt Al-Maqdis for some ten months. However, the Messenger of Allah liked to face the Qiblah of Ibrahim (Al-Ka'bah at Makkah), and he used to look to the sky and supplicate. So Allah revealed,

(Verily, We have seen the turning of your (Muhammad's) face towards the heaven) until,

(turn your faces (in prayer) in that direction) (2:144).

The Jews were disturbed by this development and said, 'What made them change the direction of the Qiblah that they used to face' Allah revealed,

(Say (O Muhammad): "To Allah belong both, east and the west") and,

(So wherever you turn (yourselves or your faces) there is the Face of Allah (and He is High above, over His Throne))."

'Ikrimah said that Ibn 'Abbas said,

(So wherever you turn (yourselves or your faces) there is the Face of Allah (and He is High above, over His Throne)) means, "Allah's direction is wherever you face, east or west." Mujahid said that,

(So wherever you turn (yourselves or your faces) there is the Face of Allah (and He is High above, over His Throne))

means, "Wherever you may be, you have a Qiblah to face, that is, Al-Ka`bah."

However, it was said that Allah sent down this Ayah before the order to face the Ka'bah. Ibn Jarir said, "Others said that this Ayah was revealed to the Messenger of Allah permitting the one praying voluntary prayers to face wherever they wish in the east or west, while traveling, when in fear and when facing the enemy." For instance, Ibn 'Umar used to face whatever direction his animal was headed and proclaim that the Messenger of Allah did the same, explaining the Ayah,

(So wherever you turn (yourselves or your faces) there is the Face of Allah)."

That Hadith was also collected by Muslim, At-Tirmidhi, An-Nasa'i, Ibn Abi Hatim, Ibn Marduwyah, and its origin is in the Two Sahihs from Ibn 'Umar and 'Amr bin Rabi'ah without mentioning the Ayah. In his Sahih, Al-Bukhari recorded that Nafi' said that whenever Ibn 'Umar was asked about the prayer during times of fear, he used to describe it and would then say, "When the sense of fear is worse than that, pray while standing, or while riding, whether facing the Qiblah or not." Nafi' then said, "I think Ibn 'Umar mentioned that from the Prophet ." It was also said that the Ayah was revealed about those who are unable to find the correct direction of the Qiblah in the dark or due to cloudy skies and, thus, prayed in a direction other than the Qiblah by mistake.

The Qiblah for the People of Al-Madinah is what is between the East and the West

In his Tafsir of this Ayah (2:115), Al-Hafiz Ibn Marduwyah recorded that Abu Hurayrah said that the Messenger of Allah said,

«مَا بَيْنَ الْمَشْرِقِ وَالْمَغْرِبِ قِبْلَةٌ لِأَهْلِ الْمَدِينَةِ وَأَهْلِ الشَّامِ وَأَهْلِ الْعِرَاقِ»

(What is between the east and the west is the Qiblah for the people of Al-Madinah, Ash-Sham and 'Iraq.)

At-Tirmidhi and Ibn Majah recorded this Hadith with the wording,

«مَا بَيْنَ الْمَشْرِقِ وَالْمَغْرِبِ قِبْلَةٌ»

(What is between the east and the west is a Qiblah.)

Ibn Jarir said, "The meaning of Allah's statement;

(Surely, Allah is Sufficient (for His creatures' needs), Knowing) is that Allah encompasses all His Creation by providing them with sufficient needs and by His generosity and favor. His statement, (Knowing) means He is knowledgeable of their deeds and nothing escapes His watch, nor is He unaware of anything. Rather, His knowledge encompasses everything."

Surah: 2 Ayah: 116 & Ayah: 117

﴿وَقَالُواْ ٱتَّخَذَ ٱللَّهُ وَلَدًا ۗ سُبْحَـٰنَهُۥ ۖ بَل لَّهُۥ مَا فِى ٱلسَّمَـٰوَٰتِ وَٱلْأَرْضِ ۖ كُلٌّ لَّهُۥ قَـٰنِتُونَ ۝﴾

116. And they (Jews, Christians and pagans) say: Allâh has begotten a son (children or offspring). Glory be to Him (Exalted be He above all that they associate with Him). Nay, to Him belongs all that is in the heavens and on earth, and all surrender with obedience (in worship) to Him.

﴿بَدِيعُ ٱلسَّمَـٰوَٰتِ وَٱلْأَرْضِ ۖ وَإِذَا قَضَىٰٓ أَمْرًا فَإِنَّمَا يَقُولُ لَهُۥ كُن فَيَكُونُ ۝﴾

117. The Originator of the heavens and the earth. When He decrees a matter, He only says to it: "Be!" - and it is.

Transliteration

116. Waqaloo itakhatha Allahu waladan subhanahu bal lahu ma fee alssamawati waal-ardi kullun lahu qanitoona   117. BadeeAAu alssamawati waal-ardi wa-itha qada amran fa-innama yaqoolu lahu kun fayakoonu

Tafsir Ibn Kathir

Refuting the Claim that Allah has begotten a Son

This and the following Ayat refute the Christians, may Allah curse them, and their like among the Jews and the Arab idolators, who claimed that the angels are Allah's daughters. Allah refuted all of them in their claim that He had begotten a son. Allah said,

(Glory is to Him.)

meaning, He is holier and more perfect than such claim;

(Nay, to Him belongs all that is in the heavens and on earth,) meaning, the truth is not as the disbelievers claimed, rather, Allah's is the kingdom of the heavens and earth and whatever and whoever is in, on and between them. Allah is the Supreme Authority in the heavens and earth, and He is the Creator, Provider and Sustainer Who decides all the affairs of the creation as He wills. All creatures are Allah's servants and are owned by Him. Therefore, how could one of them be His son The son of any being is born out of two comparable beings. Allah has no equal or rival sharing His grace and greatness, so how can He have a son when He has no wife Allah said,

(He is the Originator of the heavens and the earth. How can He have children when He has no wife He created all things and He is the Knower of everything) (6:101).

(And they say: "The Most Gracious (Allah) has begotten a son (offspring or children)." Indeed you have brought forth (said) a terrible evil thing. Whereby the heavens are almost torn, and the earth is split asunder, and the mountains fall in ruins. That they ascribe a son (or offspring or children) to the Most Gracious (Allah). But it is not suitable for (the majesty of) the Most Gracious (Allah) that He should beget a son (or offspring or children). There is none in the heavens and the earth but comes unto the Most Gracious (Allah) as a servant. Verily, He knows each one of them, and has counted them a full counting. And everyone of them will come to Him alone on the Day of Resurrection (without any helper, or protector or defender)) (19:88-95), and,

(Say: "He is Allah (the) One, Allah the Samad (the Self- Sufficent, upon whom all depend), He begets not, nor was He begotten, and there is none comparable to Him.") (112).

In these Ayat, Allah stated that He is the Supreme Master Whom there is no equal or rival, everything and everyone was created by Him, so how can He have a son from among them This is why, in the Tafsir of this Ayah, Al-Bukhari recorded that Ibn 'Abbas said that the Prophet said,

«قَالَ اللهُ تَعَالَى: كَذَّبَنِي ابْنُ آدَمَ وَلَمْ يَكُنْ لَهُ ذَلِكَ، وَشَتَمَنِي وَلَمْ يَكُنْ لَهُ ذَلِكَ، فَأَمَّا تَكْذِيبُهُ إِيَّايَ فَيَزْعُمُ أَنِّي لَا أَقْدِرُ أَنْ أُعِيدَهُ كَمَا كَانَ، وَأَمَّا شَتْمُهُ إِيَّايَ فَقَوْلُهُ لِي وَلَدًا فَسُبْحَانِي أَنْ أَتَّخِذَ صَاحِبَةً أَوْ وَلَدًا»

(Allah said, 'The son of Adam has denied Me, and that is not his right. He has insulted Me, and that is not his right. As for the denial of Me, he claimed that I am unable to bring him back as he used to be (resurrect him). As for his insulting Me, he claimed that I have a son. All praise is due to Me, it is unbefitting that I should have a wife or a son.')

This Hadith was recorded by Al-Bukhari.

It is recorded in the Two Sahihs that the Messenger of Allah said,

«لَا أَحَدَ أَصْبَرُ عَلَى أَذًى سَمِعَهُ مِنَ اللهِ: إِنَّهُمْ يَجْعَلُونَ لَهُ وَلَدًا وَهُوَ يَرْزُقُهُمْ وَيُعَافِيهِم»

(No one is more patient when hearing an insult than Allah. They attribute a son to Him, yet He still gives them sustenance and health.)

Everything is within Allah's Grasp

Allah said,

(all are Qanitun to Him). Ibn Abi Hatim said that Abu Sa'id Al-Ashaj informed them that Asbat informed them from Mutarrif, from 'Atiyah, from Ibn 'Abbas who said that,

(Qantin) (2:238) means, they pray to Him. 'Ikrimah and Abu Malik also said that,

(and all are Qanitun to Him.) means, bound to Him in servitude to Him. Sa'id bin Jubayr said that Qanitun is sincerity. Ar-Rabi' bin Anas said that,

(all are Qanitun to Him.) means, "Standing up - before Him - on the Day of Resurrection." Also, As-Suddi said that,

(and all are Qanitun to Him.) means, "Obedient on the Day of Resurrection." Khasif said that Mujahid said that, (and all are Qanitun to Him.) means, "Obedient. He says, `Be a human' and he becomes a human." He also said, "(Allah says,) `Be a donkey' and it becomes a donkey." Also, Ibn Abi Najih said that Mujahid said that,

(and all are Qanitun to Him.) means, obedient.

Mujahid also said, "The obedience of the disbeliever occurs when his shadow prostrates, while he hates that." Mujahid's statement, which Ibn Jarir preferred, combines all the meanings, and that is that Qunut means obedience and submission to Allah. There are two categories of Qunut: legislated and destined, for Allah said,

(And unto Allah (alone) falls in prostration whoever is in the heavens and the earth, willingly or unwillingly, and so do their shadows in the mornings and in the (late) afternoons) (13:15).

The Meaning of Badi'

Allah said,

(The Badi` (Originator) of the heavens and the earth.) which means, He created them when nothing resembling them existed. Mujahid and As-Suddi said that this is the linguistic meaning, for all new matters are called Bid'ah. Muslim recorded the Messenger of Allah saying,

«فَإِنَّ كُلَّ مُحْدَثَةٍ بِدْعَة»

(...every innovation (in religion) is a Bid'ah.)

There are two types of Bid'ah, religious, as mentioned in the Hadith:

«فَإِنَّ كُلَّ مُحْدَثَةٍ بِدْعَةٌ وَكُلَّ بِدْعَةٍ ضَلَالَة»

(...every innovation is a Bid'ah and every Bid'ah is heresy.)

And there is a linguistic Bid'ah, such as the statement of the Leader of the faithful 'Umar bin Al-Khattab when he gathered the Muslims to pray the Tarawih prayer in congregation (which was also an earlier practice of the Prophet) and said, "What a good Bid'ah this is."

Ibn Jarir said,

"Thus the meaning of the Ayat (2:116-117) becomes, `Allah is far more glorious than to have had a son, for He is the Owner of everything that is in the heavens and earth. All testify to His Oneness and to their submissiveness to Him. He is their Creator and Maker. Without created precedence, He shaped the creatures in their current shapes. Allah also bears witness to His servants that Jesus, who some claimed to be Allah's son, is among those who testify to His Oneness. Allah stated that He created the heavens and earth out of nothing and without precedent. Likewise, He created Jesus, the Messiah, with His power and without a father."

This explanation from Ibn Jarir, may Allah have mercy upon him, is very good and correct.

Allah said,

(When He decrees a matter, He only says to it : "Be! - and it is.) thus, demonstrating His perfectly complete ability and tremendous authority; if He decides a matter, He merely orders it to, `Be' and it comes into existence.

Similarly, Allah said,

(Verily, His command, when He intends a thing, is only that He says to it, "Be! - and it is.) (36:82),

(Verily, Our Word unto a thing when We intend it, is only that We say unto it: "Be! - and it is.) (16:40) and, (And Our commandment is but one as the twinkling of an eye) (54:50)

So Allah informed us that He created Jesus by merely saying, "Be!" and he was, as Allah willed:

(Verily, the likeness of 'Isa (Jesus) before Allah is the likeness of Adam. He created him from dust, then (He) said to him: "Be! - and he was) (3:59).

Surah: 2 Ayah: 118

﴿ وَقَالَ ٱلَّذِينَ لَا يَعْلَمُونَ لَوْلَا يُكَلِّمُنَا ٱللَّهُ أَوْ تَأْتِينَآ ءَايَةٌ كَذَٰلِكَ قَالَ ٱلَّذِينَ مِن قَبْلِهِم مِّثْلَ قَوْلِهِمْ تَشَٰبَهَتْ قُلُوبُهُمْ قَدْ بَيَّنَّا ٱلْءَايَٰتِ لِقَوْمٍ يُوقِنُونَ ﴾

118. And those who have no knowledge say: "Why does not Allâh speak to us (face to face) or why does not a sign come to us?" So said the people before them words of similar import. Their hearts are alike, We have indeed made plain the signs for people who believe with certainty.

Transliteration

118. Waqala allatheena la yaAAlamoona lawla yukallimuna Allahu aw ta/teena ayatun kathalika qala allatheena min qablihim mithla qawlihim tashabahat quloobuhum qad bayyanna al-ayati liqawmin yooqinoona

Tafsir Ibn Kathir

Muhammad bin Ishaq reported that Ibn 'Abbas said that Rafi' bin Huraymilah said to the Messenger of Allah , "O Muhammad! If you were truly a Messenger from Allah, as you claim, then ask Allah to speak to us directly, so that we hear His Speech." So Allah revealed,

(And those who have no knowledge say: "Why does not Allah speak to us (face to face) or why does not a sign come to us")

Abu Al-'Aliyah, Ar-Rabi' bin Anas, Qatadah and As-Suddi said that it was actually the statement of the Arab disbelievers:

(So said the people before them words of similar import.) He said, "These are the Jews and the Christians."

What further proves that the Arab idolators said the statement mentioned in the Ayah is that Allah said,

(And when there comes to them a sign (from Allah) they say: "We shall not believe until we receive the like of that which the Messengers of Allah had received." Allah knows best with whom to place His Message. Humiliation and disgrace from Allah and a severe torment will overtake the criminals (polytheists and sinners) for that which they used to plot.) (6:124) and

(And they say: "We shall not believe in you (O Muhammad), until you cause a spring to gush forth from the earth for us) until,

(Say (O Muhammad): "Glorified (and Exalted) be my Lord ?ý(Allah) above all that evil they (polytheists) associate with Him>! Am I anything but a man, sent as a Messenger") (17:90-93) and,

(And those who expect not a meeting with Us (i. e. those who deny the Day of Resurrection and the life of the Hereafter) said: "Why are not the angels sent down to us, or why do we not see our Lord") (25:21) and,

(Nay, everyone of them desires that he should be given pages spread out) (74:52).

There are many other Ayat that testify to the disbelief of the Arab idolators, their transgression, stubbornness, and that they asked unnecessary questions out of disbelief and arrogance. The statements of the Arab idolators followed the statements of the nations of the People of the Two Scriptures and other religions before them. Allah said,

(The People of the Scripture (Jews) ask you to cause a book to descend upon them from heaven. Indeed, they asked Musa (Moses) for even greater than that, when they said: "Show us Allah in public,") (4:153) and,

(And (remember) when you said: "O Musa! We shall never believe in you until we see Allah plainly.") (2:55).

Allah's statement,

(Their hearts are alike.) means, the hearts of the Arab idolators are just like the hearts of those before them, containing disbelief, stubbornness and injustice. Similarly, Allah said,

(Likewise, no Messenger came to those before them but they said: "A sorcerer or a madman!" Have they (the people of the past) transmitted this saying to these (Quraysh pagans)) (51:52-53).

Allah said next, (We have indeed made plain the signs for people who believe with certainty.)

meaning, We made the arguments clear, prooving the truth of the Messengers, with no need of more questions or proofs for those who believe, follow the Messengers and comprehend what Allah sent them with.

As for those whose hearts and hearing Allah has stamped and whose eyes have been sealed, Allah described them:

(Truly, those, against whom the Word (wrath) of your Lord has been justified, will not believe. Even if every sign should come to them, until they see the painful torment) (10:96-97).

Surah: 2 Ayah: 119

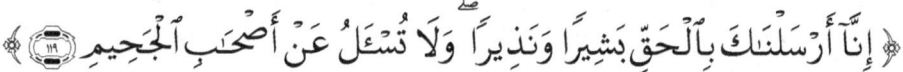

119. Verily, We have sent you (O Muhammad (peace be upon him)) with the truth (Islâm), a bringer of glad tidings (for those who believe in what you brought, that they will enter Paradise) and a warner (for those who disbelieve in what you brought, they will enter the Hell-fire). And you will not be asked about the dwellers of the blazing Fire.

Transliteration

119. Inna arsalnaka bialhaqqi basheeran wanatheeran wala tus-alu Aaan as-habi aljaheemi

Tafsir Ibn Kathir

Allah's statement;

(And you will not be asked about the dwellers of the blazing Fire.) means,

"We shall not ask you about the disbelief of those who rejected you." Similarly, Allah said, (Your duty is only to convey (the Message) and on Us is the reckoning.) (13:40)

(So remind them (O Muhammad) - you are only one who reminds. You are not a dictator over them.)(88:21-22) and, (We know best what they say. And you (O Muhammad) are not the one to force them (to belief). But warn by the Qur'an; him who fears My threat) (50:45).

There are many other similar Ayat.

The Description of the Prophet in the Tawrah

Imam Ahmad recorded 'Ata' bin Yasar saying that he met 'Abdullah bin 'Amr bin Al-'As and said to him, "Tell me about the description of the Messenger of Allah in the Torah." He said, "Yes, by Allah, he is described by the Torah with the same characteristics that he is described with in the Qur'an with: 'O Prophet! We have sent you as a witness, a bringer of good news, a warner, and as safe refuge for the unlettered people. You are My servant and Messenger. I have called you the Mutawakkil (who depends and relies on Allah for each and everything). You are not harsh, nor hard, nor obnoxious in the bazaars. He does not reward the evil deed with an evil deed. Rather, he forgives and pardons. Allah will not bring his life to an end, until he straightens the wicked's religion by his hands so that the people proclaim: There is no deity worthy of worship except Allah. By his hands, Allah will open blind eyes, deaf ears and sealed hearts.'" This was recorded by Al-Bukhari only.

Surah: 2 Ayah: 120 & Ayah: 121

﴿ وَلَن تَرْضَىٰ عَنكَ ٱلْيَهُودُ وَلَا ٱلنَّصَىٰرَىٰ حَتَّىٰ تَتَّبِعَ مِلَّتَهُمْ ۗ قُلْ إِنَّ هُدَى ٱللَّهِ هُوَ ٱلْهُدَىٰ ۗ وَلَئِنِ ٱتَّبَعْتَ أَهْوَآءَهُم بَعْدَ ٱلَّذِى جَآءَكَ مِنَ ٱلْعِلْمِ ۙ مَا لَكَ مِنَ ٱللَّهِ مِن وَلِىٍّ وَلَا نَصِيرٍ ﴿١٢٠﴾

120. Never will the Jews nor the Christians be pleased with you (O Muhammad (peace be upon him)) till you follow their religion. Say: "Verily, the Guidance of Allâh (i.e. Islâmic Monotheism) that is the (only) Guidance. And if you (O Muhammad (peace be upon him)) were to follow their (Jews and Christians) desires after what you have received of Knowledge (i.e. the Qur'ân), then you would have against Allâh neither any Walî (protector or guardian) nor any helper.

﴿ ٱلَّذِينَ ءَاتَيْنَٰهُمُ ٱلْكِتَٰبَ يَتْلُونَهُۥ حَقَّ تِلَاوَتِهِۦٓ أُو۟لَٰٓئِكَ يُؤْمِنُونَ بِهِۦ ۗ وَمَن يَكْفُرْ بِهِۦ فَأُو۟لَٰٓئِكَ هُمُ ٱلْخَٰسِرُونَ ﴿١٢١﴾

121. Those (who embraced Islâm from Banî Israel) to whom We gave the Book (the Taurât (Torah)) (or those (Muhammad's (peace be upon him) companions) to whom We have given the Book (the Qur'ân)) recite it (i.e. obey its orders and follow its teachings) as it should be recited (i.e. followed), they are the ones that believe therein. And whoso disbelieve in it (the Qur'ân), those are they who are the losers. (Tafsir Al-Qurtubî).

Transliteration

120. Walan tarda AAanka alyahoodu wala alnnasara hatta tattabiAAa millatahum qul inna huda Allahi huwa alhuda wala-ini ittabaAAta ahwaahum baAAda allathee jaaka mina alAAilmi ma laka mina Allahi min waliyyin wala naseerin 121. Allatheena ataynahumu alkitaba yatloonahu haqqa tilawatihi ola-ika yu/minoona bihi waman yakfur bihi faola-ika humu alkhasiroona

Tafsir Ibn Kathir

Ibn Jarir said, "Allah said,

(Never will the Jews nor the Christians be pleased with you (O Muhammad) till you follow their religion.) meaning, 'The Jews and the Christians will never be happy with you, O Muhammad! Therefore, do not seek what pleases or appeases them, and stick to what pleases Allah by calling them to the truth that Allah sent you with.' Allah's statement,

(Say: "Verily, the guidance of Allah (i.e. Islamic Monotheism) that is the (only) guidance") emeans, `Say, O Muhammad , the guidance of Allah that He sent me with is the true guidance, meaning the straight, perfect and comprehensive religion.'" Qatadah said that Allah's statement,

(Say: "Verily, the guidance of Allah (i.e. Islamic Monotheism) that is the (only) guidance) is, "A true argument that Allah taught Muhammad and his Companions and which they used against the people of misguidance." Qatadah said, "We were told that the Messenger of Allah used to say,

«لَا تَزَالُ طَائِفَةٌ مِنْ أُمَّتِي يُقَاتِلُونَ عَلَى الْحَقِّ ظَاهِرِينَ، لَا يَضُرُّهُمْ مَنْ خَالَفَهُمْ حَتَّى يَأْتِيَ أَمْرُ اللهِ»

(There will always be a group of my Ummah fighting upon the truth, having the upper hand, not harmed by their opponents, until the decree of Allah (the Last Hour) comes.)

This Hadith was collected in the Sahih and narrated from 'Abdullah bin 'Amr.

(And if you (O Muhammad) were to follow their (Jews and Christians) desires after what you have received of Knowledge (i.e. the Qur'an), then you would have against Allah neither any Wali (protector or guardian) nor any helper.)

This Ayah carries a stern warning for the Muslim Ummah against imitating the ways and methods of the Jews and Christians, after they have acquired knowledge of the Qur'an and Sunnah, may Allah grant us refuge from this behavior. Although the speech in this Ayah was directed at the Messenger, the ruling of which applies to his entire Ummah.

The Meaning of Correct Tilawah

Allah said,

(Those to whom We gave the Book. Yatlunahu Haqqan Tilawatih.)

'Abdur-Razzaq said from Ma'mar, from Qatadah, "They are the Jews and Christians." This is the opinion of 'Abdur-Rahman bin Zayd bin Aslam, and it was also chosen by Ibn Jarir. Sa'id reported from Qatadah, "They are the Companions of the Messenger of Allah ." Abu Al-'Aliyah said that Ibn Mas'ud said, "By He in Whose Hand is my soul! The right Tilawah is allowing what it makes lawful, prohibiting what it makes unlawful, reciting it as it was revealed by Allah, not changing the words from their places, and not interpreting it with other than its actual interpretation." As-Suddi reported from Abu Malik from Ibn 'Abbas who said about this Ayah (2:121): "They make lawful what it allows and they prohibit what it makes unlawful, and they do not alter its wordings." 'Umar bin Al-Khattab said, "They are those who when they recite an Ayah that mentions mercy, they ask Allah for it, and when they recite an Ayah that mentions torment, they seek refuge with Allah from it." This meaning was attributed to the Prophet , for when he used to recite an Ayah of mercy, he invoked Allah for mercy, and when he recited an Ayah of torment, he sought refuge from it with Allah.

Allah's statement,

(they are the ones who believe therein)

explains the Ayah,

(Those to whom We gave the Book. Yatlunahu Haqqa Tilawatihi).

These Ayat mean, "Those among the People of the Book who perfectly adhered to the Books that were revealed to the previous Prophets, will believe in what I have sent you with, O Muhammad!" Allah said in another Ayah,

(And if only they had acted according to the Tawrah, the Injil, and what has (now) been sent down to them from their Lord (the Qur'an), they would surely, have gotten provision from above them and from underneath their feet.) (5:66). The Ayah,

(Say (O Muhammad) "O People of the Scripture (Jews and Christians)! You have nothing (as regards guidance) till you act according to the Tawrah, the Injil, and what has (now) been sent down to you from your Lord (the

Qur'an).") means, "If you adhere to the Torah and the Gospel in the correct manner, believe in them as you should, and believe in the news they carry about Muhammad's prophethood, his description and the command to follow, aid and support him, then this will direct you to adhere to truth and righteousness in this life and the Hereafter." In another Ayah, Allah said,

(Those who follow the Messenger, the Prophet who can neither read nor write (i.e. Muhammad) whom they find written with them in the Tawrah and the Injil.) (7:157) and,

(Say (O Muhammad to them): "Believe in it (the Qur'an) or do not believe (in it). Verily, those who were given knowledge before it, when it is recited to them, fall down on their faces in humble prostration. And they say: "Glory be to our Lord! Truly, the promise of our Lord must be fulfilled.") (17:107-108).

These Ayat indicate that what Allah promised for Muhammad will certainly occur. Allah also said, (Those to whom We gave the Scripture (i. e. the Tawrah and the Injil) before it, they believe in it (the Qur'an). And when it is recited to them, they say: "We believe in it. Verily, it is the truth from our Lord. Indeed even before it we have been from those who submit themselves to Allah in Islam as Muslims. These will be given their reward twice over, because they are patient, and repel evil with good, and spend (in charity) out of what We have provided them.) (28:52-54) and,

(And say to those who were given the Scripture (Jews and Christians) and to those who are illiterates (Arab pagans): "Do you (also) submit yourselves (to Allah in Islam)" If they do, they are rightly guided; but if they turn away, your duty is only to convey the Message; and Allah is the Seer of (His) servants) (3:20).

Allah said,

(And whoever disbelieves in it (the Qur'an), those are they who are the losers), just as He said in another Ayah,

(But those of the sects (Jews, Christians and all the other non-Muslim nations) that reject it (the Qur'an), the Fire will be their promised meeting place) (11:17).

As recorded in the Sahih, the Prophet said,

«وَالَّذِي نَفْسِي بِيَدِهِ لَا يَسْمَعُ بِي أَحَدٌ مِنْ هذِهِ الْأُمَّةِ يَهُودِيٌّ وَلَا نَصْرَانِيٌّ ثُمَّ لَا يُؤْمِنُ بِي إِلَّا دَخَلَ النَّارِ»

(By He in Whose Hand is my soul! There is no member of this Ummah (mankind and Jinns), Jew or a Christian, who hears of me, yet does not believe in me, but will enter the Fire.)

Surah: 2 Ayah: 122 & Ayah: 123

﴿ يَـٰبَنِىٓ إِسْرَٰٓءِيلَ ٱذْكُرُوا۟ نِعْمَتِىَ ٱلَّتِىٓ أَنْعَمْتُ عَلَيْكُمْ وَأَنِّى فَضَّلْتُكُمْ عَلَى ٱلْعَـٰلَمِينَ ۝ ﴾

122. O Children of Israel! Remember My Favor which I bestowed upon you and that I preferred you to the 'Alamîn (mankind and jinn (of your time-period, in the past))

﴿ وَٱتَّقُوا۟ يَوْمًا لَّا تَجْزِى نَفْسٌ عَن نَّفْسٍ شَيْـًٔا وَلَا يُقْبَلُ مِنْهَا عَدْلٌ وَلَا تَنفَعُهَا شَفَـٰعَةٌ وَلَا هُمْ يُنصَرُونَ ۝ ﴾

123. And fear the Day (of Judgement) when no person shall avail another, nor shall compensation be accepted from him, nor shall intercession be of use to him, nor shall they be helped.

Transliteration

122. Ya banee isra-eela othkuroo niAAmatiya allatee anAAamtu AAalaykum waannee faddaltukum AAala alAAalameena 123. Waittaqoo yawman la tajzee nafsun AAan nafsin shay-an wala yuqbalu minha AAadlun wala tanfaAAuha shafaAAatun wala hum yunsaroona

Tafsir Ibn Kathir

We mentioned a similar Ayah at the beginning of this Surah, and it is mentioned here to emphasize the importance of following the Ummi Prophet and Messenger, who is described for the People of the Scriptures in their Books by his characteristics, name, the good news about him and the description of his Ummah.

Allah warned them against concealing this information, which is among the favors that Allah granted them. Allah also commanded them to remember their daily life and their religious affairs and how He blessed them.

They should not envy their cousins, the Arabs, for what Allah has given them, the Final Messenger of Allah being an Arab. Envy should not incite them to oppose or deny the Prophet or refrain from following him, may Allah's peace and blessings be upon him until the Day of Judgment.

Surah: 2 Ayah: 124

﴿ ۞ وَإِذِ ٱبۡتَلَىٰٓ إِبۡرَٰهِۦمَ رَبُّهُۥ بِكَلِمَٰتٍ فَأَتَمَّهُنَّ ۖ قَالَ إِنِّي جَاعِلُكَ لِلنَّاسِ إِمَامًا ۖ قَالَ وَمِن ذُرِّيَّتِي ۖ قَالَ لَا يَنَالُ عَهۡدِي ٱلظَّٰلِمِينَ ﴾

124. And (remember) when the Lord of Ibrâhîm (Abraham) (i.e., Allâh) tried him with (certain) Commands, which he fulfilled. He (Allâh) said (to him), "Verily, I am going to make you an Imâm (a leader) of mankind (to follow you)." (Ibrâhîm (Abraham)) said, "And of my offspring (to make leaders)." (Allâh) said, "My Covenant (Prophethood) includes not Zâlimûn (polytheists and wrongdoers)."

Transliteration

124. Wa-ithi ibtala ibraheema rabbuhu bikalimatin faatammahunna qala innee jaAAiluka lilnnasi imaman qala wamin thurriyyatee qala la yanalu AAahdee al*th*th*a*limeena

Tafsir Ibn Kathir

Ibrahim Al-Khalil was an Imam for the People

Allah is informing us of the honor of Ibrahim Al-Khalil, who He made an Imam for the people, and a model to be imitated, because of the way he conducted himself and adhered to Tawhid. This honor was given to Prophet Ibrahim when he adhered to Allah's decisions and prohibitions. This is why Allah said,

(And (remember) when the Lord of Ibrahim (i.e., Allah) tried him with (certain) commands).

This Ayah means, O Muhammad! Remind the idolators and the People of the Scriptures, who pretend to be followers of the religion of Ibrahim, while in reality they do not follow it, while you, O Muhammad, and your followers are the true followers of his religion; remind them of the commands and prohibitions that Allah tested Ibrahim with.

(which he fulfilled.) indicating that Ibrahim implemented all of Allah's orders. Allah said in another Ayah,

(And of Ibrahim (Abraham) who fulfilled (or conveyed) all that (Allah ordered him to do or convey)) (53:37)

meaning, he was truthful and he was obedient to Allah's legislation. Also, Allah said,

(Verily, Ibrahim was an Ummah (or a nation), obedient to Allah, Hanif (i.e. to worship none but Allah), and he was not one of those who were Al-Mushrikin (polytheists), (He was) thankful for His (Allah's) favors. He (Allah) chose him and guided him to a straight path. And We gave him good in this world, and in the Hereafter he shall be of the righteous. Then, We have sent the revelation to you (O Muhammad saying): "Follow the religion of Ibrahim Hanif (Islamic Monotheism - to worship none but Allah) and he was not of the Mushrikin.) (16:120-123)

(Say (O Muhammad): "Truly, my Lord has guided me to a straight path, a right religion, the religion of Ibrahim, Hanifan, and Ibrahim (to worship none but Allah, alone) and he was not of Al-Mushrikin.") (6:161) and,

(Ibrahim was neither a Jew nor a Christian, but he was a true Muslim Hanifan (Islamic Monotheism - to worship none but Allah alone) and he was not of Al-Mushrikin. Verily, among mankind who have the best claim to Ibrahim are those who followed him, and this Prophet (Muhammad) and those who have believed (Muslims). And Allah is the Wali (Protector and Helper) of the believers) (3:67-68).

Allah said, (with Kalimat (words)) which means, "Laws, commandments and prohibitions." `Words' as mentioned here, sometimes refers to what Allah has willed, such as Allah's statement about Maryam,

(And she testified to the truth of the Words of her Lord, and (also believed in) His Scriptures, and she was of the Qanitin (i.e. obedient to Allah)) (66:12). "Words" also refers to Allah's Law, such as Allah's statement, (And the Word of your Lord has been fulfilled in truth and in justice) (6:115) meaning, His legislation. "Words" also means truthful news, or a just commandment or prohibition. For instance, Allah said,

(And (remember) when the Lord of Ibrahim tried him with (certain) Words (commands), which he fulfilled) meaning, he adhered to them, Allah said,

("Verily, I am going to make you an Imam (a leader) for mankind (to follow you).") as a reward for Ibrahim's good deeds, adhering to the commandments and avoiding the prohibitions. This is why Allah made Ibrahim a role model for the people, and an Imam whose conduct and path are imitated and followed.

What were the Words that Ibrahim was tested with

There is a difference of opinion over the words that Allah tested Ibrahim with. There are several opinions attributed to Ibn 'Abbas. For instance, 'Abdur-Razzaq said that Ibn 'Abbas said, "Allah tested him with the rituals (of Hajj)." Abu Ishaq reported the same. 'Abdur-Razzaq also narrated that Ibn 'Abbas said that,

(And (remember) when the Lord of Ibrahim (Abraham) (i.e., Allah) tried him with (certain) commands) means, "Allah tested him with Taharah (purity, ablution): five on the head and five on the body. As for the head, they are cutting the mustache, rinsing the mouth, inhaling and discarding water, using Siwak and parting the hair. As for the body, they are trimming the nails, shaving the pubic hair, circumcision and plucking under the arm and washing with water after answering the call of nature." Ibn Abi Hatim said, "A similar statement was also reported from Sa`id bin Al-Musayyib, Mujahid, Ash-Sha`bi, An-Nakha`i, Abu Salih, Abu Al-Jald, and so forth."

There is a similar statement that Imam Muslim narrated from 'A'ishah who said that Allah's Messenger said,

«عَشْرٌ مِنَ الْفِطْرَةِ: قَصُّ الشَّارِبِ وَإِعْفَاءُ اللِّحْيَةِ وَالسِّوَاكُ وَاسْتِنْشَاقُ الْمَاءِ وَقَصُّ الْأَظْفَارِ وَغَسْلُ الْبَرَاجِمِ وَنَتْفُ الْإِبْطِ وَحَلْقُ الْعَانَةِ وَانْتِقَاصُ الْمَاءِ وَنَسِيتُ الْعَاشِرَةَ إِلَّا أَنْ تَكُونَ الْمَضْمَضَة»

(Ten are among the Fitrah (instinct, natural constitution): trimming the mustache, growing the beard, using Siwak, inhaling and then exhaling water (in ablution), cutting the nails, washing between the fingers (in ablution), plucking the underarm hair, shaving the pubic hair, washing with water after answering the call of nature, (and I forgot the tenth, I think it was) rinsing the mouth (in ablution).)

The Two Sahihs recorded Abu Hurayrah saying that the Prophet said,

«الْفِطْرَةُ خَمْسٌ: الْخِتَانُ وَالِاسْتِحْدَادُ وَقَصُّ الشَّارِبِ وَتَقْلِيمُ الْأَظْفَارِ وَنَتْفُ الْإِبْطِ»

(Five are among the acts of Fitrah: circumcision, shaving the pubic hair, trimming the mustache, cutting the nails and plucking the underarm hair.) This is the wording with Muslim.

Muhammad bin Ishaq reportd that Ibn 'Abbas said, "The words that Allah tested Ibrahim with, and that he implemented were: abandoning his (disbelieving) people when Allah commanded him to do so, disputing with Nimrod (king of Babylon) about Allah, being patient when he was thrown in the fire (although this was extremely traumatic) migrating from his homeland when Allah commanded him to do so, patience with the monetary and material demands of hosting guests by Allah's command, and Allah's order for him to slaughter his son. When Allah tested Ibrahim with these words, and he was ready for the major test, Allah said to him,

("Submit (be a Muslim)!" He said, "I have submitted myself (as a Muslim) to the Lord of all that exists. '') (2:131) although this meant defying and being apart from the people."

The Unjust do not qualify for Allah's Promise

Allah said that Ibrahim said,

(And of my offspring (to make leaders)) and Allah replied,

(My covenant (prophethood) includes not Zalimin (polytheists and wrongdoers)).

When Allah made Ibrahim an Imam (Leader for the faithful), he asked Allah that Imams thereafter be chosen from his offspring. Allah accepted his supplication, but told him that there will be unjust people among his offspring and they will not benefit from Allah's promise.

Thus, they will neither become Imams nor be imitated (for they will not be righteous). The proof that Ibrahim's supplication to Allah was accepted is that Allah said in Surat Al-'Ankabut (29:27),

(And We ordained among his offspring prophethood and the Book).

Hence, every Prophet whom Allah sent after Ibrahim were from among his offspring, and every Book that Allah revealed was to them. As for Allah's statement,

((Allah) said, "My covenant (prophethood) includes not Zalimin (polytheists and wrongdoers).'')

Allah mentioned that there are unjust people among the offspring of Ibrahim, and they will not benefit from Allah's promise, nor would they be entrusted with anything, even though they are among the children of Allah's Khalil (intimate friend, Prophet Abraham). There will also be those who do good among the children of Ibrahim, and these it is who will benefit from Ibrahim's supplication. Ibn Jarir said that this Ayah indicated that the unjust shall not be Imams for the people. Moreover, the Ayah informed Ibrahim that there will be unjust people among his offspring. Also, Ibn Khuwayz Mindad Al-Maliki said, "The unjust person does not qualify to be a Khalifah, a ruler, one who gives religious verdicts, a witness, or even a narrator (of Hadiths)."

Surah: 2 Ayah: 125 (continued), Ayah: 126, Ayah: 127 & Ayah: 128

﴿ وَإِذْ جَعَلْنَا ٱلْبَيْتَ مَثَابَةً لِّلنَّاسِ وَأَمْنًا وَٱتَّخِذُوا۟ مِن مَّقَامِ إِبْرَٰهِۦمَ مُصَلًّى وَعَهِدْنَآ إِلَىٰٓ إِبْرَٰهِۦمَ وَإِسْمَٰعِيلَ أَن طَهِّرَا بَيْتِىَ لِلطَّآئِفِينَ وَٱلْعَٰكِفِينَ وَٱلرُّكَّعِ ٱلسُّجُودِ ﴾

125. And (remember) when We made the House (the Ka'bah at Makkah) a place of resort for mankind and a place of safety. And take you (people)

the Maqâm (place) of Ibrâhim (Abraham) (or the stone on which Ibrâhim (Abraham) stood while he was building the Ka'bah) as a place of prayer (for some of your prayers, e.g. two Rak'at after the Tawâf of the Ka'bah at Makkah), and We commanded Ibrâhim (Abraham) and Ismâ'il (Ishmael) that they should purify My House (the Ka'bah at Makkah) for those who are circumambulating it, or staying (I'tikâf), or bowing or prostrating themselves (there, in prayer).

﴿ وَإِذْ قَالَ إِبْرَٰهِۦمُ رَبِّ ٱجْعَلْ هَٰذَا بَلَدًا ءَامِنًا وَٱرْزُقْ أَهْلَهُۥ مِنَ ٱلثَّمَرَٰتِ مَنْ ءَامَنَ مِنْهُم بِٱللَّهِ وَٱلْيَوْمِ ٱلْءَاخِرِ ۖ قَالَ وَمَن كَفَرَ فَأُمَتِّعُهُۥ قَلِيلًا ثُمَّ أَضْطَرُّهُۥٓ إِلَىٰ عَذَابِ ٱلنَّارِ ۖ وَبِئْسَ ٱلْمَصِيرُ ﴿١٢٦﴾ ﴾

126. And (remember) when Ibrâhim (Abraham) said, "My Lord, make this city (Makkah) a place of security and provide its people with fruits, such of them as believe in Allâh and the Last Day." He (Allâh) answered: "As for him who disbelieves, I shall leave him in contentment for a while, then I shall compel him to the torment of the Fire, and worst indeed is that destination!"

﴿ وَإِذْ يَرْفَعُ إِبْرَٰهِۦمُ ٱلْقَوَاعِدَ مِنَ ٱلْبَيْتِ وَإِسْمَٰعِيلُ رَبَّنَا تَقَبَّلْ مِنَّآ ۖ إِنَّكَ أَنتَ ٱلسَّمِيعُ ٱلْعَلِيمُ ﴿١٢٧﴾ ﴾

127. And (remember) when Ibrâhim (Abraham) and (his son) Ismâ'il (Ishmael) were raising the foundations of the House (the Ka'bah at Makkah), (saying), "Our Lord! Accept (this service) from us. Verily! You are the All-Hearer, the All-Knower."

﴿ رَبَّنَا وَٱجْعَلْنَا مُسْلِمَيْنِ لَكَ وَمِن ذُرِّيَّتِنَآ أُمَّةً مُّسْلِمَةً لَّكَ وَأَرِنَا مَنَاسِكَنَا وَتُبْ عَلَيْنَآ ۖ إِنَّكَ أَنتَ ٱلتَّوَّابُ ٱلرَّحِيمُ ﴿١٢٨﴾ ﴾

128. Our Lord! And make us submissive unto You and of our offspring a nation submissive unto You, and show us our Manâsik (all the ceremonies of pilgrimage - Hajj and 'Umrah), and accept our repentance. Truly, You are the One Who accepts repentance, the Most Merciful.

Transliteration

125. Wa-ith jaAAalna albayta mathabatan lilnnasi waamnan waittakhithoo min maqami ibraheema musallan waAAahidna ila ibraheema wa-ismaAAeela an tahhira baytiya liltta-ifeena waalAAakifeena waalrrukkaAAi alssujoodi 126. Wa-ith qala ibraheemu rabbi ijAAal hatha baladan aminan waorzuq ahlahu mina alththamarati man amana minhum biAllahi waalyawmi al-akhiri qala waman

kafara faomattiAAuhu qaleelan thumma adtarruhu ila AAathabi alnnari wabi/sa almaseeru 127. Wa-ith yarfaAAu ibraheemu alqawaAAida mina albayti wa-ismaAAeelu rabbana taqabbal minna innaka anta alssameeAAu alAAaleemu 128. Rabbana waijAAalna muslimayni laka wamin thurriyyatina ommatan muslimatan laka waarina manasikana watub AAalayna innaka anta alttawwabu alrraheemu

bn Kathir's Tafsir

The Virtue of Allah's House

Al-'Awfi reported that Ibn 'Abbas commented on Allah's statement,

(And (remember) when We made the House (the Ka'bah at Makkah) a place of resort for mankind) "They do not remain in the House, they only visit it and return to their homes, and then visit it again." Also, Abu Ja'far Ar-Razi narrated from Ar-Rabi' bin Anas from Abu Al-'Aliyah who said that,

(And (remember) when We made the House (the Ka'bah at Makkah) a place of resort for mankind and a place of safety) means, "Safe from enemies and armed conflict. During the time of Jahiliyyah, the people were often victims of raids and kidnapping, while the people in the area surrounding it (Al-Masjid Al-Haram) were safe and not subject to kidnapping." Also, Mujahid, 'Ata', As-Suddi, Qatadah and Ar-Rabi' bin Anas were reported to have said that the Ayah (2:125) means, "Whoever enters it shall be safe."

This Ayah indicates that Allah honored the Sacred House, which Allah made as a safe refuge and safe haven. Therefore, the souls are eager, but never bored, to conduct short visits to the House, even every year. This is because Allah accepted the supplication of His Khalil, Ibrahim, when he asked Allah to make the hearts of people eager to visit the House. Ibrahim said (14:40),

(Our Lord! And accept my invocation).

Allah described the House as a safe resort and refuge, for those who visit it are safe, even if they had committed acts of evil. This honor comes from the honor of the person who built it first, Khalil Ar-Rahman, just as Allah said,

(And (remember) when We showed Ibrahim the site of the (Sacred) House (the Ka'bah at Makkah) (saying): "Associate not anything (in worship) with Me...") (22:26) and,

(Verily, the first House (of worship) appointed for mankind was that at Bakkah (Makkah), full of blessing, and a guidance for Al-'Alamin (mankind and Jinn). In it are manifest signs (for example), the Maqam (place) of Ibrahim; whosoever enters it, he attains security) (3:96-97).

The last honorable Ayah emphasized the honor of Ibrahim's Maqam, and the instruction to pray next to it,

(And take you (people) the Maqam (place) of Ibrahim as a place of prayer). The Maqam of Ibrahim

Sufyan Ath-Thawri reported that Sa'id bin Jubayr commented on the Ayah,

(And take you (people) the Maqam (place) of Ibrahim as a place of prayer) "The stone (Maqam) is the standing place of Ibrahim, Allah's Prophet, and a mercy from Allah. Ibrahim stood on the stone, while Isma`il was handing him the stones (constructing the Ka`bah)." As-Suddi said, "The Maqam of Ibrahim is a stone which Isma`il's wife put under Ibrahim's feet when washing his head." Al-Qurtubi mentioned this, but he considered it unauthentic, although others gave it prefrence, Ar-Razi reported it in his Tafsir from Al-Hasan Al-Basri, Qatadah, and Ar-Rabi` bin Anas.

Ibn Abi Hatim reported that Jabir, describing the Hajj (pilgrimage) of the Prophet said, "When the Prophet performed Tawaf, `Umar asked him, `Is this the Maqam of our father' He said, `Yes.' `Umar said, `Should we take it a place of prayer' So Allah revealed,

(And take you (people) the Maqam (place) of Ibrahim (Abraham) as a place of prayer.")

Al-Bukhari said, "Chapter: Allah's statement,

(And take you (people) the Maqam (place) of Ibrahim (Abraham) as a place of prayer) meaning, they return to it repeatedly." He then narrated that Anas bin Malik said that `Umar bin Al-Khattab said, "I agreed with my Lord, or my Lord agreed with me, regarding three matters. I said, `O Messenger of Allah! I wish you take the Maqam of Ibrahim a place for prayer.' The Ayah,

(And take you (people) the Maqam (place) of Ibrahim (Abraham)) was revealed. I also said, `O Messenger of Allah! The righteous and the wicked enter your house. I wish you would command the Mothers of the believers (the Prophet's wives) to wear Hijab. Allah sent down the Ayah that required the Hijab. And when I knew that the Prophet was angry with some of his wives, I came to them and said, `Either you stop what you are doing, or Allah will endow His Messenger with better women than you are.' I advised one of his wives and she said to me, `O 'Umar! Does the Messenger of Allah not know how to advise his wives, so that you have to do the job instead of him' Allah then revealed,

(It may be if he divorced you (all) that his Lord will give him instead of you, wives better than you, @— Muslims (who submit to Allah)). " (66:5)

Also, Ibn Jarir narrated that Jabir said, "After the Messenger of Allah kissed the Black Stone, he went around the house three times in a fast pace and four times in a slow pace. He then went to Maqam of Ibrahim, with it between him and the House, and prayed two Rak`ahs." This is part of the long Hadith that Muslim recorded in Sahih. Al-Bukhari recorded that `Amr bin Dinar said that he heard Ibn `Umar say, "The Messenger of Allah performed Tawaf around the House seven times and then prayed two Rak`ahs behind the Maqam."

All these texts indicate that the Maqam is the stone that Ibrahim was standing on while building the House. As the House's walls became higher, Isma'il brought his father a stone, so that he could stand on it, while Isma'il handed him the stones. Ibrahim would place the stones on the wall, and whenever he finished one side, he would move to the next side, to complete the building all around. Ibrahim kept repeating this until he finished building the House, as we will describe when we explain the story of Ibrahim and Isma'il and how they built the House, as narrated from Ibn 'Abbas and collected by Al-Bukhari. Ibrahim's footprints were still visible in the stone, and the Arabs knew this fact during the time of Jahiliyyah. This is why Abu Talib said in his poem known as 'Al-Lamiyyah', "And Ibrahim's footprint with his bare feet on the stone is still visible."

The Muslims also saw Ibrahim's footprints on the stone, as Anas bin Malik said, "I saw the Maqam with the print of Ibrahim's toes and feet still visible in it, but the footprints dissipated because of the people rubbing the stone with their hands."

Earlier, the Maqam was placed close to the Ka'bah's wall. In the present time, the Maqam is placed next to Al-Hijr on the right side of those entering through the door.

When Ibrahim finished building the House, he placed the stone next to the wall of Al-Ka'bah. Or, when the House was finished being built, Ibrahim just left the stone where it was last standing, and he was commanded to pray next to the stone when he finished the Tawaf (circumambulating). It is understandable that the Maqam of Ibrahim would stand where the building of the House ended. The Leader of the faithful 'Umar bin Al-Khattab, one of the Four Rightly Guided Caliphs whom we were commanded to emulate, moved the stone away from the Ka'bah's wall during his reign. 'Umar is one of the two men, whom the Messenger of Allah described when he said,

«اقْتَدُوا بِاللَّذَيْنِ مِنْ بَعْدِي أَبِي بَكْرٍ وَعُمَرَ»

(Imitate the two men who will come after me: Abu Bakr and 'Umar.)

'Umar was also the person whom the Qur'an agreed with regarding praying next to Maqam of Ibrahim. This is why none among the Companions rejected it when he moved it.

'Abdur-Razzaq reported from Ibn Jurayj from 'Ata', "'Umar bin Al-Khattab moved the Maqam back." Also, 'Abdur-Razzaq narrated that Mujahid said that 'Umar was the first person who moved the Maqam back to where it is now standing." Al-Hafiz Abu Bakr, Ahmad bin 'Ali bin Al-Husayn Al-Bayhaqi recorded 'A'ishah saying, "During the time of the Messenger of Allah and Abu Bakr, the Maqam was right next to the House. 'Umar moved the Maqam during his reign."

This Hadith has an authentic chain of narration.

The Command to purify the House

Al-Hasan Al-Basri said that,

(And We gave Our 'Ahd (command) to Ibrahim and Isma'il) means, "Allah ordered them to purify it from all filth and impurities, of which none should ever touch it." Also, Ibn Jurayj said, "I said to `Ata', `What is Allah's `Ahd' He said, `His command.'" Also, Sa`id bin Jubayr said that Ibn `Abbas commented on the Ayah,

(that they should purify My House (the Ka'bah) for those who are circumambulating it, or staying (I'tikaf)) "Purify it from the idols." Further, Mujahid and Sa'id bin Jubayr said that,

(purify My House for those who are circumambulating it) means, "From the idols, sexual activity, false witness and sins of all kinds."

Allah said,

(for those who are performing Tawaf (circumambulating) it).

The Tawaf around the House is a well-established ritual, Sa'id bin Jubayr said that,

(for those who are circumambulating it) means, strangers (he means who do not live in Makkah), while;

(or staying (I'tikaf)) is about those who live in the area of the Sacred House. Also, Qatadah and Ar-Rabi' bin Anas said that I'tikaf is in reference to those who live in the area of the House, just as Sa'id bin Jubayr stated. Allah said, (or bowing or prostrating themselves (there, in prayer))

Ibn 'Abbas said, when it is a place of prayer it includes those who are described as bowing and prostrating themselves. Also, 'Ata' and Qatadah offered the same Tafsir.

Purifying all Masjids is required according to this Ayah and according to Allah's statement,

(In houses (mosques) which Allah has ordered to be raised (to be cleaned, and to be honored), in them His Name is remembered (i.e. Adhan, Iqamah, Salah, invocations, recitation of the Qur'an). Therein glorify Him (Allah) in the mornings and in the (late) afternoons) (24:36).

There are many Hadiths that give a general order for purifying the Masjids and keeping filth and impurities away from them. This is why the Prophet said,

«إِنَّمَا بُنِيَتِ الْمَسَاجِدُ لِمَا بُنِيَتْ لَهُ»

(The Masjids are established for the purpose that they were built for (i. e. worshipping Allah alone).)

I have collected a book on this subject, and all praise is due to Allah.

Makkah is a Sacred Area

Allah said,

(And (remember) when Ibrahim said, "My Lord, make this city (Makkah) a place of security and provide its people with fruits, such of them as believe in Allah and the Last Day.")

Imam Abu Ja'far bin Jarir At-Tabari narrated that Jabir bin 'Abdullah said that the Messenger of Allah said,

«إِنَّ إِبْرَاهِيمَ حَرَّمَ بَيْتَ اللهِ وَأَمَّنَهُ وَإِنِّي حَرَّمْتُ الْمَدِينَةَ مَا بَيْنَ لَابَتَيْهَا، فَلَا يُصَادُ صَيْدُهَا وَلَا يُقْطَعُ عِضَاهُهَا»

(Ibrahim made Allah's House a Sacred Area and a safe refuge. I have made what is between the two sides of Al-Madinah a Sacred Area. Therefore, its game should not be hunted, and its trees should not be cut.) An-Nasa'i and Muslim also recorded this Hadith.

There are several other Hadiths that indicate that Allah made Makkah a sacred area before He created the heavens and earth. The Two Sahihs recorded 'Abdullah bin 'Abbas saying that the Messenger of Allah said,

«إِنَّ هَذَا الْبَلَدَ حَرَّمَهُ اللهُ يَوْمَ خَلَقَ السَّمَوَاتِ وَالْأَرْضَ، فَهُوَ حَرَامٌ بِحُرْمَةِ اللهِ إِلَى يَوْمِ الْقِيَامَةِ وَإِنَّهُ لَمْ يَحِلَّ الْقِتَالُ فِيهِ لِأَحَدٍ قَبْلِي وَلَمْ يَحِلَّ لِي إِلَّا سَاعَةً مِنْ نَهَارٍ، فَهُوَ حَرَامٌ بِحُرْمَةِ اللهِ إِلَى يَوْمِ الْقِيَامَةِ لَا يُعْضَدُ شَوْكُهُ

«وَلَا يُنَفَّرُ صَيْدُهُ، وَلَا يَلْتَقِطُ لُقَطَتَهُ إِلَّا مَنْ عَرَّفَهَا وَلَا يُخْتَلَى خَلَاهَا»

(Allah has made this city a sanctuary (sacred place) the Day He created the heavens and earth. Therefore, it is a sanctuary until the Day of Resurrection because Allah made it a sanctuary. It was not legal for anyone to fight in it before me, and it was legal for me for a few hours of one day. Therefore, it is a sanctuary until the Day of Resurrection, because Allah made it a sanctuary. None is allowed to uproot its thorny shrubs, or to chase its game, or to pick up something that has fallen, except by a person who announces it publicly, nor should any of its trees be cut.)

Al-'Abbas said,

يَا رَسُولَ اللهِ: إِلَّا الْإِذْخِرَ فَإِنَّهُ لِقَيْنِهِمْ وَلِبُيُوتِهِمْ

'O Messenger of Allah! Except the lemon-grass, for our goldsmiths and for our graves.'

The Prophet added,

«إِلَّا الْإِذْخِرَ»

(Except lemon-grass.)

This is the wording of Muslim. The Two Sahihs also recorded Abu Hurayrah narrating a similar Hadith, while Al-Bukhari recorded a similar Hadith from Safiyyah bint Shaybah who narrated it from the Prophet .

Abu Shurayh Al-'Adawi said that he said to 'Amr bin Sa'id while he was sending armies to Makkah, "O Commander! Let me narrate a Hadith that the Messenger of Allah said the day that followed the victory of Makkah. My ears heard the Hadith, my heart comprehended it, and my eyes saw the Prophet when he said it. He thanked Allah and praised him and then said,

«إِنَّ مَكَّةَ حَرَّمَهَا اللهُ وَلَمْ يُحَرِّمْهَا النَّاسُ فَلَا يَحِلُّ لِامْرِئٍ يُؤْمِنُ بِاللهِ وَالْيَوْمِ الْآخِرِ أَنْ يَسْفِكَ بِهَا دَمًا وَلَا يَعْضِدَ بِهَا شَجَرَةً، فَإِنْ أَحَدٌ تَرَخَّصَ بِقِتَالِ رَسُولِ اللهِ صلى الله عليه وسلم فَقُولُوا: إِنَّ اللهَ أَذِنَ لِرَسُولِهِ وَلَمْ يَأْذَنْ لَكُمْ، وَإِنَّمَا أَذِنَ لِي فِيهَا سَاعَةً مِنْ نَهَارٍ وَقَدْ عَادَتْ حُرْمَتُهَا الْيَوْمَ

$$\text{كَحُرْمَتِهَا بِالْأَمْسِ فَلْيُبَلِّغِ الشَّاهِدُ الْغَائِبُ}$$

(Allah, not the people, made Makkah a sanctuary, so any person who has belief in Allah and the Last Day, should neither shed blood in it nor should he cut down its trees. If anybody argues that fighting in it is permissible on the basis that Allah's Messenger fought in Makkah, say to him, 'Allah allowed His Messenger and did not allow you.' Allah allowed me only for a few hours on that day (of the Conquest), and today its sanctity is valid as it was before. So, those who are present should inform those who are absent (concerning this fact).)

Abu Shurayh was asked, 'What did 'Amr reply' He said, ('Amr said) 'O Abu Shurayh! I know better than you about this, the Sacred House does not give protection to a sinner, a murderer or a thief.' This Hadith was collected by Al-Bukhari and Muslim.

After this, there is no contradiction between the Hadiths that stated that Allah made Makkah a sanctuary when He created the heavens and earth and the Hadiths that Ibrahim made it a sanctuary, since Ibrahim conveyed Allah's decree that Makkah is a sanctuary, before he built the House. Similarly, the Messenger of Allah was written as the Final Prophet when Adam was still clay. Yet, Ibrahim said,

(Our Lord! Send amongst them a Messenger of their own) (2: 129).

Allah accepted Ibrahim's supplication, although He had full knowledge beforehand that it will occur by His decree. To further elaborate on this subject, we should mention the Hadith about what the Messenger of Allah said when he was asked, "O Messenger of Allah! Tell us about how your prophethood started." He said,

$$\text{«دَعْوَةُ أَبِي إِبْرَاهِيمَ، عَلَيْهِ السَّلَامُ، وَبُشْرَى عِيسَى ابْنِ مَرْيَمَ، وَرَأَتْ أُمِّي كَأَنَّهُ خَرَجَ مِنْهَا نُورٌ أَضَاءَتْ لَهُ قُصُورُ الشَّامِ»}$$

(I am the supplication of my father Ibrahim, the good news of Jesus, the son of Mary, and my mother saw a light that radiated from her which illuminated the castles of Ash-Sham (Syria).)

In this Hadith, the Companions asked the Messenger about the beginning of his prophethood. We will explain this matter later, if Allah wills.

Ibrahim invokes Allah to make Makkah an Area of Safety and Sustenance

Allah said that Ibrahim said,

(My Lord, make this city (Makkah) a place of security) (2:126) from terror, so that its people do not suffer from fear. Allah accepted Ibrahim's supplication. Allah said,

(Whosoever enters it, he attains security) (3:97) and,

(Have they not seen that We have made (Makkah) a secure sanctuary, while men are being snatched away from all around them) (29:67).

We have already mentioned the Hadiths that prohibit fighting in the Sacred Area. Muslim recorded that Jabir said that the Messenger of Allah said,

«لَا يَحِلُّ لِأَحَدٍ أَنْ يَحْمِلَ بِمَكَّةَ السِّلَاحَ»

(No one is allowed to carry weapons in Makkah.) Allah mentioned that Ibrahim said,

(My Lord, make this city (Makkah) a place of security) meaning, make this a safe city. This occurred before the Ka'bah was built. Allah said in Surat Ibrahim,

(And (remember) when Ibrahim said, "My Lord! Make this city (Makkah) one of peace and security...") (14:35) as here, Ibrahim supplicated a second time after the House was built and its people lived around it, after Ishaq who was thirteen years Isma`il's junior was born. This is why at the end of his supplication, Ibrahim said here,

(All the praises and thanks be to Allah, Who has given me in old age Isma'il (Ishmael) and Ishaq (Isaac). Verily, my Lord is indeed the Hearer of invocations) (14:39).

Allah said next,

("...and provide its people with fruits, such of them as believe in Allah and the Last Day." He (Allah) answered: "As for him who disbelieves, I shall leave him in contentment for a while, then I shall compel him to the torment of the Fire, and worst indeed is that destination!")

Ibn Jarir said that Ubayy bin Ka`b commented on, (He answered: "As for him who disbelieves, I shall leave him in contentment for a while, then I shall compel him to the torment of the Fire, and worst indeed is that destination!") "These are Allah's Words (meaning not Ibrahim's)" This is also the Tafsir of Mujahid and `Ikrimah. Furthermore, Ibn Abi Hatim narrated that Ibn `Abbas commented on Allah's statement,

(My Lord, make this city (Makkah) a place of security and provide its people with fruits, such of them as believe in Allah and the Last Day.) "Ibrahim asked Allah to grant sustenance for the believers only. However, Allah revealed, `I will also provide for the disbelievers, just as I shall provide for the believers. Would I create something and not sustain and provide for I shall allow the disbelievers little delight, and then force them to the torment of the Fire, and what an evil destination." Ibn `Abbas then recited,

(On each these as well as those We bestow from the bounties of your Lord. And the bounties of your Lord can never be forbidden) (17:20).

This was recorded by Ibn Marduwyah, who also recorded similar statements from 'Ikrimah and Mujahid. Similarly, Allah said,

(Verily, those who invent a lie against Allah will never be successful. (A brief) enjoyment in this world! And then unto Us will be their return, then We shall make them taste the severest torment because they used to disbelieve.) (10:69-70),

(And whoever disbelieves, let not his disbelief grieve you (O Muhammad). To Us is their return, and We shall inform them what they have done. Verily, Allah is the Knower of what is in the breasts (of men). We let them enjoy for a little while, then in the end We shall oblige them to (enter) a great torment.) (31:23-24) and,

(And were it not that mankind would have become of one community (all disbelievers desiring worldly life only), We would have provided for those who disbelieve in the Most Gracious (Allah), silver roofs for their houses, and elevators whereby they ascend. And for their houses, doors (of silver), and thrones (of silver) on which they could recline. And adornments of gold. Yet all this would have been nothing but an enjoyment of this world. And the Hereafter with your Lord is (only) for the Muttaqin (the pious).) (43:33-35). Allah said next, (Then I shall compel him to the torment of the Fire, and worst indeed is that destination!) meaning, "After the delight that the disbeliever enjoyed in this life, I will make his destination torment in the Fire, and what an evil destination." This Ayah indicates that Allah gives the disbelievers respite and then seizes them in a manner compatible to His greatness and ability. This Ayah is similar to Allah's statement,

(And many a township did I give respite while it was given to wrongdoing. Then (in the end) I seized it (with punishment). And to Me is the (final) return (of all)) (22:48).

Also, the Two Sahihs recorded,

«لَا أَحَدَ أَصْبَرُ عَلَى أَذًى سَمِعَهُ مِنَ اللهِ إِنَّهُمْ يَجْعَلُونَ لَهُ وَلَدًا وَهُوَ يَرْزُقُهُمْ وَيُعَافِيهِم»

(No one is more patient than Allah when hearing abuse. They attribute a son to Him, while He grants them sustenance and health.)

The Sahih also recorded,

«إِنَّ اللهَ لَيُمْلِي لِلظَّالِمِ حَتَّى إِذَا أَخَذَهُ لَمْ يُفْلِتْهُ»

(Allah gives respite to the unjust person, until when He seizes him; He never lets go of him.)

He then recited Allah's statement,

(Such is the punishment of your Lord when He punishes the (population of) towns while they are doing wrong. Verily, His punishment is painful (and) severe). (11:102)

Building the Ka'bah and asking Allah to accept This Deed

Allah said,

(And (remember) when Ibrahim (Abraham) and (his son) Isma'il (Ishmael) were raising the foundations of the House (the Ka'bah at Makkah), (saying), "Our Lord! Accept (this service) from us. Verily, You are the Hearer, the Knower. Our Lord! And make us submissive unto You and of our offspring a nation submissive unto You, and show us our Manasik and accept our repentance. Truly, You are the One Who accepts repentance, the Most Merciful.")

Allah said, "O Muhammad! Remind your people when Ibrahim and Isma`il built the House and raised its foundations while saying,

(Our Lord! Accept (this service) from us. Verily, You are the Hearer, the Knower.")

Al-Qurtubi mentioned that Ubayy and Ibn Mas'ud used to recite the Ayah this way, (And (remember) when Ibrahim and (his son) Isma'il were raising the foundations of the House (the Ka'bah at Makkah), Saying, "Our Lord! Accept (this service) from us. Verily, You are the Hearer, the Knower.")

What further testifies to this statement (which adds 'saying' to the Ayah) by Ubayy and Ibn Mas'ud, is what came afterwards,

(Our Lord! And make us submissive unto You and of our offspring a nation submissive unto You).

The Prophets Ibrahim and Isma'il were performing a good deed, yet they asked Allah to accept this good deed from them. Ibn Abi Hatim narrated that Wuhayb bin Al-Ward recited,

(And (remember) when Ibrahim and (his son) Isma'il were raising the foundations of the House (the Ka'bah at Makkah), (saying), "Our Lord! Accept (this service) from us") and cried and said, "O Khalil of Ar-Rahman! You raise the foundations of the House of Ar-Rahman (Allah), yet you are afraid that He will not accept it from you" This is the behavior of the sincere believers, whom Allah described in His statement,

(And those who give that which they give) (23:60) meaning, they give away voluntary charity, and perform the acts of worship yet,

(with their hearts full of fear) (23: 60) afraid that these good deeds might not be accepted of them. There is an authentic Hadith narrated by 'A'ishah on this subject, which we will mention later, Allah willing.

Al-Bukhari recorded that Ibn 'Abbas said, "Prophet Ibrahim took Isma'il and his mother and went away with them until he reached the area of the House, where he left them next to a tree above Zamzam in the upper area of the Masjid. During that time, Isma'il's mother was still nursing him. Makkah was then uninhabited, and there was no water source in it. Ibrahim left them there with a bag containing some dates and a water-skin containing water. Ibrahim then started to leave, and Isma'il's mother followed him and said, 'O Ibrahim! To whom are you leaving us in this barren valley that is not inhabited' She repeated the question several times and Ibrahim did not reply. She asked, 'Has Allah commanded you to do this' He said, 'Yes.' She said, 'I am satisfied that Allah will never abandon us.' Ibrahim left, and when he was far enough away where they could not see him, close to Thaniyyah, he faced the House, raised his hands and supplicated,

(O our Lord! I have made some of my offspring to dwell in an uncultivable valley by Your Sacred House (the Ka'bah at Makkah)) until,

(Give thanks) (14:37). Isma'il's mother then returned to her place, started drinking water from the water-skin and nursing Isma'il. When the water was used up, she and her son became thirsty. She looked at him, and he was suffering from thirst; she left, because she disliked seeing his face in that condition. She found the nearest mountian to where she was, As-Safa, ascended it and looked, in vain, hoping to see somebody. When she came down to the valley, she raised her garment and ran, just as a tired person runs, until she reached the Al-Marwah mountain. In vain, she looked to see if there was someone there. She ran to and fro (between the two mountains) seven times." Ibn 'Abbas said that the Messenger of Allah said, "This is why the people make the trip between As-Safa and Al-Marwah (during Hajj and Umrah)."

"When she reached Al-Marwah, she heard a voice and said, `Shush,' to herself. She tried to hear the voice again and when she did, she said, `I have heard you. Do you have relief' She found the angel digging with his heel (or his wing) where Zamzam now exists, and the water gushed out. Isma`il's mother was astonished and started digging, using her hand to transfer water to the water-skin." Ibn `Abbas said that the Prophet then said, "May Allah grant His mercy to the mother of Isma`il, had she left the water, (flow naturally without her intervention), it would have been flowing on the surface of the earth."

"Isma`il's mother started drinking the water and her milk increased for her child. The angel (Gabriel) said to her, `Do not fear abandonment. There shall be a House for Allah built here by this boy and his father. Allah does not abandon His people.' During that time, the area of the House was raised above ground level and the floods used to reach its right and left sides.

Afterwards some people of the tribe of Jurhum, passing through Kada', made camp at the bottom of the valley. They saw some birds, they were astonished, and said, 'Birds can only be found at a place where there is water. We did not notice before that this valley had water.' They sent a scout or two who searched the area, found the water, and returned to inform them about it. Then they all went to Isma'il's mother, next to the water, and said, 'O Mother of Isma'il! Will you allow us to be with you (or dwell with you)' She said, 'Yes. But you will have no exclusive right to the water here.' They said, 'We agree.'" Ibn 'Abbas said that the Prophet said, "At that time, Isma'il's mother liked to have human company."

"And thus they stayed there and sent for their relatives to join them. Later on, her boy reached the age of puberty and married a lady from them, for Isma`il learned Arabic from them, and they liked the way he was raised. Isma`il's mother died after that.

Then an idea occurred to Abraham to visit his dependents. So he left (to Makkah). When he arrived, he did not find Isma'il, so he asked his wife about him. She said, 'He has gone out hunting.' When he asked her about their living conditions, she complained to him that they live in misery and poverty. Abraham said (to her), 'When your husband comes, convey my greeting and tell him to change the threshold of his gate.' When Isma'il came, he sensed that they had a visitor and asked his wife, 'Did we have a visitor' She said, 'Yes. An old man came to visit us and asked me about you, and I told him where you were. He also asked about our condition, and I told him that we live in hardship and poverty.' Isma'il said, 'Did he ask you to do anything' She said, 'Yes. He asked me to convey his greeting and that you should change the threshold of your gate.' Isma'il said to her, 'He was my father and you are the threshold, so go to your family (i.e. you are divorced).' So he divorced her and married another woman. Again Ibrahim thought of visiting his dependents whom he had left (at Makkah). Ibrahim came to Isma'il's house, but did not find Isma'il and asked his wife, 'Where is Isma'il' Isma'il's wife replied, 'He has gone out hunting.' He asked her about their condition, and she said that they have a good life and praised Allah. Ibrahim asked, 'What is your food and what is your drink' She replied, 'Our food is meat and our drink is water.' He said, 'O Allah! Bless their meat and their drink.'" The Prophet (Muhammad) said, "They did not have crops then, otherwise Ibrahim would have invoked Allah to bless that too. Those who do not live in Makkah cannot bear eating a diet only containing meat and water."

"Ibrahim said, `When Isma`il comes back, convey my greeting to him and ask him to keep the threshold of his gate.' When Isma`il came back, he asked, `Has anyone visited us.' She said, `Yes. A good looking old man,' and she praised Ibrahim, `And he asked me about our livelihood and I told him that we live in good conditions.' He asked, `Did he ask you to convey any message' She said, `Yes. He conveyed his greeting to you and said that you should keep the threshold of your gate.' Isma`il said, `That was my father, and you are the threshold; he commanded me to keep you.'

Ibrahim then came back visiting and found Isma'il behind the Zamzam well, next to a tree, mending his arrows. When he saw Ibrahim, he stood up and they greeted each other, just as the father and son greet each other. Ibrahim said, 'O Isma'il, Your Lord has ordered me to do something.' He said, 'Obey your Lord.' He asked Isma'il, 'Will you help me' He said, 'Yes, I will help you.' Ibrahim said, 'Allah has commanded me to build a house for Him there, ' and he pointed to an area that was above ground level. So, both of them rose and started to raise the foundations of the House. Abraham started building (the Ka'bah), while Isma'il continued handing him the stones. Both of them were saying, 'O our Lord ! Accept (this service) from us, Verily, You are the Hearing, the Knowing.' (2.127).'" Hence, they were building the House, part by part, going around it and saying,

(Our Lord! Accept (this service) from us. Verily, You are the Hearer, the Knower.)

The Story of rebuilding the House by Quraysh before the Messenger of Allah was sent as Prophet

In his Sirah, Muhammad bin Ishaq bin Yasar said, "When the Messenger of Allah reached thirty-five years of age, the Quraysh gathered to rebuild the Ka`bah, this included covering it with a roof. However, they were weary of demolishing it. During that time, the Ka`bah was barely above a man's shoulder, so they wanted to raise its height and build a ceiling on top. Some people had stolen the Ka`bah's treasure beforehand, which used to be in a well in the middle of the Ka`bah. The treasure was later found with a man called, Duwayk, a freed servant of Bani Mulayh bin `Amr, from the tribe of Khuza`ah. The Quraysh cut off his hand as punishment. Some people claimed that those who actually stole the treasure left it with Duwayk. Afterwards, the sea brought a ship that belonged to a Roman merchant to the shores of Jeddah, where it washed-up. So they collected the ship's wood to use it for the Ka`bah's ceiling; a Coptic carpenter in Makkah prepared what they needed for the job. When they decided to begin the demolition process to rebuild the House, Abu Wahb bin `Amr bin `A'idh bin `Abd bin `Imran bin Makhzum took a stone from the Ka`bah; the stone slipped from his hand and went back to where it had been. He said, `O people of Quraysh! Do not spend on rebuilding the House, except from what was earned from pure sources. No money earned from a prostitute, usury or injustice should be included.'" Ibn Ishaq commented here that the people also attribute these words to Al-Walid bin Al-Mughirah bin `Abdullah bin `Amr bin Makhzum.

Ibn Ishaq continued, "The Quraysh began to organize their efforts to rebuild the Ka`bah, each subtribe taking the responsibility of rebuilding a designated part of it.

However, they were still weary about bringing down the Ka'bah. Al-Walid bin Al-Mughirah said, 'I will start to bring it down.' He held an ax and stood by the Ka'bah and said, 'O Allah! No harm is meant. O Allah! We only seek to do a good service.' He then started to chop the House's stones. The people waited that night and said, 'We will wait and see. If something strikes him, we will not bring it down and instead rebuid it the way it was. If nothing happens to him, then Allah will have agreed to what we are doing.' The next morning, Al-Walid went to work on the Ka'bah, and the people started bringing the Ka'bah down with him. When they reached the foundations that Ibrahim built, they uncovered green stones that were above each other, just like a pile of spears." Ibn Ishaq then said that some people told him, "A man from Quraysh, who was helping rebuild the Ka'bah, placed the shovel between two of these stones to pull them up; when one of the stones was moved, all of Makkah shook, so they did not dig up these stones."

The Dispute regarding Who should place the Black Stone in Its Place

Ibn Ishaq said, "The tribes of Quraysh collected stones to rebuild the House, each tribe collecting on their own. They started rebuilding it, until the rebuilding of the Ka`bah reached the point where the Black Stone was to be placed in its designated site. A dispute erupted between the various tribes of Quraysh, each seeking the honor of placing the Black Stone for their own tribe. The dispute almost led to violence between the leaders of Quraysh in the area of the Sacred House. Banu `Abd Ad-Dar and Banu `Adi bin Ka`b bin Lu'ay, gave their mutual pledge to fight until death. However, five or four days later, Abu Umayyah bin Al-Mughirah bin `Abdullah bin `Amr bin Makhzum, the oldest man from Quraysh then intervened at the right moment. Abu Umayyah suggested that Quraysh should appoint the first man to enter the House from its entrance to be a mediator between them. They agreed.

The Messenger - Muhammad - was the first person to enter the House. When the various leaders of Quraysh realized who the first one was, they all proclaimed, 'This is Al-Amin (the Honest one). We all accept him; This is Muhammad.' When the Prophet reached the area where the leaders were gathering and they informed him about their dispute, he asked them to bring a garment and place it on the ground. He placed the Black Stone on it. He then requested that each of the leaders of Quraysh hold the garment from one side and all participate in lifting the Black Stone, moving it to its designated area. Next, the Prophet carried the Black Stone by himself and placed it in its designated position and built around it. The Quraysh used to call the Messenger of Allah 'Al-Amin' even before the revelation came to him."

Ibn Az-Zubayr rebuilds Al-Ka'bah the way the Prophet wished

Ibn Ishaq said,

"During the time of the Prophet, the Ka`bah was eighteen cubits high and was covered with Egyptian linen, and they with a striped garment. Al-Hajjaj bin Yusuf was the first person to cover it with silk." The Ka`bah remained the same way the Quraysh rebuilt it, until it was burned during the reign of `Abdullah bin Az-Zubayr, after the year 60 H, at the end of the reign of YazD—0d bin Mu`awiyah. During that time, Ibn Az-Zubayr was besieged at Makkah. When it was burned, Ibn Az-Zubayr brought the Ka`bah down and built it upon the foundations of Ibrahim, including the Hijr in it. He also made an eastern door and a western door in the Ka`bah and placed them on ground level. He had heard his aunt `A'ishah, the Mother of the believers, narrate that the Messenger of Allah had wished that. The Ka`bah remained like this throughout his reign, until Al-Hajjaj killed Ibn Az-Zubayr and then rebuilt it the way it was before, by the order of `Abdul-Malik bin Marwan.

Muslim recorded that 'Ata' said,

"The House was burnt during the reign of Yazid bin Mu'awiyah, when the people of Ash-Sham raided Makkah. Ibn Az-Zubayr did not touch the House until the people came for Hajj, for he wanted to incite them against the people of Ash-Sham. He said to them, 'O people! Advise me regarding the Ka'bah, should we bring it down and rebuild it, or just repair the damage it sustained' Ibn 'Abbas said, 'I have an opinion about this. You should rebuild the House the way it was when the people became Muslims. You should leave the stones that existed when the people became Muslims and when the Prophet was sent. ' Ibn Az-Zubayr said, 'If the house of one of them gets burned, he will not be satisfied, until he rebuilds it. How about Allah's House I will invoke my Lord for three days and will then implement what I decide.' When the three days had passed, he decided to bring the Ka'bah down. The people hesitated to bring it down, fearing that the first person to climb on the House would be struck down. A man went on top of the House and threw some stones down, and when the people saw that no harm touched him, they started doing the same. They brought the House down to ground level. Ibn Az-Zubayr surrounded the site with curtains hanging from pillars, so that the House would be covered, until the building was erect. Ibn Az-Zubayr then said, 'I heard 'A'ishah say that the Messenger of Allah said,

«لَوْلَا أَنَّ النَّاسَ حَدِيثٌ عَهْدُهُمْ بِكُفْرٍ، وَلَيْسَ عِنْدِي مِنَ النَّفَقَةِ مَا يُقَوِّينِي عَلَى بِنَائِهِ لَكُنْتُ أَدْخَلْتُ فِيهِ مِنَ الْحِجْرِ خَمْسَةَ أَذْرُعٍ، وَجَعَلْتُ

«لَهُ بَابًا يَدْخُلُ النَّاسُ مِنْهُ وَبَابًا يَخْرُجُونَ مِنْهُ»

(If it was not for the fact that the people have recently abandoned disbelief, and that I do not have enough money to spend on it, I would have included in the House five cubits from Al-Hijr and would have made a door for it that people could enter from, and another door that they could exit from.)

Ibn Az-Zubayr said, 'I can spend on this job, and I do not fear the people.' So he added five cubits from the Hijr, which looked like a rear part for the House that people could clearly see. He then built the House and made it eighteen cubits high. He thought that the House was still short and added ten cubits in the front and built two doors in it, one as an entrance and another as an exit.

When Ibn Az-Zubayr was killed, Al-Hajjaj wrote to 'Abdul-Malik bin Marwan asking him about the House and told him that Ibn Az-Zubayr made a rear section for the House. 'Abdul-Malik wrote back, 'We do not agree with Ibn Az-Zubayr's actions. As, for the Ka'bah's height, leave it as it is. As for what he added from the Hijr, bring it down, and build the House as it was before and close the door.' Therefore, Al-Hajjaj brought down the House and rebuilt it as it was." In his Sunan, An-Nasa'i collected the Hadith of the Prophet narrated from 'A'ishah, not the whole story,

The correct Sunnah conformed to Ibn Az-Zubayr's actions, because this was what the Prophet wished he could do, but feared that the hearts of the people who recently became Muslim could not bear rebuilding the House. This Sunnah was not clear to 'Abdul-Malik bin Marwan. Hence, when 'Abdul-Malik realized that 'A'ishah had narrated the Hadith of the Messenger of Allah on this subject, he said, "I wish we had left it as Ibn Az-Zubayr had made it." Muslim recorded that 'Ubadydullah bin 'Ubayd said that Al-Harith bin 'Abdullah came to 'Abdul-Malik bin Marwan during his reign. 'Abdul-Malik said, 'I did not think that Abu Khubayb (Ibn Az-Zubayr) heard from 'A'ishah what he said he heard from her.' Al-Harith said, 'Yes he did. I heard the Hadith from her.' 'Abdul-Malik said, 'You heard her say what' He said, 'She said that the Messenger of Allah said,

«إِنَّ قَوْمَكِ اسْتَقْصَرُوا مِنْ بُنْيَانِ الْبَيْتِ وَلَوْلَا حَدَاثَةُ عَهْدِهِمْ بِالشِّرْكِ أَعَدْتُ مَا تَرَكُوا مِنْهُ، فَإِنْ بَدَا لِقَوْمِكِ مِنْ بَعْدِي أَنْ يَبْنُوهُ فَهَلُمِّي لِأُرِيَكِ مَا تَرَكُوهُ مِنْهُ»

(Your people rebuilt the House smaller. Had it not been for the fact that your people are not far from the time of Shirk, I would add what was left outside of it. If your people afterwards think about rebuilding it, let me show you what they left out of it.) He showed her around seven cubits.'

One of the narrators of the Hadith, Al-Walid bin 'Ata', added that the Prophet said,

«وَلَجَعَلْتُ لَهَا بَابَيْنِ مَوْضُوعَيْنِ فِي الْأَرْضِ: شَرْقِيًّا وَغَرْبِيًّا، وَهَلْ تَدرِينَ لِمَ كَانَ قَوْمُكِ رَفَعُوا بَابَهَا؟»

(I would have made two doors for the House on ground level, one eastern and one western. Do you know why your people raised its door above ground level?)

She said, 'No.'

He said,

«تَعَزُّزًا أَنْ لَا يَدْخُلَهَا إِلَّا مَنْ أَرَادُوا، فَكَانَ الرَّجُلُ إِذَا هُوَ أَرَادَ أَنْ يَدْخُلَهَا يَدَعُونَهُ يَرْتَقِي حَتَّى إِذَا كَادَ أَنْ يَدْخُلَ دَفَعُوهُ فَسَقَطَ»

(To allow only those whom they wanted to enter it. When a man whom they did not wish to enter the House climbed to the level of the door, they would push him down)

'Abdul-Malik then said, 'You heard 'A'ishah say this Hadith' He said, 'Yes.' 'Abdul-Malik said, 'I wish I left it as it was."

An Ethiopian will destroy the Ka'bah just before the Last Hour

The Two Sahihs recorded that Abu Hurayrah said that the Messenger of Allah said,

«يُخَرِّبُ الْكَعْبَةَ ذُو السُّوَيْقَتَيْنِ مِنَ الْحَبَشَة»

(The Ka`bah will be destroyed by Dhus-Sawiqatayn (literally, a person with two lean legs) from Ethiopia.)

Also, Ibn `Abbas said that the Prophet said,

«كَأَنِّي بِهِ أَسْوَدَ أَفْحَجَ يَقْلَعُهَا حَجَرًا حَجَرًا»

(As if I see him now: a black person with thin legs plucking the stones of the Ka`bah one after another.) Al-Bukhari recorded this Hadith.

Imam Ahmad bin Hanbal recorded in his Musnad that `Abdullah bin `Amr bin Al-`As said that he heard the Messenger of Allah say,

«يُخَرِّبُ الْكَعْبَةَ ذُو السُّوَيْقَتَيْنِ مِنَ الْحَبَشَةِ وَيَسْلُبُهَا حِلْيَتَهَا وَيُجَرِّدُهَا مِنْ كِسْوَتِهَا، وَلَكَأَنِّي أَنْظُرُ إِلَيْهِ أُصَيْلِعَ وَ أُفَيْدِعَ يَضْرِبُ عَلَيْهَا بِمِسْحَاتِهِ وَمِعْوَلِهِ»

(Dhus-Sawiqatayn from Ethiopia will destroy the Ka`bah and will loot its adornments and cover. It is as if I see him now: bald, with thin legs striking the Ka`bah with his ax.)

This will occur after the appearance of Gog and Magog people. Al-Bukhari recorded that Abu Sa`id Al-Khudri said that the Messenger of Allah said,

«لَيُحَجَّنَّ الْبَيْتُ وَلَيُعْتَمَرَنَّ بَعْدَ خُرُوجِ يَأْجُوجَ وَمَأْجُوجَ»

(There will be Hajj and `Umrah to the House after the appearance of Gog and Magog people.)

Al-Khalil's Supplication

Allah said that Ibrahim and Isma'il supplicated to Him,

(Our Lord! And make us submissive unto You and of our offspring a nation submissive unto You, and show us our Manasik, and accept our repentance. Truly, You are the One Who accepts repentance, the Most Merciful.)

Ibn Jarir said, "They meant by their supplication, `Make us submit to Your command and obedience and not associate anyone with You in obedience or worship.'"Also, `Ikrimah commented on the Ayah,

(Our Lord! And make us submissive unto You)

"Allah said, `I shall do that.'"

(And of our offspring a nation submissive unto You)

Allah said, 'I shall do that.'"

This supplication by Ibrahim and Isma'il is similar to what Allah informed us of about His believing servants,

(And those who say: 'Our Lord! Bestow on us from our wives and our offspring the comfort of our eyes, and make us leaders of the Muttaqin) (25:74).

This type of supplication is allowed, because loving to have offspring who worship Allah alone without partners is a sign of complete love of Allah. This is why when Allah said to Ibrahim,

(Verily, I am going to make you an Imam (a leader) for mankind (to follow you)) Ibrahim said,

("And of my offspring (to make leaders)." (Allah) said, "My covenant (prophethood) includes not the Zalimin (polytheists and wrongdoers)") which is explained by,

(And keep me and my sons away from worshipping idols)

Muslim narrated in his Sahih that Abu Hurayrah said that the Messenger of Allah said,

«إِذَا مَاتَ ابْنُ آدَمَ انْقَطَعَ عَمَلُهُ إِلَّا مِنْ ثَلَاثٍ: صَدَقَةٍ جَارِيَةٍ أَوْ عِلْمٍ يُنْتَفَعُ بِهِ أَوْ وَلَدٍ صَالِحٍ يَدْعُو لَهُ»

(When the son of Adam dies, his deeds end except for three deeds: an ongoing charity, a knowledge that is being benefited from and a righteous son who supplicates (to Allah) for him.)

The Meaning of Manasik

Sa'id bin Mansur said that 'Attab bin Bashir informed us from Khasif, from Mujahid who said, "The Prophet Ibrahim supplicated, (and show us our Manasik) Jibril then came down, took him to the House and said, 'Raise its foundations.' Ibrahim raised the House's foundations and completed the building. Jibril held Ibrahim's hand, led him to As-Safa and said, 'This is among the rituals of Allah.' He then took him to Al-Marwah and said, 'And this is among the rituals of Allah.' He then took him to Mina until when they reached the 'Aqabah, they found Iblis standing next to a tree. Jibril said, 'Say Takbir (Allah is the Great) and throw (pebbles) at him.' Ibrahim said the Takbir and threw (pebbles at) Iblis. Iblis moved to the middle Jamrah, and when Jibril and Ibrahim passed by him, Jibril said to Ibrahim, 'Say Takbir and throw at him.' Ibrahim threw at him and said Takbir. The devious Iblis sought to add some evil acts to the rituals of Hajj, but he was unable to succeed. Jibril took Ibrahim's hand and led him to Al-Mash'ar Al-Haram and 'Arafat and said to him, 'Have you 'Arafta (known, learned) what I showed you' thrice. Ibrahim said, 'Yes I did.'" Similar statements were reported from Abu Mijlaz and Qatadah.

Surah: 2 Ayah: 129

﴿ رَبَّنَا وَٱبْعَثْ فِيهِمْ رَسُولاً مِّنْهُمْ يَتْلُواْ عَلَيْهِمْ ءَايَـٰتِكَ وَيُعَلِّمُهُمُ ٱلْكِتَـٰبَ وَٱلْحِكْمَةَ وَيُزَكِّيهِمْ إِنَّكَ أَنتَ ٱلْعَزِيزُ ٱلْحَكِيمُ ﴾

129. Our Lord! Send amongst them a Messenger of their own (and indeed Allâh answered their invocation by sending Muhammad (peace be upon him)) who shall recite unto them Your Verses and instruct them in the Book (this Qur'ân) and Al-Hikmah (full knowledge of the Islâmic laws and jurisprudence or wisdom or Prophethood), and purify them. Verily! You are the All-Mighty, the All-Wise."

Transliteration

129. Rabbana waibAAath feehim rasoolan minhum yatloo AAalayhim ayatika wayuAAallimuhumum alkitaba waalhikmata wayuzakkeehim innaka anta alAAazeezu alhakeemu

Tafsir Ibn Kathir

Ibrahim's Supplication that Allah sends the Prophet

Allah mentioned Ibrahim's supplication for the benefit of the people of the Sacred Area (to grant them security and provision), and it was perfected by invoking Allah to send a Messenger from his offspring. This accepted supplication, from Ibrahim, conformed with Allah's appointed destiny that Muhammad be sent as a Messenger among the Ummiyyin and to all non-Arabs, among the Jinns and mankind.

Hence, Ibrahim was the first person to mention the Prophet to the people. Ever since, Muhammad was known to the people, until the last Prophet was sent among the Children of Israel, Jesus the son of Mary, who mentioned Muhammad by name. Jesus addressed the Children of Israel saying,

(I am the Messenger of Allah unto you, confirming what is before me in the Tawrah, and giving glad tidings of a Messenger to come after me, whose name shall be Ahmad) (61:6)

This is why the Prophet said ,

«دَعْوَةُ أَبِي إِبْرَاهِيمَ وَبُشْرَى عِيسَى ابْنِ مَرْيَم»

(The supplication of my father Ibrahim and the glad tidings brought forth by Jesus the son of Mary.)

The Prophet said,

«وَرَأَتْ أُمِّي أَنَّهُ خَرَجَ مِنْهَا نُورٌ أَضَاءَتْ لَهُ قُصُورُ الشَّامِ»

(My mother saw a light that went out of her and radiated the palaces of Ash-Sham.)

It was said that the Prophet's mother saw this vision when she was pregnant with, narrated this vision to her people, and the story became popular among them. The light mentioned in the Hadith appeared in Ash-Sham (Greater Syria), testifying to what will later occur when the Prophet's religion will be firmly established in Ash-Sham area. This is why by the end of time, Ash-Sham will be a refuge for Islam and its people. Also, Jesus the son of Mary will descend in Ash-Sham, next to the eastern white minaret in Damascus. The Two Sahihs stated,

«لَا تَزَالُ طَائِفَةٌ مِنْ أُمَّتِي ظَاهِرِينَ عَلَى الْحَقِّ لَا يَضُرُّهُمْ مَنْ خَذَلَهُمْ وَلَا مَنْ خَالَفَهُمْ حَتَّى يَأْتِيَ أَمْرُ اللهِ وَهُمْ كَذَلِكَ»

(There will always be a group of my Ummah who will be on the truth, undeterred by those who fail or oppose them, until the command of Allah comes while they are on this.)

Al-Bukhari added in his Sahih,

«وَهُمْ بِالشَّامِ»

(And they will reside in Ash-Sham.)

The Meaning of Al-Kitab wal-Hikmah

Allah said,

(and instruct them in the Book) meaning, Al-Qur'an,

(and Al-Hikmah) meaning, the Sunnah, as Al-Hasan, Qatadah, Muqatil bin Hayyan and Abu Malik asserted. It was also said that 'Al-Hikmah', means 'comprehension in the religion', and both meanings are correct. 'Ali bin Abi Talhah said, that Ibn 'Abbas said that,

(and purify them) means, "With the obedience of Allah."

(Verily, You are the Mighty, the Wise).

This Ayah stated that Allah is able to do anything, and nothing escapes His ability. He is Wise in His decisions, His actions, and He puts everything in its rightful place due to His perfect knowledge, wisdom and justice.

Surah: 2 Ayah: 130, Ayah: 131 & Ayah: 132

﴿ وَمَن يَرْغَبُ عَن مِّلَّةِ إِبْرَٰهِۦمَ إِلَّا مَن سَفِهَ نَفْسَهُۥ ۚ وَلَقَدِ ٱصْطَفَيْنَٰهُ فِى ٱلدُّنْيَا ۖ وَإِنَّهُۥ فِى ٱلْءَاخِرَةِ لَمِنَ ٱلصَّٰلِحِينَ ۝ ﴾

130. And who turns away from the religion of Ibrâhim (Abraham) (i.e. Islâmic Monotheism) except him who befools himself? Truly, We chose him in this world and verily, in the Hereafter he will be among the righteous.

﴿ إِذْ قَالَ لَهُۥ رَبُّهُۥٓ أَسْلِمْ ۖ قَالَ أَسْلَمْتُ لِرَبِّ ٱلْعَٰلَمِينَ ۝ ﴾

131. When his Lord said to him, "Submit (i.e. be a Muslim)!" He said, "I have submitted myself (as a Muslim) to the Lord of the 'Alamîn (mankind, jinn and all that exists)."

﴿ وَوَصَّىٰ بِهَآ إِبْرَٰهِۦمُ بَنِيهِ وَيَعْقُوبُ يَٰبَنِىَّ إِنَّ ٱللَّهَ ٱصْطَفَىٰ لَكُمُ ٱلدِّينَ فَلَا تَمُوتُنَّ إِلَّا وَأَنتُم مُّسْلِمُونَ ۝ ﴾

132. And this (submission to Allâh, Islâm) was enjoined by Ibrâhim (Abraham) upon his sons and by Ya'qûb (Jacob) (saying), "O my sons! Allâh has chosen for you the (true) religion, then die not except in the Faith of Islâm (as Muslims - Islâmic Monotheism)."

Transliteration

130. Waman yarghabu AAan millati ibraheema illa man safiha nafsahu walaqadi istafaynahu fee alddunya wa-innahu fee al-akhirati lamina alssaliheena 131. Ith qala lahu rabbuhu aslim qala aslamtu lirabbi alAAalameena 132. Wawassa biha ibraheemu baneehi wayaAAqoobu ya baniyya inna Allaha istafa lakumu alddeena fala tamootunna illa waantum muslimoona

Tafsir Ibn Kathir

Only the Fools deviate from Ibrahim's Religion

Allah refuted the disbelievers' innovations of associating others with Allah in defiance of the religion of Ibrahim, the leader of the upright. Ibrahim always singled out Allah in worship, with sincerity, and he did not call upon others besides Allah. He did not commit Shirk, even for an instant. He disowned every other deity that was being worshipped instead of Allah and defied all his people in this regard. Prophet Ibrahim said,

(O my people! I am indeed free from all that you join as partners (in worship with Allah). Verily, I have turned my face towards Him Who has created the heavens and the earth Hanifa (Islamic Monotheism), and I am not of Al-Mushrikin.) (6:78-79). Also, Allah said,

(And (remember) when Ibrahim said to his father and his people: "Verily, I am innocent of what you worship. "Except Him (i.e. I worship none but Allah alone) Who did create me; and verily, He will guide me") (43:26-27),

(And Ibrahim's invoking (of Allah) for his father's forgiveness was only because of a promise he (Ibrahim) had made to him (his father). But when it became clear to him (Ibrahim) that he (his father) was an enemy of Allah, he dissociated himself from him. Verily, Ibrahim was Awwah (one who invokes Allah with humility, glorifies Him and remembers Him much) and was forbearing) (9:114), and,

(Verily, Ibrahim was an Ummah (a leader having all the good qualities, or a nation), obedient to Allah, Hanif (i.e. to worship none but Allah), and he was not one of those who were Al-Mushrikin. (He was) thankful for His (Allah's) favors. He (Allah) chose him (as an intimate friend) and guided him to a straight path. And We gave him good in this world, and in the Hereafter he shall be of the righteous.) (16:120-122).

This is why Allah said here, (And who turns away from the religion of Ibrahim), meaning, abandons his path, way and method

(except him who fools himself) meaning, who commits injustice against himself by deviating from the truth, to wickedness. Such a person will be defying the path of he who was chosen in this life to be a true Imam, from the time he was young, until Allah chose him to be His Khalil, and who shall be among the successful in the Last Life. Is there anything more insane than deviating from this path and following the path of misguidance and deviation instead Is there more injustice than this Allah said,

(Verily, joining others in worship with Allah is a great Zulm (wrong) indeed) (31:13).

Abu Al-'Aliyah and Qatadah said, "This Ayah (2:130) was revealed about the Jews who invented a practice that did not come from Allah and that defied the religion of Ibrahim." Allah's statement,

(Ibrahim was neither a Jew nor a Christian, but he was a true Muslim Hanifa (to worship none but Allah alone) and he was not of Al-Mushrikin. Verily, among mankind who have the best claim to Ibrahim are those who followed him, and this Prophet (Muhammad) and those who have believed (Muslims). And Allah is the Wali (Protector and Helper) of the believers.) (3:67-68), testifies to this fact.

Allah said next,

(When his Lord said to him, "Submit (i. e. be a Muslim)!" He said, "I have submitted myself (as a Muslim) to the Lord of the `Alamin (mankind, Jinn and all that exists).")

This Ayah indicates that Allah commanded Ibrahim to be sincere with Him and to abide and submit to Him; Ibrahim perfectly adhered to Allah's command. Allah's statement,

(And this (submission to Allah, Islam) was enjoined by Ibrahim upon his sons and by Ya`qub) means, Ibrahim commanded his offspring to follow this religion, that is, Islam, for Allah. Or, the Ayah might be referring to Ibrahim's words,

(I have submitted myself (as a Muslim) to the Lord of the 'Alamin (mankind, Jinn and all that exists)).

This means that these Prophets loved these words so much that they preserved them until the time of death and advised their children to adhere to them after them. Similarly, Allah said,

(And he (Ibrahim) made it ?ýi.e. La ilaha illallah (none has the right to be worshipped but Allah alone)> a Word lasting among his offspring, (true Monotheism)) (43:28).

It might be that Ibrahim advised his children, including Jacob, Isaac's son, who were present. It appears, and Allah knows best, that Isaac was endowed with Jacob, during the lifetime of Ibrahim and Sarah, for the good news includes both of them in Allah's statement,

(But We gave her (Sarah) glad tidings of Ishaq (Isaac), and after Ishaq, of Ya`qub (Jacob)) (11:71).

Also, if Jacob was not alive then, there would be no use here in mentioning him specifically among Isaac's children. Also, Allah said in Surat Al-'Ankabut,

(And We bestowed on him (Ibrahim), Ishaq and Ya`qub, and We ordained among his offspring prophethood and the Book.) (29:27), and,

(And We bestowed upon him Ishaq, and (a grandson) Ya`qub) (21:72), thus, indicating that this occurred during Ibrahim's lifetime. Also, Jacob built Bayt Al-Maqdis, as earlier books testified. The Two Sahihs recorded that Abu Dharr said, "I said, 'O Messenger of Allah! Which Masjid was built first' He said, (Al-Masjid Al-Haram (Al-Ka`bah).) I said, 'Then' He said, (Bayt Al- Maqdis.) I said, 'How many years later' He said, (Forty years.)" Further, the advice that Jacob gave to his children, which we will soon mention, testifies that Jacob was among those who received the advice mentioned in Ayat above (2:130-132).

Adhering to Tawhid until Death

Allah said,

((Saying), "O my sons! Allah has chosen for you the (true) religion, then die not except as Muslims.") meaning, perform righteous deeds during your lifetime and remain on this path, so that Allah will endow you with the favor of dying upon it. Usually, one dies upon the path that he lived on and is resurrected according to what he died on. Allah, the Most Generous, helps those who seek to do good deeds to remain on the righteous path.

This by no means contradicts the authentic Hadith that says,

«إِنَّ الرَّجُلَ لَيَعْمَلُ بِعَمَلِ أَهْلِ الْجَنَّةِ حَتَّى مَا يَكُونُ بَيْنَهُ وَبَيْنَهَا إِلَّا بَاعٌ أَوْ ذِرَاعٌ فَيَسْبِقُ عَلَيْهِ الْكِتَابُ فَيَعْمَلُ بِعَمَلِ أَهْلِ النَّارِ فَيَدْخُلُهَا. وَإِنَّ الرَّجُلَ لَيَعْمَلُ بِعَمَلِ أَهْلِ النَّارِ حَتَّى مَا يَكُونُ بَيْنَهُ وَبَيْنَهَا إِلَّا بَاعٌ أَوْ ذِرَاعٌ فَيَسْبِقُ عَلَيْهِ الْكِتَابُ فَيَعْمَلُ بِعَمَلِ أَهْلِ الْجَنَّةِ فَيَدْخُلُهَا»

(Man might perform the works of the people of Paradise until only a span of outstretched arms or a cubit separates him from it, then the Book (destiny) takes precedence, and he performs the works of the people of the Fire and thus enters it. Also, man might perform the works of the people of the Fire until only a span of outstretched arms or a cubit separates him from the Fire, but the Book takes precedence and he performs the works of the people of Paradise and thus enters it.) Allah said, (92:5-10),

(As for him who gives (in charity) and keeps his duty to Allah and fears Him. And believes in Al-Husna. We will make smooth for him the path of ease (goodness). But he who is a greedy miser and thinks himself self-sufficient. And belies Al-Husna (none has the right to be worshipped except Allah). We will make smooth for him the path for evil),

Surah: 2 Ayah: 133 & Ayah: 134

﴿ أَمْ كُنتُمْ شُهَدَآءَ إِذْ حَضَرَ يَعْقُوبَ ٱلْمَوْتُ إِذْ قَالَ لِبَنِيهِ مَا تَعْبُدُونَ مِنْ بَعْدِى قَالُوا۟ نَعْبُدُ إِلَـٰهَكَ وَإِلَـٰهَ ءَابَآئِكَ إِبْرَٰهِـۧمَ وَإِسْمَـٰعِيلَ وَإِسْحَـٰقَ إِلَـٰهًا وَٰحِدًا وَنَحْنُ لَهُۥ مُسْلِمُونَ ۝ ﴾

133. Or were you witnesses when death approached Ya'qûb (Jacob)? When he said unto his sons, "What will you worship after me?" They said, "We shall worship your Ilâh (God - Allâh), the Ilâh (God) of your fathers, Ibrâhim (Abraham), Ismâ'il (Ishmael), Ishâq (Isaac), One Ilâh (God), and to Him we submit (in Islâm)."

$$\left\{ \text{تِلْكَ أُمَّةٌ قَدْ خَلَتْ لَهَا مَا كَسَبَتْ وَلَكُم مَّا كَسَبْتُمْ وَلَا تُسْئَلُونَ عَمَّا كَانُواْ يَعْمَلُونَ} \right\}$$

134. That was a nation who has passed away. They shall receive the reward of what they earned and you of what you earn. And you will not be asked of what they used to do.

Transliteration

133. Am kuntum shuhadaa ith hadara yaAAqooba almawtu ith qala libaneehi ma taAAbudoona min baAAdee qaloo naAAbudu ilahaka wa-ilaha aba-ika ibraheema wa-ismaAAeela wa-ishaqa ilahan wahidan wanahnu lahu muslimoona 134. Tilka ommatun qad khalat laha ma kasabat walakum ma kasabtum wala tus-aloona AAamma kano yaAAmaloona

Tafsir Ibn Kathir

Ya`qub's Will and Testament to His Children upon His Death

This Ayah contains Allah's criticism of the Arab pagans among the offspring of Isma`il as well as the disbelievers among the Children of Israel Jacob the son of Isaac, the son of Ibrahim. When death came to Jacob, he advised his children to worship Allah alone without partners. He said to them,

("What will you worship after me" They said, "We shall worship your Ilah (God - Allah) the Ilah of your fathers, Ibrahim, Isma`il, Ishaq,")

Mentioning Isma`il here is a figure of speech, because Isma`il is Jacob's uncle. An-Nahas said that the Arabs call the uncle a father, as Al-Qurtubi mentioned).

This Ayah is used as evidence that the grandfather is called a father and inherits, rather than the brothers (i.e. when his son dies), as Abu Bakr asserted, according to Al-Bukhari who narrated Abu Bakr's statement from Ibn `Abbas and Ibn Az-Zubayr. Al-Bukhari then commented that there are no opposing opinions regarding this subject. This is also the opinion of `A'ishah the Mother of the believers, Al-Hasan Al-Basri, Tawus and `Ata', Malik, Ash-Shaf`i and Ahmad said that the inheritance is divided between the grandfather and the brothers. It was reported that this was also the opinion of `Umar, `Uthman, `Ali, bin Mas`ud, Zayd bin Thabit and several scholars among the Salaf and later generations.

The statement,

(One Ilah (God)) means, "We single Him out in divinity and do not associate anything or anyone with Him."

(And to Him we submit), in obedience meaning, obedient and submissiveness.

Chapter 2: Al-Baqarah, Verses 001-141

Similarly, Allah said,

(While to Him submitted all creatures in the heavens and the earth, willingly or unwillingly. And to Him shall they all be returned) (3:83).

Indeed, Islam is the religion of all the Prophets, even if their respective laws differed. Allah said,

(And We did not send any Messenger before you (O Muhammad) (but We revealed to him (saying): La ilaha illa Ana (none has the right to be worshipped but I (Allah)), so worship Me (alone and none else)) (21:25).

There are many other Ayat - and Hadiths - on this subject. For instance, the Prophet said,

«نَحْنُ مَعْشَرَ الْأَنْبِيَاءِ أَوْلَادُ عَلَّاتٍ دِينُنَا وَاحِدٌ»

(We, the Prophets, are brothers with different mothers, but the same religion.)

Allah said,

(That was a nation who has passed away) meaning, existed before your time,

(They shall receive the reward of what they earned and you of what you earn).

This Ayah proclaims, Your relationship to the Prophets or righteous people among your ancestors will not benefit you, unless you perform good deeds that bring about you religious benefit. They have their deeds and you have yours, (And you will not be asked of what they used to do)."

This is why a Hadith proclaims,

(Whoever was slowed on account of his deeds will not get any faster on account of his family lineage.)'

Surah: 2 Ayah: 135

﴿ وَقَالُواْ كُونُواْ هُودًا أَوْ نَصَـٰرَىٰ تَهْتَدُواْ ۗ قُلْ بَلْ مِلَّةَ إِبْرَٰهِـۧمَ حَنِيفًا ۖ وَمَا كَانَ مِنَ ٱلْمُشْرِكِينَ ﴾ ﴿١٣٥﴾

135. And they say, "Be Jews or Christians, then you will be guided." Say (to them, O Muhammad (peace be upon him)) "Nay, (we follow) only the religion of Ibrâhim (Abraham), Hanifa (Islâmic Monotheism, i.e. to worship none but Allâh (Alone)) and he was not of Al-Mushrikûn (those who worshipped others along with Allâh - see V.2:105)."

Transliteration

135. Waqaloo koonoo hoodan aw nasara tahtadoo qul bal millata ibraheema haneefan wama kana mina almushrikeena

Tafsir Ibn Kathir

Muhammad bin Ishaq reported that Ibn `Abbas said that `Abdullah bin Suriya Al-A`war said to the Messenger of Allah, "The guidance is only what we (Jews) follow. Therefore, follow us, O Muhammad, and you will be rightly guided." Also, the Christians said similarly, so Allah revealed,

(And they say, "Be Jews or Christians, then you will be guided.") Allah's statement,

(Say (to them O Muhammad), "Nay, (we follow) only the religion of Ibrahim, Hanif) means, "We do not need the Judaism or Christianity that you call us to, rather,

((we follow) only the religion of Ibrahim, Hanif) meaning, on the straight path, as Muhammad bin Ka`b Al-Qurazi and `Isa bin Jariyah stated. Also, Abu Qilabah said, "The Hanif is what the Messengers, from beginning to end, believed in."

Surah: 2 Ayah: 136

﴿ قُولُوٓاْ ءَامَنَّا بِٱللَّهِ وَمَآ أُنزِلَ إِلَيْنَا وَمَآ أُنزِلَ إِلَىٰٓ إِبْرَٰهِۦمَ وَإِسْمَٰعِيلَ وَإِسْحَٰقَ وَيَعْقُوبَ وَٱلْأَسْبَاطِ وَمَآ أُوتِيَ مُوسَىٰ وَعِيسَىٰ وَمَآ أُوتِيَ ٱلنَّبِيُّونَ مِن رَّبِّهِمْ لَا نُفَرِّقُ بَيْنَ أَحَدٍ مِّنْهُمْ وَنَحْنُ لَهُۥ مُسْلِمُونَ ﴾

136. Say (O Muslims), "We believe in Allâh and that which has been sent down to us and that which has been sent down to Ibrâhim (Abraham), Ismâ'il (Ishmael), Ishâq (Isaac), Ya'qûb (Jacob), and to Al-Asbât (the offspring of the twelve sons of Ya'qûb (Jacob)) and that which has been given to Mûsâ (Moses) and 'Isâ (Jesus), and that which has been given to the Prophets from their Lord. We make no distinction between any of them, and to Him we have submitted (in Islâm)."

Transliteration

136. Qooloo amanna biAllahi wama onzila ilayna wama onzila ila ibraheema wa-ismaAAeela waishaqa wayaAAqooba waal-asbati wama ootiya moosa waAAeesa wama ootiya alnnabiyyoona min rabbihim la nufarriqu bayna ahadin minhum wanahnu lahu muslimoona

Tafsir Ibn Kathir

The Muslim believes in all that Allah `revealed and all the Prophets

Allah directed His believing servants to believe in what He sent down to them through His Messenger Muhammad and in what was revealed to the previous Prophets in general. Some Prophets Allah mentioned by name, while He did not mention the names of many others. Allah directed the believers to refrain from differentiating between the Prophets and to believe in them all. They should avoid imitating whomever Allah described as,

(And wish to make distinction between Allah and His Messengers (by believing in Allah and disbelieving in His Messengers) saying, "We believe in some but reject others," and wish to adopt a way in between. They are in truth disbelievers) (4:150-151).

Al-Bukhari narrated that Abu Hurayrah said, "The People of the Book used to read the Torah in Hebrew and translate it into Arabic for the Muslims. The Messenger of Allah said,

«لَا تُصَدِّقُوا أَهْلَ الْكِتَابِ وَلَا تُكَذِّبُوهُمْ وقُولُوا: آمَنَّا بِاللهِ وَمَا أُنْزِلَ إِلَيْنَا»

(Do not believe the People of the Book, nor reject what they say. Rather, say, `We believe in Allah and in what was sent down to us.)"

Also, Muslim, Abu Dawud and An-Nasa'i recorded that Ibn `Abbas said, "Mostly, the Messenger of Allah used to recite,

(We believe in Allah and that which has been sent down to us) (2: 136), and,

(We believe in Allah, and bear witness that we are Muslims (i.e. we submit to Allah)) (3:52) during the two (voluntary) Rak`at before Fajr."

Abu Al-`Aliyah, Ar-Rabi` and Qatadah said, "Al-Asbat are the twelve sons of Jacob, and each one of them had an Ummah of people from his descendants. This is why they were called Al-Asbat." Al-Khalil bin Ahmad and others said, "Al-Asbat among the Children of Israel are just like the tribes among the Children of Isma`il." This means that the Asbat are the various tribes of the Children of Israel, among whom Allah sent several Prophets. Moses said to the Children of Israel,

(Remember the favor of Allah to you: when He made Prophets among you, made you kings) (5:20). Also, Allah said,

(And We divided them into twelve tribes) (7:160).

Al-Qurtubi said, "Sibt is the group of people or a tribe all belonging to the same ancestors."

Qatadah said, "Allah commanded the believers to believe in Him and in all His Books and Messengers. " Also, Sulayman bin Habib said, "We were commanded to believe in the (original) Torah and Injil, but not to implement them."

Surah: 2 Ayah: 137 & 2 Ayah: 138

﴿ فَإِنْ ءَامَنُواْ بِمِثْلِ مَآ ءَامَنتُم بِهِۦ فَقَدِ ٱهْتَدَواْ ۖ وَّإِن تَوَلَّوْاْ فَإِنَّمَا هُمْ فِى شِقَاقٍ ۖ فَسَيَكْفِيكَهُمُ ٱللَّهُ ۚ وَهُوَ ٱلسَّمِيعُ ٱلْعَلِيمُ ۝ ﴾

137. So if they believe in the like of that which you believe, then they are rightly guided; but if they turn away, then they are only in opposition. So Allâh will suffice you against them. And He is the All-Hearer, the All-Knower.

﴿ صِبْغَةَ ٱللَّهِ ۖ وَمَنْ أَحْسَنُ مِنَ ٱللَّهِ صِبْغَةً ۖ وَنَحْنُ لَهُۥ عَـٰبِدُونَ ۝ ﴾

138. (Our Sibghah (religion) is) the Sibghah (Religion) of Allâh (Islâm) and which Sibghah (religion) can be better than Allâh's? And we are His worshippers. (Tafsir Ibn Kathîr.)

Transliteration

137. Fa-in amanoo bimithli ma amantum bihi faqadi ihtadaw wa-in tawallaw fa-innama hum fee shiqaqin fasayakfeekahumu Allahu wahuwa alssameeAAu alAAaleemu   138. Sibghata Allahi waman ahsanu mina Allahi sibghatan wanahnu lahu AAabidoona

Tafsir Ibn Kathir

Allah said, if they, the disbelievers among the People of the Book and other disbelievers, believe in all of Allah's Books and Messengers and do not differentiate between any of them,

(then they are rightly guided) meaning, they would acquire the truth and be directed to it.

(but if they turn away) from truth to falsehood after proof had been presented to them,

(then they are only in opposition. So Allah will suffice you against them) meaning, Allah will aid the believers against them,

(And He is the Hearer, the Knower). Allah said,

(The Sibghah of Allah). Ad-Dahhak said that Ibn `Abbas commented, "The religion of Allah." This Tafsir was also reported of Mujahid, Abu Al-`Aliyah, `Ikrimah, Ibrahim, Al-Hasan, Qatadah, Ad-Dahhak, `Abdullah bin Kathir, `Atiyah Al-`Awfi, Ar-Rabi` bin Anas, As-Suddi and other scholars. The Ayah,

(Allah's Fitrah (i.e. Allah's Islamic Monotheism)) (30:30) directs Muslims to, "Hold to it."

Surah: 2 Ayah: 139 Ayah: 140 & Ayah: 141

﴿ قُلْ أَتُحَاجُّونَنَا فِى ٱللَّهِ وَهُوَ رَبُّنَا وَرَبُّكُمْ وَلَنَآ أَعْمَـٰلُنَا وَلَكُمْ أَعْمَـٰلُكُمْ وَنَحْنُ لَهُۥ مُخْلِصُونَ ۝ ﴾

139. Say (O Muhammad (peace be upon him) to the Jews and Christians), "Dispute you with us about Allâh while He is our Lord and your Lord? And we are to be rewarded for our deeds and you for your deeds. And we are sincere to Him in worship and obedience (i.e. we worship Him Alone and none else, and we obey His Orders)."

﴿ أَمْ تَقُولُونَ إِنَّ إِبْرَٰهِـۧمَ وَإِسْمَـٰعِيلَ وَإِسْحَـٰقَ وَيَعْقُوبَ وَٱلْأَسْبَاطَ كَانُوا۟ هُودًا أَوْ نَصَـٰرَىٰ ۗ قُلْ ءَأَنتُمْ أَعْلَمُ أَمِ ٱللَّهُ ۗ وَمَنْ أَظْلَمُ مِمَّن كَتَمَ شَهَـٰدَةً عِندَهُۥ مِنَ ٱللَّهِ ۗ وَمَا ٱللَّهُ بِغَـٰفِلٍ عَمَّا تَعْمَلُونَ ۝ ﴾

140. Or say you that Ibrâhim (Abraham), Ismâ'il (Ishmael), Ishâq (Isaac), Ya'qûb (Jacob) and Al-Asbât (the offspring of the twelve sons of Ya'qûb (Jacob)) were Jews or Christians? Say, "Do you know better or does Allâh (knows better ... that they all were Muslims)? And who is more unjust than he who conceals the testimony (i.e. to believe in Prophet Muhammad (peace be upon him) when he comes, as is written in their Books (See Verse 7:157)) he has from Allâh? And Allâh is not unaware of what you do."

﴿ تِلْكَ أُمَّةٌ قَدْ خَلَتْ ۖ لَهَا مَا كَسَبَتْ وَلَكُم مَّا كَسَبْتُمْ ۖ وَلَا تُسْـَٔلُونَ عَمَّا كَانُوا۟ يَعْمَلُونَ ۝ ﴾

141. That was a nation who has passed away. They shall receive the reward of what they earned, and you of what you earn. And you will not be asked of what they used to do.

Transliteration

139. Qul atuhajjoonana fee Allahi wahuwa rabbuna warabbukum walana aAAmaluna walakum aAAmalukum wanahnu lahu mukhlisoona   140. Am

taqooloona inna ibraheema wa-ismaAAeela wa-ishaqa wayaAAqooba waal-asbata kanoo hoodan aw nasara qul aantum aAAlamu ami Allahu waman athlamu mimman katama shahadatan AAindahu mina Allahi wama Allahu bighafilin AAamma taAAmaloona   141. Tilka ommatun qad khalat laha ma kasabat walakum ma kasabtum wala tus-aloona AAamma kanoo yaAAmaloona

Tafsir Ibn Kathir

Allah directed His Prophet to pre-empt the arguments with the idolators: (Say (O Muhammad to the Jews and Christians), "Dispute you with us about Allah) meaning, "Do you dispute with us regarding the Oneness of Allah, obedience and submission to Him and in avoiding His prohibitions, (while He is our Lord and your Lord) meaning, He has full control over us and you, and deserves the worship alone without partners.

(And we are to be rewarded for our deeds and you for your deeds.) meaning, we disown you and what you worship, just as you disown us. Allah said in another Ayah, (And if they belie you, say: "For me are my deeds and for you are your deeds! You are innocent of what I do, and I am innocent of what you do!") (10:41), and, (So if they dispute with you (Muhammad) say: "I have submitted myself to Allah (in Islam), and (so have) those who follow me") (3:20). Allah said about Ibrahim, (His people disputed with him. He said: "Do you dispute with me concerning Allah") (6:80), and,

(Have you not looked at him who disputed with Ibrahim about his Lord (Allah)) (2:258). He said in this honorable Ayah, (And we are to be rewarded for our deeds and you for your deeds. And we are sincere to Him.) meaning, "We disown you just as you disown us,"

(And we are sincere to Him), in worship and submission.

Allah then criticized them in the claim that Ibrahim, the Prophets who came after him and the Asbat were following their religion, whether Judaism or Christianity. Allah said, (Say, "Do you know better or does Allah") meaning, Allah has the best knowledge and He stated that they were neither Jews, nor Christians. Similarly, Allah said in the Ayah, (Ibrahim was neither a Jew nor a Christian, but he was a true Muslim Hanifa (to worship none but Allah alone) and he was not of Al-Mushrikin) (3:67) and the following Ayat. Allah also said,

And who is more unjust than he who conceals the testimony he has from AllaOh2:140(؟(. Al-HJasan Al-BasJri said, They used to recite the Book of AllaOh He sent to them that stated that the true religion is IslaOm and that MuhJammad is the Messenger of AllaOh. Their Book also stated that IbraOhOm, Isma0 Ol, IshJa0q, Ya qu0b and the tribes were neither Jews, nor Christians. They testified to these facts, yet hid them from the people. AllaOh s statement,

(And Allah is not unaware of what you do), is a threat and a warning that His knowledge encompasses every one's deeds, and He shall award each accordingly. Allah then said,

(That was a nation who has passed away.) meaning, existed before you,

(They shall receive the reward of what they earned, and you of what you earn.) meaning, they bear their deeds while you bear yours,

(And you will not be asked of what they used to do) meaning, the fact that you are their relatives will not suffice, unless you imitate their good deeds. Further, do not be deceived by the fact that you are their descendants, unless you imitate them in obeying Allah's orders and following His Messengers who were sent as warners and bearers of good news. Indeed, whoever disbelieves in even one Prophet, will have disbelieved in all the Messengers, especially if one disbelieves in the master and Final Messenger from Allah, the Lord of the worlds, to all mankind and the Jinns. May Allah's peace and blessings be on Muhammad and the rest of Allah's Prophets.

www.ingramcontent.com/pod-product-compliance
Lightning Source LLC
Chambersburg PA
CBHW081104080526
44587CB00021B/3447